In the NAME *of* GOD

Also by Selina O'Grady

And Man Created God

In the NAME *of* GOD

THE ROLE OF RELIGION IN THE MODERN WORLD

A History of Judeo-Christian and Islamic Tolerance

SELINA O'GRADY

PEGASUS BOOKS
NEW YORK LONDON

In the Name of God

Pegasus Books, Ltd.
West 37th Street, 13th Floor
New York, NY 10018

First Pegasus Books hardcover edition June 2020

ISBN: 978-1-64313-507-6

10 9 8 7 6 5 4 3 2 1

Printed in the United States of America
Distributed by Simon & Schuster

To Tony for his endless capacity to amaze intellectually

To Anna and Sibby who went way beyond tolerating me

And to Graeme Mitchison 1944–2018

CONTENTS

ILLUSTRATIONS

First section

Second section

Portrait of Martin Luther by Cranach the Younger, 1564 (*The Picture Art Collection/Alamy Stock Photo*)

Portrait of John Calvin by Titian, sixteenth century (*Historic Images/Alamy Stock Photo*)

Portrait of Charles V by Titian, 1548 (*Artepics/Alamy Stock Photo*)

Engraving of Michael Servetus (*Science History Images/Alamy Stock Photo*)

A Young Woman and Her Little Boy by Angelino Bronzino, *c.* 1540 (*Widener Collection, National Gallery of Art, Washington D.C., USA*)

Portrait of Suleiman I by Sinan Bey, sixteenth century (*World History Archive/Alamy Stock Photo*)

Portrait of Shah Ismail I (*The History Collection/Alamy Stock Photo*)

The Hanging by Jacques Callot, 1633 (*Wikimedia Commons*)

The Ratification of the Treaty of Münster, 15 May 1648 by Gerard ter Borch, 1648 (*Wikimedia Commons*)

Print of Roger Williams (*Bettman/Getty Images*)

Portrait of Muhammad Baqir Majlisi, *c.* 1670–80 (*The Picture Art Collection/Alamy Stock Photo*)

Portrait of Voltaire by Maurice Quentin de La Tour, 1735 (*The Picture Art Collection/Alamy Stock Photo*)

Portrait of Jean-Jacques Rousseau by Maurice Quentin de La Tour, 1753 (*Heritage Image Partnership Ltd/Alamy Stock Photo*)

Portrait of Robespierre, *c.* 1790 (*The Picture Art Collection/Alamy Stock Photo*)

Bonaparte Before the Sphinx, 1867 by Jean-Leon Gerome, 1868 (*Photo by DeAgostini/Getty Images*)

Lavater and Lessing Visit Moses Mendelssohn by Moritz Daniel Oppenheim, 1856 (*Wikimedia Commons*)

Portrait of Dorothea Schlegel by Anton Graff, *c.* 1790 (*Heritage Image Partnership Ltd/Alamy Stock Photo*)

Photograph of Alfred Dreyfus taken on 5 January 1895, the day he was dishonourably discharged and demoted (*Photo by Apic/Getty Images*)

Theodor Herzl (*Granger Historical Picture Archive/Alamy Stock Photo*)

Mustafa Kemal Atatürk (*Pictorial Press Ltd / Alamy Stock Photo*)

Hassan al Banna (*Historic Collection/Alamy Stock Photo*)

The 'Three Pashas' (*Photo by DeAgostini/Getty Images*)

The signing of the Reichskonkordat on 20 July 1933 (*akg-images/WHA/World History Archive*)

TIMELINE

303–5 CE	Christians persecuted under the Roman emperor Diocletian
312	The emperor Constantine has a vision of the cross
320	The emperor Theodosius declares that the Roman Empire is officially Christian
610	Muhammad begins preaching
622	The hijra, Muhammad's flight from Mecca to Medina
634–718	Islamic conquests of the Byzantine and Persian empires
711–1492	Muslim rule in the Iberian Peninsua. At its largest, al-Andalus, as the Muslim-controlled territory was called, extended from Portugal through most of Spain to what is now part of southern France
718–1492	The Reconquista. A series of sporadic campaigns by the Christian kings of northern Spain to recapture territory from the Muslims in al-Andalus
c. 786–1258	The Islamic golden age, often dated from the reign of the Abbasid caliph Harun al-Rashid to the capture of Baghdad by the Mongols
800	Charlegmagne is crowned Holy Roman emperor by Pope Leo III
833–47	Islam's inquisition, the Mihna
851	The first of the 'Cordoba Martyrs' is burned to death
909	Cluny Abbey founded
1066	Granada Massacre; 4,000 Jews murdered by a Muslim mob
1073–1122	The Investiture Controversy; Pope Gregory VII does battle with the Holy Roman emperor Henry IV over the right of lay rulers to appoint senior churchmen

1077	Pope Gregory VII forces the Holy Roman emperor Henry IV to stand in the snow before the gates of Canossa Castle and beg forgiveness
1090	Almoravids, Berber muslims from Morocco, conquer al-Andalus; by 1172 the Almohads have wrested al-Andalus from them. Both dynasties preside over the most intolerant regimes ever to rule Muslim Spain and Portugal
1095	Pope Urban II launches the First Crusade
1096	The Rhineland massacres; on their way to Jerusalem, Crusaders massacre thousands of Jews in the Rhineland towns of what is now Germany
1099	The Crusaders conquer Jerusalem and massacre Jews, Muslims and Latin Christians
1145	Pope Eugenius III calls for a Second Crusade
1147	Pope Eugenius III gives his blessing to the Reconquista by calling for a crusade to recapture al-Andalus from the Muslims. Pope Eugenius also launches the 'Baltic Crusade' against the pagans in north-eastern Europe on Germany's borders
1162	Thomas Becket, Archbishop of Canterbury, is murdered
1187	Saladin conquers Jerusalem
1190	York massacre; 150 Jews are killed or commit mass suicide
1206–1405	Mongol invasions and conquest of Asia and Europe
1208–27	Albigensian Crusade; the crusade is fought against one of the most vigorous heretical movements in Europe, Catharism based in southern France
1258	Mongols conquer Baghdad
1264	Charter of Jewish Liberties, the Statute of Kalisz, Poland; unprecedented document in medieval Europe that treated Jews as legally equal to Christians
1290	Edward I expels Jews from England; they are excluded from England until 1656
1300–17	Ibn Taymiyya delivers three fatwas on the Mongols

1306	King Philip the Fair of France expels Jews. They are invited back in 1315 but expelled again in 1394
1347–53	The Black Death kills about 100 million people in the Christian and Islamic worlds
1469	Marriage of King Ferdinand II of Aragon and Queen Isabella I of Castile unites Spain
1483–1834	Spanish Inquisition
1492	Fall of Granada – the end of Muslim Spain
1492	Jews expelled from Spain
1501	Shah Ismail, founder of the Safavid dynasty, declares Shiism to be the official religion of the Iranian empire
1517	Martin Luther writes his 95 theses criticizing the Catholic Church
1541–64	Calvin 'rules' Geneva
1553	Calvin has Michael Servetus executed for heresy and blasphemy
1555	Pope Paul IV establishes a ghetto for Jews in Rome and recommends all secular rulers do the same
1561	Gracia Mendez and her nephew Joseph are leased land by the Ottoman emperor to establish a homeland for Jews in Palestine
1572	St Bartholomew's Day Massacre; an estimated 5,000 to 20,000 French Calvinist Protestant (Huguenots) are massacred by Catholics in France
1598	Edict of Nantes settles the French Wars of Religion between Huguenots and Catholics
1609	Muslims expelled from Spain
1618–48	Thirty Years' War between the Catholic and Protestant states of Europe; 8 million die
1620–42	About 21,000 Puritans leave England and settle in New England
1636	The Puritan Roger Williams, pioneer of religious tolerance, establishes the New England colony of Providence (Rhode Island). Rhode Island becomes the first polity

	in the modern world to separate Church and State and guarantee religious liberty
1642–51	English Civil Wars
1644	Roger Williams' argument for religious tolerance, *The Bloudy Tenent*, is published
1648	Peace of Westphalia ends the Thirty Years' War
1656	Jews allowed back into England under Oliver Cromwell
1685	Revocation of the Edict of Nantes – freedom of worship for Huguenots in France withdrawn
1687	Muhammad Baqir Majlisi is appointed Shaykh al-Islam, religious leader, and becomes the most powerful figure in Iran and a hugely influential figure in Shiite doctrine
1689	John Locke's *A Letter Concerning Toleration* is published; it was one of the seventeenth century's most influential arguments in favour of religious toleration
1744	The puritanical religious reformer Muhammad ibn Abd al-Wahhab makes a pact with Muhammad ibn Saud founder of the Saudi dynasty. The alliance between the House of Saud and the descendants of Ibn Abd al-Wahhab still continues in Saudi Arabia today
1776	The United States' Declaration of Independence justifies the North American colonies' rebellion against England on the grounds of natural rights and the equality of 'all men'
1788	The Constitution of the United States is ratified; the word 'God' is not mentioned in the constitution
1789	France's Declaration of the Rights of Man and of the Citizen
1789–99	The French Revolution
1791	Jews in France are emancipated
1791	The First Amendment to the United States Constitution guarantees freedom of religion and expression and forbids Congress from making any religion the official religion of the country. The United States becomes the first country in the world to make religious intolerance illegal

1794	Robespierre's Cult of the Supreme Being is made the established religion of France
1798	Napoleon invades Egypt
1810	Reform Judaism's first synagogue is established in Germany
1839	The Edict of Gülhane issued by the Ottoman emperor, Sultan Abdulmejid I, initiates the period of the Tanzimat (reform, reorganization) and recognizes the equal rights of *dhimmis* with Muslims
1881	Wave of pogroms following the assassination of Alexander II, Tsar of Russia
1884	Jamal al-Din Afghani and Muhammad Abduh, leaders of the pan-Islamic and modernist movements, found the newspaper *al-Urwa al-Wuthqa* ('the firmest bond')
1894	Captain Dreyfus a Jewish officer in the French army is falsely accused of leaking information to the Germans and convicted of treason. The Dreyfus Affair divided France and revealed the anti-Semitism at the heart of the French establishment
1896	Theodor Herzl publishes *Der Judenstaat* (*The Jewish State*), his manifesto for political Zionism
1905	France declares itself a secular state, the only European country so far to have done so
1915–23	The Armenian Genocide; about 1.5 million Christians in the Ottoman Empire are slaughtered
1926	Mustafa Kemal (Atatürk), the first president of Turkey, announces that Turkey will no longer be ruled according to the sharia
1928	Hassan al-Banna founds the Muslim Brotherhood
1933	Hitler establishes an absolute dictatorship
1933	Vatican signs a concordat with Nazi Germany – the Nazi government agrees to respect the Church's autonomy and the Church agrees that its priests in Germany would not get involved in politics
1948	David Ben-Gurion proclaims the establishment of the State of Israel

1948 Universal Declaration of Human Rights is adopted by the newly formed United Nations

1969 The Universal Islamic Declaration of Human Rights is adopted by the newly created Organization of Islamic Co-operation

INTRODUCTION

'To tolerate is to insult.'

– Goethe

THE ABILITY OF ALL of us to live together – that is what the terrorist attacks of the past twenty years seem designed to make us question. That, at its most basic level, is the reason for this book.

When the morning radio announces another violent atrocity close to home, I go through an automatic checklist that I am sure has become part of the experience of many of us: What's the chance that someone I love has been affected? Is it a Muslim or a white supremacist terrorist attack? And then the wider questions: How have we reached this point? What has gone wrong? … A moment of grief for the victims and their loved ones. Then I get on with my day.

If it is Muslim-linked terrorism, I am left with a niggling feeling of unease, wondering whether this atrocity is more than a matter of terrorists harnessing their religion to their political anger but is a fundamental and irresolvable clash of religions and civilizations.

I am middle class, white, educated and urban. I rebelled in the 1970s against my hyper-traditionalist Catholic father and my spiritually absorbed mother. My intellectual atheism was one of many hardly noticed acts of rebellion. I shook off God and got on with being a liberated feminist. Until religion returned to our world with a bang on 9/11 in 2001. This book is a result of that bang. I needed to answer the question that my liberal self finds almost inadmissible even to ask: Is it possible for Muslims and people like me to live together – one country, one home, one set of rules?

What Western woman who prides herself on her tolerance and

liberalism – and I should say that as a white, middle-class woman I do – has not felt her hackles rise when she sees a veiled woman with nothing but her eyes visible, walking down the street several steps behind her man. My female forebears have fought for centuries, and the fight is not over yet, I think, for equality with men. Yet these women accept such visible signs of their subjection; and these men so unquestioningly accept their right to dominate, not because of any virtue they possess but solely because they are men. My feminism finds itself at uncomfortable odds with my liberalism. At these moments I want to ban the burqa. Yet I also believe in religious freedoms and respect for the beliefs of others.

From the fear of violence in our countries inspired by ISIS or al-Qaeda to the repressive regimes in Iran, Saudi Arabia and parts of Afghanistan, many of the West's nightmares are haunted by Islam. But does Islam pose a threat to the liberal values of the West? Are Muslim habits of thought and behaviour at odds with Western ones? The policies necessary for the stability and harmony of Western countries, with their growing Muslim minorities, depends on how we answer such questions.* For a wide range of people in the West – whether on the right or the left politically, middle class or working class, intellectual or anti-intellectual, the answer is a resounding 'yes': Muslims pose a threat. That answer is expressed in different ways in different places – at its worst in vicious acts of religious/racial hatred and violence: anything from burning down mosques to hissing at women in burqas. But it is also expressed in policy – in banning the veil in public places, as has happened in France, or challenging the right of Muslims to run their own schools and conduct segregated swimming classes (UK) or their right to build minarets (Switzerland).

Can we live together? That question very quickly turns into a debate about tolerance – that highest of liberal political virtues, the one that

---

* According to the Pew Research Center's latest report compiled in 2016, there are about 44 million Muslims living in Europe, about 4.9 per cent of the population, of which about 4 million live in the UK (about 6.3 per cent of the population), 5.7 million in France (8.8 per cent of the population) and 5 million in Germany (6.1 per cent of the population). As of 2017 the United States has about 3.45 million Muslims, making up about 1.1 per cent of the population.

purports to distinguish our civilized West from the rest. Those who believe that Islam does indeed pose a threat to Western values argue that it is the West's tolerance that underwrites our liberty. The post-Christian Western emphasis on the freedom and rights of the individual allows each of us to pursue our own life choices – to be, for instance, gay or straight, followers of one religion or another, or of no religion at all. Admittedly the West still has a long way to go, but the freedoms that we have so far won as individuals depend on allowing everyone to pursue their own path to fulfilment (within the law, of course) – in other words, they depend on tolerance. Islam is, according to this view, inimical to such Western laissez-faireism. It is a religion based on submission to authority (in particular to Allah and the Quran), on the rejection of rational inquiry in favour of belief, and on following traditional patterns of social behaviour which require the submission of women to men and which are firmly opposed to sexual freedoms (in particular homosexuality). However, those who see no essential clash of values dispute this picture of Islam, claiming that it represents only a small proportion of Muslims who follow a distorted form of Islam. It is in fact Islam that has been exceptionally tolerant; Western political virtue is recent, contingent – and anyway much over-valued.

In this book I examine these questions by unpicking the story of religious intolerance in the Christian West (America as well as Europe) and in the Islamic world closest to Europe – Spain, the Middle East and North Africa. In doing so I hope to disentangle the West's assumptions and prejudices about Islam from the reality.

I trace the different paths both religions have taken – and why they did so – through the stories of both the persecutors and the persecuted. Amongst them are the ninth-century caliph in gloriously cosmopolitan Baghdad who was defeated by an austere Muslim scholar; the Spanish Christians who deliberately provoked their own martyrdom; the English king who thought of converting his country to Islam; the Puritan hero, friend of Oliver Cromwell and author of the first study of American Indians, who established America's first non-persecutory state; Robespierre, the most bloodthirsty of the French revolutionaries who founded his own religion, and Ibn Abd al-Wahhab, his near contemporary, the epitome of Islam's intolerance in Western eyes. My story ends in 1945 after the Armenian genocide in the Muslim world and the Holocaust in the Western one, when all religion's capacities to unleash hatred were transferred onto nationalism and racism.

In the course of working on this book several points became glaringly obvious to me. Firstly, that for many centuries Christendom and Islamdom both thought that intolerance was godly and tolerance sinful. Monotheisms are by their nature intolerant. It is almost impossible for a monotheism to be otherwise, given that each believes itself to be following the sole God who possesses the sole truth.* And since religion and politics were historically inseparable, secular authority, like its religious counterpart, deemed tolerance to be more of a vice than a virtue, liable to create dissension and rebellion, as well as to encourage evil beliefs and practices contrary to God's will.

It is also clear that Islam has unquestionably scored better than Christianity in the tolerance game. Anti-Semitism and Christianity have gone hand in hand since around one hundred followers of Jesus broke away from Judaism soon after his crucifixion. Islam, too, has had its massacres and persecutions. But it can also vaunt its golden age in the Muslim Spain of the eighth to eleventh centuries, and its millet system of semi-autonomous religious communities in the Ottoman Empire, which were the wonder of Christian visitors and the delight of Jewish refugees fleeing Europe's expulsions and pogroms. Admittedly, Muslim tolerance has been to some extent mythologized by those anxious to shame Christendom in comparison. Nonetheless, the image of tolerance is in large part accurate.

But the truth, as my book will show, is that no one *wants* to be tolerated. If this sounds surprising, ask yourself this simple question: think of someone whom you believe cherishes and appreciates you, and whose love or friendship you treasure; now imagine finding out that they *tolerate* you; how would you feel? Hurt, disappointed and probably angry. This is the meaning of Goethe's pithy maxim that 'to tolerate is to insult'. When you tolerate someone, you put up with them. And if you are in a position to

* Until the twentieth century, Judaism was rarely in a position to possess a state through which it could exert tolerance or intolerance. But when it did, Judaism too showed the propensity of monotheisms to persecute those who disagreed with them.

put up with them, rather than they with you, then you are by default their superior. At an extreme, perhaps one could say that you can only tolerate what you despise. To be tolerated is better than being persecuted or killed, but it is not to be wished for. The price of being tolerated is accepting your inferiority. Toleration depends on the tolerators' belief in their own superiority. Tolerance is easy to dispense when a ruler and people feel confident of their own superiority. But when that sense of superiority feels threatened, toleration turns to hatred and intolerance, whether exercised by the State or the mob, or both. The tolerated can never rely on their tolerators.

What we all want is not to be tolerated but to be treated as equals. Many in the West believe that the post-Christian world has gone much further towards reaching that goal than the Islamic world, thanks to the Enlightenment. The West claims a particular ownership of equality, tracing its path from imperial pagan Roman and Judaic origins through the small Jewish cult of Christians which developed at odds with the empire, to Christianity's dominance of the Western world through the institution of the Catholic Church, on to the Protestant Reformation, and ending triumphantly with the Enlightenment, which the Islamic world never experienced.

Many Muslims, however, reject this view. The Islamic world, they argue, did indeed go through its own Enlightenment – a claim I will examine in this book. And many Christians, as well as Muslims, are sceptical about the blessings of the Enlightenment, arguing that religious equality or pluralism has been bought at the price of religious indifference; precisely what Muslims and Christians predicted back in the seventeenth and eighteenth centuries.

I will be teasing apart the histories of tolerance and equality, from the time when the Roman Empire became Christian to the genocides of the twentieth century. That is a span of 1661 years and might feel as if I am delving into a very distant past. However, it is worth noticing that this is only sixty-six generations. An averagely fortunate human will, over their own lives, know and have some direct understanding of their grandparents and their grandchildren – a span of five generations. Thought of in those terms, we could identify just thirteen people whose lives and personal memories connect the whole period represented by this span of 1661 years.

Think now of the relatively slow pace of change when it comes to beliefs and attitudes between the three, four or five generations you know. I say this only to point out that even apparently distant history is alive with us today. It lives in institutions, in beliefs, in language. The past is handed down through contact and memory. We cannot return to it and we know it imperfectly. But it is all around us and does a lot to make us what we are. The effort to come to some understanding of that history, an effort to which I hope this book contributes, is essential if we are to act wisely for the future and create the history that we will in turn hand down.

Some disclaimers. This is not intended to be a comprehensive comparative history of Christian and Muslim tolerance. Given the vastness of the topic, I have restricted myself to Europe, America, North Africa and the Middle East – venturing as far as Iran – and to the Latin/Western Church. And even within those parameters I have only looked at a few events, those which I feel shed the most illuminating light on the changing attitudes of Christendom and Islamdom to their religious 'others'.

Just as the terms Islam, Sunni, Shia, Christianity and Protestantism cover a range of shades of beliefs so does the term Judaism. For ease of reading I have used these broad umbrella terms, but readers should be aware that the many different religious movements covered by these terms differ from each other in the specifics of their beliefs.

Using broad umbrella terms to refer to religious groups is tricky in itself, especially when writing about tolerance, because doing so can appear to be an insensitive lumping together, a symbolic violence akin to the actual violence that I describe. I try to use phrases like 'the Jews' only in cases where the context makes it clear that they are in fact being targeted as a group. Otherwise, I try to drop the definite article. And similarly for Christians and Muslims.

Note on the Quran: I have used the translation of the Quran by M. A. S. Abdel Haleem, Oxford University Press, 2004. It is well thought of by scholars and is admirably clear. I have used the King James version of the Bible because it is the most beautiful translation and there are no significant scholarly objections to it.

CHAPTER 1

THE BIRTH OF PERSECUTION: THE ROMAN EMPIRE TURNS CHRISTIAN

'It is one thing to take on willingly the contest for immortality, quite another to enforce it with sanctions.'

– Constantine in *Life of Constantine* by Eusebius, *c.*337–39 CE

'Of all religions, the Christian is without doubt the one which should inspire tolerance most, although up to now the Christians have been the most intolerant of all men.'

– Voltaire, *Philosophical Dictionary*, 1764

IN 284 CE THE Roman army was marching home after campaigning in the Sasanian (Persian) Empire. At their head the young emperor Numerian was being carried in a litter hidden from sight behind drawn curtains. Soldiers who asked about him were told that he was suffering from an eye infection and had to be protected from the sunlight. As days passed, a terrible stench began to seep from the litter. When soldiers pulled back the curtains to peer inside, they found the rotting body of the emperor.

News of his death was announced to the army at Nicomedia (Izmit, in today's Turkey on the borders of the Sea of Marmara). On a hill outside the city, the army lifted up their swords and unanimously acclaimed their general Diocles as their new emperor. Diocles raised his sword in acknowledgement. Then he turned and thrust it into the man standing beside him, Lucius Flavius Aper, commander of the Praetorian Guard, who was, Diocles declared, guilty of murdering the former emperor. Historians now believe that it was Diocles who had been responsible for the assassination, as he probably had been of the previous emperor, Numerian's father Carus.*

Diocles, Diocletian as he then became, would be the saviour of the empire. He would also be pagan Rome's most savage persecutor of Christians. Did success require the persecution of this minority group? Diocletian thought it did.

Though Christians through the ages have liked to magnify the numbers of their early martyrs, pagan Rome had mostly turned a blind eye to what was becoming an increasingly popular cult. It is in the nature of imperial states to accept the differences, including religious ones, of their diverse peoples. Most empires, after a phase of expansionary conquest, find their *raison d'être* in tax collection, which is by its nature indifferent to most things but the bottom line.

But it was particularly easy for a pagan empire like Rome to adopt a laissez-faire attitude towards religious diversity. Pagan Rome did not care how many gods its subjects believed in. The pagan god required minimal beliefs, and little in the way of constraining behaviour, just a sacrifice now and again. It was a straight quid pro quo between worshipper and worshipped: a *do ut des* as the Romans said, 'I give so that you might give.' When Rome conquered a new piece of territory, it preferred to co-opt the gods of its conquered people and fuse them with the Roman gods rather than destroy them. In Britain, Sulis, the Celtic goddess of the thermal springs in Bath, became Sulis Minerva; in Gaul the healing god Lenus latched on to the Roman god of war Mars to become Lenus Mars; in

---

* This anecdote is referred to by several fourth-century CE sources (Eutropius, *Breviarium Historiae Romanae*, Abridgement of Roman History Book IX. 18–20, and Aurelius Sextus Victor *Liber de Caesaribus*, *Book on the Caesars*, 38). It is also recounted in the *Historia Augusta*, a collection of biographies of Roman emperors probably written before 425 CE. The *Historia Augusta* has, however, to be treated with some suspicion as its authors are known to have inserted fake information (for propaganda purposes, or perhaps even for the fun of it). But modern historians still rely on it as a source for the emperors of the second and third centuries CE.

Egypt the goddess Isis merged with Roman Venus. Rome left its peoples free to worship whom and what they pleased – just as long as they were good subjects and paid their taxes.*

But Rome *did* test its subjects' loyalty: they must sacrifice to the divine empire and the emperor, just as they must pay tax. Most of Rome's subjects had no problem with adding the divine emperor to their pantheon of gods. In the glory days of Rome, during its riotous festivals when spectators packed the amphitheatres to watch chariot races, when gladiatorial stars fought each other and became sexual trophies for senators' wives, the emperor simply joined the numerous gods whose images were paraded down the paved streets.

For pagans there was no such entity as a 'false' god, just as there was no such being as a heretic. But the empire's Jews, the world's first monotheists, could not sacrifice to the divine emperor. While the pagan gods could make room for another addition to their ranks, the single Jewish God is a jealous god who brooks no rivals. But as the largest minority in the empire after the Greeks, Jews had the bargaining power to extract a remarkable concession.† It was most probably engineered in about 6 CE by Herod the Great, King of Judea. Rome agreed that the Jewish Temple priests (the Temple in Jerusalem was the Jews' holiest building and place of pilgrimage, just as the Kaaba in Mecca would later be for Muslims) would not have to offer daily sacrifices to the divine emperor. Instead they would offer a daily sacrifice (two lambs and a bull) to their own God for the emperor's well-being.[1]

Periodically the Romans evicted Jews from Rome or closed down their synagogues. But it was not for religious reasons. The Jews' belief in a single all-powerful God – laughable as it seemed to the Romans – put their loyalty to the emperor in doubt. When it came to a choice between

---

* There were occasional exceptions to this freedom, such as the suppression of the Druids in Gaul and Britain. That cult involved human sacrifice, which was offensive to Roman notions of good order, although the Romans themselves had indulged in human sacrifice much earlier in their history.

† It is impossible to give an accurate figure of Jewish numbers, although many historians estimate that there were about 6 million Jews living in the Roman Empire, constituting about 10 per cent of the population.

God and emperor, it was not clear which the Jews would opt for. The same was true of the cult of Jesus, the group that had broken away from its Jewish parent and had a much more active programme of recruitment.

But the authorities usually followed the pragmatic logic of empires and extended to Christians the same tolerance they showed Jews. Christians had, in fact, far more to fear from their pagan neighbours, who would denounce Christians to the authorities for failing to sacrifice or even take matters into their own hands and beat them up, stone them or lynch them. As closely knit communities who refused to honour the Roman gods, Christians were often subjects of suspicion. The same was true for Jews, but Christians had none of the advantages of being so well established and were easy scapegoats in bad times. As Tertullian, the Early Church theologian from North Africa put it, pagan Romans 'suppose that the Christians are the cause of every public disaster, every misfortune that happens to the people. If the Tiber overflows or the Nile doesn't, if there is a drought or an earthquake, a famine or a pestilence, at once the cry goes up, "The Christians to the lion".'[2]

As this book will show, the status of being tolerated is an extraordinarily fragile and precarious one. Can you trust those who are putting up with you? When they feel powerful, they can afford to be generous; once they feel threatened, their tolerance evaporates. By the third century CE, not just ordinary pagans, but the Roman authorities themselves, were feeling very threatened indeed. Their once invincible empire was disintegrating. Almost every week a revolt broke out or a frontier was threatened – in the west by Germanic tribes from across the Danube and in the east by the rival Sasanian (Persian) Empire. Smallpox was rampant. Cities emptied of people, fields were left untended. Skyrocketing prices and starvation were followed by riots and civil war as general contended with general for the ever-thinner pickings associated with the imperial throne. Between 235 and 284 CE, the year that Diocletian took the imperial throne, twenty-six emperors had come and gone, assassinated by their own troops, casualties of the plague or dying in mysterious circumstances.

*

Diocletian had fought on many frontiers and in many civil wars. To staunch the flow of breakaway movements and revolts, he turned, as many rulers looking for an edge will do, to religion. It was the greatest weapon of social control available to him. Diocletian was convinced that it was essential to rekindle in Rome's subjects a sense of unity and of pride in their empire, which had been lost in the chaos of the preceding years. A reaffirmation of the old gods would restore the martial ethos that had made Rome great.

The rapid increase in converts to Christianity, especially in the army, concerned Diocletian. Their numbers had been growing during the anarchy of the second and third centuries. More and more people turned away from the gods who seemed to be failing them and towards a god who offered kindness, social justice, inclusion in a community of believers and the wonderful prospect of an eternal life of blissful love.

The Christians' version of the Jews' monotheism was proving dangerously appealing. Yahweh's promise that he would bring Jews back to their homeland if they worshipped only him, the jealous one, and followed his law, had preserved Jews as a united and distinct group since their Babylonian exile in the sixth century BCE. But that very distinctiveness posed a constant problem for Jews when the demands of their god conflicted with the demands of Rome.

Jesus – and Paul after him – had tried to solve that problem by claiming there were two separate realms: Caesar's and God's. But for most Jews, their law, Halakha, which applied to every aspect of life, from sex to trading, farming to praying, made it impossible to disentangle the two realms, just as the Islamic equivalent, sharia, would make it impossible for Muslims in later centuries.

After Jesus's death, his cult, as it evolved under Paul, did away with the law and universalized Yahweh. While Yahweh was the Jews' God and they were his chosen people, the Christian God was a god for Jew and non-Jew alike; nor did the Christian God require his followers to observe the detailed rules of behaviour that Yahweh expected of his followers.

At the time of Jesus's death in about 32 CE his followers numbered about one hundred. By 250 CE, that number had swelled to around 6 million. Christians made up about 10 per cent of the empire's population of 60 million, the same proportion as Jews.* The Gospel was being preached in every corner of the conquered world. Christians were becoming increasingly visible; they no longer worshipped in the privacy of their own homes but in large churches occupying prominent positions in the major imperial cities. In the case of Nicomedia, which Diocletian was turning into the capital of the eastern part of his empire, the church was on a hill facing his palace. *Aulae ecclesiae* – 'halls of the Church' as they were called – were attracting large crowds.

Diocletian saw with alarm that an increasing number of his soldiers were turning their backs on the pagan Roman gods and all that they stood for. Instead of giving their loyalty to him, the emperor, and to Rome, Christian soldiers were giving their loyalty to the one God. In *c.*295 CE he demanded that every soldier should sacrifice to the Roman gods and to the emperor. Those who refused were dismissed.

In 303, he went further and embarked on a policy to eradicate Christianity altogether. He ordered the destruction of all Christian churches, banned all meetings for worship and ordered that all copies of the scriptures and Christian liturgy should be burned. The following year, he decreed that any Christian who refused to make sacrifice to the Roman gods should be executed.

It is not known how many Christians died during the 'Great Persecution'. Enforcement was very uneven, with Gaul and Italy being less affected than the East. Eusebius, Bishop of Caesarea, the most important city in Roman Palestine (its ruins lie near modern Caesarea between Tel Aviv and Haifa), claimed there were about 20,000 Christian martyrs. But writers at the time were always loose with numbers. And it was, of course, in Eusebius's interests to exaggerate the number of 'these truly astounding champions of pure religion' – many martyrs make good advertisements for the power of their beliefs. Certainly Eusebius claims to have personally witnessed the miracles that took place in the arena

* Most historians seem to agree with this figure, although as with the number of Jews, accurate figures for the Christian population are impossible to come by.

during the *damnatio ad bestias*. This was a form of execution particularly appreciated by the crowd, in which the victim was tied naked to a pole and attacked by panthers, bears, wild boars or bulls who had been starved, or goaded with red-hot irons. 'For some time the man-eaters did not dare to touch or even approach the bodies of God's beloved,' Eusebius recorded in his *History of the Church*, 'as they stood naked and in accordance with their instructions waved their hand to attract the animals to themselves [but] were left quite unmolested: sometimes when the beasts did start towards them they were stopped short as if by some divine power, and retreated to their starting-point ... so that in view of the ineffectiveness of the first, a second and third beast were set on to one and the same martyr.'[3]

But the martyrs notwithstanding, even Eusebius admitted that 'numbers of men, women and children crowded up to the idols and sacrificed'. Mass apostasies took place all over the empire.

Diocletian died in 311, leaving the empire militarily and economically stronger than when he had ascended to the throne. But if Diocletian believed he had killed off Christianity, he had misread the mood of his subjects. That very same year his successor Galerius, who had been an assiduous persecutor of Christians, announced that he was rescinding all measures against them. Henceforth they would be allowed to worship. It was an admission of defeat: Christians had become too big a force to be destroyed. Galerius died soon after, and the struggle for the throne resumed.

On 27 October 312, Constantine, the junior emperor in the eastern part of the empire, was marching with his troops to do battle with his rival for control of Rome. As they looked up at the sky, a light appeared with the message 'In this sign conquer'. When he first recounted this event, Constantine would say that the sign had been sent by his guardian deity Apollo and the goddess Victory. Several years later he made a politically advantageous alteration: what he had seen etched against the sky was a vision of the cross. Or so Constantine told Eusebius, his friend and biographer. From that time on, Constantine became the protector and friend of the Christians. Perhaps he had seen that this once scapegoated group, the 'enemy within', held the key to military and political victory.

The following year, in 313, freedom of religion was enshrined in imperial legislation for the first time in the history of the Roman Empire. Constantine and his co-emperor, the pagan Licinius, announced that they were granting the Christians 'free and unrestricted opportunity of religious worship'. On top of that they 'also conceded to other religions the right of open and free observance of their worship, that each one may have the free opportunity to worship as he pleases'.[4] The 'Edict of Milan', as it has become known, was issued, as both emperors acknowledged, 'for the sake of the peace of our times'. Tolerance was always adopted by Muslim and Christian empires alike for pragmatic reasons, not moral ones.

Although Constantine called himself the thirteenth apostle and claimed his horse's bridle was made with one of the nails which had crucified Christ, he was never a wholehearted Christian. He did not discontinue the practice of emperor worship and even considered himself to be divine. Indeed, he could not afford to antagonize the pagans who still formed the majority of his subjects. Polytheists were free, he said, to 'celebrate the rites of an outmoded illusion', if they were foolish enough to want to do so.

But by 324 Constantine had defeated his co-emperor Licinius and his concern now was to reunite the empire which had been divided between them. Christianity, the religion that was proving so popular across the empire, would be his instrument. That meant that the divisions amongst Christians themselves had to be eliminated.

Constantine still believed that he was, as all emperors had been before him, Pontifex Maximus, head of Church and State. And in those early days of the State's non-rivalrous relationship with Christianity, when the emperor was a Christian but the empire was not officially so, the institutional Church did not demur. After 300 years, Christians could finally shelter under the protecting wing of an emperor who did not treat them with suspicion. But it had no idea how to conduct that relationship. For the moment the Church was happy to accept the inferior position that being protected gave it. Its future was still too uncertain for it to do anything else.

In 325 Constantine invited a number of bishops from throughout Christendom, from Britain to Jerusalem, to meet at Nicaea in today's Turkey, all travel expenses and accommodation paid. Their brief was to thrash out what Christians should believe, in particular to agree on the arcane matter of the divine and human nature of Christ, the son of God, and of his relationship to God, the Father. The resulting statement of belief, the Nicene Creed, heralded the official birth of the heretic. Never before had a Roman religion been formulated in terms of a set of beliefs with which followers must either agree or disagree.

The Catholic orthodoxy laid down at Nicaea was that God and Christ were 'consubstantial', that is, different but of the same substance. The most popular alternative belief, Arianism, that Jesus was created by God and inferior to him, was declared heretical. The political ramifications were rapid and draconian: Constantine and the royal family were sympathetic to Arianism, but a unified Christianity was more important. He exiled those bishops who refused to sign the settlement at Nicaea and also those who signed it but refused to condemn Arian doctrines. Arian books were burned along with those written by Gnostics, Donatists and all the other Christian factions who now found themselves branded as heretics and forbidden to hold assemblies.

The persecuted had turned persecutor. Christians had begun to hound their fellow Christians, although they had not yet turned on the true polytheist, the pagan. Periodically Constantine ordered pagan temples to be pulled down and forbade public sacrifices, but this never amounted to a systematic persecution. He was still happy to allow pagans to practise their rites and worship their gods. There were, after all, still more pagans than Christians in his empire.

Nonetheless, Constantine was now powerful enough to acquire the patronizing tone – one that will become familiar throughout this book – that the tolerant deign to adopt towards their inferior but tolerated subjects. 'Let them have, if they please, their temples of lies,' Constantine announced, 'we have the glorious edifice of Thy truth.' As for the Jews,

Constantine wrote to the bishops who had been unable to attend the meeting at Nicaea: 'Let us … have nothing in common with the Jews, who are our adversaries … lest your pure minds should appear to share in the customs of a people so utterly depraved.'[5] If he was tolerant of some 'others', he was certainly not respectful.

Systematic persecution and intolerance began in earnest on 28 February 380 when the emperor Theodosius issued an edict announcing that the empire was to become officially Christian. The edict was in effect a declaration of intolerance: 'It is Our will', Theodosius declared, 'that all the peoples who are ruled by the administration of Our Clemency shall practise that religion which the divine Peter the Apostle transmitted to the Romans… The rest, whom We adjudge demented and insane, shall sustain the infamy of heretical dogmas, their meeting places shall not receive the name of churches, and they shall be smitten first by divine vengeance and secondly by the retribution of Our own initiative.'[6]

The Nicene brand of Christianity which had been hammered out under Constantine was now imposed as the orthodoxy throughout the empire. The heretic and the non-Christian had been criminalized.

Theodosius came from Hispania (modern Spain and Portugal). He was urbane, courteous and charming, according to his admirers, but 'addicted to indolence and other vices', according to his critics such as the fiercely pagan historian Zosimus. Theodosius, according to Zosimus, employed 'whole legions of cooks, butlers, and other attendants' to serve the imperial table, and had so many eunuchs that 'the whole government was, in effect, at their disposal; the emperor being guided by their pleasure, and changing his sentiments at their desire'.

Theodosius was no friend of paganism or pagans. Certainly he had good reasons to fear them. The invasions of Germanic tribes, pushed westwards and southwards by Hun tribesmen advancing from Mongolia, seemed unstoppable. For Theodosius, the pagan within the empire was as much the enemy as the pagan Germanic barbarians without. In the western part of the empire, his enemies were gathering under the banner of paganism in support of a rebel emperor, Eugenius.

So it was not perhaps surprising that when he defeated Eugenius and his Frankish general Arbogast in 392, Theodosius set about exterminating paganism with a ruthlessness worthy of Diocletian's persecution of the Christians at the beginning of the century. There is nothing new in the persecuted turning persecutor.

He began with a direct attack on sacrifices, the very heart of pagan practice; few pagan gods required that their followers should follow any set of beliefs, but they all demanded sacrifices. Theodosius decreed that anyone caught performing or attending a pagan sacrifice would be put to death; any pagan who worshipped the statue of a god or hung a votive offering on a tree could lose their house; even in the privacy of their own homes, pagans were forbidden to offer wine, or burn incense to their household gods.

Theodosius was battling for control of the empire and that was intimately bound up with control of the spiritual realm. Like Diocletian, like Constantine, like so many rulers we will find throughout this book, Theodosius thought that if he could impose a single religion on the subjects of Rome, he could create a unified state. The single all-powerful monotheist God was the perfect reflection in the supernatural world of Theodosius's vision of the emperor's position in the material world.

Ordinary Christians, with the backing of some of the most important figures in the Church, were happy to co-operate in the extermination of pagans and heretics. Christians defaced statues of the gods, roamed the countryside destroying temples and shrines where the local farmer on his way to work had once placed a daisy chain, a wreath or a libation; they fought pagans in the streets, in the name of a religion that was based on 'love thine enemy'.

In a letter to Theodosius, the pagan rhetorician Libanius described rampaging gangs of monks, 'this black-robed tribe', he called them, 'who eat more than elephants and, by the quantities of drink they consume, weary those that accompany their drinking with the singing of hymns'. They attacked temples 'with sticks and stones and bars of iron, and in some cases, disdaining these, with hands and feet... Then utter desolation follows, with the stripping of roofs, demolition of walls, the tearing down of statues and the overthrow of altars… After demolishing one, they scurry to another, and to a third, and trophy is piled on trophy'.[7]

This was mob violence sanctioned by both the State and the Church. But whereas the empire has good pragmatic reasons to be tolerant and usually resorts to intolerance only when it feels threatened, monotheistic religion has intolerance built into it. *My God is the sole true God. Therefore anyone who denies my God by worshipping other gods or by having different views on the nature of my God, is not just wrong but evil.* Augustine, the North African Bishop of Hippo in today's Algeria and the greatest of the Early Church theologians, urged his own flock to smash all evidence of paganism. More than three centuries later Islam would make a similar move from tolerance to intolerance, though never as violently or as viciously as Christianity.

Theodosius's battle extended beyond pagans to Christian heretics. If the purpose is to make a single mind, an *esprit de corps*, then sharing the name of a god is not enough: you need to agree on the nature of the god and how to worship it. Theodosius banned all Christian heresies in a list which reads to us today as a roll call of the dying and the dead heresies. The Manicheans, the Donatists and the Arians still live on in historical memory if not in practice, but who beside the scholar has heard of the Pneumatomachs, the Eunomians, the Encratites, the Apotactites, the Saccophori or the Hydroparastatae?

Augustine had argued in favour of tolerating the heretic, but changed his mind, he said, when he saw how effective Theodosius's edicts were in suppressing heresy. Intolerance worked. Augustine was one of the first major Church figures to justify religious persecution. He was not, however, in favour of killing heretics, preferring instead that they should be fined, flogged, imprisoned or exiled. It was not until the eleventh century that Europe's Church and State agreed that heretics should be burned to death.

*

In 387, seven years after Theodosius's declaration of intolerance, a priest in the city of Antioch in today's Turkey preached a series of venomous sermons to his Christian flock. These sermons, known as *Adversus Judaeos* or Homilies Against the Jews, have formed the backbone of Christian anti-Jewish literature ever since.

John Chrysostom had just spent two years living as a hermit in a mountain cave outside Antioch. Ill health brought on by putting his body through the ascetic trials of fasting, sleep deprivation and standing praying for hours on end, had forced him back to the city. After Rome and Alexandria, Antioch was probably the most magnificent and cosmopolitan city in the Roman Empire, where Jews and Christians mixed freely. Far too freely in John's view. Christians were celebrating Jewish festivals, observing Jewish fasts, feasting with Jews and going to the synagogue.

John Chrysostom's hate-filled diatribes were fuelled by a fear that Judaism was putting Christianity's newly won position as the religion of the empire at risk. As usual, it was fear that prompted intolerance. That Christians in Antioch, the cradle of Christianity where Paul had set up his missionary base, should still find the faith of the Jews attractive was a clear sign that Christianity was in danger of losing its followers to Judaism.[8]

But, John reminded his flock, even the Old Testament prophets had likened the Jews to the heifer and the calf, and 'although such beasts are unfit for work, they are fit for killing'. Jews were 'the odious assassins of Christ and for killing God there is no expiation possible… Christians may never cease vengeance, and the Jew must live in servitude for ever.' Jews, the Christ-killers: it would be the spur and justification for every Christian mob that fell upon Jews. It is the running sore that has so profoundly damaged Christian attitudes to Jews and whose effects we are still feeling today. John Chrysostom (*chrysostom* means golden-mouthed in Greek) is still honoured as a saint today. The Vatican did not remove the reference to Jews killing Christ, a charge repeated every year in the Good Friday service's Prayer for the Jews, until 1962. It is an accusation which the third monotheism that emerged in the seventh century explicitly denies: 'They [the Jews] did not kill him, nor did they crucify him,' says the Quran (4:157). Muslim scholars explain that God replaced Jesus's body on the cross with an illusion. Allah, however, did not forgive the Jews for refusing to submit to him: 'For those of them that reject the truth we have prepared an agonizing torment,' he says later in the same sura (chapter), 4:161.

Anti-Judaism was to some extent an essential part of Christianity. Christianity was the child of Judaism and as such needed to proclaim its distinctness. That need became even more pressing in the wake of the disastrous Jewish Wars against the Roman Empire of 66–73 and 132–135 CE. Christians were eager to emphasize to the Romans how different they were from the disloyal, rebellious Jews. The Gospel of Matthew, written almost immediately after the Romans had crushed the Jews' first war of independence in 73 CE, portrays the Jews as the enemies of Jesus who persecuted him during his lifetime and were responsible for his death. 'His blood be on us and on our children,' Matthew's gospel has Jews say when they are given the choice between reprieving Jesus or Barabbas from the sentence of crucifixion.

With the Church's blessing, Christian mobs looted and burned down synagogues, although the emperor Theodosius tried to prevent these dangerous outbreaks of lawlessness. When in 415, at the urging of their bishop, Christians in Callincium (present-day Raqqa in Syria), burned down the local synagogue, Theodosius insisted that they pay for rebuilding it. 'The sect of the Jews is forbidden by no law,' he told one official. Jews were not threatening the integrity of the empire as the pagans were.

But the Church – in the shape of the stocky, black-bearded scourge of Jews and pagans, Ambrose, Bishop of Milan – urged Theodosius back onto the path of intolerance. 'Should not the rigour of the law yield to piety?' he asked Theodosius. Under pressure from Ambrose, Theodosius withdrew his order that Callincium's Christians rebuild the Jews' synagogue.

Ambrose, who had baptized Augustine, was perhaps the most influential Christian figure of the late fourth century. A former governor of an Italian province, he had switched his ambitions and energy into the Church. From there he exerted extraordinary influence over three successive emperors and pushed them in a much more intolerant direction than they would ever have taken on their own.

Ambrose had in fact convinced Theodosius's predecessor, Valentinian II, to resist one of the most moving pleas for religious respect ever recorded. It was made by Symmachus, member of an old patrician family and a passionate defender of Rome's old traditions and gods. The Altar of Victory in the Senate House, which had been intimately associated with the business of Roman life for centuries, where offerings were made before any senatorial business could begin, had been removed. It symbolized pagan Rome and Symmachus, speaking on behalf of Rome's pagans, was urging the emperor to reinstall it. 'We look on the same stars, the sky is common, the same world surrounds us,' Symmachus argued, just as centuries later Shylock would try to persuade a hostile court that Jews and Christians shared a common humanity. 'What difference does it make by what pains each seeks the truth? We cannot attain to so great a secret by one road.'

Symmachus's argument that there are many, equally valid, paths to truth, was of course one that no monotheist could accept. Bishop Ambrose persuaded Valentinian to be deaf to such a plea; Symmachus made two further appeals to Valentinian's successor, Theodosius, but again Ambrose was at the emperor's shoulder. Symmachus was exiled in 390.

Ambrose's power went far beyond influence. In April 390 a riot broke out in Thessalonica (Salonica in northern Greece), possibly because a popular charioteer had been arrested on charges of homosexual rape by the commander of the city garrison. In the course of the riot, the commander and several officers were killed and their bodies dragged through the streets. Theodosius ordered a swift and brutal retaliation. At the next races, when about 5,000 to 7,000 spectators had gathered in the circus at Thessalonica to cheer on their chariot teams, the gates were barred. Soldiers then fell on the spectators and massacred them. 'Innocent and guilty alike … without any forms of law … like ears of wheat in the time of harvest, they were alike cut down,' the theologian and Church historian Theodoret recorded.

Ambrose was so outraged that he refused to celebrate Mass in Theodosius's presence or give him Communion until Theodosius repented. Five months later Theodosius did so in a public ceremony of penance and humiliation. 'He threw on the ground all the royal attire that he was wearing,' Ambrose reported, no doubt with great satisfaction. 'He wept publicly in church for his sin... He prayed for pardon with groans and with tears. What private citizens are ashamed to do, the emperor was not ashamed to do, namely, to perform penance publicly.'[9]

Ambrose rescinded his excommunication and Theodosius was once more allowed to receive Communion. The spirit had shown its superiority over the sword. Theodosius became the first emperor to relinquish his title of Pontifex Maximus, head of both Church and State. It was a landmark in the history of Christendom.

Theodosius may well have been genuinely contrite, but for pragmatic reasons alone he had to capitulate. He could not afford to alienate the Church; it had too many followers. A God who determines the eternal fate of his people is a powerful ally; the weapon of ideology is often more powerful than real weaponry.

The Church's power over minds was its principal asset, but it had also found it useful to add some very earthly wealth to its balance sheet. Constantine had been an extremely generous benefactor and had launched the Church on its way to becoming the richest institution in western Europe. He had also exempted the clergy from having to pay taxes – with the unintended consequence that wealthy pagans flocked to the priesthood in order to claim the tax break. The Church's fusion with – and then superiority over – secular power set the framework and aspirations of the institution which would seek to dominate the Western world for the next thirteen centuries.

Now it is time to move south-eastwards, to Mecca, the birthplace of that other monotheism which would seek to dominate the Eastern world.

CHAPTER 2

MUHAMMAD'S EDICT OF TOLERATION

'You have your religion and I have mine.'

– Quran 109:6

'Wherever you encounter the idolaters [polytheists], kill them, seize them, besiege them, wait for them at every lookout post; but if they repent, maintain the prayer, and pay the prescribed alms, let them go on their way, for God is most forgiving and merciful.'

– Quran 9:5

IN THE HEAT OF the noonday sun an African slave named Bilal was pinned down on the desert sands outside Mecca in western Arabia while his master whipped him and crushed him with a huge boulder shouting, 'You will stay here till you die or deny Muhammad and worship Al-Lat and al-Uzza.' 'One, one,' screamed Bilal as he endured his pagan master's torture. 'There is no god but Allah.'

Bilal ibn Rabah was one of the first followers of the Meccan merchant turned preacher/prophet Muhammad. To the fury of most of his fellow tribesmen Muhammad was claiming that the many gods they worshipped did not exist and that there was only one God. Muhammad was so impressed by Bilal's refusal to renounce Allah that he sent his Companion Abu Bakr to free Bilal in exchange for a black slave who was 'tougher and stronger' than Bilal but, more importantly, was only 'a heathen'.* The heathen slave has followed the majority of humanity into oblivion. But Bilal will forever be remembered as the first muezzin to call Muhammad's followers to prayers and as the treasurer of Islam's first state.†

In barely twenty years, between 610 and 632, Muhammad welded together a number of warring tribes to form a united Arabia from which tribesmen would issue forth to build one of the largest empires the world would ever see. He did so thanks to monotheism. Muhammad created a community united by belief in the same god rather than split apart into tribes where membership rested on blood relationships and the blood feud ruled. As the sociologist Max Weber put it with his usual insight: 'The great achievement of the ethical religion ... was to shatter the fetters of the kinship group ... [by establishing] a superior community of faith and a common, ethical way of life in opposition to the community of blood.'[1] The Israelite tribes had been united by the one warrior god Yahweh who had evolved from being a supreme god amongst other gods to being the only god; under him they had conquered Canaan between 1250 and 1050 BCE. Constantine and Theodosius had used a universal monotheism, Christianity, to prevent their empire's disintegration.

Monotheism is a supremely effective glue. Ironically this is in part because of its ability to create the enemy. Constantine had used Christianity to unite the two halves of his empire. In doing so, he had virtually created the Christian heretic at Nicaea. Theodosius also used Christianity to unify the empire and stamp out his pagan enemies. A universalist monotheism, all-embracing as it purports to be, can be

* Muhammad's first followers are known as 'Companions'. This story is recounted in the earliest of the *sira* (Muslim biographies of Muhammad) by Ibn Ishaq in the mid eighth century. His *Life of the Prophet of God* is lost but survives in edited versions by the ninth-century scholar Ibn Hisham and the tenth-century scholar al-Tabari. Apart from the *sira* the most important sources for the life of Muhammad are the hadiths, the collections of the sayings and deeds of Muhammad, said to have been witnessed by Muhammad's first followers and passed on orally down the generations. Fragmentary references to the prophet's life are also found in the Quran.

† For simplicity's sake I will refer to 'Islam', even though it took several centuries for Muhammad's revealed messages to be systematized.

used as much to exclude as to include. The creation of 'one mind' by the elimination of the 'other' is, as we will see, an ever-present use to which monotheisms are put.

Muhammad was charisma and energy personified. According to Ibn Ishaq, his first biographer, Muhammad's whole body conveyed action. He was broad-shouldered and powerfully built with big feet and hands. When he turned, he turned not just his head, but his whole body. He leaned forward as he walked, as if he was running downhill, so that his companions were exhausted trying to keep up with him. He turned red when he was angry and showed the gap between his front teeth when he laughed. Aisha, his favourite wife, said he always helped with the household chores, mended his own clothes, repaired his shoes and swept the floor. He also, apparently, had beautiful, long, thick eyelashes.

In 610 CE, when Muhammad was forty, he announced to his immediate family and close friends that the angel Gabriel had revealed to him a message from God. Over the next twenty-two years, Muhammad continued to receive these messages. In their bare essence they said that there is no god but Allah; that the way to gain fulfilment and everlasting life in paradise and to avoid eternal hell was to follow His commands on how to live a righteous life. *Islam* means 'surrender', or 'submission'; a *Muslim* is someone who has submitted to Allah's law. Obedience to one supreme leader who transcends all petty loyalties to tribal chiefs, and who promises infinite rewards – what a call to unity!

Muhammad repeated these messages publicly to a growing band of listeners who learned them by heart. The angel Gabriel had delivered the first message in writing. But, when Muhammad confessed he could not read, the angel switched to transmitting God's words orally in verse. In the twenty years following Muhammad's death, those verses were written down and collected. The result is the Quran, meaning 'recitation'. For Muslims, it is the word of God verbatim. Uniquely amongst the monotheisms, Islam considers its entire holy book to be the literal words of God, which is what makes 'interpretation' of the Quran so fraught.

In a region as inhospitable as the north of Arabia, causes for conflict were everywhere. Tribes fought for scarce resources – for water, grazing grounds, animals – and for tribal glory. Whether they were nomadic, semi-nomadic, or permanently settled, Arabs' lives were governed by the tribe to which they belonged – or at least one of the highly competitive clans of which the tribe was composed. There was no such thing as 'law', in the sense of State-imposed punishment exacted according to a certain set of rules. 'Law' meant vengeance, which was inherently unstable and potentially never-ending: a crime inflicted on one member of a clan reflected on the dignity of the whole of the clan and therefore implicated every man in the duty to exact vengeance on the offending clan.

Unexpected encounters between men from different tribes were so fraught with potential danger that they would signal their intentions in advance. If they meant no ill will, they presented the butt ends of their spears towards one another; to signal aggression they presented the points, often tipped with poison. The two neighbouring superpowers – the Byzantine (the eastern half of the former Roman Empire) and Sasanian (Persian) empires* – only exacerbated tribal hostilities. In their own version of the Cold War, the two empires competed for dominance over the region by making alliances with local tribes and playing 'divide and rule'.

Mecca, set in a narrow valley surrounded by desert and mountains, was probably the safest place in Arabia. When Muhammad lived there and was beginning to reveal his messages from the one God, it was the pagans' holiest city, as it is for Muslims today. Pagan pilgrims journeyed

* The eastern Roman Empire, based on Byzantium (later renamed Constantinople after Constantine), was not called the 'Byzantine' Empire until the sixteenth century, a hundred years after Constantinople had fallen to the Ottomans. I use 'Byzantine' and 'eastern Roman Empire' interchangeably. 'Persia' is the name by which the Western world has referred to Iran since the fifth century BCE when Cyrus the Great ruled his vast empire. Ancient Greeks called the whole of Iran 'Persis' after the region in south-west Iran which was Cyrus's homeland. 'Iran', meaning land of the Aryans (the Indo-European people who settled the area between 1800 and 1600 BCE) is what its inhabitants have always called the region. 'Iran' and 'Persia' are now both used.

to Mecca and circled around the Kaaba as Muhammad himself did and as over a million Muslims still do every year while performing the hajj (the pilgrimage to Mecca that every Muslim is required to do at least once in their lifetime).

In pre-Islamic times, the Kaaba was venerated as the shrine of Allah, the name already in use for the high god of the local pagan pantheon. It was also home to 360 gods whose wooden effigies, statues and sacred stones were worshipped inside and outside the building.* Pilgrims adorned their gods with necklaces, earrings and ostrich eggs and gave them offerings of crops, milk and sacrificial animals. Amongst the sacred images were Jesus and Mary – Mecca was also a place of pilgrimage for Arabia's substantial number of Christians.

Mecca was an important trading as well as religious centre. It was on the caravan route that brought slaves, spices and incense – the oil of its day – from Yemen in the south to Syria in the north, and wine, cereal and weapons on the reverse journey.

The only way men from rival tribes could meet amicably in Mecca as fellow pilgrims and traders was to declare it a fight-free zone. No violence was allowed within thirty-two kilometres of the Kaaba. Every spring, after 'the sea without water', as Bedouin poets called the desert, had been transformed into a meadow by the winter rains, when 'ostriches and gazelles brought forth their young, and wide-eyed oryx stand peacefully over their newborn' as the warrior poet and early Muslim convert Labid described it, all the tribes recognized a truce. They could travel without fear of being ambushed, robbed or killed. Springtime rains meant that pasturage and water were plentiful enough for large groups to share an encampment; pilgrims to Mecca set out from their acacia-shaded encampments, leaving behind a clean-swept hearthstone, a few pieces of charred firewood, shreds of dyed wool and 'the dung of gazelles scattered like peppercorn', in the words of Imru' al-Qays, the most famous of all the pre-Islamic Bedouin poets. Arabic

* *Sahih al-Bukhari*, 2478. *Sahih al-Bukhari* is considered to be the most important of the six major hadith collections of Sunni Islam. It was compiled by the Muslim scholar Muhammad al-Bukhari in around 846 CE.

tribesmen had a veneration for poetry that would be inherited by their Muslim descendants.

Women too made the pilgrimage. Musk-scented and with indigo spirals painted on their flesh, they rode atop their camels, if they were wealthy enough, sheltering behind curtains of brocaded wool and gauze.

As both religious and economic centre, Mecca was extremely profitable for Muhammad's own tribe, the Quraysh, whose clans dominated Mecca. The Quraysh were guardians of the Kaaba, and consequently had a status in Arabia which stretched way beyond the small mud-bricked houses of Mecca and its environs. But Muhammad wanted to claim the Kaaba for his sole God, declaring that anyone who worshipped other gods was profoundly sinful. As the ranks of his followers swelled beyond the members of his immediate family, close friends, slaves and social outcasts, so opposition grew.

Muhammad and his followers were threatening not just the Quraysh's gods but their business and their prestige. 'We will boycott your goods and reduce you to beggary,' one prominent Meccan warned Muhammad's merchant followers. Meccans were forbidden to sell food or medicine to Muslims.* Woe betide the convert who was a 'man of no social importance' and belonged to one of the poorer of the Quraysh clans, with no fearsome family connections to protect him. He would often be beaten up so badly 'that he could hardly sit upright because of the violence they had used on him, so that in the end he would do whatever they said'.[2]

Muhammad's message that everyone was equal in the eyes of Allah was particularly appealing at a time when tribes were swapping their nomadic life for a settled life in the city, and disparities of wealth were becoming more glaring. Survival as a nomad requires equality, the sharing of scarce resources amongst your own small group which is united by blood ties. But the settled life fosters economic competition, the accumulation of property (and, for some, debt). The battle of war is replaced by the battle for economic dominance.

---

* The Arabic prexfix 'mu' means one who practises, so Muslim means one who practises Islam.

According to the tenth-century Quranic scholar and historian al-Tabari, relying on an incident recorded in Ibn Ishaq's original biography of Muhammad, Muhammad was so troubled by the antagonism of his fellow tribesmen and was so eager to convert them that he allowed himself to be deceived: he accepted as a revelation from God what was actually 'the prompting of Satan'. One day, when a group of the leading Quraysh of Mecca were gathered together before the Kaaba, Muhammad is said to have pronounced these so-called 'satanic verses': 'Have ye thought upon [the goddesses] al-Lāt and al-Uzzá and Manāt, the third, the other? These are the high-flying gharāniq [cranes] and their intercession is to be hoped for.'

In essence, Muhammad was uttering a shocking blasphemy. He had recognized the three goddesses worshipped by the pagan Quraysh. The 'satanic verses' were, perhaps, an extraordinarily generous attempt to escape monotheist exclusivity and move to a religious egalitarianism where the sole god accepts the existence of other gods. Believing that Muhammad had backed down on his claim that there was only one god, the delighted Quraysh promptly prostrated themselves before the Muslims' God, saying, according to al-Tabari, 'Muhammad has referred to our gods most favourably.' What was perhaps worse was that the Muslims too believed that their one and only god had acknowledged these other gods, because 'the Believers trusted in their prophet [Muhammad]'. But not long after Muhammad had uttered the 'satanic verses', the angel Gabriel 'came to the Prophet and said, "O Muhammad, what have you done! You have recited to the people something which I have not brought you from God, and you have spoken what He did not say to you."' Muhammad was bitterly repentant, according to al-Tabari, and God took mercy on him.

The blasphemous verses were expunged from the collection of Muhammad's revelations which were being memorized by his followers and written down and collected in what became the Quran. The majority of Islamic scholars had decided that since the Prophet was immune from error he could not have been prompted by Satan into uttering the satanic verses. Instead, in sura 53 of the Quran Muhammad tells the

Quraysh that their three goddesses are 'nothing but names you have invented yourselves, you and your forefathers. God has sent no authority for them,' (Quran 53:23–24). The memory of those 'satanic verses' might linger on in tradition, but if Muhammad had ever publicly recited them, they had mercifully been erased. Al-Tabari himself, who had reported them, is still respected as a religious scholar who was if anything proving the sacred nature of the Quran by showing that it could not contain anything erroneous or evil. 'God removes what Satan insinuates,' says the Quran (22:52).

By 619 Quraysh hostility towards Muhammad and his followers had intensified. According to Ibn Ishaq, 'The Quraysh showed their enmity to all those who followed the apostle … imprisoning them, and beating them, allowing them no food or drink, and exposing them to the burning heat of Mecca, so as to seduce them from their religion. Some gave way under pressure of persecution, and others resisted them, being protected by God.' Amongst those brave latter was, of course, the ex-slave Bilal.

Muhammad's life was now in serious danger. But 275 miles to the north, he had made converts amongst the Khazraj tribesmen in Medina. Unable to resolve their bloody conflict with a rival pagan tribe and with the three Jewish tribes who were the biggest landowners in the area but were losing their dominant position, the Khazraj asked Muhammad to mediate. They offered him their protection if he came to live in Medina. It was not uncommon for holy men to be called in as arbitrators when tribal quarrels had reached an impasse.

Muhammad agreed. One night in the spring of 622, he slipped out of his house, which according to his biographer was surrounded by Quraysh threatening to kill him, and set out for Medina. With him was his faithful Companion, the emaciated and slightly hunched Abu Bakr whose daughter Aisha was about to become Muhammad's favourite wife. The flight, the hijra, from Mecca to Medina, marks the true birth of Islam. As Christians begin their calendar with the birth of Jesus, Muslims begin theirs with the hijra.

While Mecca was predominantly a trading and religious centre,

Medina (Yathrib as it was then known) was a cluster of agricultural settlements and fortresses, surrounded by wheat fields, pasture land and above all by great groves of date palms. When the dates ripened, nomadic tribesmen appeared in Medina on their 'silent great shuffle-footed beasts'[3] to claim a portion of the huge date harvest. The nomads had negotiated a deal: dates in return for protecting the lives and property of the more sedentary tribesmen of Medina, who were unable to settle their inter-tribal conflicts grounded in disputes over land and harvests.

It is crucial to the story of Islam that when Muhammad arrived in Medina at the age of fifty-three, he was not seen as a powerless fugitive from persecution, but as a respected figure capable of putting an end to war. His role was to unite the warring tribes. Nonetheless, he and his group of seventy followers were a defenceless minority amongst Jews, pagans and Christians. The Muslims were bereft of the only protection that was available to Arabs in those days – the protection of their own clan. They were vulnerable both to the Medinans and to the continuing hostility of the Quraysh from Mecca. The Khazraj had offered to protect them, but how much that offer could be relied upon was questionable when it was kinship that bound a group together and made its members capable of laying down their lives for each other.

Muhammad, however, had the unifying power of Islam on his side. As far as he was concerned, Jews and Christians did not present a problem. Muhammad, in fact, assumed that the Jews and Christians of Medina would accept his revelations. He did not so much conceive of himself as the founder of a new monotheistic religion, but as the purifier of the two monotheist religions, Judaism and Christianity, which had preceded Islam but had gone astray and been corrupted. According to tradition, Jews and Arabs were both descended from Abraham, who had built the Kaaba in Mecca (Quran 2:127) though it had now been defiled by pagans. Muhammad was the last link in the chain of prophets which stretched from Adam, through Noah, Abraham and Moses, to Jesus. As the last of the prophets, Muhammad would give God's final message to humankind. But he was still close enough in spirit to the Jews to receive a revelation after the hijra that Muslims should pray towards Jerusalem, and that it was lawful for Muslims to eat Jewish food and marry Jewish women (Quran 5:5). Muhammad even adopted the Jewish fashion and let his thick hair hang loose to his shoulders rather than parting it with a comb as was customary among Arabs.

Christianity, by contrast, was far more at loggerheads with its mother, Judaism. Jews after all rejected the fundamental tenet of Christianity, that Christ was the Messiah. Not only that but the Jews had been responsible for Jesus's crucifixion. This difference in Islam's attitude to the other monotheisms profoundly affected how it treated its monotheistic 'others' when it came to rule over them.

Muhammad's relations with the pagans of Medina, however, were indeed oppositional. The Christian and Jewish tribes needed reforming, but their basic beliefs were correct and they would surely soon opt for his perfected monotheism and be united. But the pagans of Medina, each household with their god placed on a shelf shrouded with a veil, rejected the very idea of a single exclusive god.

In about 622, soon after his arrival in Medina, Muhammad set out the ground rules for establishing peace between the warring tribes and for safeguarding the Muslims' position within Medina's tribal network. The rules have become known as the 'Constitution of Medina', though it was probably a collection of agreements rather than a single treaty. The 'faithful covenanters', as Muhammad called those who agreed to the 'Constitution', consisted of nine pagan and Jewish tribes, the Muslims who had emigrated from Mecca and the Muslim converts in Medina, who were now organized in their own clans.

The faithful covenanters were 'bound to help one another against any attack on Yathrib [Medina]' and forbidden to offer protection to Muhammad's enemies the Quraysh of Mecca; only Muhammad could authorize war and all disputes were to be 'referred to God and to Muhammad the apostle of God'.[4] The tribal egalitarianism of the many gods was being replaced by the all-powerful rule of the one and only God.

The new Islamic 'state' was beginning to reflect the growing move in Arabia from the nomadic to the sedentary, the egalitarian to the hierarchical. Muhammad preached that all Muslims were brothers, but they were brothers under the ultimate authority of God. Muhammad, as God's mouthpiece, was that authority on earth. The nomadic way of life determined an egalitarian form of decision-making where the chief's role was very different from a king's. A king dictated terms to his subjects and his role was to protect them. A chief, on the other hand, was first among equals: his role was to act as arbitrator of disputes and to preside over meetings attended by all the adult males of the tribes. Decisions were made not on the chief's diktat but on the basis of an emerging consensus. Muhammad had won for himself a position somewhere between king and tribal chief. The Constitution on which the Medinan state rested had been agreed upon by all the tribes and Muhammad ruled with their consent. But the terms of the Constitution were his, and ultimately the real power, that is, the control of violence, was in his hands – he decided when Medina should go to war. God and king, or in the case of Muhammad 'demi-king', are better at putting a lid on warfare than gods and chiefs.

Allah, through his messenger Muhammad, was bringing peace to Medina's warring tribes. He was creating 'one nation [*umma*] separate [distinct] from all peoples', as the preamble to the Constitution declared. This, however, was an *umma* based on territory, not on a shared god; it was only when Muhammad became more powerful that the *umma* took on its present incarnation as a community made up exclusively of Muslims linked by their submission to the one God.

By necessity the Constitution made no religious demands: it sought only to establish the peaceful cohabitation of tribes whether pagan, Jewish or Muslim. No covenanter was required to acknowledge Muhammad's Allah. But in the light of Muhammad's view that Judaism was a corrupted form of Islam, and that Jews would soon recognize this and convert, the Constitution explicitly puts Jews on an equal religious footing with 'the Believers', that is, Muslims, declaring that 'the Jews have their religion, and the Muslims [in some translations 'the Believers'] have theirs'.

This declaration of religious pluralism is thought to find its counterpart in sura 109:1–6 of the Quran, believed to have been transmitted to Muhammad when he was still living in Mecca: 'Disbelievers, I do not worship what you worship, you do not worship what I worship, I will never worship what you worship, you will never worship what I worship: you have your religion and I have mine.' The verse is often cited as exemplifying the tolerant spirit of the Quran. But Muhammad's biographer, Ibn Ishaq, whose version of the Constitution of Medina is the one most regularly cited, interprets the verse as meaning precisely the opposite. The disbelievers Muhammad addresses were two senior Quraysh whom Muhammad encountered while he was still living in Mecca. In a spirit of compromise they had said to him: 'Let us worship what you worship and you will worship what we worship … if what you worship is better than what we worship we will take a share of it; and if what we worship is better than what you worship, you can take a share of that.' Muhammad's response – 'O disbelievers, I will never worship what you worship, you will never worship what I worship: you have your religion and I have mine' – in fact meant, according to Ibn Ishaq, 'If you disbelievers will only worship God on condition that I worship what you worship, I have no need of you at all. You can have your religion, all of it, and I have mine.' Muhammad might have been prepared to compromise politically with pagans, but not religiously.

Muhammad was now officially recognized as the chief of all the tribes of Medina. He was the political leader of Medina and religious leader of the Muslims, the founder of a state as well as of a religion. In this, of course, he was radically different from Jesus, who was seen as an enemy of the State, and was indeed killed by the state under whose laws he lived. Christianity started its life in an antagonistic relationship with the state, and remained as such for over two centuries. From the Start Christianity has been a religion of separations – Church from State; body from soul; this world from the next world; the individual from the collective. Islam, on the other hand, has from the start been a religion of unity – Muhammad embodying the unity of Church and State, Islam concentrating its gaze on the *umma*, the worldwide body of Muslims, rather than on the individual soul and conscience; seeing body and soul as seamlessly interconnected. Except for its twelve years as a persecuted minority in

Mecca, Islam experienced no conflict with the State: Muhammad, its founder, *was* the State.

Muhammad was far more akin to Moses than to Jesus. Moses was also both spiritual and political leader; he also handed down laws from his sole God, laws which made no distinction between an inner world of the spirit and an outer world of activity and ordinary living, between the spiritual and the mundane, the city of God and the city of man, as Augustine put it. In fact, sharia, the Islamic divine law, and Halakha, the Judaic divine law, both mean 'path' or 'way'.

Within a year of his arrival in Medina in 622, Muhammad had established himself as ruler. With money provided by his faithful follower, Abu Bakr, he acquired land on which he built a mosque, its roof covered in palm branches, its columns made from tree trunks. Muhammad considered but rejected the idea of using a trumpet as the Jews did to call the faithful to prayer; instead he chose Bilal, the faithful slave who opened this chapter, to be muezzin and call out with his fine voice: 'Allahu Akbar! Allahu Akbar! ... There is no God but God.'

But Muhammad had one major problem. He and his followers from Mecca had been forced to abandon their land and possessions and were now finding it difficult to support themselves. In Mecca, they had never put up any physical resistance to their Qurayshi persecutors. Allah had instructed Muhammad to refrain from fighting his enemies. 'Repel evil with good,' Muslims were told (23:96), and 'patiently endure what they say, ignore them politely and leave to Me those who deny the truth and live in luxury' (73:10). But soon after his arrival in Medina, Muhammad received the verse: 'Those who have been attacked are permitted to take up arms because they have been wronged' (Quran 22:39), and the Muslim exiles from Mecca had certainly been wronged by the Quraysh.

This of course contradicted Allah's earlier counsel of forbearance. But how could Allah, the omnipotent all-perfect God, contradict himself? Islamic scholars had solved that problem back in the mid eighth century when they began assembling the Quran. Allah himself had provided the answer – *naskh*, abrogation. 'Any revelation We cause to be superseded or forgotten, We replace with something better or similar' (Quran 2:106).

Abrogation follows the logic of chronology: revelations received earlier in Muhammad's life, when he was living in Mecca, the 'Meccan suras', chapters, were abrogated or superseded by the 'Medinan suras' that were revealed to him later in Medina, when he was facing very different circumstances. This is not, however, obvious to the novice reader, since the Quran is not arranged chronologically but according to the length of the sura, with the longest appearing first.

The 'permission to fight' verse is the first instance in the Quran when jihad, that word which today carries such an undertow of violence and hatred, is associated with physical struggle. In pre-Islamic literature jihad had meant a struggle or effort of any sort, but had no military connotation; jihad 'by the sword' is an Islamic innovation. For Muslims jihad is invested with a double meaning, signifying both an internal struggle to purify the soul and an external struggle against Islam's enemies. To this day, emphasis shifts from one to the other, as we all know to our cost. But the word itself occurs only four times in the Quran, although exhortations to fight occur many times.[5]

Muhammad and his followers had turned the other cheek in Mecca; now, with Allah's permission, they began plundering the great Quraysh caravan trains that plodded between Mecca and Syria. Up to 2,000 camels, each laden with precious goods, would regularly pass near Medina. They were guarded by horsemen, but Muhammad was a brilliant military tactician and proved to be so time and time again. From small groups of about eight followers, the raiding parties soon grew as increasing numbers of local tribesmen joined them, attracted by their success. Raids to seize booty from enemy clans was a normal part of Arabian life. Muhammad was particularly successful, however, perhaps because he had elevated the raid into a fight sanctioned by Allah. Those who took part in the raids were transformed from plunderers into holy warriors, fulfilling the wishes of their God, Allah. In just the same way, late eleventh-century Christian kings battling over Muslim Spain would be transformed from warriors fighting for territory and personal glory, into Christian warriors fighting for the glory of their God (see Chapter 7).

Muhammad was defeating his Quraysh enemy while providing for his followers and gaining new ones. He could now add the promise of wealth to the promise of peace on this earth and paradise in the next.

In March 624, news reached Mecca that Muhammad's forces were planning to ambush a particularly valuable Quraysh caravan from Syria in which nearly all Mecca's merchants were invested. As well as merchandize it was carrying 50,000 gold dinars – a vast treasure. Anxious to preserve their investment, about 950 of Mecca's chiefs and fighting men rode out to confront Muhammad's forces at Badr, a regular watering place for camel caravans.

At daybreak on March 13, the Quraysh, mounted on camels and horses, confronted Muhammad's men. The Quraysh were confident of victory – Muhammad was outnumbered three to one; according to tradition he had about 300 men, just seventy camels, and only two horses.

As was the custom of war, a Quraysh nobleman issued a challenge to single combat by sword; three of Muhammad's men stepped forward to answer the challenge and dispatched three Meccans. Muhammad, an arrow in his hand, threw a handful of pebbles towards the Meccans, a gesture which was probably the traditional prelude to Arab battles, and which all pilgrims to Mecca now make. Shouting 'Foul be those faces!' he ordered his forces to charge. Then, according to Ibn Ishaq, he retired with his faithful Companion Abu Bakr to a shelter made of palm branches where he had a 'light sleep'.

Horses 'snorting under the weight of the spearmen', warriors in coats of mail, wearing helmets that left only their eyes visible, or with cloths bound round their heads, and ostrich feathers on their breasts, hacked at each other with their swords; one combatant remembered cutting off a man's foot and seeing it flying through the air like 'a date-stone flying from the pestle when it is beaten'. Through clouds of dust 'each man advanced towards his enemy walking as though to shake hands'.[6] Indeed, the enemy knew each other intimately. The Quraysh and many of the Muslims they were fighting belonged to the same tribe; they were killing each others' relatives. Knowing that his uncle was fighting with the Quraysh enemy, Muhammad ordered that his life should be spared on the grounds that he had been forced to fight against his will;

Muhammad also spared several others whom, he said, had never insulted him in Mecca.

By early afternoon the battle was over. As vultures circled overhead and black-faced hyenas feasted on human flesh, the victorious Muslims threw the dead Quraysh into a pit, and quarrelled over the booty, until Muhammad intervened. The Quraysh who had driven Muhammad and his followers out of Mecca and who had thought they would have an easy victory, had been humiliated. Muhammad's forces had beaten a far larger army, killing forty-five Meccans at the cost of only fourteen of their men.

An army has to be united if it is to be a serious fighting force. This may be the monotheist's greatest asset: the ability, even in the face of the ultimate personal sacrifice, to create group cohesion. 'A hundred of you, if steadfast, will overcome a thousand of the disbelievers,' Allah told Muhammad in sura 8, which is dedicated to the victory at Badr.

Muhammad's triumphant forces set off back to Medina taking with them seventy 'unbelieving prisoners' whom they intended to ransom in exchange for gold or camels – pregnant camels being particularly valuable. Amongst the prisoners was Umayyah ibn Khalaf, a prominent Quraysh, who had been the former master and tormentor of Bilal. When Bilal caught sight of him, he screamed 'Worst of infidels! Let me die if he be allowed to live!' Umayyah was promptly stabbed to death by Muhammad's troops.[7]

The victory at Badr was a decisive moment for Muhammad and Islam. It was convincing proof that theirs was the side to join, and it established Muhammad as a force to be reckoned with. Tribes beyond Medina submitted to him; if they did not willingly submit, he was now powerful enough to enforce their submission. Shortly after the Battle of Badr, Muhammad expelled two of Medina's three most important Jewish tribes, the Nadir and the Qaynuqa.

When Muhammad first arrived in Medina in 622 he had happily adopted Jewish religious practices, confident that the Jews would soon convert to Islam. But only sixteen months later he had recognized that some Jews were never going to accept him as a prophet. On the contrary, the rabbis would 'laugh and scoff at their [the Muslims'] religion', according to Ibn Ishaq. The Jews were opposing Muhammad both religiously and politically. They had made alliances with his enemy the Quraysh, which under the Constitution of Medina they were forbidden to do.

The two tribes were given the choice of death or exile. Most chose exile. In a wonderful gesture of defiance the departing Nadir filed through the town on 600 camels, to the sound of pipes and timbrels. The women, dressed in their finest clothes, proudly took off their veils to show their faces. Following the tribes' expulsion, Muhammad parcelled out their land – they had owned some of the most fertile palm groves in the oasis – between himself and his fellow exiles. They had arrived landless and without possessions in Medina. The immediate problem of their livelihood was solved.

In the same year that Muhammad triumphed over the pagans at the Battle of Badr, he received a revelation: Muslims should stop facing northwards towards Jerusalem when they prayed, as they had been doing, and instead face south towards Mecca. Muslims ceased to share the Jews' fast day of atonement held in the first month of the Islamic calendar; in its stead they instituted their own fast in Ramadan, the ninth month of the Islamic calendar, the month in which the Quran was first revealed to Muhammad and in which the Battle of Badr was fought. The hajj, the pilgrimage to Mecca, was now declared to be a necessary part of Muslim ritual.

Islam and Judaism had parted company. In the Quran (3:12–13) Allah commands Muhammad to:

> ... say to the disbelievers, 'You will be defeated and driven together into Hell, a foul resting place. You have already seen a sign in the two armies that met in battle, one fighting for God's cause and the other made up of disbelievers. With their own eyes [the former] saw [the latter] to be twice their number, but God helps whoever He will.'

The rules and rituals that would distinguish Islam from its adversaries and competitors were being formulated. The days of accommodation with other monotheists were over. Indicatively, Muhammad abandoned the

Jewish fashion of wearing his shoulder-length hair loose and began to part it with a comb.

In 627, just five years after his arrival, Muhammad fell on the third and only surviving Jewish tribe left in Medina, the Qurayza. The Qurayza had also been guilty of allying with the Quraysh against Medina. But this time Muhammad did not let the Jews make a defiant exit from the city. According to Ibn Ishaq, all the men of the tribe – about 600 to 800 men – were beheaded in the marketplace. Their bodies were thrown into specially dug trenches, while the women and children were sold into slavery – standard practice at the time.

After the massacre, hardly any Jews remained in Medina, certainly too few to pose any threat to Muhammad. Medina was now effectively a Muslim state. Muhammad went on to conquer the Jewish tribes in nearby oasis settlements, including the Nadir, the tribe he had expelled from Medina. The head of the tribe had already been executed. His beautiful nineteen-year-old daughter Safiyya was enslaved as part of the war booty acquired by Muhammad. But as a goodwill gesture he proposed marrying her if she would convert to Islam. Muhammad had already taken another Jewish slave, Rayhana, under the same conditions, after her husband had been killed in the massacre of Qurayza men in Medina. Safiyya readily agreed to convert: she had little to lose, she told Muhammad, because all her family had been killed. After the wedding, Safiyya covered her face with a veil as Muhammad told all his wives to do, and became a prestigious 'Mother of Believers'.

In 630 Muhammad had his sweetest victory: the conquest of Mecca, the town which had expelled him. On the day that Mecca surrendered, Muhammad went to the Kaaba and encompassed it seven times on his camel. Then he ordered that all of the Kaaba's 360 idols should be smashed and burned – only the images of Jesus and Mary were to be preserved.

'O Quraysh, God has taken from you the haughtiness of paganism,' Muhammad told his erstwhile persecutors. The Qurayshi men paid homage to the seated Muhammad and promised to obey God and his apostle 'to the best of their ability'; the women were asked to go one step further and had to admit that there is no god but Allah, after which Muhammad plunged his hand in a vessel of water, a gesture repeated by the women. Muhammad's pagan enemies in Mecca had formally surrendered: they had accepted Islam.

From then on increasing numbers of pagan, Jewish and Christian tribes submitted to him, often without even a fight. Under the terms of their surrender they were given the choice of converting to Islam or continuing to practise their own religion but on two conditions: they must accept Muslim supremacy, and pay a tribute, *jizya*. If the Jewish and Christian tribes refused to be converted or to pay the *jizya*, they would be killed. Muhammad had moved from *accepting* religious pluralism as embodied in the Constitution of Medina to *bestowing* religious tolerance.

After their submission to Muhammad, the large and established community of Christian merchants in Najran, in today's Saudi Arabia, were guaranteed the 'protection of God and the *dhimma* [guarantee of protection] of Muhammad the prophet, the Messenger of God, for themselves, their community, their land, and their goods ... and for their churches and services (no bishop will be moved from his episcopate, and no monk from his monastic position)'. In return they had to hand over 2,000 robes and support the Muslim army when necessary by lending 'thirty coats of mail, thirty horses, and thirty camels'. The Jews of Khaybar had to submit half of their date palm harvest. The Jewish tribe of a fishing town had to pay annually: 'a quarter of what your palm trees produce, a quarter of what your fishing rafts [or fishermen] catch and a quarter of what your women weave' plus 'all the fine cloth and all the slaves among you and all the horses and the armour'. Such arrangements would form the template for how Jews and Christians would be treated throughout the Islamic Empire, which at its largest extended from Spain through North Africa and across the Middle East to the borders of China. In essence, Jews and Christians were told 'we will put up with you, if you will pay up'. They lived under such a system until the Ottoman empire was forced to abandon it by the European Great Powers in the nineteenth century (see Chapter 20).

Muhammad, like Theodosius over 300 years earlier, was far more severe on the pagans. As far as he was concerned Jews and Christians may have been perversely refusing to recognize the truth of Islam, but they did at least believe in a single God. Paganism's multiple gods worshipped by multiple warring tribes had to be eradicated in order to create a new dispensation of an Arabia united by belief in one God, one law and one law-giver.

'Wherever you encounter the idolaters, kill them, seize them, besiege them, wait for them at every lookout post; but if they repent, maintain the prayer, and pay the prescribed alms, let them go on their way, for God is most forgiving and merciful,' Allah tells Muhammad (Quran 9:5).

The 'sword verse', as it is called, is perhaps the most well known and contentious verse in the Quran. Today it is used by Islam's critics to highlight the violent and antagonistic nature of Islam. But scholars have been arguing over its meaning for over 1,300 years and are still doing so. Some take the view that it is a general injunction to kill all non-Muslims. According to their argument, the sword verse was revealed to Muhammad in Medina in 631, the year before he died. It therefore can be seen as abrogating the many earlier tolerant Meccan suras such as 'there is no compulsion in religion' (2:256) or indeed what can be interpreted as an embrace of religious pluralism, 'Had your Lord willed, all the people on earth would have believed. So can you [Prophet] compel people to believe?' (10:99). In the Meccan suras, Allah had instructed Muhammad not to fight the Quraysh. They were too powerful and Muhammad and his small group of followers were in no position to confront them; patience was their best tactic. By 631, however, Muhammad's position in Medina was secure enough that he could spread the message of his God aggressively. Indeed, later in the sura, believers who refuse to fight are threatened with hellfire (9:81).

Pagans, according to this interpretation, had to choose between conversion or death. On the other hand, the People of the Book, as Jews, Christians and often Zoroastrians were called, should not be killed if they did not convert to Islam, but only if they flouted the conditions of their protection (9:29):

> Fight those of the People of the Book who do not [truly] believe in God and the Last Day, who do not forbid what God and His Messenger have forbidden, who do not obey the rule of justice, until they pay the tax [the *jizya*] promptly and agree to submit.

Many scholars, however, including Abdel Haleem whose well-respected translation of the Quran I use in this book, argue that the sword verse applied specifically to the pagans who had just violated their peace treaties with Muhammad and waged war against the Muslims. The verse should not therefore be understood as a general command to wage war against non-Muslims.

Judaism, too, has its bloodthirsty injunctions from Yahweh to exterminate the idolaters – the Canaans and Amalekites – from the Land of Israel and 'not leave anything alive that breathes' (Deuteronomy 20:16–18). Fundamentalist Jewish groups like the defunct but still influential radical Zionist settler movement Gush Emunim in Israel, identify Palestinian Arabs, and Arabs generally, with the Canaanites or Amalekites and therefore claim that Jews have a duty to make war on them. But most rabbinic scholars consider that the holy wars commanded by Yahweh were limited in time and target to the idolaters of the biblical era – the same argument used by liberal Islamic scholars.

Nonetheless, the sword verse has been used as a terrible weapon in the hands of Islamic terrorists. And certainly it is true that there is nothing as bloodthirsty in Christianity's holy scripture, the New Testament. Warfare is part and parcel of Islam in a way that it is not in Christianity – perhaps inevitably so. As political leader as well as prophet, Muhammad had to be a warrior, and a good one, in order not just to protect his people (it would be entirely inappropriate to call them his flock) but to ensure the victory of Islam, as God had ordered him to do. Muhammad's military campaigns and raids were essential to the survival and success of Islam. Ibn Ishaq's biography was, in fact, initially called *Kitab al-Maghazi* (Book of Campaigns).

*

Muhammad died in 632 at the age of about sixty-two. His favourite wife Aisha laid him on her lap and beat her breast and slapped her face in grief. He was washed, laid on a bed in his house and visited by mourners who argued over where he should be buried.

Uniquely amongst the founders of the three major monotheisms, Muhammad died triumphant. Whereas Moses had died outside the Promised Land after forty years of wandering in the desert, and Jesus had suffered the common fate of ordinary criminals and been crucified as a rebel, Muhammad was probably the most renowned, feared and venerated figure in Arabia. He had triumphed religiously, militarily and politically. He had united Arabia under Islam; his forces were about to conquer much of the known world.

The state created by Muhammad may have begun as a multi-religious state, but it ended as a theocracy, which recognized God as its ultimate ruler. The Medinan state created by Muhammad in the seventh century is the model by which even today many Muslims judge their governments.

After Muhammad's death, a struggle broke out over who should succeed him as leader of the Muslim community. The choice was between Abu Bakr, Muhammad's father-in-law and close companion who had fled with him from Mecca, and Ali, Muhammad's 31-year-old cousin and son-in-law, married to Muhammad's daughter Fatima. Abu Bakr won. His victory would form the basis of the schism which slowly developed between those who began to define themselves as Sunnis (people of the sunna) and Shiites (the 'partisans' of Ali).* The Sunni–Shia schism has killed and is still killing countless Muslims, although it is worth noting that over the centuries Christians have killed far more of their co-religionists than Muslims have theirs.

Shiites claim that Abu Bakr and his supporters engineered a coup in defiance of Muhammad's dying wishes; Sunnis claim that Muhammad had never chosen Ali to be his successor. According to Sunnis, Abu Bakr was elected by his fellow Muslims in Medina on the sound political

* Sunna, meaning traditions, refers to the normative example set by Muhammad in his words and deeds as recorded in the Hadith.

grounds that he had been the most senior of Muhammad's followers and was best able to preserve the unity of the Muslim State. Around these opposing views of the succession would develop very different attitudes as to the relationship between political and religious leadership, resulting in a different understanding of the Quran and the role of the ulema, the religious scholars.

Abu Bakr gave himself the title 'Successor [caliph, from the Arabic *khalifa* meaning deputy or successor] of the Prophet of God'. By this he meant that he had inherited from Muhammad the leadership of the Muslim community, the *umma*. But what was the nature of the authority he had inherited? Sunnis believed that Abu Bakr had not inherited Muhammad's spiritual perfection – that had died with him. Nonetheless he would still be the religious ruler of the *umma*, ensuring that it observed the law and defending it from attack. How far the caliph or imam (the titles were interchangeable) was entitled to pronounce on religious matters and interpret the law would be a matter of dispute with the ulema for the following two centuries. The struggle over the ownership of religious power would also be crucial to the history of Christendom though in significantly different ways, as we will see.

Shiites, however, believed that since Muhammad had chosen his cousin Ali, the Prophet had clearly intended that the imam should inherit, literally, his own spiritual perfection as the mouthpiece of God. That meant that the imam would be the political leader of the *umma*, but would also be its infallible religious guide.

Ali did indeed become the fourth caliph, though as far as Shiites are concerned the preceding three caliphs were illegitimate. But he was assassinated in 661 by a group of his own followers. Civil war had broken out between Ali and the governor of Syria, Muawiyah, but after an indecisive battle in 657 Ali had been forced to agree to arbitration. This concession so enraged some of his followers that they formed a breakaway group. The Kharijites, as they were called (from *kharaja*, to secede), believed they were justified in killing Ali because by resorting to settling the matter by human arbitration he was contradicting the Quranic verse 'Judgement is for God alone' (6:57). Ali was therefore, according to the Kharijites, a *kafir*, an unbeliever or apostate, and the punishment for apostasy was death. By declaring a Muslim to be an apostate, a practice known as *takfir*, the Kharijites had sidestepped the Quranic ban on killing fellow Muslims. In fact it was a duty to wage jihad against them and kill them. The Kharijites had broken new ground. They had taken upon themselves the right to declare who was and was not a believer. *Takfir*, as a theological justification for murdering their co-religionists, would later be practised by modern extremists to devastating effect.

Since his assassination by the Kharijites in 661, the followers of Ali, the Shiites, have venerated him as martyr and saint. They insist that only the descendants of the murdered Ali and Fatima can be legitimate rulers, governing as semi-infallible priest-kings. But by the tenth century they believed that Ali's descendant, who should have been the rightful ruler, had been forced to withdraw from the world and go into hiding (occultation) because of Sunni persecution. Although Shiites disagree as to which imam was forced to do so, they do agree that he will return at the end of time as the Mahdi, the equivalent of the Jewish Messiah, who will restore peace and justice on earth and rule over a world converted to Islam. In the meantime they have accorded to their most respected religious scholars the authority to act as the occulted imam's earthly spokesmen.

Within a few decades of Muhammad's death, illiterate Muslim tribesmen were conquering the most sophisticated cities of the Mediterranean world. Muhammad had moulded a religion for empire builders. He had used the binding power of monotheism to turn warring pagan tribes into united Muslim warriors. Their victories within the Arabian peninsula had convinced more and more tribes to submit to Allah. Allah had told them to fight against the unbeliever wherever he might be found; they had been rewarded richly for obeying him. Why should they confine their conquests to Arabia?

Monotheism, especially in its more explicitly universal forms of Christianity and Islam, had already proved that it would not tolerate competition. The monotheistic God loved everyone. But Allah, Yahweh and the Christian God were mutually exclusive. Muhammad had never assumed an egalitarian attitude towards the Jewish and Christian religions. He had first assumed that they would inevitably recognize the superiority of Islam, which was after all the perfected version of their religions. But when they failed to do so he had extended tolerance towards them – that is to say, he would put up with them. By definition that meant they were inferiors.

As the following chapters will repeatedly demonstrate, intolerance is not the opposite of tolerance, but its essential concomitant. To tolerate is to dislike and that can easily turn to hate. Tolerance and intolerance are on a continuum. Both Christian and Muslim empires alternated between the two; but the Muslim empire would rely on the pragmatic advantages of tolerance far more than the Christian empire did. And although it is demeaning to be put up with, nonetheless, as Jews and Christians in the Muslim world discovered, it is much better to be allowed to exist, even if grudgingly, than to be persecuted.

CHAPTER 3

THE PRICE OF TOLERATION: THE *DHIMMI* IN THE ISLAMIC EMPIRE

'Humiliate them, but do them no injustice.'

– Umar I (caliph 634–644)

'Toleration is not the opposite of intoleration, but is the counterfeit of it. Both are despotisms. The one assumes to itself the right of withholding liberty of conscience, and the other of granting it.'

– Thomas Paine, *Rights of Man*, part 1, *Life 6:101–6*, 1791

IN 634, TWO YEARS after the death of Muhammad, about 20,000 Arab tribesmen laid siege to the Byzantine empire's great walled city of Damascus in Syria.

The desperate Damascans managed to smuggle out a letter to their emperor Heraclius, begging for help. And on the twentieth day of the siege, help came. Wearing glittering armour, and brandishing their flags and crosses, Byzantine reinforcements arrived. The Arab forces were heavily outnumbered, according to the early ninth-century historian al-Waqidi. But undaunted, Dirwar, the Muslim general, advanced bare chested on his horse, shouting the great rallying cry of 'Allahu Akbar' ('God is Great'). Behind him his spearmen, with their leather shields, gilded helmets, their faces half covered with the tail of their turbans, closed ranks forming a protective wall behind which the archers fired their arrows. Damascus – where 600 years earlier, Saul, the persecutor of the Jesus cult, had become Paul, the founder of Christianity – surrendered. It was the first major city of the Byzantine empire to fall to the Arabs.

Over the following ten years Arab forces rearranged the Mediterranean world and became its military superpower. And yet in creating their new empire, the Arabs actually followed much the same path that their Roman predecessors had used when they created their empire – one that oscillated between the 'multicultural' tolerance of the taxman and secure ruler to the monocultural/monotheist intolerance of the leader who fears that power is slipping from him and so attempts to forge a unified people.

By 642, under the leadership of their caliph Umar I, Arab forces had achieved the unthinkable. A mere ten years after Muhammad's death, they had conquered two thirds of the Byzantine Empire, including its two most important provinces, Egypt, the breadbasket of the empire, and Syria/Palestine, the heartland of Christianity. They had also conquered almost the whole of the Persian Empire.

The extent of the Arabs' victories, achieved, as even the seventh-century Christian bishop and chronicler Sebeos conceded, 'in the twinkling of an eye', was proof indeed that Allah was on their side, that Islam was the true religion. But such victories could never have been so easily achieved without the support of the Christians and Jews who had no love for either the Byzantine or the Persian empires. They had been abused, exploited, persecuted and massacred by both empires and caught up for far too long in the incessant and devastating wars between the two.

Not surprisingly, the Arab invaders exploited the bitter resentment felt by Jews and those Christian communities who were persecuted by the Byzantine authorities for refusing to follow the orthodox line on the nature of Christ's divinity formulated at the Council of Nicaea (see Chapter 1).* The Byzantine emperor Heraclius, 'the Misbeliever' as the

* Since the Persian Empire's Zoroastrian shahanshah ('King of Kings') believed in a supreme god amongst many gods, rather than *the* supreme God amongst no others, they were more tolerant towards their religious minorities than the Christian Byzantine Empire.

Copts (Egyptian Christians) called him, had expelled the head of the Coptic Church, Patriarch Benjamin, from Alexandria. The Muslim commander, 'Amr ibn al-'As, used the expulsion to his advantage. Before laying siege to the city in 641, he wisely made sure to announce that he would welcome the patriarch back. And he was as good as his word. After capturing this huge prize – Alexandria was the biggest trading city in the Roman world – the patriarch, Benjamin, was allowed to return, his Coptic Church was declared the official church and 'the people and the whole city rejoiced', according to the ninth-century Muslim historian al-Baladhuri. The same story of benevolence played itself out in Jerusalem, where Heraclius had expelled Jews from the city and where the Arab invaders welcomed them back.

'We like your rule and justice far better than the state of oppression and tyranny under which we have been living,' the Jews of Emesa (Homs in today's Syria) told the invading Muslim army, as reported by al-Baladhuri. Everywhere Christians and Jews shut the gates of their cities against the Byzantine forces and greeted the Arabs with music and dancing. And in some ways the Arabs, following the arc of tolerance taken by all empire builders, justified the hopes placed in them.

In about 637 the caliph Umar I, who was bald and stout despite his ascetic diet, was fond of wrestling and dyed his beard orange with henna as Muhammad had done, signed two peace treaties, one with the Christians of Syria and one with the Jews and Christians of Jerusalem. Out of those two treaties Muslim jurists (the scholars who were experts in Islamic law) would later create the set of regulations known today as the Pact of Umar. It would be the template for how Muslim rulers would treat the 'People of the Book'. Humiliating as it was, the pact would always be regarded as having been modelled on treaties to which the Jews and Christians had themselves allegedly agreed.

When Muhammad drew up his Constitution of Medina he was in a very different position vis-à-vis non-Muslims than Umar was when he drew up the Pact of Umar. Muhammad did not enter Medina with an army behind him. He was no victor able to dictate terms, as Umar was, but a man whose only weapons were the respect he commanded and his God. The constitution was the result of negotiation and agreement. This was not tolerance, since tolerance entails that one party has the power to bestow or withdraw it, and Muhammad had none. The Pact of Umar, on the other hand, was a set of regulations drawn up by the victors. Tolerance requires an asymmetry of power between groups, and the pact, in many ways the quintessential document of tolerance, makes that very plain. Tolerance is an attitude of the powerful. When you are weak, you make alliances with others; when you are strong, you may find it opportune to tolerate them. It is why tax-farming empires tend to be tolerant. Their concern is to keep the empire together, and that depends on maintaining the flow of taxes which fund it, which in turn depends on not unnecessarily antagonizing the different communities of which an empire is comprised.

But although Umar had conquered, he was nevertheless dependent on his newly created subject communities. He and his Arab forces were a tiny minority in a sea of Christians, Jews and Zoroastrians. Arabs numbered about 500,000 out of a total population of about 30 million, spanning three continents from Egypt, through the Middle East, to Iran, Afghanistan and Pakistan. The Jewish community in Alexandria alone numbered about 40,000. Apart from the ordinary Christian Copt peasants and city-dwellers, thousands of Christian hermits led their ascetic lives in the desert to the south where they lived in caves, although a few took their asceticism to the next level and perched atop pillars (the 'pillar saints' or 'Stylites', from the Greek meaning 'pillar dwellers'). While the hermits may not have been particularly useful to a new empire, Umar *did* need the Christians and Jews for their craftsmanship, scholarship and to cultivate the land. Above all, he needed their administrative know-how and their taxes. These people had been living in and running sophisticated empires for centuries. Like the Germanic tribesmen who conquered the Roman Empire over the course of the third to fifth centuries, the Arabs were in the sometimes awkward position of being far less technically and culturally equipped than the peoples they had conquered – except in the techniques of war and brute force.

The Arab invaders came from an oral, not a literary culture; their cities were small oasis trading settlements. A predominantly pastoral, nomadic people, they found themselves in command of cities whose inhabitants numbered in the hundreds of thousands, whose scholars could look back on centuries of written learning, whose language, god and customs were totally alien. Even the all-conquering Arab general who had captured Alexandria in 641 was dazzled by its grandeur. 'It is impossible for me to enumerate the variety of its riches and beauty,' he wrote to the caliph Umar, 'and I shall content myself with observing that it contains 4,000 palaces, 4,000 baths, 400 theatres or places of amusement, 12,000 shops for the sale of vegetable food, and 40,000 tributary Jews.' It would take less than a century for Islamic cities to equal their Byzantine and Persian predecessors in intellectual and artistic achievements. But until then the Islamic Empire had to rely on the skills of its conquered peoples; convenience therefore dictated that they should be tolerated.

But to be tolerated meant, of course, that they were not equal to Muslims: *dhimmis*, as the People of the Book were known because they were given protection (*dhimma*) under the Pact of Umar, had to pay a special tax, the *jizya*, in exchange for their protection. As we have seen, such a tax was not new. Muhammad had imposed it on the Jewish and Christian tribes who had surrendered to him in Arabia. Before Umar's conquests, the Persian empire had similarly allowed its non-Zoroastrian communities freedom to practice their own religion and have their own schools and law courts, on the condition that they paid tribute; Jews had to do the same in the Christian Roman Empire.

It is not surprising that the Pact of Umar was in many ways an adaptation of the rules by which the two empires that Umar was conquering had previously dealt with their Christian and Jewish minorities. The newly emerging Islamic Empire was simply following the pragmatic tolerance required of an empire. But Umar's pact most closely resembled Christian Rome's Theodosian Code, a collection of all the laws enacted by the Christian emperors against Jews since 312 CE. Indeed, in many ways the pact seems to be an Islamicized version of the Theodosian Code. Grudging in tone, reeking of superiority, it epitomizes what makes tolerance preferable to intolerance but still not something to be wished for. Monotheism may be prepared to put up with other monotheists, but it is clear that they in no way celebrate each other's existence.

'I will not honour them [the *dhimmis*] when God has degraded them; I will not glorify them when God has humiliated them; I will not bring them near when God has set them far away,' Umar is alleged to have told the governor of Kufa in Iraq.[1] *Dhimmis* should never feel themselves to be equals with Muslims, just as the Roman Empire's Theodosian Code insisted that Jews should never feel equal to Christians.

'We [*dhimmis*] shall show deference to the Muslims and shall rise from our seats when they wish to sit down,' is one of the stipulations imposed in the pact. Both physically and metaphorically the *dhimmis* should never be at the same level, and certainly never above, that of a Muslim. For this reason *dhimmi* men were forbidden to ride horses or camels: instead they had to ride the lowly (literally) ass and sit side-saddle like a woman. They always had to yield the centre of the road to Muslims. They were not allowed to build their homes higher than a Muslim's.

Dhimmis 'must not attempt to resemble the Muslims in any way with regard to their dress' or hairstyle. That was not difficult to comply with in the early days of conquest: desert Arabs dressed completely differently from their new Byzantine and Persian subjects. Arab men wore turbans and sandals and parted their long hair; to avoid any doubts, however, *dhimmi* men had to cut their hair short at the front and wear a belt in order that they should be easily distinguishable from Muslims.

While Muslim women were required to cover their faces with a veil when they went outside, *dhimmi* and slave women could go barefaced. In some instances they were actually forbidden to wear the veil. Virtue and propriety belonged only to Muslim women.* *Dhimmi* men were of course

* While the Quran insists that women dress modestly, it refers only once to the hijab, and this in the sense of a screen or curtain, and only with reference to the Prophet's wives: 'When you [the Believers] ask his wives for something, do so from behind a screen: this is purer both for your hearts and for theirs' (Quran 33:53). The Quran also enjoins women when in public 'to make their outer garments hang low over them so as to be recognized and not insulted' (33:59).

forbidden to marry or touch a Muslim woman, just as the Theodosian Code had forbidden Jews to marry Christians. They were not allowed to carry weapons, a real symbol of inferiority in a society where it was normal if not essential to do so. *Dhimmis* were not to be considered legally equal with a Muslim; they could not give evidence in court against a Muslim, and their oaths were unacceptable in an Islamic court.

Dhimmis were forbidden on pain of death to mock or criticize the Quran, Islam or Muhammad. They were forbidden to proselytize, or, as one version of the pact puts it, 'use your idolatrous language about Jesus, the son of Mary, to any Muslim'. They were told not to 'parade your idolatry':[2] they were allowed to worship as long as they did so inconspicuously, which meant they could not display crosses in public, hold public religious processions, build new places of worship or pray too loudly. The Theodosian Code had similarly banned Jews from building new synagogues and from praying or chanting if they could be heard by Christians in neighbouring churches.

'Humiliate them, but do them no injustice,' Umar is alleged to have said of the *dhimmis*. And that about sums up 'tolerance': a scrupulous and fair application of rules concerning minorities which protect them but insist on their inferiority.

The *dhimmis* bought their safety and their freedom to practice their own religion at the price of the *jizya* and their humiliation.* If tolerance entailed humiliation, that was perhaps a small price to pay for life, and the liberty to worship one's own god. But the problem with tolerance is that because it is bestowed, it can equally well be withdrawn. As we have already had cause to note, intolerance is not the opposite of tolerance but simply a nastier version of it. To tolerate is to put up with what you don't like; the inferiority, the distastefulness, of the tolerated is a given.

---

* Although the Ottoman Empire officially abolished the status of *dhimmi* in the nineteenth century, non-Muslims are still severely discriminated against in some Muslim states, such as Saudi Arabia, Iran and Pakistan; restoration of the *dhimmi* system is, of course, the aim of extremist Muslim groups such as the Taliban, al-Qaeda and the Islamic State (ISIS).

Islam, Christianity and Judaism might preach equality; but equality between rival monotheisms would have amounted to theological absurdity. 'Verily, this is the authentic religion of truth,' could have been the words of Jew, Christian or Muslim although they were actually written by the twelfth-century rabbinic scholar and philosopher Maimonides, who was referring to Judaism. It is the potential fate of all monotheists to think their brand of monotheism is the best and the only.

Umar's vision of his new empire was that the Arabs would live as a military elite in their garrison towns segregated from the corrupting influence of the *dhimmi* who would provide the peasant labour force, the skilled artisans, the administrative know-how and the taxes to fund the empire. Fustat, now part of today's Cairo in Egypt, began its life in 643 as a tented garrison town centred around a Byzantine fortress. Soon Copts and Jews were moving into the town. Payment – bribes – to the right authorities solved the problem of the ban on building new places of worship, so churches and synagogues soon appeared along with mosques. As long as they paid the *jizya*, the Copts were allowed their churches and monasteries and to live under their patriarch and administer their own affairs – a freedom that had legally been denied them under the Byzantine Empire.

As the years wore on, the conquered and the conquerors inevitably began to intermingle. The garrison towns developed into ordinary towns and cities where Jews and Christians migrated to service the needs of the townspeople. The new Muslim rulers imported thousands of Arab Bedouins to farm the land. They lived side by side with their fellow Christian and Jewish peasants. They worked under the same landowners and often rebelled with them against the hardships they jointly endured, especially the land tax that was becoming more onerous with each passing year. *Dhimmi* women married Muslim men (the other way round was forbidden under the Pact of Umar). Muslims and *dhimmis* were mixing together, much to the concern not just of Muslims but of Christians also. 'A terrible report about dissipated Christians has come to the hearing of our humble self,' wrote Patriarch Athanasius of Balad to his archbishops in 683. 'Greedy men, who are slaves of the belly, are heedlessly and senselessly taking part with the pagans [as Christians called Muslims] in feasts together, wretched women mingle anyhow with the pagans unlawfully and indecently.' Athanasius, the seventh-century patriarch of Antioch, could have been John Chrysostom talking about Christian relations with Jews in Antioch three centuries earlier.

The Pact of Umar was interpreted leniently or stringently according to the waxing and waning of the fortunes of the empire and its rulers. Christendom's treatment of Jews – the only visible minority in Christendom – similarly fluctuated, though far more violently.

In the early days of the Muslim empire, the emphasis was less on the humiliations to be imposed on the *dhimmis*, than on the money that was to be extracted from them. 'No one of the people of the *dhimma* should be beaten in order to exact payment of the *jizya*, nor made to stand in the hot sun, nor should hateful things be inflicted upon their bodies ... Rather, they should be treated with leniency,' wrote one of the celebrated Islamic jurists of the eighth century, Abu Yusuf. In later, less tolerant, times, the collector of the *jizya* might be required to slap the *dhimmi*'s neck when he handed over his tax, which was usually paid in goods such as ropes or needles.

But no minority – in Christendom or Islamdom – would have expected an equality of respect. If part of monotheism's appeal was precisely its message of the equality of humankind, that equality really only applied to those who belonged to the same monotheism, not to those who followed a different monotheistic god. Tolerance was the most that any minority could hope for.

Arab forces committed the inevitable violence of conquerors towards their enemy's religion – they burned down churches, destroyed monasteries, desecrated crosses. But the Arab invaders rarely tortured Christians, nor forced them to convert on pain of death; even prisoners of war were left unmolested. Jews and those Christians who under their former Byzantine Christian rulers had been branded as heretics – Copts in Egypt, Nestorians in Iraq, Jacobites in Syria – would have compared their lot favourably with what they had experienced under the previous regime and with what the Jews were beginning to experience in Europe, the western half of the old Roman Empire. Christians and Jews were in general left unmolested to flourish economically and intellectually.

Testament to the comparative benignity of the new Arab Muslim rulers was the extraordinarily slow rate of conversion to Islam on the part of Christians and Jews – for the wealthier, being a *dhimmi* was not so uncomfortable that they needed to convert. Nor was it in the interests of the Arab rulers to force them to do so: more Muslim converts diluted the status of the Arabs, and more importantly the fewer the *dhimmis*, the lower the tax revenues. Money was preferable to faith. And from the *dhimmis'* point of view, there was not even a tax advantage to converting. Non-Arab converts to Islam still had to pay the *jizya*.

A little more than a hundred years after Muhammad's death in 632, the Islamic world had established itself from Spain to North Africa, the Middle East (Egypt, Iraq, Syria, Palestine and Iran) to the Central Asian lands of what is now Uzbekistan and Tajikistan, and to India. Only Alexander the Great's empire could rival the new Muslim empire in geographic scope and the speed with which it was acquired.

But by 685, when Abd al-Malik (the fifth caliph of the Umayyad dynasty) came to the throne, the empire was reaching its limits. Or at least it was expanding into the less profitable parts of the former Roman Empire. And as expansion slowed down, and the profitability of conquest decreased, intolerance towards the *dhimmis* increased.

The Arab warriors who in 634 had halted in amazement before the vast dazzling cities of the empires they were about to conquer, had been recruited from tribes across Arabia. Thanks to Muhammad, they had been united to fight under a single all-powerful God. But the prospect of the spoils of war had also been a powerful incentive. Indeed, the fact that Muslims were forbidden to fight each other was an added incentive to embark on foreign conquest for those Arab tribesmen who had converted to Islam, since raiding other tribes had previously been an important source of livelihood. But the booty was drying up. The Muslim rulers of this new empire, well aware that they must keep their soldiers united when there was less in the way of war spoils with which to bribe them, turned to their religion. It was the best way of uniting their men – and keeping them united. The men's reward would be in the conviction of the superiority of their God, and therefore of themselves.

In 696 Abd al-Malik, nicknamed the 'fly killer' for his appalling bad breath, ordered the minting of a new coinage. On one side of the new gold coins was the inscription 'There is no god but God alone, He has no associate', and on the other 'Muhammad is the messenger of God whom He sent with guidance and the religion of truth that He might make it prevail over all religion'. Only a year before, the coins had shown the figure of a bearded Abd al-Malik, with curly, shoulder-length hair, wearing Arab robes, a Bedouin scarf headdress and an ornately decorated sword at his waist. Abd al-Malik the man had been replaced by the word of Allah. Henceforth every transaction that every subject of the new empire made would remind them that Islam was the religion of the empire. Abd al-Malik went on to declare that Arabic was now to become the administrative language of the empire, replacing Greek, Coptic, Aramaic and Persian.

It was a sign of the times that an Arab Christian, one of the most famous poets of his day, fell out of favour. Al-Akhtal had been a regular at the court of Abd al-Malik's father, partly on the strength of the panegyrics to the caliph that he had very sensibly written. He had clearly not been expected to honour any of the regulations specified in the Pact of Umar by which *dhimmis* were expected to show themselves inferior to Muslims, since he dressed in a silk *jubba*, the short jacket which was specifically banned under the pact's regulations, wore a gold cross round his neck and rode on a horse rather than the far smaller ass. He also appeared before the caliph with his beard dripping with wine. But Abd al-Malik's new assertion of the Islamic nature of his empire made such behaviour no longer acceptable at court.

Al-Walid, Abd al-Malik's son, gave even more evidence of the intolerance *dhimmis* could now expect under their rulers' determination to impose the Islamic nature of the empire. Islamic dominance meant Christian and Jewish subjection.

In the early days of the empire, it had been common practice for the conquering Muslims to worship in a Christian church and later negotiate with the Christian owners to buy the building. Under al-Walid's great-great-grandfather, Muawiyah, Christians in his capital city of Damascus shared the Church of St John with Muslims. In 651, the caliph asked for permission to extend that part of the church which was used as a mosque. The Christians refused; Muawiyah accepted their decision.

Not so his great-grandson al-Walid, fifty years later. In 711, when the Christians refused his request for an extension, al-Walid had the church smashed to pieces. The Umayyad Mosque was built on the rubble. To add insult to injury al-Walid used skilled craftsmen imported from Constantinople (today's Istanbul), the capital of what remained of the Christian Byzantine empire following the Islamic conquests of the seventh century. The Christian craftsmen decorated the mosque with gold and marble and richly coloured mosaics of trees and buildings set beside a flowing river; it was a depiction of Paradise, though a paradise that was empty of human figures.*

The new empire was rubbing the old empire's nose in its defeat. The Umayyad caliphs, triumphant rulers of an expanding empire, were riding high.

In 717 al-Walid's cousin and successor, Umar II, insisted on enforcing and extending the regulations of the Pact of Umar, which had been largely ignored by his predecessors. As far as the conquerors were concerned, the *dhimmis* were not sticking to their side of the tolerance bargain, so clearly articulated in the Pact of Umar – the acceptance of their inferiority. *Dhimmis* were even beginning to look like Muslims, from their curly shoulder-length hair to their Arab-like robes and silk *jubba*, strapped sandals and Bedouin scarf or turban. Periodically, over the centuries,

* Although several hadiths disapprove of figurative representation, it is nowhere forbidden in the Quran, which only forbids idolatry. For Jews and Christians, the Second Commandment also forbids idolatry but whether the prohibition on making images of any living thing applies only if they are made in order to be worshipped has been, and still is, open to either a strict or loose interpretation. Following the Reformation, the Protestant iconoclasts took the commandment very literally indeed.

this would become such a subject of resentment and concern on the part of Muslims that *dhimmis* would be forced to wear some distinguishing mark. In the twelfth century one caliph would insist that Jews wear a yellow badge. 'Inspired' by this example, the Catholic Church followed suit in 1215, the year of Magna Carta, by stipulating that all Jews and Muslims must wear distinctive dress.

But Umar II was the first caliph who demanded that *dhimmis* actually observe the *ghiyar*, that is, bear the physical signs of their inferiority by looking different from Muslims. *Dhimmis* had to wear a thick cord round their waist, a quilted sleeveless cloak, a tall cap and sandals with distinctive twisted thongs. They were forbidden to wear silk, sandals with straps or turbans, or have their hair long or appear in public unless they had cut the hair on their forehead short. When travelling from place to place they had to carry a lead seal round their neck, a sign that they had paid the *jizya*. Umar became the first caliph to order the dismissal of all *dhimmi* government officials in his empire – repeating the Jews' exclusion from government service under Byzantine rule. 'God honoured, exalted and strengthened His people with Islam, and put humiliation and shame on their opponents,' Umar told his governors, and then, obviously revelling in the success of his new policy: 'I do not know a secretary or official … who was not a Muslim but I dismissed him and appointed in his stead a Muslim.'

Dhimmis were not to be trusted. Had not Allah himself said 'do not take the Jews and Christians as allies' (Quran 5:51)? Ibn Umar, a Companion and brother-in-law of Muhammad, reported that Muhammad had warned Muslims to be on their guard when greeting a Jew: Jews were notorious for muttering 'may poison afflict you', *al-sammu 'alayka*, instead of the standard Arabic greeting 'peace be upon you', *as-salāmu 'alaykum*. Muhammad had recommended that the safest reply to the greeting should be an ambiguous 'may it be upon you too'.[3]

Dhimmis were now rated legally at half the value of a Muslim. According to a number of traditions, Muhammad was said to have fixed the blood money, the *diya*, payable to the relatives of a murdered Jew or Christian at the same price as that due the relatives of a murdered

Muslim – 1,000 dinar. Umar II, however, reduced the *diya* of a Jew or Christian to half that payable for a Muslim. Jurists, however, demurred. They argued that in fairness the *dhimmis*' and Muslims' *diya* should be equal, since the *dhimmi* had paid the *jizya* precisely in order to secure full protection.

As being a *dhimmi* became increasingly uncomfortable, the prospect of becoming a Muslim became that much more attractive, especially as Umar announced a financial incentive for converting. Previously *dhimmis* who accepted Islam still had to carry on paying the *jizya*. At some time during his short reign between 717 and 720 Umar decreed that non-Arab converts were exempt.

It was partly for this reason that Jewish and Christian peasants were converting in their droves. For those teetering on the margins of existence, the *jizya* combined with the increasingly onerous *kharaj*, the land tax, tipped them over the edge into starvation. 'Without blows or torture they [the Christian peasants] slid down in great eagerness toward denial,' records the *Zuqnin Chronicle*, written by a Syrian monk in the latter half of the eighth century. 'Forming groups of twenty, thirty and a hundred men, two and three hundred, without any kind of compulsion to this [though some might think the threat of starvation was a kind of compulsion], they went … to the governors and became Muslims.'

The Islamicization of the empire was in full flow. Turreted mosques pierced the city skylines of Alexandria, Damascus, and Jerusalem. Islamic designs and motifs flowered on Damascus's newly built palaces, surrounded by their shady, fountain-filled pleasure gardens.

By the mid eighth century Islamic expansion was finally at an end. In 711 Muslim troops had failed to wrest Constantinople from the Byzantines who were still clinging to the remnants of their empire. In western Europe, Muslims had conquered most of Christian Spain but their expansion north into Gaul had been halted at Poitiers in 732 by the Frankish king Charles Martel. The once indivisible Islamic Empire had split between the Abbasid dynasty who ruled the greater part of the empire (essentially Egypt, Syria, Iraq, Iran and the Central Asian steppes) from their new capital Baghdad in Iraq, and the Umayyads in Cordoba who ruled most of Spain and Portugal, al-Andalus (Muslim Spain), as it was called.

When Muslim Berbers from North Africa and Muslims from Arabia began their forays into Spain at the beginning of the eighth century, Jews welcomed them as liberators from their oppressive Christian rulers, just as in the sixth century Jews in the Byzantine empire had welcomed the Muslim invaders as liberators from *their* Christian rulers.

Jews had been living in western Europe since at least the first century BCE. Their lot had not significantly changed with the coming of Christianity in the late second century CE. Western Europe was far from the reach of Rome, and the Theodosian Code's regulations against Jews were largely ignored. Nor had the Jews' circumstances changed much with the great wave of Germanic tribesmen that overran the western Roman Empire during the following century. Jews lived in the same areas as their pagan or Christian neighbours. They farmed, grew vines or traded as merchants in the Mediterranean city ports; they fought together with pagans and Christians to defend their towns and dressed like the rest of the local population in knee-length tunics with cloth or skins bound about their legs by cross-gartering.

But on Christmas Day 498 the Jews' lot changed. The town of Reims was decked out with tapestried canopies. Its church was adorned with white curtains and sweet-smelling candles in honour of Clovis, pagan king of the Germanic tribe of Franks and the founder of France. With his long plaits hanging down on each side of his face as was his Merovingian clan's custom, Clovis advanced to the baptismal font and became the first Germanic king in the West to convert to Catholicism. Three thousand of his tattooed warriors not surprisingly followed their chief and converted also.

With the king on its side, and its bishops as his chief counsellors, the Church could now enforce the anti-Jewish regulations which it had not previously had the power to enforce. Jews began to be radically separated from the growing Christian population. They suffered the same fate in what was then Hispania (now Spain and Portugal) when their Visigoth ruler converted to Catholicism in 587. Church councils decreed that no Christian could marry a Jew; Christians were forbidden to eat with Jews or celebrate the Jewish Sabbath. The Talmud* and sharia also had interfaith marriage restrictions and discouraged sharing meals. The Talmud forbade Jews from marrying Christians, and prohibited eating food cooked by gentiles. Sharia law forbade Muslim women from marrying non-Muslim men, although Muslim men were allowed to marry Christian or Jewish women, and Islam's strict dietary laws effectively meant Muslims could not eat with Christians. The Church also decreed that no Jew was to be appointed to any official post that might put him in a position of superiority over a Christian. A similar stipulation, though with Muslims in the superior position, was included in the Pact of Umar. But because Christians held Jews responsible for Christ's crucifixion, Church council decrees against Jews were filled with a particular religious hatred missing from Islamic regulations. Jews were forbidden to leave their homes during Easter week because, said the Church synod of Orleans in 538, 'their appearance is an insult to Christianity'.

In the early seventh century King Sisebut in Hispania and King Dagobert in Gaul presented their Jewish communities with a choice: convert to Catholicism or be expelled. It was an ultimatum that Jews would be given all too often in the following centuries. To what extent these seventh-century ultimatums were put into effect is not clear. Certainly, over the course of the century Catholic legislation in Spain against Jews became more savage. They were forbidden to trade, forbidden to observe the Sabbath or circumcise their sons, were subjected to punitive taxation and forcibly baptized. It is not surprising then that Jews in Spain at the beginning of the eighth century welcomed the Muslim invaders.

By the beginning of the ninth century, the Islamic world, from Baghdad in the east to Cordoba in the west, had embarked on an era of cultural glory. Its artistic and intellectual achievements would rival those of Europe's

---

* The Talmud contains the teachings and opinions of thousands of rabbis and forms the basis of Halakha, Jewish law. It was compiled in two versions, the earlier Jerusalem Talmud in the fourth century CE and the later Babylonian Talmud, considered to be more definitive, compiled in about 500 CE.

Renaissance during the fifteenth and sixteenth centuries. Indeed, the European Renaissance owed its existence to this earlier Islamic flowering of the eighth to eleventh centuries.

After the Jews had been expelled from Spain in the late fifteenth century, they would look back with longing to this 'golden age' in al-Andalus when ancient Greek, Christian, Indian, Persian, Egyptian, North African, Byzantine and Muslim art, science, theology and philosophy mixed as gloriously as the Christians, Jews and Muslims who studied them.

In the light of their treatment under Christians, the 'Golden Age' – *La Convivencia* as it has been called – under Muslim rule became ever more golden to Jews. It was the jewel in the tolerant crown of Islam held up to shame Christendom for its savage intolerance. In nineteenth-century Europe eminent Jews such as the British prime minister Benjamin Disraeli and the German poet Heinrich Heine, would use the example of medieval Muslim Spain in order to reproach Christendom for its exasperatingly slow and reluctant progress towards Jewish emancipation and integrating Jews more fully into society. Andalusian Jews, like Andalusian Christians, however, had still been *dhimmis*, never certain when their relatively comfortable relationship with their Muslim overlords and neighbours would break down, but always aware that it could. The life of the tolerated is always precarious.

CHAPTER 4

ISLAM'S INQUISITION

'Any grave where lies a follower of innovation, even one who renounced the world, is a pit inside the Fire.'

– Ibn Hanbal 780–855 CE

EARLY NINTH-CENTURY BAGHDAD UNDER the Abbasid caliph Harun al-Rashid (one of the heroes of the *One Thousand and One Nights*) was the largest city in the world outside China. It was the heart of the Islamic Empire, which was now vaster in size than the Roman Empire had ever been. It was probably the world's most cosmopolitan city – and for the gilded elite, its most civilized. Jews, Christians, Zoroastrians, Sunnis and Shias, Arabs, Turks, Persians, Indians, North Africans, Greeks and Central Asians packed a city which had long sprawled beyond its city walls. The Abbasids were extraordinarily tolerant of their minorities. Jews and Christians scarcely felt the humiliations of those subject to *dhimma*.

The Muslim state and its elite were quite prepared to put commerce and knowledge – and therefore tolerance – before faith and the imposition of the superiority of Islam. But Baghdad, the city of tolerance, was also home to the religious scholar who pitted intolerant moral authority against tolerant pragmatic power – and won.

Straddled between the two banks of the great Tigris river, Baghdad was a city of water, criss-crossed by canals like an early Venice. Thousands of pinnaces ferried goods and people under its arched bridges; occasionally a magnificently decorated barge swept by bearing the almost godlike figure of the caliph to one of his great palace complexes on the banks of the Tigris.

Bridges of boats spanning the two banks split and re-formed to allow the passage of great barges carrying goods from Egypt, Syria, India and China. The bridges also served a more gruesome purpose – as places of public execution. Abbasid Baghdad may have been flourishing culturally, but across the empire countless plots and rebellions were flaring up like so many rockets as the frontier provinces sought greater independence from imperial control. Rebels were dragged onto the wooden walkways that topped the pontoon bridges, where they were crucified; their severed heads were then stuck up on poles to the dismay or titillation of passersby.

As for the poor, their numbers ever swelled by new immigrants from across the empire and beyond, they made their living servicing the city as canal diggers, reed weavers, soap boilers, craftsmen and traders. Each craft and trade had its own separate market. There was the Market of Cooked Meat Sellers, the Market of the Thorn Sellers, who sold thorn used for kindling ovens and heating the hammams, markets for pomegranates, poultry and textiles. Markets were an essential feature of Baghdad's daily life.[1]

At the centre of this city of canals, with its streets of wooden and mud-brick windowless houses opening into internal courtyards, was the vast palace complex and mosque. The mosque was allegedly big enough to hold 14,000 men; the palace was said to be four times bigger. In comparison, the western European cities ruled by Harun's contemporary, Charlemagne, king of the Franks and self-styled emperor, were poor and provincial, homogenous and dull.

A large Jewish community had lived in Iraq, or Babylon as Jews called it, since the days of the Babylonian exile. By the beginning of the ninth century, Jews had become the international traders of the Muslim empire, criss-crossing the world from the land of the Franks to India and China, dealing in spices, pearls, coral, gold and slaves. They were left relatively free to govern their own affairs, as they had been under the Umayyads and before them the Persians. The Exilarch, a Jew chosen by the Jews, was recognized by the Abbasids as the leader of Jewry across the empire, though how far the Exilarch was actually able to control Jewish affairs outside

Baghdad is not clear. But within Baghdad his power was impressive and visibly shown to be so. He had his own court and courtiers, servants and slaves. He appointed the judges who settled most Jewish legal matters, though Jews sometimes preferred to take their complaints to the *qadis*, the Muslim judges, if they felt they could get a fairer or better deal there.

If anything, Christians were more vulnerable to Muslim intolerance than Jews. Christians made up a far greater proportion of the population than Jews and were therefore more visible. More importantly, in Muslim eyes Christians were always suspect: for the sake of their faith, Christians might betray the Islamic Empire to its enemy, the Christian Byzantine Empire that was always fighting to claw back the territories it had lost to the Muslims. Jews had no such potentially conflicting loyalties. Besides, Jews were far closer religiously to Muslims in the importance they gave to the law, in their looser and more egalitarian religious structure and in their distaste for what they perceived as the polytheism of the Christian doctrine of the Trinity. On the whole, however, Christians were also left relatively free to manage their own affairs under their patriarch.

For the elite, Baghdad under the Abbasids was a paradise of tolerance, as it was for the elite in al-Andalus under the Umayyads. Christians, Jews and Muslims discussed mathematics, science, philosophy and history and took part in joint theological debates They shared all-night drunken erotic parties held on the lawns and patios of the great palaces, the revellers drinking from their own crystal goblets or sharing a cup passed from drinker to drinker by a wine pourer. They vied with each other in poetic contests – the Jewish poets, who are now considered to have been the greatest in Jewish literary history, modelled their poems on Arabic poetic forms. Jewish and Christian scholars from as far away as Scotland journeyed to Baghdad and to the Andalusian cities of Granada, Toledo and Cordoba (which had perhaps the biggest library in the world, housing more than 400,000 volumes). It is thanks to the Arabic translations made by these Muslim, Jewish and Christian scholars that the works of Aristotle, Euclid, Ptolemy, Galen and Hippocrates were saved from oblivion.

In the courtyards and halls of Baghdad's five hospitals, which doubled as medical schools, doctors of the three faiths worked together as partners, assistants or students, and studied each other's works. Muslim scientists and mathematicians excelled in algebra, geometry, astronomy and marine navigation. The Islamic world was intellectually superior to Christendom in almost every field of intellectual endeavour. Christendom did not begin to catch up until the beginning of the twelfth century when Aristotle's writings started to be translated from Arabic, and Greek.

Arabic became the international language of science, philosophy and high culture. Jews across the Islamic world spoke and wrote in Arabic, though they used Hebrew characters to make it easier for other Jews to read. It was in striking contrast to medieval Christendom, where the Jews made very limited use of Greek and virtually none of Latin, the language of a hostile Church. Jewish scholars even translated the Bible into Arabic. One of the greatest rabbis of the Middle Ages, Saadia Gaon, would later refer naturally to the Torah as 'sharia', the Hebrew bible as 'Quran' and the Jewish prayer leader (*hazzan*) as imam.

Presiding over this Islamic renaissance was the caliph Harun al-Rashid. He glittered and gleamed with jewelled tiara, jewel-encrusted shoes and gold-brocaded robes. But he was also said to have been a shy and pious Muslim – allegedly, he performed a hundred prostrations daily and went on the two-month pilgrimage to Mecca a record eight times – despite his predilections for wine, boys and women.

Harun al-Rashid's harem housed 2,000 women. His son Ali recalled that during the scorching heat of summer, the caliph would have seven slave girls brought to the pavilion where he took his siesta. They would undress and put on linen shifts which had been dipped in a mixture of perfumes, saffron and rose water. Then each in turn would sit on a stool perforated with holes under which aloes and amber burned, until her shift dried and the room became 'permeated with the fragrant incense and the perfume'.[2]

It was typical of Harun al-Rashid's extravagant gestures that when Charlemagne sent a delegation to his court the caliph presented the unfortunate envoy with an elephant which he had to cart all the way back to Aachen, in Germany, the favoured base for Charlemagne's court. Worth noting is that the delegation seems to have been headed by Isaac, a Jew who clearly occupied a prominent position at court, though he might not have relished his journey home from Baghdad. It took three years before the elephant, named Abul Abbas, lumbered through the streets of Aachen, where he became an object of wonder and delight. Abul Abbas died in 810, on his way to fight on the Danish frontier, but had obviously been so admired that his bones were carefully preserved, not to be discovered until the eighteenth century.

Privileged guests to a feast at Harun al-Rashid's palace would progress through a series of sombre brick corridors, emerge into the sudden blazing sunlight of a courtyard where fountains splashed, plunge back into the gloomy corridors until they arrived in the great domed and vaulted audience hall. Only the privileged few could get beyond the eunuchs (mainly white Slavs though there were some black Africans), ministers and chamberlain who guarded the curtain separating the caliph from his subjects.

Dressed in brocades and tunics with long trailing sleeves, the guests sat on sumptuous rugs. Candles lit up the marble panels and rich tapestries that lined the walls; the air was filled with the scent of burning ambergris and musk; musicians played behind a curtain while Harun al-Rashid sat cross-legged being fed by a slave girl. Guests were served with dishes of meats and fruits laid on palm leaves or animal skins spread on the floor. Singing girls, who were expected to be highly skilled sexually, musically and conversationally, strummed their lutes and sang (although pious Muslims deeply disapproved of music). But no freeborn woman ever attended these male gatherings. Some of the more observant guests drank sherbet or sugared water scented with rose, violet or orange flowers, but most drank wine and drank it copiously, despite the Quranic prohibition on drinking grape wine.

This *Arabian Nights* world with its intoxicating tolerance of different behaviours and ideas was of course one available only to the elite. It was also one which was inherently vulnerable to the countervailing pull of intolerance, as it proved. In 812 Harun al-Rashid died and a vicious civil war broke out between his two sons, al-Ma'mun and his dissolute eunuch-loving brother al-Amin.

Baghdad descended into physical and moral chaos before its half-starving inhabitants' eyes. Much of the city was reduced to ruins and Harun al-Rashid's palace was burned to the ground. Gangs roamed the city streets, looting, kidnapping, and attacking women.

It took six years for al-Ma'mun to best his brother and take control of Baghdad. But his hold on the throne was frighteningly insecure. Civil war had created deep fissures within the empire, and in the early years of his reign rebellions continued to erupt from Medina, Mecca and Yemen, to Egypt, Syria and in Iraq itself.

Al-Ma'mun's overriding concern was to restore, maintain and if possible enhance the authority of the caliph. Paradoxically, Islam's greatest patron of Greek philosophy was also the initiator of Islam's only formal inquisition against its co-religionists. Intolerance is the almost inevitable response to a breakdown in the social order. It is a tactic used to impose or reimpose authority, adopted as much by today's rulers as it was by those in the past.

Ever since Abu Bakr had succeeded Muhammad in 632, the idea that the caliph inherited Muhammad's political role but not his divine relationship with God had come to be accepted by the Sunni majority. As the caliphs gained a reputation for decadence and extravagance and seemed to be diverging further and further from the ideal set by Muhammad, the authority of the ulema – the experts in Islamic doctrine and law – grew, as the people looked to them increasingly for religious leadership and guidance. The ulema might not possess the institutional power of the Church, they might not have an Ambrose who could bring an emperor to do public penance for his sins (see Chapter 1), but with the moral authority bestowed on them by the people, the Mosque had the power to criticize the State.

Al-Ma'mun was determined to deprive them of that power by remodelling himself as the caliph who was 'inheritor of the prophethood … direct recipient of knowledge from God'. He would be the 'salvation of the souls of Muslims' as well as the 'Commander of the Faithful' (as the caliphs styled themselves). In effect he would be the imam envisioned by the Shiites, the fount of religious as well as of political authority (see Chapter 2). Only as the supreme head of all authority did al-Ma'mun think he could ensure the survival of the caliphal institution.

It was as a rationalist that al-Ma'mun waged his battle for authority with the ulema. Al-Ma'mun was a poet and mathematician; he was enthralled by Greek science and philosophy, and the learning of all the cultures that had been incorporated into the Islamic Empire. Once a week he held debates on Greek philosophy, medicine or theology at which Sunnis, Shiites, Christians and Jews argued their positions. Often he would join in, accompanied by his bored or attentive courtiers, dressed in their long black cloaks, a sword dangling at their side. Al-Ma'mun founded a library-institute, the 'House of Wisdom', dedicated to the study and translation of Greek philosophical and scientific works; in charge was his chief physician, the Christian scholar Hunayn ibn Ishaq, who had measured the circumference of the earth and was also an indefatigable translator of Hippocrates' and Galen's medical works.

Al-Ma'mun was naturally sympathetic to a religious/philosophical movement which had developed in the intellectual ferment of the times. The Mu'tazilites believed that reason rather than divine revelation was the best way to understand their religion and its moral principles, which put them at direct variance with most of the ulema who put faith before reason. The true believer, they argued, accepts the Quran as the word of God and does not speculate about it. Something was good because God said that it was so; killing was wrong because God forbade it. For the 'rationalists', however, it was the other way around: God forbids killing because it is wrong.

In 833 al-Ma'mun ordered Ishaq ibn Ibrahim, the governor of Baghdad, to interrogate all of his officials on a matter of doctrine: did they believe that the Quran was created? This question, so astonishingly abstract to modern ears, had a clear political purpose. It would sort out the Mu'tazilite sheep from the traditionalist goats. The Mu'tazilites, like the Shia with whom they shared many beliefs, argued that the Quran had been created. Created by Allah, of course. Nonetheless it meant that if the Quran was a creation of Allah's, it was separate and not co-eternal with Allah who alone was uncreated. And since the Quran was created, it could be interpreted. The traditionalists, however, believed that the Quran, like God himself, was uncreated and had existed through all eternity; it could not be challenged, interpreted or modified in any way. The uncreated nature of the Quran was a fundamental tenet of the traditionalists and has become accepted Sunni doctrine.*

It was these traditionalists, the 'deluded ... depraved ... untrustworthy ... heretics ... making a pretense [sic] of piety and knowledge' who according to al-Ma'mun 'deliberately lead the masses astray', that he was determined to root out. 'The Commander of the Faithful does not regard any of them suited for holding an office of trust ... or men to exercise authority over any aspect in the lives of the subjects,' he told Baghdad's governor.[3] Those who refused to accept that the Quran was created would lose their jobs, risk imprisonment and in a few cases face death. Henceforth the 'Commander of the Faithful' would be just that.

'When the Prophethood came to an end ... God made the mainstay of the religion and the ordering of the government of the Muslims reside in the [Deputyship].' He, al-Ma'mun, had been appointed by God to be guardian of his religion and his laws – not the ulema. It was the caliph who would be in control of religious matters, who would determine what was true Islamic doctrine, and even which were authentic hadith and which were not.

Compared to the Spanish and Europe-wide inquisitions, the Muslim world's version, the Mihna (from the Arabic 'test' or 'trial') was a minor affair. It lasted only fourteen years (833–847) while the Church's inquisitions spanned more than three centuries, starting in 1478 and ending at the beginning of the nineteenth century. The European inquisitions interrogated at least 150,000 people, of whom at least 3,000–5,000 were executed. Al-Ma'mun's inquisition probably killed less than twenty people: it targeted only the elite, and left ordinary people alone.

Of those who were interrogated by the *qadis*, by the governor of the

---

* Similarly, in rabbinic literature it is taught that the Torah was one of the six or seven things created prior to the creation of the world.

province, by influential Mu'tazilites at court and by al-Ma'mun himself, most were prepared to save their official positions and avoid imprisonment by declaring in favour of the created Quran. But amongst those interrogated was Ahmad Ibn Hanbal, the most prominent and respected of the traditionalists, or 'proponents of farce' as the rationalists called them. Learned, austere, renowned for his piety, Ibn Hanbal took Sunnism to the people. His name lives on as founder of the Hanbali school of law, one of the four schools of Sunni law (*madhahib*).* Today's Wahhabis and Salafis like to trace their ideological roots back to Ibn Hanbal.

Ibn Hanbal was deeply opposed to the Mu'tazilites' reason-based theology (*kalam*). To discuss religious beliefs about God, good and evil on the basis of rational criteria was to put human reason above divine revelation according to Ibn Hanbal. That, he thought, was nothing short of blasphemy. The Mu'tazilites argued that the rational faculty was a God-given faculty and that to use it in the service of Islam could not therefore be blasphemous. But for Ibn Hanbal, everything a believer needed to know in faith and practice was to be found in the Quran and the sunna.† They were the only sources of sharia, the divine rules by which Allah intended humanity to live.

Ibn Hanbal was one of the pre-eminent scholars engaged in the mammoth task of collecting the hadiths and sifting out the authentic from the fabricated and distorted. He aimed to live exactly as the

* The four schools of law, named after their founding scholars, Abu Hanifa, Malik ibn Anas, al-Shafi'i and Ahmad Ibn Hanbal, developed between the eighth and tenth centuries, based on different legal opinions. All four agree as to the general principles by which legal judgements should be derived from the Quran and sunna (see footnote below). But they disagree as to the weight and order that should be given to each of the principles. Each school has developed its own body of legislative rulings accordingly. (The Shia have their own separate schools of law.) The principles are: *ijma'* (the consensus of Muslim jurists); *qiyas*, finding analagous cases in the Quran or sunna; and *ijtihad*, reasoning by the jurist, which was highly contentious at the time and remains so to this day. Ibn Hanbal was deeply suspicious of unregulated *ijtihad*.

† For Sunnis, the sunna is the summation of Muhammad's opinions, practices, comments and instructions, as recorded in the Hadith. It is Islam as lived and thought by Muhammad. Shiites believe imams are also sources of sunnaic practice.

Prophet and his Companions had lived, eschewing any luxuries that the Prophet had never seen, eating only what Muhammad and his Companions had eaten. Any innovation was, for Ibn Hanbal, to contradict the will of Allah. The true Muslim must follow the principles and practice laid out by the Quran and the sunna. And Ibn Hanbal meant that literally. His growing number of followers might be wilting in the baking heat of Baghdad, but Ibn Hanbal forbade them to drink from the city's roadside wells on the grounds that in several hadiths Muhammad forbade his followers to drink water while standing up or impede a public thoroughfare. Ibn Hanbal debated whether he and his followers should vomit up food if they were not sure where it had come from; he recalled one Companion who had done so. He worried about whether he should keep a few coins in his room in case that would show a lack of trust in Allah, and would sit reading in his shabby room in exactly the way a hadith report had described Muhammad sitting, his feet flat on the floor, knees against his chest.

Careless of how he looked, Ibn Hanbal did not perhaps present the most attractive appearance. One of his followers remembered seeing him sitting on a dirt floor: 'The dye in his hair had run [Ibn Hanbal dyed his hair and beard with henna, following the example of Muhammad], and I could see the white roots of his hair. He was wearing a small, dirty breechclout [turban] of white cotton and a coarse shirt with a smudge on the shoulder and sweat stains on the collar.'[14]

Ibn Hanbal was a married man, but he seems to have been a harsh and exacting father and an unloving husband. Just two days after the mother of his son died, he married again. 'I detest spending the night as a celibate,' he is said to have remarked. Though, putting good behaviour before sensuality, he went on to marry a one-eyed woman rather than her more beautiful sister because the former was said to be better behaved.

Ibn Hanbal was, however, a beneficent landlord; he lived on rents from the properties he owned but often waived the rents when his tenants were in difficulties. He was generous to the poor, for whom 'he had a great liking, preferring them to the people [who were immersed in the life] of this world', and lived a life of extreme austerity, according to al-Mirwazi, one of his contemporaries. 'Many times I saw him shake the dust off pieces of dried bread and put them in his bowl,' his son Salih recalled.[5]

Ibn Hanbal's ascetic life in one of the richest cities on earth where the unbelievably wealthy reclined in their palaces while beggars, lepers, cripples and the very poor squatted under bridges or in vast shanty towns, made him a source of veneration amongst the people. If the reports collected by his thirteenth-century biographer Ibn al-Jawzi are to be believed, crowds of up to 5,000 would gather to hear him speak. The piety and rigours of his life could not but be an implicit criticism of the caliph's decadence, pious Muslim though al-Ma'mun tried to be.

In 833, Ibn Hanbal and twenty-four other men were hauled in for questioning by al-Ma'mun's inquisitors. When they all refused to say that the Quran was created, al-Ma'mun ordered that they be tortured, and threatened with execution. All of them recanted except for Ibn Hanbal and one other man, a scholar called Muhammad ibn Nuh. Al-Ma'mun (the self-styled 'slave of God') was, however, reluctant to carry out his threat. He had physical force on his side, but Ibn Hanbal had the passionate support of the people. Al-Ma'mun could offer the standard bribe of an emperor – tolerance. But while that may have suited the elite, it was of little benefit to the Muslim majority who deferred to Ibn Hanbal's religious certainties. Knowing that popular opinion was against him, al-Ma'mun commuted the sentence of execution to imprisonment.

After al-Ma'mun's death in 833, the Mihna continued under his brother al-Mu'tasim who was as anxious as al-Ma'mun had been to assert his religious authority over the ulema. In 834, Ibn Hanbal again refused to recant, and was flogged so mercilessly that he fell unconscious. There was such public outcry that al-Mu'tasim was forced to release him, though he was banished from Baghdad. The caliph was no match for Ibn Hanbal who had the people behind him. Ibn Hanbal was their hero: he lived like them, sympathized with their plight, championed traditional Islam against Mu'tazilism, the alien doctrine espoused by the caliph and many of his court. Early Sunnism was discovering the power of populism.

Rebellion against the caliph was brewing. The rebels asked Ibn Hanbal to join them. He refused. Just as well for him. The signal for the rebellion was meant to be the simultaneous beating of drums around the city. One group of conspirators got so drunk, however, that they started beating the drums in their part of the city a day too early. They were rounded up and executed. The rebellion had failed. Nonetheless it was a clear sign that the caliph was losing, not gaining, authority.

In 847, the new caliph al-Mutawakkil, dressed in a gold-worked velvet robe embroidered with Arabic inscriptions, silk waistcoat and turban, bowed to reality and called a halt to the inquisition. He gave up the attempt to impose Mu'tazilism and acknowledged that he could not compete with the traditionalist ulema. The Mihna had lasted sixteen years. Ibn Hanbal, by now a frail old man, had defeated four successive caliphs. His victory signalled the failure of the caliphate's bid for religious authority.

Ibn Hanbal was welcomed back from exile to the delight of the cheering crowds in Baghdad. Erstwhile Mu'tazilite courtiers flocked to him, begging to be forgiven for their implicit connivance in the inquisition. But Ibn Hanbal's first-hand experience of religious persecution had done nothing to soften his own intolerance towards those he considered to be heretics: they should be killed. Such intransigence was not surprising. After all, it was his religious zeal that had motivated his stand against the inquisitors and that had garnered him the overwhelming support of the people against which the caliph was powerless.

In an effort to placate his former adversary, al-Mutawakkil summoned Ibn Hanbal to his palace. Ibn Hanbal, the hero of the Mihna, was old and ill but reluctantly complied with the summons. His visit was not a success. Neither the luxury of the palace nor the caliph's behaviour were likely to please him. Al-Mutawakkil was said to have had a harem of 4,000 eunuchs and concubines – and to have had sex with every one of them. Ibn Hanbal was immune to blandishments and proved himself to be generally unco-operative. He turned down the prize position of tutor to al-Mutawakkil's son, refused to touch the palace delicacies and would eat only a few loaves of bread. Al-Mutawakkil, quick-witted and sharp-tongued though he was, admitted defeat and allowed Ibn Hanbal to return to Baghdad from where he regularly refused the caliph's gifts of food and money.

When Ibn Hanbal died in 855, a record number of mourners attended his funeral. Al-Mutawakkil officially embraced Ibn Hanbal's Sunni traditionalism and turned his back on the speculative shores of Muta'zilism. It was perhaps the moment when traditionalism and anti-rationalism became the dominant mode of Islamic thought. The formulation and application of the law, not speculation, became the main concern of scholars and determined the future shape of Sunnism. The use of *ijtihad*, rational conjecture, by religious judges when making their judgements, became more regulated and restricted. When the philosopher Ibn Rushd (known in the West as Averroes) died in 1198 the Islamic philosophical tradition, which had combined Aristotelian and Islamic thought, died with him.*

In abandoning the Mihna, al-Mutawakkil had acknowledged that it was the ulema, and in particular Ibn Hanbal and the Sunni traditionalists, who were in control of religious affairs. Popular opinion had backed the Sunni traditionalist scholars, rather than the Mu'tazilite caliph. Henceforth, the caliph would be the religious leader of the Islamic world in terms of being its protector and upholding Islamic law, but he would have no say in doctrine and belief.

At the end of the fourth century CE Archbishop Ambrose had forced the emperor Theodosius to relinquish his title of Pontifex Maximus, head of Church and State. Ibn Hanbal had forced al-Mutawakkil to do likewise and concede religious authority to the ulema. But Ibn Hanbal and the ulema could never have forced the caliph to publicly beg for forgiveness as Ambrose did, nor would the ulema ever have been able to forbid a caliph to marry, as several Christian popes would later forbid kings. The ulema did not have the power.

---

* Mu'tazilism did not, however, die out entirely. In fact, the Turko-Mongol warrior-intellectual Timur Lenk (Tamerlane) is said to have taken a Mu'tazilite theologian with him on his campaigns in the fourteenth century.

*

Political rulers in Islamdom, as in Christendom, recognized that the possession of physical force was not enough to rule successfully. They needed to be seen as having God's blessing. And if they did not possess it in their own right, then they were prepared to bargain with those who could confer it – the Church or the Mosque. Al-Mutawakkil yielded the spiritual realm to the ulema, but he gave them moral power only. Christian kings on the other hand conceded earthly power as well.

The Church had the immense bargaining strength of an institution which spoke for Catholic Christians across the whole of Europe (the struggle with the Eastern Church was yet to come). The ulema had no comparable institutional structure that could give them such coherence and strength. They never had the power to compete with the State and therefore could never make themselves entirely distinct from it. They had no leader who was meant to speak for them, no equivalent of a bishop or archbishop. The origins of Christianity as a suspect cult liable to persecution had encouraged the creation of an institution, within one hundred years of the death of Jesus, that could preserve and protect its members from the State. The Christians had their pope* or their patriarch, their archbishops, bishops, priests, deacons, subdeacons, lectors, psalmists, acolytes and doorkeepers, and their synods, where certain beliefs were consigned to heretical hell; the ulema, by contrast, had no leader and no ultimate authority to determine orthodoxy.

Recognizing the power of the Church, and his need of its support, Constantine had begun endowing the Church with land after his conversion to Christianity in 312, and by the early seventh century the Church had become the largest landowner in the West. Bishops were as powerful as lay magnates and, like their lay counterparts, mustered their soldiers for the king as good vassals had to do. Caliphs and wealthy Muslims were generous patrons to individual scholars, and to the schools

---

* In the ninth century the pope had not yet, however, established himself as the supreme head of the Catholic Church; he was bishop of Rome, senior bishop, but not the ultimate authority that he would become in the eleventh century.

of law that were beginning to develop around eminent scholars such as Ibn Hanbal, the hero of the inquisition. But the schools of law had their differing views and never spoke with one voice.

In 754 the Church became a state in its own right. Pope Stephen II in effect made a deal with the new king of the Franks: land in exchange for the Church's support. Pepin the Short (alas, so called not because of his stature, but because of a mistranslation of the Latin 'minor': Pepin was a younger, not a tiny, son) had usurped the kingdom of Gaul and needed the legitimacy bestowed by the pope and his religion. On his side, Pope Stephen wanted control of the lands in and around Rome which the pope/bishop of Rome had once owned and then lost to the Germanic tribe of Lombards. Pepin duly handed over Rome and other cities and lands to the pope. In return the pope anointed Pepin as king of the Franks and bound them by a solemn vow never to recognize any other royal family.

By 800, when Pope Leo III crowned Pepin's son, Charlemagne, as Holy Roman emperor 'crowned by God', the pope was temporal ruler of the duchies of Rome, Ravenna, parts of Corsica, Tuscany and Lombardy, and had his own army. The Papal States comprised some of the most important states in the Italian peninsula. They would remain under papal control for almost 1,000 years, until Italy was unified in 1871.

Nothing perhaps more graphically illustrates the difference in institutional power between Islam and Christianity than the coronation of Charlemagne in 800 CE and the accession to the throne forty-seven years later of the Islamic caliph al-Mutawakkil, not long before he called a halt to the Mihna inquisition. On the day of his coronation, 10 August 847, al-Mutawakkil crossed the vast courtyards of his palace and walked down the mile-long processional corridor to the Public Audience Hall. There he offered the usual bribes made by the incoming caliph to the courtiers and army and accepted pledges of allegiance from those whose support was considered most crucial – members of his Abbasid family, the most influential governors, senior officials, such as the vizier, and members of the ulema. The ulema's backing was needed of course, but they had no special role in the coronation.

By contrast to the near invisibility of the Mosque at al-Mutawakkil's coronation, the Church turned Charlemagne's coronation into an overt display of its power. Charlemagne, a literally towering figure, was crowned Holy Roman emperor in the most important church in Western Christendom, St Peter's in Rome. By placing the crown on the emperor's head, the pope was symbolically representing the dependence of the emperor on the pope. Indicatively, the Church and the imperial accounts of the ceremony differed in one significant detail. The Frankish Royal Annals relate that the pope then 'worshipped Charles according to the manner of the ancient princes', that is, he kissed the ground before Charlemagne, the customary obeisance made to an emperor. The Church's account, in the *Liber Pontificalis* (Book of the Popes), however, records no such act of deference.

On top of the vast lands the Western Church already owned and the immense hierarchy of religious officials that it already managed, the pope was now sovereign ruler of his own territory. The Church had not effected a separation between Church and State; it had simply become a state itself, vying with the Holy Roman Empire which, thanks to Pepin and Charlemagne's conquests, now ranged from Gaul, through northern Spain and northern Italy to most of what is now Germany.

The Church's very power would lead to a competition with the State in which the loser would be tolerance. Ibn Hanbal had made a deal with the caliph that won the ulema moral authority but left the caliph relatively undisturbed in his political authority. The relationship between caliph and ulema never degenerated into the endless battle that took place in Christendom, where the Church had material as well as spiritual power. It became a state competing with a state and as a result inevitably used the tool always available to a monotheist religion – intolerance. The Church whipped up religious fervour and support by uniting its followers against its religious enemies. Jews, Muslims and heretical Christians would be the victims.

CHAPTER 5

THE PROBLEMS OF ASSIMILATION: WILLING MARTYRS

'Persecutions make proselytes.'

– Voltaire, *Philosophical Dictionary*, 1764

IN 827 AGOBARD, THE archbishop of Lyons, wrote a letter to the Carolingian emperor Louis the Pious (Charlemagne's son), protesting against Louis' treatment of the Jews. Louis was treating them too well, Agobard complained:

> They boast of being dear to the king and of being received by him with favour, because of their descent from the Patriarchs; they exhibit costly garments which, they say, have been presented to them by the relatives of the king, and gowns which their wives have received from the ladies of the palace; contrary to the law, they take the liberty of building new synagogues; ... and the commissioners of the king have ordered a change of the market day, in order that the Jews might be able to observe their day of rest.

The Jews, he said, were even stealing Christian children in order to sell them as slaves. Louis, ruler of the Christian Holy Roman Empire, following in his father Charlemagne's footsteps, was being too tolerant: the Jews were getting above themselves. The Church wanted Louis to treat Jews in the same way as the caliph did – tolerate them only on the condition that they accepted their inferiority.

The letter is in fact almost identical in tone to the fulmination against the Christians written in Baghdad some twenty years later by the Islamic scholar Abu Uthman al-Jahiz during the reign of the caliph al-Mutawakkil:

> We know that they [the Christians] ride highly bred horses and dromedary camels, play polo, wear silken garments and have attendants serve them. They call themselves Hasan, Husayn, Abbas, Fadl and Ali and employ also their forenames. There remains but that they call themselves Muhammad.[1]

This chapter follows the story of three religious bigots in the first half of the ninth century. Agobard, Archbishop of Lyons, al-Jahiz, adviser to Caliph al-Mutawakkil, and Paulus Alvarus, Christian poet, theologian and inciter of martyrdom in Muslim Spain. All three wanted their rulers to be more intolerant. All three were responding to the problem of assimilation, to how the minority community related to the majority.*

As far as Agobard and al-Jahiz were concerned, their respective *dhimmis* had committed two unforgivable sins: they were not only following the wrong god and turning their back on the true God, but they had broken the rules of the tolerance game, which the religious authorities only reluctantly accepted in any case. *Dhimmis* were getting above themselves; they were assimilating too well with the majority. And their respective rulers, Louis and al-Mutawakkil, were letting them get away with it.

Louis, a dour, irritable and ascetic character, unlike his father Charlemagne, was as insecure on his throne as al-Mutawakkil was on

* 'Assimilation' is now considered a dated and politically incorrect term, 'integration' being the preferred term. I prefer to use both terms so as to capture the uneasy undertones implied in 'assimilation', that is to say that the minority melts into the majority and thereby loses its own identity; I use the word 'integration' as a more value-neutral term for a minority adjusting to the majority but not necessarily at the expense of its own separate identity.

his. During his twenty-seven-year reign Louis was embroiled in two civil wars with his sons; there were rebellions by his lawless aristocracy, skirmishes with the Muslims on his doorstep in al-Andalus and the constant risk of Viking raiding parties nosing along the coast or upriver in their sleek and menacing ships. In Baghdad al-Mutawakkil had just been defeated by Ibn Hanbal. Not only had the caliph been forced to recognize the power of the ulema, but he was also in danger of losing political control as his Turkish slave soldiers became dangerously powerful.

But while al-Mutawakkil responded to the urgings of al-Jahiz, Louis ignored Agobard. Al-Mutawakkil thought that by acting harshly against the *dhimmis* he would gain public support and with it a firmer grasp on his throne. Louis thought he would do better by tolerating the Jews and ignoring the Church, strong though it was.

Until the eleventh century, the majority of Jews lived in the Islamic world. Within Europe many more Jews lived in southern Italy and Sicily, lands which were still controlled by the Byzantine Empire. In the Carolingian empire, Jews were a tiny minority (8,000 out of a population of at least 10 million) living mostly in southern France, in Narbonne, Arles and Marseilles. But urban Jews did not pose much of a threat to the majority. In marked contrast to the Islamic world, status, wealth and the webs of power in western Europe were still based on land rather than the city. Some Jews were landowners with fields, orchards and vineyards; they were major producers of wine in the Rhône Valley, and around Paris, even selling Communion wine to priests. But most Jews were concentrated in the cities, where they specialized in commerce. So it was unlikely that Louis would antagonize popular feeling unduly by being tolerant to Jews. And besides, they were invaluable.

Few Christians ventured further than their own settlement. The world beyond their doorstep was unknown, dangerous brigand-infested territory. Christians tended to trade in foods, such as grains, wine and cheese. But Jews, with their contacts in Jewish communities around the known world, were masters of long-distance trade. They imported luxuries – pepper and cinnamon, dates, ivory, incense, brocades and precious metals – from Italy,

Spain, Egypt, Iraq, Palestine, Syria, Arabia, India and China. They traded in male and female slaves who were captured in their thousands in the newly conquered Slavic (Eastern European) lands and exported to the Carolingian empire or to Baghdad, North Africa and al-Andalus. Other than Northern European slaves, there was very little else Muslims wanted from the poverty-stricken West.

In the future, Jews would be despised as rootless cosmopolitans, but in the ninth century their cosmopolitanism made them strange but extremely useful. While the Franks mostly spoke a bastardized form of Latin, the Jewish international traders spoke Greek, Persian and Arabic as well as the languages of the Franks, the Spanish and the Slavs. This made them invaluable when ambassadors and their suites arrived from the caliph of Baghdad, the emir (ruler) of al-Andalus, the Byzantine emperor, the kings from Britain or the Scandinavian chieftains, or when the Carolingians sent their own envoys off on diplomatic missions.

King Louis, like his father Charlemagne, granted Jews privileges to entice them to settle permanently, especially on the volatile frontiers with Muslim Spain and in the Rhineland (in what is now Germany). The Rhineland was the heart of the empire and the centre of rudimentary urban life. Aachen (Aix-la-Chapelle) was as near as the Carolingians got to a capital city. Charlemagne had built a palace complex there on the site of a Roman settlement. Though they had given way to the Franks and other Germanic 'barbarians' at the end of the fifth century, the Romans still made their presence felt in the crumbling ruins, patched up roads, in the columns and pillars cannibalized from temples and villas and incorporated into new churches and royal residences.

In this primitive empire Jews were clearly useful and King Louis wanted to encourage them. He instituted a special oath which did not require Jews to swear by the Christian God but by 'the living and true God and by the holy law that the Lord has given to the blessed Moses on Mount Sinai'. It was a verbal sleight of hand similar to the pagan Roman emperors' permission for Jews to sacrifice to the *health* of the emperor rather than *to* the emperor. Louis exempted Jews from all the financial burdens incurred by the ordinary traveller. They did not have to pay the tolls exacted at town gates, bridges and ports, nor did they have to pay compensation for the damage caused by horses or mules as they dragged their cartloads of goods across frozen or muddy fields.

It was the Church that fomented anti-Jewish feeling. The Church feared Jews as rivals in the competition for souls, and resented them for becoming the social equals, if not the betters, of Christians. Easter and the run-up to it was always the worst time of the year for Jews in Christian Europe. On Good Friday, every church would echo to the sound of the prayer for the 'perfidious' Jews (in the sense of faithless, though it was always understood as meaning 'treacherous'), the *pro perfidis Judaeis*:

> Let us pray also for the faithless Jews: that Almighty God may remove the veil from their hearts; so that they too may acknowledge Jesus Christ our Lord... Almighty and eternal God, who dost not exclude from thy mercy even Jewish faithlessness: hear our prayers, which we offer for the blindness of that people; that acknowledging the light of thy Truth, which is Christ, they may be delivered from their darkness.

The Catholic Church removed the word 'perfidious' from the Good Friday prayers in 1959.

With anti-Jewish feelings inflamed by the local priest who stood up in his pulpit to narrate the sufferings of Christ at the hands of the Jews, and pointed to the paintings on his church walls which depicted Jews mocking Jesus, Christians would attack Jews and their homes. In Italy the attacks had clearly laid-out rules; stones could be thrown, but only at the walls of Jewish homes, not at windows or doors.

Every Palm Sunday in the southern French town of Béziers the bishop preached a sermon urging his congregation to attack the Jews – though he made sure to stress only with stones, since the Jews had stoned Jesus. In Chalon-sur-Saône in northern France it was the custom to throw stones at Jews on Palm Sunday. On Easter Sunday in Toulouse, a Jew would be singled out and forced to stand before the church in the town square, where he would be slapped in the face to avenge the crucifixion of

Jesus. In 1020, the victim was struck so violently that he lost an eye and died. The 'Toulouse slap' was only stopped in 1077 when the Jews paid off the clergy with a special tax.

Nonetheless, despite this annual orgy of anti-Jewish violence whipped up by the Church, relations between Jews and Christians had not yet hardened into segregation. Neither Jews nor Christians seem to have paid much heed to the prohibitions against mixing with each other laid down by their religious authorities. Indeed, Jews of the Carolingian Empire in the ninth century probably mixed more with Christians than they would do again until the nineteenth century.[2]

In vain did Church councils continually reissue the regulations collected in the Theodosian Code which the Church synods in Orleans had sought to impose back in the sixth century (see Chapter 3). Christians were forbidden to live side by side with Jews, to eat with them, or marry them. But Catholics and Jews persisted in mingling. Some Christians even went to the synagogue, saying they preferred the sermons of the rabbis to those of the clergy, wrote the fearful and resentful Archbishop Agobard to the emperor Louis, 'while we, with all the humanity and goodness which we use toward them, have not succeeded in gaining a single one to our spiritual beliefs'. Born out of Judaism, Christianity felt the constant need to assert its difference and its superiority. But that assertion was totally undermined by Christians celebrating Jewish holidays, observing the Sabbath and eating kosher food.

Agobard, who as a young man had fled Muslim Spain for Christian Europe, was concerned that Louis' tolerant policy was only encouraging the blurring of the boundaries between Jews and Christians. It was, he wrote, 'unworthy of our faith that the sons of light [the Christians] should associate with the children of darkness'. Any physical contact with a Jew was polluting, according to Agobard. A priest who shared a meal with a Jew would be contaminated and would pass on that impurity to anyone who received the Eucharist from his hands.

Papal policy itself continued to be ambivalent, as Christianity's policy towards the Jews always had been (see Chapters 1 and 3). Popes followed the line adopted by Augustine: Jews must be rejected because they rejected Christ as the Messiah. But they must not be subjected to unwarranted physical brutality, because the New Testament foretold that the conversion of the Jews would herald the Second Coming and be the final witness to the truth of Christianity. In other words: tolerate, do not treat as equal.

Agobard, however, feared that Louis' benevolence towards Jews was threatening the status of the Church and of Christians. Louis appointed Jews as tax collectors and government officials. He was ignoring Church regulations which banned Jews from employing Christians (slave or free). Christians worked the lands and vineyards that enabled Jews to become wealthy merchants of meat and wine. Jews employed Christian artisans, servants, maids, even wet-nurses; there were Jewish doctors at court taking blood from Christian veins. Jews were allowed to preach in public. They managed Church estates and advised bishops and abbots on their financial affairs. Louis had even appointed a special magistrate (*magister Judaeorum*) whose role was to adjudicate disputes between Jews and non-Jews.

It was the *magister*'s ruling against Archbishop Agobard in favour of a Jew that was the final straw. In 822 Agobard had baptized a slave despite the opposition of her Jewish owner who had previously converted the slave to Judaism (the slave presumably having very little say in the matter). The *magister* ruled in the Jewish owner's favour. Agobard refused to accept the decision, seized the slave, and travelled to the palace of Aachen to argue his case. To his fury, the *magister*'s decision was upheld. Louis not only dismissed him from the palace but granted a charter to the Jews of Lyons, Agobard's own diocese, making it mandatory for clergymen to get the consent of the owner before baptizing any slave in a Jewish household.

The struggle simmered on for several years. Priests in Lyons, backed by Agobard, converted slaves despite the protests of their Jewish owners. Imperial emissaries arrived, forcibly returned the slaves to their owners and threatened the priests. Agobard wrote yet another letter of protest to Louis. Louis issued further edicts reaffirming Jewish privileges and threatening punishment for anyone who resisted. It was said that in gratitude the Jews supported Louis in the civil wars which plagued the final ten years of his reign when his sons were fighting over his empire.

Compared to Christendom's later treatment of Jews, Louis was indeed remarkably tolerant. His tolerance exemplifies the pragmatic attitude of political rulers down the ages when they see no need to enlist the aid of the binding and unifying powers of religious absolutism.

Louis did, of course, respect the Church. He was not called 'Louis the Pious' for nothing. When he inherited the throne he had cleared his father Charlemagne's concubines from the imperial court at Aachen and shut up his sisters in a nunnery as punishment for having lived sexually loose lives. It was, of course, hard to tell where Louis' spiritual spring-cleaning of the court ended and the purging of Louis' real or suspected opponents began; certainly few of Charlemagne's administrators remained in place.

Louis himself lived an almost monastic life. According to the bishop Thegan, who wrote a biography of Louis in 836, 'Every morning it was his custom to enter the church, and there, throwing himself on his knees, to touch the pavement with his forehead, continuing long in prayer, and often shedding tears.' He dressed plainly except on great festival days when 'he was covered with gold, and carried a sceptre in his hand, and his crown upon his head'.[3]

Even at his banquets, when Church and lay dignitaries grew red-faced on wine and beer, when serried rows of bakers and cooks loaded the table with honeyed and spiced meats and loaves of white bread, and the seated or standing guests crammed food into their mouths with their hands, Louis 'never showed his white teeth in laughter', though harpists, flautists, mime artists and jesters were straining every nerve to amuse the guests.[4] Louis picked most of his advisers from the ranks of the Church, more because they were literate and educated than because of their faith. Bishops were often so wealthy that, like mini-kings, they had their own court and courtiers; they were amongst the leading men in the empire, equivalent in power to the lay aristocrats, in a way that was inconceivable under Islam.

But the Church was still subordinate to the State. Despite the opposition of Carolingian churchmen such as Agobard, Louis persisted in appointing archbishops and controlling the distribution of abbacies and bishoprics, with all the lands attached to them. And wealthy landowners, like their contemporaries in Anglo-Saxon England, had their own 'proprietary churches' – churches which were their own private property and which they felt they could control in any way they pleased.

Like all secular rulers, Louis was more concerned with the worldly than the spiritual affairs of his empire. He was eager to use Christianity to solidify his empire but quite prepared to tolerate, protect and even encourage religious minorities as long as they were financially useful and obedient. But for Archbishop Agobard the Christianization of the empire was an end in itself. He believed intolerance was necessary for the sake of asserting Christianity's dominance, just as al-Jahiz, the Islamic scholar, believed intolerance was necessary to preserve Islam's superior position in relation to the minority rival monotheisms, the religions of the *dhimmis*.

As far as al-Jahiz ('jahiz' means bulging eyes) was concerned, *dhimmis* were assimilating far too much; they were becoming not just the equals but the superiors of Muslims. *Dhimmis* in the Islamic world were involved in the business of state in ways that were unimaginable for Christendom's religious minority, the Jews. This was partly because in the Islamic Empire's earliest days Arab Muslims had had to rely on the administrative skills of the Christian and Jewish elites they had conquered to run the new empire. (By contrast the Carolingian empire relied on the education and administrative skills provided by churchmen.) Christians and Jews were prominent at Muslim courts as physicians and financial advisers, though contrary to the Jewish stereotype, most of the great bankers of the eighth century were Christians; it was Christians, not Jews, who remained the archetypal men of money in Arabic literature and lore.

As commerce flourished in the ninth century, Jews and Muslims shared workshops and were business partners, so much so that the rabbinic authorities were often needed to solve the resulting problems. What to do, for instance, about the profits from transactions concluded on Saturday, the Jewish Sabbath: the answer was that Saturday's profits belonged to the non-Jewish partner, but the Jewish partner would be compensated by receiving more of the profits from another day's trade. World trade was dominated by trading associations of Muslims, Jews and Christians from Islamic lands. One of the reasons why so many houses in Baghdad were in ruins was because Jews, Christians and Muslims often owned them as joint landlords and nothing could be done without the consent of the other, who might be away travelling on business or involved in other affairs.

In Muslim cities most Jews and Christians chose to live amongst their own communities – it was usually more convenient, since they would be in walking distance of their synagogue, *mikveh* (ritual bath) or church. But the neighbourhoods were rarely exclusively Jewish or Christian and no stigma was attached to a primarily Jewish area as it would be in Christendom from the eleventh century on. In Fustat, the business capital of Egypt a couple of miles north of Cairo, at least half the houses in Jewish neighbourhoods were inhabited by gentiles. *Dhimmis* and Muslims lived in apartments in the same compounds despite the inevitable friction that entailed: the presence of Muslims interfering with the Jews' observance of the Sabbath; the greater visibility of Jewish or Christian women offending Muslim sensibilities. The Jewish authorities' ban on the sale or rent of parts of houses to Muslims clearly had little effect. However, Jews usually avoided siting their synagogues too near a large concentration of Muslims and preferred to bypass predominantly Muslim neighbourhoods when they processed to the Jewish cemetery. *Dhimmi* funeral processions could be the object of occasional harassment, sometimes minor, sometimes serious.

In Baghdad and Cairo, as in Cordoba, Muslims celebrated Christian festivals and joined in the dancing and drinking that accompanied them. Pilgrims of all three faiths visited the same shrines – the birthplace of Abraham outside Damascus, the cave where Cain killed Abel, and the home of Jesus and Mary. Jewish and Muslim dietary laws, however, made it difficult for them to share a meal with a Christian.

But despite the fraternization, non-Muslims could never be on a level of total equality with their Muslim neighbour, business partner or even friend. Jews and Christians could never entirely shake off their *dhimmi* status. A legal manual of the time, for instance, stressed that 'The *jizya* is to be given in a humiliating manner. At the moment of remittal, the *dhimmi* should incline his head, whereupon the [Muslim] official should seize him by the beard and deliver him a blow on the temple.'

There was always a line, but one which was perpetually moving, beyond which the *dhimmi* risked bringing down the outrage and resentment of Muslims. The *dhimmis* had crossed that line, according to al-Jahiz, and were no longer accepting their inferiority. They had been allowed to assimilate too much.

When he abandoned Mu'tazilism and the inquisition in 847, al-Mutawakkil had publicly ordered a return to 'submission and the acceptance of tradition'. The failure of the inquisition had demonstrated the power of the traditionalist ulema and shown that the people were behind them. Eager to regain public support and assert his traditionalist credentials, al-Mutawakkil played the intolerance card. He would adhere faithfully to the principle of the Pact of Umar and assert the superiority of Muslims.

In 850, about three years after he had dismantled the inquisition, al-Mutawakkil wrote to all his officers in the provinces and cities and to the governors of the frontier towns. 'Wishing to find favour with God', he ordered that they 'should cease to employ *dhimmis* in any of their work and affairs or to adopt them as associates'. The *dhimmis*, he went on to say, must be reduced 'to the station which God has assigned to them'.

Al-Mutawakkil's ban on *dhimmis* holding public office was followed up with such a battery of orders that he became the first caliph fully to implement the humiliating restrictions on *dhimmis* laid down in the Pact of Umar. He ordered that all churches and synagogues that had been built after the Muslim conquests had to be torn down or turned into mosques. And – just to strengthen his orthodox Sunni credentials – the Shiite shrine to Husayn, the martyred grandson of Muhammad, was also to be demolished. One tenth of the houses owned by *dhimmis* were to be confiscated, and turned into mosques, if they were spacious enough; Jewish and Christian processions were banned; *dhimmi* graves had to be levelled to a height lower than that of Muslim graves. *Dhimmis* had to wear yellow so that they would be clearly differentiated from Muslims – their large cloaks, the men's turbans and the women's veils, if they wore them, must all be yellow; poorer *dhimmis* who could not afford such clothes had to wear two yellow patches on their cloaks, one on the front and one on the back. (In 1215 the Church would copy the Muslims and force the Jews of Europe to wear distinguishing clothing.) Al-Mutawakkil insisted that *dhimmis* must ride mules or donkeys and forbade them to ride horses. *Dhimmis* and Muslims were ordered to use separate public baths.

The 'hater of Christians', as al-Mutawakkil was called, commanded that wooden images of devils be nailed to the doors of Christian homes to distinguish them from the homes of Muslims. As well as being denied employment in government offices they were forbidden to conduct 'any official business whereby they might have authority over Muslims' (just as the Church synods had decreed regarding Jews). Jews and Christians had to talk to Muslims with eyes cast down.

We do not know how strictly the *dhimmis* were forced to comply with al-Mutawakkil's edicts. The dress codes were certainly enforced and some Christians were ousted from public office. But it was impossible to apply a wholesale ban on the employment of *dhimmis* because Christians and Jews were such experienced administrators.

Al-Mutawakkil's clampdown on the *dhimmis* does not, however, seem to have been accompanied by mob violence against them – nothing like the violent assaults that would be unleashed upon the Jews of Christendom in the coming centuries. The caliph had miscalculated. He had hoped his assertion of Muslim superiority would please the ulema, whom he needed to get back on his side, and would also be a crowd pleaser. But as an attempt to strengthen his own position, al-Mutawakkil's recourse to intolerance failed utterly.

In the early hours of 11 December 861 he and his courtiers were blind drunk – as they often were; al-Mutawakkil was so drunk that he had slumped over and his eunuchs had to prop him up again, as was their custom. At that moment Bugha, head of the palace bodyguard, appeared accompanied by ten guards. 'Their faces were veiled and the swords which they were holding in their hands glittered in the light of the candles,' according to the poet al-Buhturi, who witnessed the event. The guards made straight for the caliph while guests and courtiers fled. Only his faithful friend and adviser Al-Fath remained. When the guards slashed at al-Mutawakkil with their swords, Al-Fath 'threw himself on the body of the caliph and they died together'.[5]

The assassination was probably carried out with the connivance of al-Mutawakkil's son. It revealed just how far the caliph had lost control to the Turkish slave soldiers who formed his bodyguard and were the crack troops of his army. Al-Mutawakkil's two predecessors, his younger brother al-Mu'tasim, and al-Mu'tasim's son al-Wathiq, had unwisely decided to enslave the nomads who roamed the vast grasslands of central Asia, import them into the empire, convert them to Islam and train them up to be the empire's slave army. For these men slavery was the passport to success, to education and membership of a highly trained military elite. The caliph believed slave soldiers (mamluks) would have no loyalty to anyone but him. He was wrong. It was a mistake that Islam's rulers would make time and time again. The ruler would import his foreign soldiers, who would overthrow him, only to be supplanted in their turn.

Caliphs had the financial resources to use what were in effect foreign mercenaries. By contrast, rulers in medieval Europe had to recruit soldiers from their own territories and reward them with land since they had no other means of paying them. Soldiers morphed into great landholders. And since part of their feudal contract with the king – land in exchange for service – included providing a body of armed men when required, these barons had both territorial and military power.

The presence of this landed aristocracy was crucial in the development of western Europe. It meant that neither King nor Church could ever hold the monopoly of power because there was always this third party, the landed military aristocracy, to be reckoned with. The triangulation of power, as sociologist Max Weber pointed out, motored innovation in western Europe. All three had to do deals with each other in order to defend and enhance their own position; parliament, according to Weber, was one result. But the tripartite struggle was a brutal one. Intolerance, the invention of the 'enemy other', became one of the standard tools that all three parts of the Weberian triangle would rely on. The consequences for the evolution of tolerance were profound.

In the ninth century the Abbasids further choked off the development of a landed aristocracy by rewarding mamluks and officials with the non-hereditary deed to land (an *iqta'*). In exchange for an annual rent the deed entitled them to collect the taxes from the peasants and keep the profits and a portion of the peasants' crops. But they were not given ownership of the land, and consequently had no stake in it; indeed, they often lived in towns far from their agricultural holdings. They were considered to be and often felt themselves to be aliens. Tax-farming mamluks in particular were disliked anyway for their difference, their fair skin, their use of a foreign language, and often for their inability to even speak Arabic.

Shortly after al-Mutawakkil's assassination al-Jahiz, the religious scholar who had fulminated against the Jews' pretensions to equality with Muslims, died. Appropriately, he was killed by an avalanche of books which fell on him from his library shelves.

As for his counterpart in Christendom, Agobard's worst fears were realized: 'something to be bewailed by all the children of the Catholic Church', as the chronicler of the *Annals of St-Bertin* put it. In 839, Bodo, the royal chaplain at Louis' imperial court, went on a pilgrimage to Rome. On the way he sold all his companions into slavery except his nephew, and headed to Zaragoza (Saragossa) in Muslim Spain where he 'had himself circumcised, allowed his hair and beard to grow long, changed his name, and boldly assumed the name of Eleazar'. If an eminent Churchman could convert to Judaism, how many more Christians might the Church lose?

Bodo/Eleazar had been 'seduced by the enemy of the human race' according to the *Annals of St-Bertin*; Eleazar himself claimed that he had been appalled by the laxity of Louis' court (despite Louis' piety) and had suffered theological scruples. Soon after his move to Zaragoza, where there was a substantial Jewish community, he married a Jewish woman and began trying to convert Spanish Christians to Judaism, much to their dismay.

A year after Bodo/Eleazar's conversion, he engaged in a theological debate by letter with one of Muslim Spain's most fervent and radical Christians, the lay theologian and poet Paulus Alvarus. Although their correspondence began with controlled politesse on both sides – Alvarus writing to 'my dear' Eleazar, and Eleazar calling Alvarus a 'good man' – it rapidly degenerated in tone, until Alvarus called Eleazar an 'enemy of God' and a 'wailing fox' whose 'foul letter' was 'full of lies, rotten with insults'. Eleazar, on his side, described one of Alvarus's last letters to him as the 'barking of mad dogs'. Like many converts, Bodo/Eleazar and Alvarus (who was probably Jewish) were more fervent than their co-religionists who had been born into their faith.

Agobard and al-Jahiz – fellow 'austerians' as I like to think of them – had tried to resist what they considered to be the ill effect of toleration – assimilation. Assimilation threatened the superior status of the dominant religion and those who practised it. However, Louis, the Carolingian emperor, refused Agobard's plea to discriminate against the Jews. Louis needed the Jews more than he needed the backing of his archbishop; anti-Jewish measures would not be that popular anyway, given that Jews were not in serious competition with Christians. Al-Mutawakkil, on the other hand, was more receptive to al-Jahiz's similar call for intolerance because he believed it was in his interests to do so. He willingly imposed intolerance on Jews and Christians, thinking that by calling a halt to assimilation he would gain the support of the ulema and the majority of his people.

In Muslim-controlled al-Andalus, however, opposition to assimilation came not from the dominant religion but from within the minority that was doing the assimilating. A small group of Christians set out to halt what they perceived as the haemorrhaging of Christians to Islam. They chose a tactic still used by today's Islamic terrorists – of provoking intolerance as a way of uniting the Christian community against the Muslims and making assimilation impossible.

Assimilation is the common response to being tolerated. Since toleration requires the minority to accept its inferior status, some members of the minority naturally try to escape the discomforts and humiliations of being 'put up with' by merging with the superior majority. Assimilation, however, is problematic for the majority who both demand that the minority assimilate but at the same time fear that they, the majority, are losing their superior status as a result. But assimilation is also deeply problematic for the minority itself who see increasing numbers of their group disappearing into the majority and fear they are losing their communal and religious identity. In Europe the dilemma of assimilation has been felt most acutely by Jews and today by Muslims. It is why 'ghettoes', in the sense of members of a particular religion or ethnicity living together in the same area, may be created by the minority itself out of preference and the desire to preserve its own identity. (A ghetto in this voluntary, self-created sense is of course very different from the ghettoes imposed by European states from the sixteenth century onwards, when Jews were *forced* to live apart from the majority; see Chapter 14)

Neither the ruling group nor the subordinate group necessarily wants assimilation; and the minority group can be just as harsh as the majority in insisting that both groups should maintain their distance. Talmudic lawyers imposed segregation just as Church canon lawyers did: Jews were to avoid attending Christian ceremonies or employing gentile servants, and a Jew's lips should never touch anything touched by gentile lips, which made socializing with Christians fraught with difficulty.

In the mid ninth century al-Andalus witnessed a huge increase in the number of Christian converts to Islam. And if they had not actually converted, Christians were becoming indistinguishable from Muslims. Soon there would be no Christians left in al-Andalus. That was what Alvarus feared, anyway. He and his close friend, the priest Eulogius, inspired fifty men and women to provoke the Muslim authorities into burning them to death in Cordoba – the biggest city in western Europe and the most tolerant. The 'Cordoba Martyrs' believed their deaths would smash the growing union between Muslims and Christians and so preserve the Christian community from disappearing into the world of Islam.

The benefits for Mozarabs ('would-be Arabs', as Christians disparagingly called those Christians considered to have become contaminated by Muslim customs) and Jews of converting to Islam, or 'passing themselves off' as Muslims, often far outweighed the cost of losing their own faith. Ambitious Mozarabs at the court of Abd al-Rahman II in Cordoba made sure to be seen to follow enough of the sharia to avoid giving offence to Muslims. Christians could not hope for serious advancement at court otherwise. It was why they underwent circumcision, 'the mark of the devil' according to Alvarus. Circumcision, painful though it was, was a price worth paying for promotion at court. A Christian who was uncircumcised was considered to be physically polluted, so were Christians who ate pork; as a result many Christians stopped eating pork and raising pigs. Drinking wine, however, was not a problem at the court of the Umayyad Abd al-Rahman II – it was common practice. Wealthier Christian women adopted the Muslim custom of going out with their faces veiled. Christian men looked to Arabic, not Latin, as the source of their culture and daily life. 'They have forgotten their own language,' Alvarus lamented. 'For every one who can write a letter in Latin to a friend, there are a thousand who can express themselves in Arabic with elegance and write better poems in this language than the Arabs themselves.' Of course, the Christians were right to embrace Arabic. It was not just the global language of power, essential for anyone who wanted a career, but it was also the language of high culture, of poetry, philosophy, science, commerce, even of theology, Christian and Jewish as well as Islamic. Jews too wrote and spoke in Arabic.

In a period of relative peace and stability, marred by the occasional Viking fleet that came prowling down the Mediterranean coast, and by skirmishes with the Christian kingdoms to the north, Abd al-Rahman turned Cordoba into one of the most tolerant cities in the world. In this flourishing city surrounded by streams and olive groves, the court rivalled the Abbasids' court at Baghdad in its culture and opulence.

Jews and Christians who did not convert did not suffer unduly. Most of the regulations contained in the Pact of Umar were not enforced, although *dhimmis* were required to wear distinctive clothing – Jews wore yellow woollen caps and were forbidden to wear turbans; and, of course, like the Christians, they had to pay the *jizya*.

Alvarus and Eulogius believed that if the Muslim authorities could be goaded into behaving harshly enough, Christians would unite against them and assimilation would stop. 'Muhammad enjoyed the wives of other men like a pimp,' Alvarus wrote, 'concealing the scabbiness of his filth behind an angelic command, promising as a gift for those who believe in him harlots for the taking, scattered about in the paradise of his God.' Eulogius described Muhammad as the Antichrist and pseudo prophet. Insulting Muhammad was a sure way to enrage Muslims.

In June 851, a monk called Isaac descended from his monastery in the mountains and headed for the emir's palace in Cordoba where he asked to speak to the chief *qadi* (the chief judge).* To the *qadi*'s utter astonishment, Isaac launched into an unprovoked attack on Islam claiming that Muhammad was languishing in hell. 'Are you drunk or mad?' the enraged *qadi* asked, to which Isaac replied that he was compelled to speak by the 'zeal of righteousness' and that he was prepared to die for his remarks.† The *qadi* promptly had Isaac arrested, reported the case to the emir Abd al-Rahman II, and sentenced him to death for blaspheming.

On 3 June Isaac was decapitated and suspended upside down for the public to gawp at. He was the first of the Cordoban 'martyrs' and set the style by which they courted death. Most of them would walk into the *qadi*'s court and denounce Muhammad as a liar or madman. Or they would try to preach the gospel in Cordoba's vast central mosque,

* The Umayyad rulers of Cordoba called themselves emirs (rulers) but did not claim for themselves the title 'caliph', meaning leader of the global community of Muslims, until 929.

† Under sharia law death is one of the penalties for blasphemy, although the Quran itself never actually specifies what the punishment should be; a few hadiths do refer to execution but it is unclear whether that is exacted for the crime of blaspheming or for the crime of inciting violence and treason. As in the pagan Roman Empire, so in the Christian and Islamic empires – treason and sedition usually took a religious form. In the Book of Leviticus Yahweh tells Moses that the blasphemer should be stoned to death (24:16).

renowned even then for its pillared prayer hall topped with arches decorated in a dazzling pattern of red bricks and white stone. (The mosque was in fact built on the site of a Christian church which in turn had been built on the ruins of a Roman temple.)

Abd al-Rahman issued an edict in which he reminded his subjects of the Islamic prohibition on blasphemy and that capital punishment was the penalty. But over the next four days, seven Christians appeared before the *qadi* repeating Isaac's blasphemies. 'Now hand down the sentence,' they told the *qadi*. 'Multiply your cruelty, be kindled with complete fury in vengeance for your prophet. We profess Christ to be truly God and your prophet to be a precursor of Antichrist and an author of profane doctrine.' They were duly decapitated. The emir then ordered the arrest of the local Church leaders, amongst them Eulogius, but released them after only four months.

One week before Abd al-Rahman's death, a monk together with a Syrian pilgrim entered the Great Mosque of Cordoba during worship. In the prayer hall, the two men preached the gospel and proclaimed the falsehood of Islam. Furious worshippers tried to kill them, but the authorities saved them for an equally dreadful death: their hands and feet were amputated while they were still alive and then, like the other Christian martyrs, they were decapitated.

But the emir had not been a very effective persecutor, and the candidates for martyrdom were anyway not that numerous. When Abd al-Rahman died in September 852, ten martyrs had followed Isaac to their deaths – four monks, two priests, two women, a young soldier in the emir's army called Sanctius and the pilgrim from Syria. Abd al-Rahman's successor, his son Muhammad I, however, proved to be far more satisfactory, as far as Alvarus and Eulogius were concerned.

Muhammad I was facing widespread revolts; in a bid to assert their independence, local landlords erected fortresses and stopped paying taxes to Cordoba. According to Eulogius, Muhammad contemplated 'killing all Christian men and dispersing their women by selling them into slavery, except those who spurned their religion and converted to his cult'. But he was apparently dissuaded by his counsellors who convinced him that it was unfair to punish the majority for the sins of the few.

Instead, like al-Mutawakkil in Baghdad, he began to enforce the Pact of Umar more rigorously. Christians were expelled from office (Jews were exempted, since they were not the ones causing the trouble). When more Christians were inspired to volunteer for having 'their necks struck', as decapitation was euphemistically called, Muhammad shut down monasteries and convents and ordered that all churches built after the Arab occupation should be destroyed.

In 859 Eulogius gave refuge to a Muslim girl called Leocritia who had converted to Christianity and run away from her parents. Both were arrested, Eulogius for proselytizing and assisting in the 'abduction' of a Muslim girl and Leocritia for apostasizing and refusing to return to the faith of her parents. On 11 March Eulogius was beheaded; Leocritia was beheaded four days later. She was the last of the Cordoba 'martyrs'.

Alvarus, unlike his beloved friend Eulogius, never attacked Islam in a public place where he might be arrested and chose not to become a martyr. Instead he lived on to become the sort of Christian assimilationist he had despised, currying favour with an influential courtier in order to get help when a monastery sued him over a land grant.

Alvarus's and Eulogius's hopes of putting a brake on assimilation backfired. At the time, most Andalusian Christians, including the clergy, had little sympathy for these self-styled martyrs and thought of them instead as fanatical suicidees who jeopardized the modus vivendi which most Christians had established with Muslims. The senior bishop of al-Andalus, Reccafred of Seville, even declared that they were not true martyrs since they had deliberately sought their own deaths. Reccafred made a point of contrasting the true martyrs – the early Christians executed under Diocletian in the fourth century – with Cordoba's brand. The early Christians had refused to worship a pagan religion imposed on them by imperial Rome. Cordoba's 'martyrs', on the other hand, were free to practise Christianity; Muslim authorities were not forcing them to convert to Islam or demonstrate their loyalty to it. Reccafred was indeed so opposed to the Cordoba martyrs that he backed a proposal to imprison clerics suspected of being sympathetic to or inciting martyrdom and named them to the authorities. According to Alvarus 'he fell upon churches and clergy like a violent whirlwind and threw as many priests as he could in jail'.[6]

The 'martyrs' had succeeded in provoking the Muslim authorities to behead them, but that had not produced the desired result of turning the tide of assimilation. On the contrary, it had made the urge to assimilate – the response of the minority to the petty humiliations of toleration – even stronger. Large numbers of Christians converted to Islam in a bid to distance themselves from the troublemakers. During the tenth century, the Christians, once a majority in Cordoba, were reduced to a small minority.

Eulogius and Alvarus had used martyrdom in an attempt to unite their group and prevent its disappearance under the pressures of assimilation. Their attempt had failed, but 200 years later, in the eleventh century, the 'Cordoba Martyrs' would be resuscitated. Transformed into heroic symbols of resistance to cruel Islam, the martyrs became a powerful propaganda weapon in the Christian effort to reconquer al-Andalus from the Muslims (see Chapter 7).

CHAPTER 6

AUSTERITY IN ENGLAND AND THE PAPAL BATTLE FOR SUPREMACY

'Monks give themselves to greed and luxury indecent even for godly layfolk. Nay more, in consecrated houses of God lay abbots are living with their wives, their sons and their daughters, with their soldiers and their dogs.'

– Recorded at an assembly of bishops, early tenth century

'The pope alone can depose emperors; he can absolve subjects from their allegiance; all princes should kiss his feet.'

– Pope Gregory, *Dictatus papae*, 1075

FEW PEOPLE TODAY HAVE heard of the mid-tenth-century English monk Dunstan. At the time he was the most powerful man in Wessex, religiously and politically. A century separates this stern, harsh monk from Pope Gregory, 'the devil in a cowl' as he was called by his enemies, who, as we will see, had the power to force an emperor to stand in the snow for three days. But both men were embarked on the same mission: to enhance the power and the glory of the Church. And both men join the ranks of the 'austerians' who discovered the power of religious zealotry, of a passionate intolerance towards their co-religionists, as a tool for enhancing the power and glory of the Church. Ibn Hanbal's religious zealotry had done the same for the Mosque; it had led to the defeat of the caliph's inquisition and the consequent enhancement of the ulema's power. But it was a moral power only. In Christendom that rise in moral power was translated into political power. Dunstan and Pope Gregory learned that spiritual authority can be converted into power, material as well as moral, and that the most effective way of generating unity and fervour is to create a common enemy. In their case the enemy was the lax churchman and they were ruthless in rooting him out, both using the same means, the shining example of Cluny Monastery which had set the Christian world alight.

When Dunstan took holy orders in about 939 at the age of thirty, 'England' was a set of semi-pagan warring kingdoms and the Church was a demoralized, shattered institution. Once great monasteries lay in ruins after being looted by the Vikings; in those monasteries that had survived, monastic life had become so debased that it had virtually ceased to exist. A mere sixteen years later in 955 Dunstan and the Church's standing was so high that he could dictate the behaviour of the young and handsome King Edwy at his coronation banquet.

After hours of feasting with the 200 greatest men of the land, when drunkenness – at which Anglo-Saxon men, like their modern counterparts, excelled – had reached fever pitch, King Edwy disappeared. His absence was spotted by Dunstan, chief adviser and treasurer, sitting at the feast in his hooded black monk's habit. Dunstan went in search of the king and found him upstairs with his consort the beautiful Elgiva and her mother, all three 'pressed in close with desire, like pigs wallowing in a pit', according to one of Dunstan's earliest biographers and near contemporaries. Appalled at the sight of this troilism, Dunstan ordered the king to return to the feast. Edwy refused. Snatching up the heavy gold and silver crown which had rolled into a corner of the room, Dunstan crammed it onto Edwy's head and dragged him back to the feast. Embroidered though this juicy gossip might have been over the centuries, it is an extraordinarily graphic display of undiluted Church power.

Dunstan had raised the English Church to this position of dominance by following the example of the Benedictine Abbey at Cluny in Burgundy. Cluny Abbey was becoming famous across Europe during the tenth century for its creation of the pure Christian life on earth, for, in fact, its monastic rigour – none of those fat, licentious monks who fed their appetites and not their souls. Cluny's monks followed a strict regime of prayer, silence, and work. They slept in dormitories where a candle was kept burning to prevent any illicit behaviour and took their meagre meals in utter silence while a monk read devotional works to them. Their days and nights were punctuated by prayers. They were flogged if they were found deviating from the monastery's strict rules.

The medieval Christian view was that the world was fallen; it had evil built into it and was essentially corrupting. Cluny enforced the strictest separation between the spiritually pure world of God and the corrupt material world of Caesar. By contrast Islam never saw humankind as inherently sinful, and never made a sharp distinction between the spiritual and physical realms. The Christian assumption was that only by living apart from the world was it possible to lead a truly Christian life. The Islamic assumption was that all of society – not just a specialized few whose pure living would help save the rest of humanity – would live according to sharia law. Ibn Hanbal had insisted that the good Muslim must live strictly according to the sharia and follow the ways of Muhammad and his Companions. Cluny did not insist that all Christians should follow the strict regime of its monks. But its religious rigour, and its intolerance towards monks who strayed from the monastic ideal created a renewed and purified model of the Christian life which filled ordinary Christians with a new religious fervour.

The Cluniac model was adopted by sister monasteries in France, Italy and Germany, and by Dunstan in England. Dunstan and his senior bishops (Aethelwold, Bishop of Winchester, and Oswald, Bishop of Worcester, the son of Viking pagans) set about cleansing the monasteries of dissolute monks. A strict monastic rule of silence and prayers was established. Those monks who refused to abide by the new rule were expelled along with their women. Bishop Aethelwold had appeared at the doors of his cathedral with a king's officer at his side and told his reluctant monks, 'Either you take hold of discipline here and now, or here and now you leave your stalls in this Cathedral Church!' A number of them walked out. Later they tried to poison him, but, according to his biographer-hagiographer, Aethelwold survived by a miracle.

By reforming the monasteries and making them the showcases of the Church's spiritual excellence, Dunstan restored the moral stature of the Church in England. That gave it a power with which the king was eager to ally himself. King Edgar, who took the throne in 959 after civil war and the death of his troilist brother Edwy, was struggling to unite the kingdoms of Mercia and Northumbria in the north with Wessex and Kent in the south. These were lawless violent kingdoms where blood feuds could last for generations, where kings – and bishops, too – died in drunken brawls, and a stranger could be legitimately killed if he did not announce his presence by shouting or blowing a horn. Edgar understood that while physical power could force people to behave, moral power was a far more effective way to unite a people, and to mould behaviour and feelings.

For the whole of his sixteen-year reign Edgar gave Dunstan his unreserved support. Edgar made him both head of the Church, Archbishop of Canterbury; and chief minister, head of the Witan, the king's council. He lavished land and endowments on the monasteries. (Pepin, the founder of the Holy Roman Empire, had set the precedent for this in 754 by 'donating' territory in Italy to the pope.) With Edgar's support, Dunstan transformed the Church into an immensely powerful institution, a quasi-state powerful enough to impose its vision on England.

In 973 Edgar received the inestimable gift of God's blessing at his coronation ceremony. It was in fact his second coronation, but this time had all the dignity and pomp conferred by the Church through the all-powerful Dunstan. The king processed to the high altar and prostrated himself before Dunstan – a reflection of the nature of the relationship between Church and State which was in distinct contrast to Pope Leo III's alleged obeisance before Charlemagne in 800. In Edgar's case, however, the prostration more accurately reflected the true relationship of Church and State at the time.

Dunstan's standing was such that when he discovered Edgar had raped a nun, he was able to forbid the king from wearing his crown for seven years. When Edgar died in 975, Dunstan forced a reluctant Witan to back the king's bastard son Edward and crowned him as king.

A monk had elevated the Church to be as powerful as the king, if not more so. Dunstan had turned England into a virtual theocracy thanks to the moral power that his piety gave him. That England did not become a permanent theocracy, that western Europe's kings did not succumb to the supranational rule of the Church, was in large part thanks to the military-landed aristocracy, the third element in Weber's triangulation of power (see Chapter 5). The existence of a third source of power prevented a straight two-way fight between Church and State where the outcome was likely to be either a Caesaro-papist state in which religious affairs were controlled by the political administration, or a theocratic state where Church controlled State.

In the tenth century, Dunstan, the Archbishop of Canterbury, crammed a crown on the head of one king, and forbade another to wear a crown because of their sexual misconduct; in 1077 Pope Gregory VII of Rome forced the Holy Roman emperor to stand shivering barefoot in the snow for three long days, not for committing a crime against morality, but for his 'unheard of insolence' in defying the Church. Never an emollient man, the 'devil in a cowl' declared war against the State, putting Church and State in direct competition for power, for who should rule. The outcome was all the more crucial because both pope and Holy Roman emperor felt their hold on their respective thrones to be so precarious.

Before his election as pope in 1073 when he took the name Gregory, Cardinal Hildebrand, as he then was, had been one of the key figures in a factional fight within the Church. It had ended with the election of two different popes and a one-year battle between them for control of Rome. Moreover, Christendom itself was splitting apart. In Constantinople, 852 miles east of Rome, the patriarch, the most senior Christian figure of the Byzantine (Eastern) Church was contesting the pope's claim to be both head of the Latin (Western) and of the Byzantine Church.

The Holy Roman emperor, Henry IV, was in an equally vulnerable position. Henry was struggling to keep control over what remained of his empire. It had shrunk since the ninth century when Charlemagne and his son Louis the Pious had restored the western Roman Empire and ruled over a united western Europe. By the eleventh century what we now know as France had gone its separate way. Henry still ruled northern Italy and modern-day Germany, but only just. Germany's princes, rulers of their local territories, were always snapping at his heels, fighting for their independence.

Like Dunstan, Gregory learned from Cluny's monastic austerity. Thanks to its austerity, Cluny had created a spiritual elite who inspired the Christian world. It was an elite defined by monastic purity. That meant the monks must distinguish themselves from the impure, who had to be expelled. The Church discovered a passionate sense of unity, by pitting itself – the pure – against the impure in its midst. The creation of the enemy proved to be an extraordinarily useful tool, which the Church would harness and apply to ever-broader categories of people – not just lax monks but heretics, Jews, and Muslims – as the following chapters will show. It is through this spiral of intolerance that the Church became the most powerful institution in Europe. And it is also, as we shall see, a pattern its enemies had to imitate in order to bring it down.

Intolerance had turned Cluny into a model of spiritual perfection in the eyes of Christendom. Kings and noblemen eagerly donated their fortunes and their land to this exemplar of the Christian life. In return the 'black monks' (Benedictines wore a long, black hooded robe) saved them from the flames of hell, a real and terrifying possibility. Donors like Alfonso VI, King of León in northern Spain, gave the equivalent of millions of pounds to 'the monks fighting for God and St Peter … for the assistance of the souls of myself, my father and mother, and my brothers, for my wife and children in order that it may help the living to deserve eternal life and the dead to have eternal rest'. For Alfonso it was a good bargain. His generosity to Cluny gave him the reassurance that his and his family's souls were safe in the hands of the monks who spent eight hours of the day and night raising their voices in prayer to the barrel-vaulted ceiling of their dimly lit, cold stone abbey, pierced by its tall, narrow arched windows.

By the middle of the eleventh century Cluny had created a network of 2,000 monasteries across Europe, under the overall control of Cluny's abbot, Hugh. The bishops and cardinals of France and the Holy Roman Empire were former Cluniac monks. They were among the most highly esteemed advisers of kings, bishops and nobles. Abbot Hugh was connected to every important figure in Europe and had a hand in virtually every major event in late eleventh-century Europe. He was, of course, a friend of Pope Gregory.

One of the many ways in which Islamdom confounds Western expectations is on the separation of Church/Mosque and State. From its beginnings Christianity split Church from State, and yet the Church would for centuries play a major political role. Islam, by contrast, had from the start emphasized the unity of Mosque and State, and yet the Sunni ulema would for centuries remain broadly aloof from the State. Ibn Hanbal, in his stained white cotton shirt, made a point of distancing himself from the caliph, despite all al-Mutawakkil's blandishments and invitations to his palace, whereas Dunstan in his monk's long, black habit was at the centre of government affairs, head of State as well as Church.

Ironically Cluny's strict separation of the monastic from the secular world attracted to it the material wealth and authority which resulted in it becoming thoroughly enmeshed with the political secular world. In Christendom the most powerful positions in government were occupied by Church figures.

Cluny's spiritual authority had given it power and wealth. Gregory and his reformers pursued the same path as Cluny. Their enemy, however, was not just the greedy monk with his mistress, but senior church figures who had become too worldly; men like Manasses, the Archbishop of Reims, who purportedly said that 'the archbishopric would be a fine thing, if only one did not have to sing Mass for it'.* Gregory's enemies were the sleek, corrupt churchmen who bought and sold clerical offices (committing the sin of simony), who were more interested in the world than in the spirit. No wonder. They were appointees of the local prince, magnate,

* According to the early twelfth-century Benedictine Abbot Guibert of Nogent.

or ruler, selected for their political usefulness, not for their spirituality. Naturally they were more loyal to the layman who appointed them than to the Church and its head, the pope.* Fortunately Gregory's spiritual and material interests coincided perfectly. By attacking lay investiture (the appointment of churchmen by laymen), Gregory was both reforming the Church and striking a blow for papal supremacy.

This was no minor matter. Archbishops, bishops and abbots were vast landowners, controlling not just the spiritual but the economic lives of the peasants and townspeople who lived in their diocese. In what is now Germany but was then part of the Holy Roman Empire, bishops were legally recognized as prince-bishops, the rulers of their own territory. If lay investiture were to be abolished, it would entail a serious loss of political control for emperor, king, prince or magnate, and a significant increase in power for the Church and above all for the pope. In 1073 Gregory announced that senior churchmen who received their appointments from lay rulers would be excommunicated.

In one of his innumerable letters, Gregory set out his vision: a theocracy where

> ... the pope alone can depose and restore bishops; he alone can make new laws, set up new bishoprics and divide old ones... He alone can call general councils and authorize canon laws; he can depose emperors; he can absolve subjects from their allegiance; all princes should kiss his feet; his legates ... have precedence over all bishops.[1]

Inevitably, Pope Gregory locked horns with the Holy Roman emperor Henry IV, who was struggling to control the rebellious German princes in his empire. The pope made common cause with many of them while the emperor found allies among many of the bishops who felt the pope's attacks on the emperor had gone too far (Gregory was also enforcing

* Cluny was the exception. It had been explicitly exempted from any secular control since its foundation in 909. It was answerable only to the pope.

celibacy on his reluctant bishops). Henry refused to give up his right to appoint bishops – and popes too. In January 1076 Henry called on Gregory, 'not pope but false monk', to step down from the papal throne.

The following month, on 22 February, Gregory retaliated and excommunicated the emperor. Gregory's excommunication was not just depriving the emperor of the consolations of the Church, although that alone was a terrible sentence for a Christian; it was an incitement to rebellion.

> In the name of Almighty God, Father, Son and Holy Ghost I withdraw, through Thy power and authority, from Henry the king, son of Henry the emperor, who has risen against Thy Church with unheard of insolence, the rule over the whole kingdom of the Germans and over Italy. And I absolve all Christians from the bonds of the oath which they have made or shall make to him; and I forbid any one to serve him as king.[2]

Faced by an overwhelming coalition of German princes, lay magnates and bishops, who threatened to depose him if he did not seek absolution from the pope, Henry caved in. In December 1076 he made his famous trek across the Alps to Canossa Castle in north Italy where the pope was staying. It was the harshest winter the chroniclers could recall. Henry and his entourage, including his wife and young son, were, according to the chronicler Lampert of Hersfeld, reduced to 'crawling on their hands and feet, now clinging to the shoulders of their guides and also occasionally, when a foot slipped on an icy surface, falling and rolling down for a considerable distance'. A month later, on 25 January, they reached the walled castle which was perched on the white cliffs of the Apennines. But the pope ordered the castle's gates to be closed. Henry could not be trusted, the pope claimed, though no doubt Gregory also wanted to demonstrate just how powerful the Church was. For three days and nights Henry stood shivering in a hair shirt outside the castle walls, as the pope smugly told the German princes:

> Laying aside all royal insignia, barefooted and in coarse attire, he [Henry] ceased not with many tears to beseech the apostolic help and comfort until all who were present or who had heard the story were so moved by pity and compassion that they pleaded his cause with prayers and tears. Indeed, they marvelled at our hardness of heart. Some even complaining that our action savoured rather of heartless tyranny than of chastening severity.

Amongst those who pleaded Henry's cause was his godfather, Hugh, the well-connected and extraordinarily influential Abbot of Cluny who was in the papal entourage.

Having made his point Pope Gregory finally allowed the gates to be opened. Henry knelt before the pope and begged his forgiveness – a humiliating genuflection to papal power. How Islam's ulema in Cordoba, Baghdad and Cairo must have gasped in astonishment when they heard the news. Henry swore an oath promising 'to satisfy the grievances which my archbishops, bishops, dukes and other princes of Germany or their followers may have against me' and never to 'hinder or molest' the pope.[3] The pope lifted his excommunication. Seven years later, in 1084, Henry's troops captured Rome and imprisoned Gregory.

He died the following year in 1085.

Sixteen years later, in 1111, an agreement was hammered out between a new pope and a new emperor, Henry V. It was astonishingly radical. The emperor agreed to give up lay investiture; in exchange Germany's churches would return to the Holy Roman emperor all the vast lands with which they had been endowed; bishops would renounce their secular positions and become simple pastors once more, living on the tithes and free gifts of the faithful. Shorn of its wealth, and its secular powers, the German Church would no longer be a competitor with the State – pope and Holy Roman emperor would stop meddling in each other's affairs. It was a deal which Pope Paschal II, who was genuinely devoted to the monastic ideals of poverty, as well as being politically naive, felt he was too weak to refuse.

Alas, during the coronation ceremony at St Peter's in which Pope Paschal II was to have crowned Henry as legitimate emperor, the agreement was read out and was shouted down in anger. Cardinals and the German bishops attending the ceremony were outraged. The Abbot of Cluny was amongst the vociferous opponents of a settlement which would have done more to return the Church to its monastically simple roots than any of Cluny's monasteries. Ideological struggles are, after all, intimately connected to material ones. If the Concordat of 1111 had been accepted, of course, the Church would have become much more like the ulema, and the emperor much more like the caliph. But the point had passed when this was conceivable – perhaps it never was, post-Constantine, for the Roman Church.

The pope abandoned the coronation. He and sixteen of his cardinals were seized by Henry's soldiers. It took ten years for the ensuing civil war to be finally resolved with the far less radical Concordat of Worms of 1122. The Church would keep hold of its wealth; the emperor would abandon his right to select abbots and bishops who would be appointed by ecclesiastical election. Lay investiture had in theory been abolished. But, crucially, the emperor would have a representative present at the elections and would arbitrate in the case of disputed elections. The emperor would give up his right to invest bishops with the spiritual symbols of their office, the ring and crozier. Instead he would invest them with a new symbol of office, the sceptre. The sceptre signified the secular privileges and lands which the emperor was officially granting and for which the appointees still paid homage. The Concordat had in reality changed little in Germany.

Forty years after the Concordat, England had its own version of the investiture struggle. In 1162, the highly irascible, flame-haired king, Henry II, appointed his close friend Thomas Becket as Archbishop of Canterbury. Becket now combined his role as head of the Church in England with his previous role as Chancellor, the most senior political figure in the realm, rather as Dunstan had done 200 years earlier. And like Dunstan, Becket was implacable and uncompromising. To the fury of the king, Becket, his formerly pleasure-loving friend, opposed him at every turn. In 1170 Henry had him murdered. When it came to it, victory still went to the side with physical force. As Henry said when an unfortunate bishop protested that only the pope could deprive him (the bishop) of his office: '"Very true; he can't be deposed; but look" (and at this Henry gave the bishop a violent shove with his hands) "he can be given the push."'[4]

True, the State had physical force to call upon. But that rival state, the Church, had the priceless ability to capture the hearts and minds of the people with the power of a God who ruled this world and the next. The Concordat of Worms of 1122 had clearly not solved the struggle for dominance between Church and State, although it had, temporarily, called a halt to it. But in the endless bargaining between pragmatic political force and religious dogmatic force, Europe's Church had steadily accumulated land and wealth. The Church was becoming a state powerful enough to threaten the secular state. Tragically, it was doing so by creating a common enemy – unleashing the demons of intolerance and uniting its flock against its religious 'others'.

Al-Andalus, ostensibly the Muslim model of tolerance, had taken a similar route to the European Church. In 1066 – the same year that William of Normandy encouraged Jews to settle in his newly conquered territory of England – a Muslim mob killed 4,000 Jews in Granada, one of the most civilized and tolerant city states in Muslim Spain, and home to the largest community of Jews in the Muslim world.

Mob violence against a people does not spring out of nowhere. It is the physical expression of resentments and fears which have built up over time, often encouraged by religious or secular rulers trying to get 'the people' on their side. This was certainly the case in Granada.

Al-Andalus had for centuries rightly felt itself to be superior – in wealth, culture and military prowess – to its Christian neighbours to the north. But the Umayyad caliph was losing control of Muslim Spain and it was shattering into small city states (*taifas*) at constant war with each other. Small, quarrelling states made relatively easy pickings for their land-hungry neighbours. There had always been skirmishes on the borders between Christian and Muslim Spain, but the Muslims had usually won. Now their despised Christian neighbours were battening on al-Andalus, demanding tribute from the *taifas* and invading them if payment was denied.

Muslims were beginning to suffer the humiliations of what Christendom has dubbed the 'Reconquista', the reconquest of Muslim Spain by Christian kings (see Chapter 7). Muslims now felt all too aware that a once glorious Islamic Spain was increasingly coming under threat. Their unease was only exacerbated by the sight of Jewish *dhimmis* occupying the highest official state posts.

Josef Naghrela, the Jewish vizier to the Berber King of Granada, was a case in point. Josef had succeeded his father Samuel as vizier in about 1056. First the father and now the son was occupying the most powerful administrative position in the state of Granada. It did not help that Josef Naghrela refused to play by the rules of the game: if a *dhimmi* achieved a position of power, he should at least be circumspect. But Josef 'did not know the humbleness of the *dhimmi* or the filth of Jewishness', according to Ibn Idhari, the early fourteenth-century historian of al-Andalus and the Maghreb (north-west Africa). Josef apparently insisted on displaying his extraordinary wealth and behaving as spoilt sons of inherited privilege do.

Resentment of the Jews' wealth and success, fear that Jews were taking over – it was rumoured that Josef mentally enslaved the Berber ruler with a special Jewish potion and was plotting to turn Granada into a Jewish state – was given its lethal dose of religious justification. It was not just that according to the Pact of Umar no non-Muslim should exercise authority over a Muslim; by insinuating themselves into the heart of government, Jews were preventing the establishment of a true Islamic state and laying it waste like locusts. 'They collect all the revenues, they munch and they crunch,' wrote the Muslim religious scholar and poet Abu Ishaq whose animus against the Jews was no doubt in part the result of having been passed over at court in favour of Josef Naghrela.

In his nasty, hate-filled ode against Josef's appointment as vizier, Abu Ishaq gave vent to all the frustrated ambitions, the jealousy, the fear, the political and religious disquiet, felt by Muslims in Granada:

> He [the Berber ruler, Badis ibn Habus] has chosen an infidel as his secretary when he could, had he wished, have chosen a Believer.
>
> Through him, the Jews have become great and proud and arrogant...
> And how many a worthy Muslim humbly obeys the vilest ape among these miscreants...

And in a final burst of venom:

> Hasten to slaughter him [Josef Naghrela] as an offering,
> Sacrifice him, for he is a fat ram
> And do not spare his people...
> Do not consider it a breach of faith to kill them –
> the breach of faith would be to let them carry on.[5]

It was an incitement to murder. On 30 December 1066, a Muslim mob broke into Joseph Naghrela's white marble palace. Abd Allah ibn Buluggin, the last Berber ruler of Granada and grandson of Badis, described the event in his memoirs: 'The Jew fled into the interior of the palace, but the mob pursued him there, seized him, and killed him [in fact they crucified him]. Then they put every Jew in the city to the sword and took vast quantities of their property.'[6] Muslim sources, who had good reason to underestimate the number of Jews massacred by Granada's Muslims, put the number killed at 4,000.

But, as many historians of Islam have pointed out, hate-filled diatribes against Jews, such as Abu Ishaq's, and massacres such as took place in Granada, were rare in the Muslim world. Jews and Christians would suffer systematic persecution, massacres and forced conversions under the Muslim ultra-traditionalist Almohads in mid-twelfth-century Spain and North Africa. But on the whole the *dhimmis* of the Islamic world tended to be subjected to a stricter enforcement of the Pact of Umar – rules which were already in place – rather than the extreme end of intolerance such as physical violence or even murder, which was often incited and condoned in Europe by Church or State. Horrendous though the Granada massacre was, it had few parallels in Islamic history – in contrast to Christendom's dreadful record in Europe.

By the end of the eleventh century the Cluniac abbots, the warriors who had knitted Christendom together in support of a spiritual crusade, had elevated the Church to new heights of political power and wealth. Now they would help create an aggressive, triumphalist Christendom which would inspire a physical crusade against God's enemies. The Church was about to ride to battle on the back of intolerance. Christendom was becoming a 'persecuting society'.[7]

CHAPTER 7

THE CRUSADES: THE CHURCH FINDS ITS ENEMY

'Vast and powerful empires are founded on religion. This is because dominion can only be secured by victory, and victory goes to the side which shows most solidarity and unity of purpose.'

– Ibn Khaldun, *The Muqaddimah*, 1377

If you want an insight into the creation of the Muslim enemy and how it helped the Church, read the *Chanson de Roland* (*Song of Roland*).

The *Chanson* started life as a popular ballad which did the rounds orally in France for several centuries. But at some time, probably in the mid eleventh century, it was transformed into the great propaganda myth and rallying call for the Crusades and the 'Reconquista' (the recapture of Muslim Spain by kings from the Christian north).

The original ballad recounted a real event, the eighth-century battle of Roncevaux Pass between Charlemagne's army and Basque rebels in the Pyrenees mountains on the border between Spain and France. Charlemagne and his men were returning from an unsuccessful venture in Muslim Spain where he had joined forces with the Muslim ruler of Saragossa. As they made their way home across the Pyrenees, the rear-guard was separated from the main body of Charlemagne's army and slaughtered by Basques at Roncevaux Pass.

But under the godlike hand of the author of the *Chanson*, probably a Cluniac monk, the Basques are recreated as Muslims. The battle is no longer a battle of Christians fighting Christians (most Basques had been Christianized, although paganism still survived). It becomes a holy war of Christians fighting Muslims, or 'pagans' as the *Chanson* often calls them, the enemies of God. A minor defeat scarcely mentioned at the time becomes a glorious martyrdom in which 10,000 heavily outnumbered Christian soldiers are massacred by 400,000 Muslims. Roland, the leader of the rearguard and probably an imaginary figure, becomes a warrior Christ surrounded by his twelve apostles represented by his twelve magnates; the thirteenth, his stepfather, had betrayed Roland to the Muslims. '*Paien unt tort e crestiens unt dreit*' (Pagans are wrong and Christians are right) is Roland's rallying cry.

Since its earliest days the Church had had a problem with war in a way that Islam never had. War was built into Islam from the start – Muhammad could never have established Islam in Medina had it not been for his military triumphs. Jihad – not just the internal battle to cleanse the soul but the external battle to conquer the heretic – was a positive duty. But for the Church, war, though often considered necessary, seemed to fly in the face of Jesus's insistence on turning the other cheek and loving your enemy. Killing in battle was murder, for which the soldier must do penance, however just the war was deemed to be, and whether the enemy were heretics or Christians. After the Norman conquest of England in 1066, Pope Alexander II had ordered the victorious Norman soldiers to observe a strictly graded pattern of penances: forty days for each man they had wounded and possibly killed; if the soldier did not know how many men he had killed or wounded, then he had to do penance one day a week for the rest of his life, or give alms for the rest of his life. Even if a soldier 'had willed' to kill but 'had not actually struck a man', he still had to do penance. Intention was as bad as action.[1]

But the same pope who ordered that the Norman soldiers do penance for actions which they had been commanded to carry out – killing and maiming the enemy – also declared that soldiers fighting to reconquer Muslim Spain had to do no such penance. Instead soldiers would be cleansed of their previous sins by these actions: they would either jump straight to paradise or at least have quite a considerable time shaved off their sojourn in purgatory, the realm poised between heaven and hell. Ironically, the Church may well have borrowed this extraordinarily potent bribe from the Muslims' promise to their warriors for Islam: jihadis who died on the battlefield went straight to paradise, where they would enjoy the additional bonus of seventy-two wide-eyed (also translated as dark-eyed) virgins. The Church was creating a Christian version of jihad.

For centuries the Church had held an essentially pacifist view that war was wrong though sometimes necessary. But in the *Chanson de Roland* it is the archbishop Turpin, from Cluny Abbey of course, who fights side by side with Roland to the very end when 10,000 Christians lie dead. Besides Roland himself and Roland's great friend the nobleman Oliver, Turpin is the most important hero of the *Chanson* – and the most warlike. No one could accuse Turpin of loving his enemy. In this war for Christendom, hatred of the Muslim enemy was praiseworthy. 'No mortal hates he with hate so fell,' the *Chanson* says admiringly of Turpin's relish for slicing up Muslims with his sword. 'Fight for the succour of Christendom,' Turpin tells the doomed Christian soldiers, and then, says the narrator, 'In God's high name the host he blessed, / And for penance gave them – to smite their best.'[2] The more 'heathens' they killed, the greater the soldiers' chances of getting into heaven. Turpin was announcing, or reflecting, a sea change in the Church's attitude to war. Warfare was no longer a sin but praiseworthy in the eyes of God if it was waged against God's enemies, the Muslims.

The *Chanson* reflects Christianity transforming itself into an aggressive, triumphalist religion; it reveals, like the much earlier Roman epic the *Aeneid* and the Anglo-Saxon epic *Beowulf*, a world hovering on the cusp between paganism and Christianity. But while the *Aeneid* and *Beowulf* range Christian and pagan warrior virtues against each other, the *Chanson* marries the two with chivalry. The chivalric knight is the warrior turned Christian: his code of honour combines Christian and warrior virtues: loyalty, courtesy, generosity, courage and above all devotion to Christ.

The *Chanson* was hugely popular in the eleventh century. It was sung by minstrels in town squares and in the banqueting halls of great noblemen; over the course of the century, it was written down. Ever since Muslims had conquered southern Spain in the eighth century, Christian kings in northern Spain had periodically tried to reconquer pieces of al-Andalus. In the eleventh century the number of Christian and Muslim clashes increased as Christian rulers took advantage of the shattering of al-Andalus into small warring city states (*taifas*). But these attacks on the *taifas* had been little more than a series of unco-ordinated land grabs. The *Chanson* turned them into the 'Reconquista'. Self-interested Christian kings and their adventure warriors, vying with each other for the rich pickings of al-Andalus, could now clothe themselves in the far nobler costume of the Christian warrior. Instead of mere territory and wealth, they were fighting for 'the honour of Christ and the glory of the holy cross, that God may give us victory over the barbarians through the triumph of the cross', according to the Barcelonan count, Ramon Berenguer I.

In May 1085 Alfonso, King of León and Castile, and one of Cluny's most generous donors, conquered the Muslim city of Toledo after an eight-month siege. True, the city surrendered with hardly a murmur, indeed with some relief since it had sunk into civil war under its incompetent ruler al-Qadir; true also that Toledo had already been paying tribute to Alfonso. But Toledo was a city far greater, richer, more cosmopolitan and cultured than anything in the Christian north. Its loss 'sent a great tremor through al-Andalus and filled the inhabitants with fear and despair', wrote Abd Allah ibn Buluggin in the same memoirs in which he had recorded the massacre of the Jews in Granada nine years earlier (see Chapter 6).

Muslims had always seen themselves as belonging to the *umma*, the worldwide community of Muslims, and had put a premium on preserving its unity. But that had been more in theory than reality. In al-Andalus the warring *taifa* rulers had never presented a united front against the attacks from their Christian neighbours; indeed they had often allied with one Christian king to defend themselves against each other. Now they united as Muslims to fight against the Christian enemy.

In the summer of 1086, Mu'tamid, ruler of the *taifa* of Seville, headed a delegation that crossed the Mediterranean to beg for military aid from the rising new power in North Africa. 'In so doing, I dug my own grave,' Mu'tamid admitted years later in bitter exile in Morocco. The *taifa* rulers had put power into the hands of the Almoravids. They and their successors, the Almohads, would be the most intolerant set of rulers that the Islamic world ever experienced.

The Almoravids were Berber warriors drawn from different tribes in the Sahara Desert who followed a particularly hard-line form of Sunnism ('Almoravids' derives from 'morabites', champions of the faith). The Almoravid brand of Sunni Islam stressed the primacy of a strict interpretation of the religious law. It rejected alcohol, music, womanizing or any compromise with the infidel non-Muslims and those they considered to be 'heretical' or lax Muslims. Wielding their brand of purist Islam and devoted to the ideals of jihad, these nomads were united by religion rather than by membership of the same tribe. Armed with their religion and their swords, lances and tall shields, they conquered Morocco and Algeria. The Almoravids were building an empire.

In the mid seventh century the Muslim Arab tribesmen, who conquered the Byzantine and part of the Persian empires, pursued a policy of tolerance towards their religious others – Jews, Christians and Zoroastrians. In the eleventh century their counterparts, the Almoravids, who conquered North Africa, were notably intolerant towards Christians, Jews and Muslims who did not follow their brand of Islam. The difference of course was that the earlier Muslim conquerors had been a minority; they needed to placate the Christian and Jewish majority and had relied on the administrative skills of the conquered. The Almoravid tribesmen, on the other hand, were conquering territory which had been in Muslim hands since those earlier Muslim conquests four centuries before. They had no need to be tolerant.

Indeed, it was their particular brand of strict traditionalist Islam that unified them into such an effective fighting force, as the fourteenth-century philosopher-historian Ibn Khaldun pointed out: 'In the Maghrib [Maghreb, that is North Africa], there existed many tribes equalling or surpassing them in numbers and group feeling,' he wrote. 'However, their religious organization doubled the strength of their group feeling through their consciousness of having the right religious insight and their willingness to die ... and nothing could withstand them.'[3]

The Almoravids were fighting a jihad – just as the Reconquista warriors were fighting a crusade to cleanse the world of the infidel. And it was to the Almoravids that the *taifa* rulers, led by Mu'tamid the ruler of Seville, looked for military help against the Reconquista. But though the Andalusians and the Almoravids were fellow Sunnis, a desert separated them. The Almoravids' harsh form of Islam was well suited to the simpler, harsher conditions under which the Saharan nomads had had to live. But it was very different from the laxer, accommodating Islam of the Muslims of Spain. Yusuf ibn Tashufin, ruler of the expanding Almoravid Empire, was, as far as Mu'tamid was concerned, an illiterate, uncultured zealot, albeit a militarily extremely useful one. Ibn Tashufin represented everything the Andalusian rulers, with their centuries of civilized (that is, urban) culture behind them, despised.

There is, of course, no essential contradiction between military imperial success and the barbaric, or what seems barbaric to the civilized. Ibn Khaldun, the Max Weber of the Islamic world, but writing five centuries earlier, developed a theory of the rise and fall of empires in which the 'barbarian', the nomadic warrior, played an essential role. According to Ibn Khaldun, the barbarian's life engenders particular virtues – aggression, bravery, loyalty, endurance, egalitarianism – which are precisely those that are conducive to imperial success. For Ibn Khaldun, it is the barbarians who create the empire. But it is the decadence of the city culture that the empire then creates which eventually corrupts and softens the barbaric spirit, thereby leading to the fall of the empire. (Gibbon and Nietzsche would follow a similar though more accusatory line. They 'blamed' the fall of the Roman Empire on the rise of a civilizing, peaceful Christianity which lauded meekness and turning the other cheek as opposed to the old pagan warrior values of bravery and aggression.) For Ibn Khaldun, the rise – and fall – of the Almoravids was the paradigm for his cyclical theory of the rise and fall of empires.

Following the custom of many Saharan tribesmen Ibn Tashufin and his men wore veils – unlike the women who went unveiled. Only their gleaming black eyes were visible; Ibn Tashufin's were said to be particularly piercing. He dressed only in animal skins – none of the rich brocades and silks of the Andalusian princes. He ate only meat and drank only camel's milk, in contrast to the wine that was served in golden goblets in the courts of al-Andalus. Many of the Andalusian princes came from Arab patrician families and claimed to be descended from settlers who had conquered al-Andalus nearly four centuries earlier. They vied to outdo each other in the splendour and brilliance of their courts, which were probably the most splendid in Europe. They surrounded themselves with the most learned scholars, the wittiest and most mellifluous of poets. Mu'tamid was himself one of the most outstanding of al-Andalus's many poets. For his part, Ibn Tashufin despised the wine-drinking Andalusian *taifa* rulers who listened to music and the singing of their female slaves. He considered they were not true Muslims. Nonetheless he yielded to Mu'tamid's argument that it was the Almoravids' duty to wage jihad against the Christian infidels.

In July 1086, 1,200 veiled Berbers from the Maghreb, along with tribesmen from inner Africa, rode their camels and horses, or tramped on foot through the lemon, orange and olive groves of a sun-parched al-Andalus to meet the Christian enemy, Alfonso VI, conqueror of Toledo.

In the strange game of war where violence and chaos are meant to be played out according to certain rules, there was a problem as to when battle should commence. Alfonso proposed Monday, since Friday was a holy day for the Muslims, and Sunday was for the Christians, while Saturday was a holy day for the Jews. But the rules were broken. While Ibn Tashufin was apparently saying his prayers on Friday morning, battle commenced. It was called the Battle of Sagrajas in Spanish, *Zallaqa* in Arabic, meaning 'slippery ground', because so much blood was shed that the warriors could not keep their footing.

Accompanied by the booming thud of drums (a highly effective use of psychological warfare, said to have been pioneered by Ibn Tashufin), warriors on horses and camels, veiled in loose blue robes with only the slits of their eyes showing, charged mail-clad knights on horseback. Javelins and arrows were pitted against swords, short spears and shields covered with hippopotamus hide. And Ibn Tashufin rode through the ranks of his army, shouting over the din of battle: 'Muslims, be strong and patient in this jihad against the infidel enemy of God; those of you who die today will go to Paradise as martyrs.' It was the same cry uttered by Turpin, the Cluniac warrior archbishop, urging the doomed Christian soldiers to fight until the bitter end in the *Chanson de Roland*:

'Beyond this day shall no more live one man;
But of one thing I give you good warrant:
Blest Paradise to you now open stands.'[4]

Inevitably, Ibn Tashufin added the more materialist incentive, 'and those who do not die will be rewarded in booty'. Rewards on earth as well as in heaven are a heady mixture.

The Muslims won and inflicted huge losses on the Christians. At least half Alfonso's army was killed.

In the ninth century the Abbasid caliphs in Baghdad had imported Turkic tribesmen as slave soldiers. But the soldiers turned on their caliphs (see Chapter 5). The *taifa* rulers made the same mistake with the North African Almoravids. The Almoravids came to al-Andalus at the invitation of its desperate rulers; they stayed to conquer, armed with a fatwa (a legal ruling on a point of Islamic law by a religious judge) which declared that it was Ibn Tashufin's duty to dethrone the *taifa* kings. The *taifa* kings' decadent, non-Islamic behaviour meant they could not be considered as Muslims. By 1091 Ibn Tashufin had conquered Seville and all the Muslim *taifas* in Spain except Zaragoza.

The Almoravids had owed their success in large part to their strict religious fervour. That did not ease off when they conquered al-Andalus. Jews and Christians were banned from public office, forced to convert, pay brutally punitive taxes and expelled to North Africa, or made to live in special quarters (harbingers of ghettoes, see Chapter 14). Muslims saw their 'heretical' works burned by the Almoravids and joined the large numbers of Jews and Christians seeking refuge in Christian Spain.

The regulations governing how Seville's market should be conducted were indicative of the Almoravid attitude to *dhimmis*, even if they may not have been strictly enforced. Jews and Christians must wear a distinguishing sign 'by which they are recognized to their shame'; they must be 'shunned and not greeted with the customary formula "Peace be upon you"', for 'the devil has gained mastery over them and has made them forget the remembrance of God'; 'A Muslim must not massage a Jew or a Christian nor throw away his refuse nor clean his latrines. The Jew and the Christian are better fitted for such trades, since they are the trades of those who are vile.' Muslim women were forbidden to enter the Christians' 'abominable churches for the priests are evil-doers, fornicators, and sodomites'. Any Muslim found disobeying the rules was to be denounced.[5]

But Christian rulers were no less intolerant. In such turbulent times, when rulers were trying to cling on to their states or establish themselves in new ones, the enemy was only too salient and it was only too useful to escalate hostility against them. Indeed, it was so difficult for hard-pressed *dhimmis* to judge which set of rulers was the worse that many ended up switching back and forth between Muslim and Christian Spain. Judah Halevi, one of the most famous Jewish poets of the time, lived sometimes in Christian Toledo, sometimes in Islamic al-Andalus, according to the severity of the discrimination imposed.

Bernard, the new Bishop of Toledo, converted the city's principal mosque, 'the dwelling place of demons', into the Cathedral of Santa Maria. Bernard who had been, of course, a monk at Cluny, went on to close down all the mosques in every village in his diocese, or converted them into parish churches. This brutally triumphalist gesture was repeated wherever the Reconquista forces scored a victory over the Muslims. Converting a mosque into a church even acquired its own phrase: *eliminata spurcicia Mahometi*, 'eliminating the filth of Muhammad'.

In March 1088 Bernard's former prior at Cluny Abbey was elected Pope Urban II by his supporters. But it took nine months before Urban was strong enough to dislodge the alternative pope, Clement III, who was backed by the Holy Roman emperor, Henry IV. Urban was even more determined to assert his papal supremacy than his mentor Pope Gregory had been (see Chapter 6). Handsome, less belligerent in manner and more charming than Pope Gregory, Urban II would take Western Christendom to new heights of intolerance.

On 27 November 1095 Pope Urban rose to his feet in a field outside the city gates of Clermont, in central France, and addressed the 300 or so French noblemen, archbishops, bishops and abbots gathered before him. His speech has affected Muslim–Christian relations ever since.

Urban called on the knights of France to rescue Jerusalem from 'an accursed race ... utterly alienated from God'.* Holy war, as Steven Runciman, historian of the Crusades, pointed out, is no more than war in the Church's interests. There could be no better way for Urban to assert his leadership over the Church, over Christendom and over the temporal world than by launching a war against 'the enemies of God', and convincing all Western Christendom to take part. Not even emperors could do that.

Muslim rule of Jerusalem was nothing new. It stretched back 400 years to 638 when Umar II conquered the city. What gave the pope his opportunity to overthrow the Muslims was the massive defeat inflicted on what remained of the Christian Byzantine Empire by a confederation of Turkish nomadic tribes from Central Asia led by the Seljuks. The Seljuks, who had converted to Sunni Islam, were conquering Islamic lands from Syria to Afghanistan. Their latest conquest was the greater part of Anatolia (modern Turkey), the most eastern part of the Byzantine Empire.

Western and Eastern Christendom were still at odds; the Byzantine emperor, Alexius Comnenus, had been excommunicated by Pope Gregory for supporting the Holy Roman emperor Henry IV. But this was no time for niceties. Alexius appealed to Gregory's successor, Pope

---

* In some versions of the speech it is not Jerusalem but the Christians of the East who are to be rescued.

Urban, for help. This was a god-sent opportunity for Urban. Anxious that Alexius might recognize Henry IV and his antipope, eager to heal the rift between the two churches and establish himself as unrivalled head of Christendom, Urban turned a battle over territory into a battle for God. (The *Chanson de Roland* had done the same.)

He offered the bribe that was becoming a papal commonplace: 'All who die by the way, whether by land or by sea, or in battle against the pagans, shall have immediate remission of sins.' Urban, of course, also promised material rewards, as Turpin did in the *Chanson de Roland*, and as Ibn Tashufin, the Almoravid, had done with his warriors in al-Andalus in 1086: 'The possessions of the enemy, too, will be yours, since you will make spoil of their treasures.'

Urban's call to war resonated across Europe, appealing to both rulers and ruled, rich and poor. Rulers were keen to show themselves as lining up behind God and the Church. Besides which the Crusade, it was hoped, would put a stop to the unrelenting battles fought in the fields and villages of Europe between the unruly troops of warring barons. Instead of fighting each other, the barons and their peasant armies would direct their violence outside the boundaries of the Christian world and onto the pagan Muslim enemy. 'You rage against your brothers and cut each other in pieces,' Urban had harangued the noblemen at Clermont:

> You, the oppressors of children, plunderers of widows; you, guilty of homicide, of sacrilege, robbers of another's rights; you who await the pay of thieves for the shedding of Christian blood – as vultures smell fetid corpses… If, forsooth, you wish to be mindful of your souls, either lay down the girdle of such knighthood, or advance boldly, as knights of Christ, and rush as quickly as you can to the defence of the Eastern Church … restrain your murderous hands from the destruction of your brothers, and in [sic] behalf of your relatives in the faith oppose yourselves to the Gentiles.[6]

As is common with the demagogue who is trying to whip up hatred, Urban, with tears running down his cheeks, dwelt on how physically disgusting the Muslims were. They polluted the holy places 'with their filthiness', they forcibly circumcised Christians and spread their blood on the altar or poured it into the baptismal font – an accusation prefiguring the 'blood libels' against Jews which would soon become rife in Europe.

By the time he ended his speech, bishops and lay noblemen were, according to eyewitnesses, crying and seized with convulsive trembling. They queued up to pledge themselves to this 'holy war', soon to be known as the First Crusade. It was the first of nine shabby ventures to conquer the 'Holy Land', which stretched over 200 years, and finally petered out in 1291.

Urban's speech ignited France. A huge array of archbishops, bishops and abbots, including Abbot Hugh of Cluny, travelled around the country towns of France, calling on Christians to resist both the claims of property and 'the alluring charms of your wives', to fight for Christ. Peasants and nobles made their vow and were given strips of cloth to sew on to their mantle, cassock, tunic or surcoat, in the shape of a cross ('crusade' derives its name from the old French *croisée,* 'cross'). They received their symbols of pilgrimage – the purse and staff – and made their arrangements for the longest journey many of them would ever make and from which they might never come back.

The gains might be huge in terms of entry to heaven and the riches that might be acquired on earth. But the risks were also huge. A major nobleman would be spending the equivalent of four or five times his annual income, given that he would be travelling for thousands of miles with a retinue of thousands of knights and infantrymen, his wife, her maids, household servants, stable boys and surgeons. Raymond Count of Toulouse, the wealthiest and mightiest of all the Crusader lords, led a contingent of 10,000 or so knights and infantry.[7] Knights often had to sell their possessions and mortgage their properties. The beneficiaries were often Cluniac monasteries, though also Jewish moneylenders. But numerous surviving charters from those mortgaging their properties bear witness to the genuinely religious fervour which at least in part motivated the armed pilgrims. Stephen of Neublen mortgaged his property and received from Cluny's dean 'fifty shillings and two excellent mules' so that he could go to Jerusalem 'where God the man was seen and lived with men'. Abbot Hugh then 'put the sign of salvation, that is the holy cross, on my shoulder and a ring on my finger' and promised that 'he would have me inscribed so that my memory would endure for all time at Cluny' in the event of Stephen's death on crusade.

For the peasants the Crusade was a chance to escape a harsh life tied to the land, where they were caught up in the anarchic warfare of opposing barons and their lawless soldiers; it was a chance to win fame and fortune, or to vault over purgatory and in one leap pass into heaven, as Urban put it.*

Urban had asked his bishops to preach the Crusade; but populist preachers soon also got involved. In Germany, the monk Peter the Hermit, so called because he wore a hermit's mantle down to his ankles and went barefoot, claimed to have been appointed to preach by God himself; Peter even had a divine letter to prove it. Riding his donkey through the towns and villages of northern France and Germany, his passionate sermons persuaded thousands of peasants to take the cross.

On 12 April 1096 Peter set off from Cologne on the banks of the Rhine in what is now western Germany with an 'army' of thousands.† The army was in fact a motley collection of armed peasants, townsmen and women and children on foot, dragging their household possessions behind them in carts. One month later another peasant army, allegedly of 10,000, set off from the Rhineland, led by a local count, Count Emich. These murderous and disastrous journeys east became known as the People's or Paupers' Crusade.

It began in the city of Speyer near Count Emich's estates on the river Rhine. On 3 May 1096 the Crusaders, supported by many of Speyer's Christian burghers, gave the Jews of the city a familiar choice: baptism

---

* The idea of purgatory (from the Latin *purgare*, to purge) was fully developed by the late eleventh century. It was conceived as an intermediary place between heaven and hell, where souls could be purged of their sins and could be helped by the prayers – and alms – of the living.

† Medieval chroniclers put the number at 20,000. But they loved to exaggerate numbers; modern historians prefer to say only that the army numbered in the thousands.

or death. Eleven Jews preferred death. The rest either accepted baptism or fled to the countryside, though thanks to Speyer's bishop, they later returned to the city under his protection.

The People's Crusaders went on to murder and pillage their way through other wealthy cities on the Rhine. The Rhine was one of Europe's major trade routes, where Jews had established large communities and were prospering. On 18 May the Crusaders arrived at the city of Worms. According to a Jewish chronicler the Crusaders whipped up the fury of the Christian townsmen by taking a corpse which had been buried thirty days earlier and parading it through the city claiming that it was a comrade who had been boiled alive by the Jews. Enraged Crusaders and Christian townsmen marched through the streets waving their swords and crying: 'Behold the time has come to avenge him who was crucified, whom their ancestors slew. Now let not a remnant or a residue escape, even an infant or a suckling in the cradle.' Around 800 Jews were murdered or committed suicide with their children because they refused to be converted.

In Mainz, home to the largest community of Jews in western Europe, Count Emich's Crusaders murdered about 1,000 men, women and children who were sheltering in the archbishop's palace. The Crusaders then stripped them and hurled their naked bodies to the ground through the palace windows, 'heap upon heap, mound upon mound... Many were still alive as they threw them', according to the twelfth-century chronicler, Albert of Aix.[8] The archbishop himself had fled the palace, abandoning the Jews to their fate.

The pope had used hatred of the mutual Christian enemy to reignite the loyalty of his Catholic flock. Having done so, he could not turn round and tell his flock that they must hate *this* enemy of God (the Muslim) and not *that* one (the Jew). As the Crusaders themselves put it, according to Guibert of Nogent who wrote a history of the First Crusade in 1108: 'We wish to attack the enemies of God in the East, after travelling great distances. However, before our very eyes are the Jews, and no people is more hostile to God than they are.'

For centuries the Church had declared that Jews should not be attacked while at the same time denouncing their religion, condemning them as heretics and making sure Christians did not get too near them. How were ordinary Christians to interpret this? For the crusading bands stirred up by Peter the Hermit, Count Emich and others, the answer was clear. The slaughter of the Jews in the Rhineland was, as the Crusaders said, 'their duty against the enemies of the Christian faith'.[9]

The attitude of the Christian chroniclers – all of whom were monks and priests – to the perpetrators of the massacres perfectly illustrates the Church's contradictory thinking on Jews. Frutolf of Michelsberg describes with admiration how 'zealously devoted to the Christian religion' Emich and his troops were as they 'destroyed the execrable race of the Jews … or forced them into the bosom of the Church'. Albert of Aix blamed the People's Crusaders because they 'had slaughtered the exiled Jews through greed of money, rather than for the sake of God's justice, although the Jews were opposed to Christ'. The slaughter had been committed by a rabble of 'the chaste as well as the sinful, adulterers, homicides, thieves, perjurers, and robbers: indeed, every class of the Christian profession, nay, also, women'. This 'intolerable company' were inspired by base motives. They were very different, according to Albert of Aix, from the true Crusaders who set out as planned in August 1096, their banners fluttering, a cross emblazoned on every garment. These Crusaders were led by the papal legate Archbishop Adhemar and the great secular lords of western Europe.

'Who ever heard such a mixture of languages in one army?' wrote Fulcher of Chartres, the only chronicler to have actually taken part in the Crusade. He wrote of his experience:

> There were Franks, Flemish, Frisians, Gauls, Allobroges, Lotharingians, Alemanni, Bavarians, Normans, Angles, Scots, Aquitanians, Italians, Dacians, Apulians, Iberians, Bretons, Greeks and Armenians. If a Breton or Teuton questioned me, I would not know how to answer either. But though we spoke diverse languages, we were, however, brothers in the love of God and seemed to be nearest kin. For if one lost any of his possessions,

> whoever found it kept it carefully a long time, until, by inquiry, he found the loser and returned it to him.[10]

Unity had been achieved by the invention of a common enemy. This was the unity the pope had dreamed of: Western Christendom united under the papal banner.

But it was indeed a dream. In fact, this 'official' Crusade was not much more disciplined than the People's Crusade. It was a series of armies under the command of their respective feudal lords who were almost all Franks. Most notable were: Robert Duke of Normandy, the son of William the Conqueror; the tall, fair-haired and bearded Godfrey of Bouillon, Duke of Lower Lorraine; his white-skinned, haughty brother, Count Baldwin of Boulogne; Stephen of Blois who shamed himself by deserting the Crusade, though he later became King of England; Raymond Count of Toulouse, the wealthiest of them all, and Robert Count of Flanders. They had embarked on this war against the Muslims not just for the glory of God, but also for their personal glory, and inevitably squabbled amongst themselves over the leadership of the Crusade.

That the 'official' Crusade didn't massacre the Jews was mainly because most of the armies chose a different route, encouraged to do so by generous bribes offered to them by the Jews of the Rhineland cities. Before setting out, Godfrey of Bouillon had declared that 'he would not depart on his journey without avenging the blood of the Crucified with the blood of Israel and that he would not leave a remnant or residue amongst those bearing the name Jew'.[11] Godfrey was paid 500 pieces of silver by the Jews of Cologne and then by the Jews of Mainz to keep his army away from their cities.

Once they had crossed into the Byzantine Empire the Crusaders behaved like invaders, not protectors. 'The whole West … was bursting forth into Asia in a solid mass, with all its belongings,' wrote Anna Comnena, historian and daughter of the emperor, Alexius Comnenus. Modern historians reckon that between 60,000 and 100,000 knights, infantry and non-combatants ravaged the land in search of provisions and killed any peasant who stood in their way. Eastern Christendom's troops fought the troops of Western Christendom; the one side fighting what they considered to be an army out of control; the other outraged that, as Raymond Count of Toulouse declared, they should be attacked by those they considered to be 'our brothers and helpmates'. Comnena and her father suspected that the Crusade was a ploy to disguise Western Christendom's real motive – the takeover of the Eastern Church and the empire. The emperor, the man whose appeal for help against the Turks' conquest of Anatolia had sparked off the Crusade, now pushed the Crusaders as quickly as he could across the Bosphorus straits into Anatolia and the arms of the Seljuk Turks.

The Muslims, however, did not present a united front as the Almoravids and Andalusians had tried to do against the Reconquista ten years earlier in 1086. Not only were the Seljuks fighting amongst themselves, but for fifty years they had also been fighting their neighbour, rival and religious enemy, the Shiite empire of the Fatimids based in Cairo. Both Sunni Seljuk Turks and Shiite Arabic Fatimids were struggling for control over Syria and Palestine. The Fatimids, profiting from Seljuk disarray, had just taken Jerusalem from the Seljuks.

The result was that the Christian armies, though far from home, often outnumbered the Seljuk enemy. Nevertheless, the Crusaders' advance on Jerusalem was a desperate and gruelling one. Men, women and children died of sunstroke, thirst and hunger along the route, together with their horses and pack animals. Four out of five knights, having abandoned their dead or dying horses, were reduced to walking, like the common people, carrying their weighty armour on their backs. Many Crusaders deserted, including England's future king, Stephen of Blois, prompting the pope to declare that he would excommunicate any deserter.

In June 1099 a decimated army of Crusaders finally reached their journey's end, their numbers reduced from about 40,000 to about 13,000. The holy city of Jerusalem was a place of pilgrimage for Jews, Christians and Muslims (it was from Jerusalem that Muhammad was said to have ridden on a winged steed to visit paradise) and was home to about 20,000 Jews, Christians and Muslims.

The Crusaders pitched their tents outside Jerusalem's walls and the siege began. Day after day, amidst the heat, the dust stirred up by the wind and the stench of rotting animals who had died of thirst, engineers tunnelled under the ramparts, men filled in the moats with stones so that the battering rams could do their work and smash the walls down, while others began constructing the great wooden siege-towers whose skeletal silhouettes, lit up by thousands of campfires, loomed larger every night.

On 15 July 1099, after a one-month siege, Jerusalem, 'the navel of the world', fell to the Christians. Fuelled with religious passion and the triumph of war, the Crusaders embarked on an orgy of killing. Muslims who had taken refuge in their mosque were massacred; Jews who had done the same in their synagogue were locked inside and burned to death; others were flayed while they were still alive; children were dashed against stones; even Christian monks, Eastern not Latin of course, were mown down when they tried to protect the shrine of the Holy Sepulchre from being looted. 'Indeed, it was a just and splendid judgement of God that this place [Jerusalem] should be filled with the blood of the unbelievers, since it had suffered so long from their blasphemies,' wrote Raymond of Aguilers, chaplain to Raymond Count of Toulouse. By the time the Crusaders had finished, the entire Muslim population of Jerusalem had either been killed or enslaved.

Church criticism of the Crusaders' behaviour was muted to say the least. Urban was in fact beatified by the Catholic Church in 1881. But it may have been a petition from the Jews for greater protection following these massacres that prompted Pope Calixtus II to issue the *Sicut Judaeis* ('and thus to the Jews') in 1120. This papal bull forbade Christians, on pain of excommunication, to molest or kill Jews, steal their property, deface their cemeteries, forcibly convert them or 'disturb in any way, with clubs or stones' the Jews' religious festivities. However, the edict emphasized that the Church extended its protection only to those Jews who 'do not plot to subvert the Christian faith'. The *Sicut Judaeis* was reaffirmed by successive popes until the fifteenth century.

Nothing had changed in the Church's Janus-faced policy towards the Jews since the time of Pope Gregory in the late sixth century.

Jewish faithlessness must be condemned, but Christian forbearance was necessary. As far as the Latin Church was concerned, the Crusade was a 'success'. It was in fact the only one of the nine Crusades that achieved its objective – to conquer Jerusalem.

As for the Muslims, since the Shiite Fatimids and the Sunni Seljuks were at odds over their religion and fighting over Syria and Palestine, they did not join forces against the Crusaders. The Seljuks may even have been quite pleased to see the Fatimids defeated in Jerusalem. The pope had shown he had the authority to launch a crusade, but the ulema did not have a commensurate institutional power, nor did they speak with one voice. And the caliph, the supposed head of the Muslim community, was equally powerless. Neither the Sunni caliph in Baghdad nor the Shia imam-caliph in Cairo could or would wage jihad.

After their conquest of Jerusalem in 1099, the Crusaders went on to conquer and rule over more territory in the eastern Mediterranean. The four 'Crusader states', based around the cities of Jerusalem, Antioch and Edessa (both in modern Turkey), and Tripoli (in modern Libya), attracted thousands of immigrants from western and central Europe, hoping to make a new and better life for themselves.

But though the Crusaders had arrived pumped up with hatred against the Muslims, they were in fact surprisingly tolerant as rulers of their new kingdoms. After the terrible Jerusalem massacre, there are no reports of outrages against Jews in the Crusader states. Jews were banned from living in Jerusalem, but on the whole they did not suffer from the discriminatory laws and persecutions which were increasingly being practised against Jews in Europe, above all in England (see next chapter).

The Crusaders treated Jews and Muslims much as the Muslims treated their *dhimmis*. That included exacting a tax similar to the *jizya* in exchange for which Muslims and Jews were guaranteed protection and the freedom to practise their own religion. As usual, the reason for the Crusader states' tolerance was pragmatism. The militant, holy-war rhetoric of Pope Urban II was quite simply impractical. The Franks, as the Muslims called all the Crusaders, were vastly outnumbered by Muslims as well as by Christians of the different eastern sects. The new rulers could not afford to alienate this majority on whom they were economically dependent for food, and revenue from taxes.

Tolerance had its limits, of course. Muslims were not always allowed to keep their mosques. Nor were Latin Christians always tolerant of their Eastern counterparts. At the Church of the Holy Sepulchre in Jerusalem, Greeks, Georgians, Armenians, Copts and Syrians who used to officiate there jointly were expelled. Orthodox bishops and Copts were banned, like Jews, from the city.

Practical necessity ensured that the Crusader states were relatively tolerant not just of their *dhimmis* but also of neighbouring Muslim states. Christian and Muslim rulers needed to transport goods through each other's territories. Muslim states needed access to ports such as Acre and Tripoli which were held by the Crusader kings. Indeed Christian–Muslim trade had become so important that it threatened the enmity between the two faiths which the Church had tried to nourish. Successive popes would in fact try to stop Venice, Genoa and the other Italian maritime republics who dominated the Mediterranean from trading with the Muslims of the Near East. But the popes were continually ignored: trade was too profitable. Trade may not fully erase tribal and religious hatreds but it is perhaps the best antidote we have so far discovered.

But trade notwithstanding, hostilities between the Crusader and Muslim states still continued. In 1144 the Crusader county of Edessa was captured by the Seljuks or at least by an ambitious military leader appointed by them. His conquest of Edessa was relatively easy – the Crusader states were too at odds with each other to come to Edessa's aid. The Church seized its chance to reassert itself. Pope Eugenius III called for a second Crusade – this time targeting Damascus.

The Latin Church was on the march again, not just in the East but in Spain and northern Europe. In al-Andalus the Almoravids' fundamentalism had cost them all the support they had enjoyed when they had been invited over by the *taifa* kings. That invitation had been backed by most of the ulema, but they had since withdrawn their support and the

Almoravids and their power declined rapidly as a result. They had alienated Muslims and *dhimmis* alike. By around 1125, barely forty years after their arrival, the Almoravids were losing their grip on Muslim Spain.[12] They were an alien minority who never captured the affection or respect of the Andalusians. On the city streets, they stood out as a menacing barbaric presence, still wearing the light-blue robes and veil that covered all but their eyes which they had worn in the Sahara.

Rebellions broke out all over al-Andalus. Taking advantage of its vulnerability, Christian rulers in northern Spain launched another phase of their Reconquista. They asked the pope to call a crusade against Muslim Spain. At the same time German nobles petitioned the pope to call for a crusade against their pagan neighbours so that a battle over territory could be ennobled by becoming a fight against the pagan enemies of God. Between 1147 and 1148, with Pope Eugenius's blessing, five Crusader armies set out for the East, four armies of 'Baltic Crusaders' marched across north-eastern Europe and four Crusader expeditions were launched in Spain and Portugal.[13] Secular rulers well understood how useful God's enemies were.

This time the pope made efforts to ensure that 'religious over-enthusiasm' did not adversely affect Jews, and there was indeed little violence against European Jewry. Most of the assaults that did occur were perpetrated by individuals or small bands; there were no crusading armies bent specifically on attacking Jews, and apparently no villainous leader to match Count Emich. Nonetheless, Jews in the Rhineland, and probably in northern France, endured repeated small-scale assaults.[14]

The Second Crusade ended in a storm of recrimination between its leaders, King Louis VII of France, King Conrad III of Germany and King Baldwin III of Jerusalem. Having failed to capture Damascus, the Crusaders limped home in 1149. But the Crusaders in al-Andalus scored notable victories, capturing the city of Lisbon, the *taifa* of Tortosa and the rich port city of Almería. The Almoravids were incapable of defending al-Andalus against the Reconquista; they were concentrating their resources on defending their empire in North Africa. The empire was under attack from the Almohads, a new and even more hard-line group of nomadic Berbers from the Atlas Mountains of southern Morocco.

The Almohads and Almoravids rose and fell by the same weapon of intolerance. Members of different Berber tribes had united under the Almoravids' ultra-traditionalist (in Christian terminology 'fundamentalist') form of Islam. The same happened with the Almohads, only they outflanked the Almoravids by being even more puritanical. Their founder Ibn Tumart indeed believed that he had a mission to bring the Almoravids back to strict Islamic orthodoxy through his own brand of Islam, a mix of Sunni and Shia Islam. In 1121 he announced that he was the Mahdi (the Messiah whose coming would inaugurate the rule of true Islam on earth and herald the end of time). Resistance to Ibn Tumart therefore meant resistance to God. Ibn Tumart and his growing band of followers toured the cities of North Africa preaching and enforcing their form of Islam. They beat up groups of men and women who were mixing together on the streets; in Fez they smashed up musical instruments – drums, castanets, flutes, and guitars; in Marrakech they overturned vats of wine; Ibn Tumart even publicly insulted the Almoravid ruler Ali ibn Yusuf, by calling him a veiled woman.

Fuelled by religious fervour against the moral laxity of their fellow Berbers, the Almohads saw their battle to gain control of the Almoravids' empire as jihad. By the 1170s, the Almohads had seized virtually the whole of the Almoravids' empire including al-Andalus where the people were caught between invading Christian 'crusaders' from northern Spain and the new triumphalist Muslim 'barbarians'. The Almohads were more brutal than the Almoravids towards the *dhimmis*; Christians and Jews had never experienced such unremitting savagery. In 1147 Abd al-Mu'min, the first Almohad caliph, told Jews and Christians that since their ancestors had denied the mission of the Prophet they would no longer be allowed to continue in their infidelity. In each city the Almohads conquered, they forced Jews and Christians either to go into exile, convert or be killed until 'there was no Jew left from Silves [in Portugal] to Mahdia [in today's Tunisia]', wrote one appalled Jewish eyewitness.[15] Given the Reconquista and that it had been sanctified by the pope as a crusade, Andalusian Christians were not surprisingly treated as the enemy. But it would be wrong to think of Abd al-Mu'min as an 'uncivilized' traditionalist. He built richly ornamented monuments and palaces in al-Andalusia; and Ibn Rushd (Averroes), the great Muslim philosopher/theologian, flourished during his reign.

Nonetheless, the Christian communities of North Africa were virtually wiped out; those Christians who had not chosen a martyr's death fled to Christian Spain. Synagogues were destroyed, Hebrew books burned and observance of the Sabbath and other Jewish festivals forbidden. One foreign Jewish merchant described a forced conversion that he witnessed in Aden (modern-day Yemen) on a Friday in August 1198. The market-crier rang his bell and shouted: '"Community of Jews, all of you, anyone who will be late in appearing in the audience hall after noon, will be killed." Moreover, he ordered that anyone returning to the Jewish faith would be killed. Thus all apostatized.'[16]

'No nation has ever been so intent on humiliating and degrading us, and on hating us,' the Jewish rabbi-philosopher Maimonides wrote of the Almohads. He and his family lived under Almohad rule in Cordoba. They may well have been amongst the thousands of Christians and Jews who outwardly converted to Islam.* They dressed and behaved like Muslims publicly, even going to the mosque occasionally, while continuing to practise their real faith in secret. Conversion to Islam required only that the convert recite the basic statement of the Islamic faith: there is no god but God and Muhammad is his messenger. Many Jews, including Maimonides, believed it was justifiable to pretend to convert to Islam if it was done under duress. Shiites similarly condoned the practice of *taqiyya*, hiding their true beliefs to avoid Sunni oppression. Both Muslims and Jews, however, thought conversion to Christianity was never permissible. Christians were polytheists and idolaters: they worshipped three gods – the Trinity – and venerated images. Nevertheless, many Jews did outwardly convert to Christianity during the Reconquista. It was, in fact, the suspect nature of their conversion that prompted the establishment of the Spanish Inquisition (see Chapter 12).

* Although Maimonides' feigned conversion is questioned by scholars, it is reported by Ibn al-Qifti, twelfth-century historian and friend of a pupil of Maimonides. See Kraemer, pp.118 ff.

Feigned converts or not, Maimonides and his family soon followed the journey taken by many Andalusian and North African Jews to Christian Spain or headed east to the more tolerant Muslim lands of Egypt and Syria. Maimonides eventually settled in Cairo in 1165, where he rose to become an eminent rabbi, philosopher and physician to the devout Muslim ruler Salah ad-Din.

Salah ad-Din or Saladin, a Kurd from Tikrit (in today's Iraq) was the new power in the Islamic world. Small and frail, with a melancholy face and a short, neat beard, he was a fearless and brilliant strategist. He had risen through the ranks of the Fatimid government thanks to his military skills against the Crusaders. Appointed vizier, he overthrew the Shiite Fatimids and proclaimed his allegiance to Sunni Islam and the Abbasid caliph in Baghdad.

Saladin was a usurper and needed the legitimacy conferred by the religious scholars (*Salah* meaning 'righteousness' and *Din* meaning faith or religion). It was important that his conquests should be seen not as the self-interested actions of a man bent on power for himself and his family but as the actions of a man fighting for Islam and the *umma*. Even when he was fighting his fellow Sunni Muslim rivals – and Saladin probably spent more time fighting them for control of Syria and Egypt than he did fighting the Christians – he always presented his struggles as jihad. Whether he was attacking Muslim or Christian, 'to wage war in God's name was a veritable passion', wrote Baha al-Din ibn Shaddad, in his contemporary account *Life of Saladin*. 'His whole heart was filled with it, and he gave body and soul to the cause.' It's not clear how much the *Life*, one of the most important sources for what we know about Saladin, is biography and how much hagiography – every commissioned biography has that problem. But certainly its author was a close friend and counsellor, who accompanied Saladin on his later campaigns and was appointed *qadi* of the army; he would have been keen not to offend.

On 2 October 1187 Saladin conquered Jerusalem, the city which had been won by the Crusaders almost a century previously in 1099. It was a shattering blow to the pope, Urban III, who apparently collapsed and died when he heard the news. Except for a few brief interludes in the thirteenth century, the city remained in Muslim hands until the defeat of the Ottoman Empire in 1917, when the British took over.

Jerusalem was not a strategically important city but it was of hugely symbolic religious significance for both Muslims and Christians. As Saladin pointed out in a letter to Richard I, known as Richard the Lionheart: 'Jerusalem is to us as it is to you. It is even more important for us since it is the site of our Prophet's nocturnal journey [to paradise] and the place where the people will assemble on the day of judgement.'

It took Saladin a little more than a month to capture the city. The Christians were heavily outnumbered and divided. Despite the tolerance meted out by the Crusader Kingdom of Jerusalem, Eastern Christians had little reason to support it, and every reason to favour Saladin. They had been despised and treated as heretics by the Latin clergy who had banned Orthodox bishops and Copts from entering the city. Tolerance only went so far.

Expecting the same treatment from the Muslim conquerors as had been meted out to Muslims and Jews when the Crusaders had conquered Jerusalem in 1099, the city's Latin Christians panicked. The chronicler Emoul witnessed Saladin's triumph:

> The people crowded to the churches to pray and confess their sins; beat themselves with stones and scourges, supplicating the mercy of God. The women cut off their daughters' hair, and plunged them naked in cold water, in the hope of averting their shame. The priests and monks paraded the city in solemn procession, bearing the Corpus Domini and the Cross, and chanting the Miserere.

The entire population took part in the procession, according to Emoul, except for the very old men who shut themselves inside their homes.[17]

And indeed, Saladin's first thought was revenge: 'I shall deal with you only in the way you dealt with its inhabitants when you conquered it,' he told the Franks (Latin Christians), according to one of the greatest chroniclers of medieval Islam, Ibn al-Athir, who travelled with Saladin's army.[18] But Saladin relented when Balian, one of the most powerful barons in the Kingdom of Jerusalem, threatened to pre-empt Saladin by killing every inhabitant – Christian and Muslim (the Christians owned around 5,000 Muslim slaves) – in the city. In the end, there was no repeat of the bloodbath of 1099. When Saladin's soldiers entered Jerusalem, he explicitly forbade them to harm a single Christian and posted a solder on every street to ensure his orders were carried out.

Saladin agreed that he would allow all the Franks to leave the city unharmed if they paid a ransom. But he ordered his guards to proclaim that all the old people who could not afford the ransom were free to leave. At each city gate, queues of Christians formed, men, women and children, rich and poor. Soldiers checked to make sure they had paid their ransoms. Then, escorted by Saladin's cavalry, they marched away from Jerusalem with their wagonloads of household goods, family treasures, church ornaments and relics.

In marked contrast again to the Crusaders, Saladin allowed Orthodox bishops and Copts to return to Jerusalem; he agreed to the Byzantine emperor's request to convert all the churches in the city back from the Latin to the Orthodox Church; other sects were allowed to pray freely in their churches. He refused to listen to pleas to destroy the Church of the Holy Sepulchre, and even allowed Latin monks to remain and look after it.

Why were Saladin and his troops so much less savage than the Crusaders had been in 1099? Muslim chroniclers of the time thought the answer was simply that the Franks were less civilized. They were 'animals possessing the virtues of courage and fighting, but nothing else; just as animals have only the virtues of strength and carrying loads', according to the diplomat and one-time member of Saladin's court, Usama ibn Munqidh.

There is perhaps some truth in that. But the real answer lies in the fact that Saladin's mission was very different from that of the Crusaders. The ostensible goal of the First Crusade had been to rescue the Byzantine Empire from the attacks of Seljuk Turks and recapture Jerusalem. But in reality the First Crusade was designed to assert Church supremacy, and did so in a way that suited State as well as Church. As the chronicler Fulcher of Chartres put it, Urban's plan for the Crusade was to 'turn against the pagans the strength formerly used in prosecuting battles among themselves'. From the outset the Crusade was conceived of by Pope Urban as a religious war between 'a people which has the faith of omnipotent God and is made glorious with the name of Christ' against 'a despised and base race, which worships demons'. The Crusaders were deliberately fired up with a hatred of the religious enemy, whether Muslim, Jew or even other Christians.

Saladin's jihad, on the other hand, was not a religious war against Christians per se, but a war to take back control of a prosperous city – righteousness was a means to a simple military and economic end. But for the Crusaders who slaughtered the inhabitants of Jerusalem, the slaughter of 'God's enemy' had become an end in itself.

Despite the failure of the Second Crusade and the loss of Jerusalem, the pope's ability to muster the kings of Europe and the men and women of Christendom in a battle for God had demonstrated the Church's power. Furthermore, the Reconquista had made major inroads into al-Andalus. By the early thirteenth century the Almohads had lost the great cities of Cordoba, Valencia and Seville to Christian Spain. In the newly conquered Christian territories Muslims were expelled or were forbidden to give the call to prayer from minarets, to go on pilgrimage or to practise their faith in public. High taxes led to an increasingly low standard of living for Muslims. The ground was being laid for the final expulsion of Islam from the land of al-Andalus at the end of the fifteenth century.

The pope headed an institution that in power and territorial reach had no equivalent. Secular authority in Western Christendom was divided between many state kings; religious authority was in the hands of one overarching Church-emperor, the pope, whose reach was 'global', not just restricted to one territory. The Church's immense wealth, its legal courts, its administrative bureaucracy, the alliances and deals it struck with its neighbours, all made it a state in its own right, with which the secular state had to negotiate. The popes may not have won their battle for supremacy but they had certainly succeeded in creating an institution powerful enough to oppose and influence the secular state.

Islam had no comparable institution. Moral-religious power belonged to the ulema, but the ulema would never speak with one voice – it was too democratic. The ulema sprang from the egalitarianism of Islam's tribal roots; the Church, from the hierarchical organization of imperial Rome. Popes Gregory and Urban saw themselves as moral 'emperors', speaking for the whole of Western Christendom. The ulema were members of a number of intellectual and ideological movements each with their differing beliefs, and different charismatic scholars with their own students and supporters. The ulema could never present a concerted opposition against the secular ruler.

An individual member of the ulema might have the ear of the caliph and might exert huge influence. But he rose and fell by the strength of his own individual authority, not because he was part of a formidable institution with which every ruler of the time had to come to terms. Church officials were often also the highest officials of the Christian state. But because the institutional strength of the Church resulted in conflict with secular monarchs, churchmen of principle, like Thomas Becket, sometimes had to choose between loyalty to their Church or to their king.

The Crusades created the sense of a united Western Christendom, with the pope as its leader. Western Europe's diverse peoples began to see themselves as part of a new entity defined by their religion. Despite their different languages, their centuries-old battles for slices of each other's territory, the ridicule that the Franks poured on the English and the English on the Franks, they were united as fellow members of 'the Christian Republic' as it was often called. And yet paradoxically the Church and its offspring the Crusades both inspired a sense of belonging to a new overarching entity, Western Christendom (a sort of early EU), but also inspired a sense of nationhood and national pride.

The idea of the nation chosen by God rings out clearly in the *Chanson de Roland*. The *Chanson* becomes integral to the creation of France's national myth. 'Land of France, thou art soothly fair,' are Roland's dying words. In a scene that rivals any World War II film for its heart-stirring patriotism, Roland blows a last feeble call for help on his horn. It is heard by Charlemagne across the mountains, who orders his troops to sound

A graffiti artist in 200 CE mocked Christianity in this earliest surviving representation of the crucifixion. Christ is shown with a donkey's head above the scribbled words 'Alexamenos worships [his] God'.

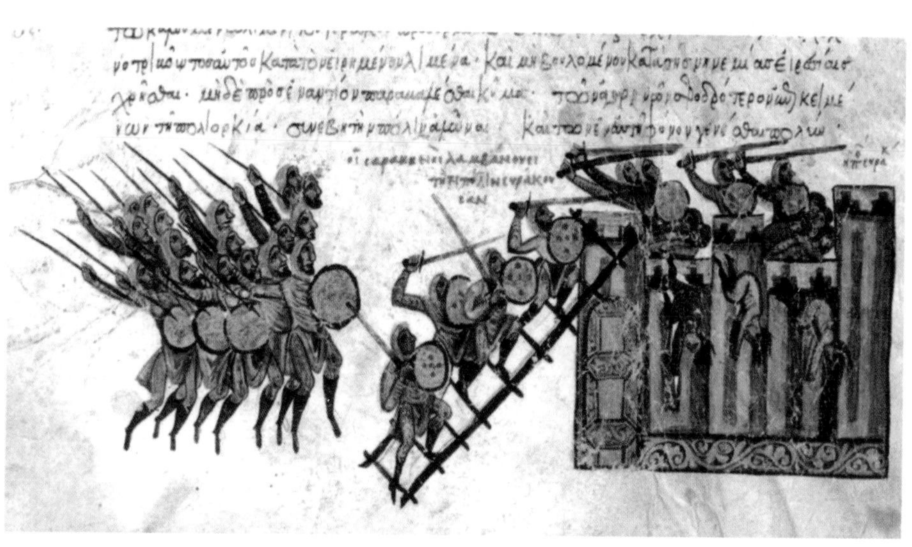

Arab armies besiege and conquer Syracuse, Sicily (from the twelfth-century illuminated manuscript the *Madrid Skylitzes*). After the death of Muhammad in 632 Arab tribesmen conquered the Byzantine and Persian empires. By 750 the Muslim empire stretched from Spain to Iran.

(*Top left*) The period of Muslim rule in Spain from the eighth to the end of the fifteenth century has been dubbed *La Convivencia* (Coexistence) by some historians who view it as a period of extraordinary religious tolerance and cultural intermingling between Muslims, Christians and Jews. A Christian and a Muslim play ouds together (in a miniature from *Cantigas de Santa Maria of Alfonso X*, c. 1221–84). (*Above right*) A caravan of pilgrims on the way to Mecca (in a miniature by Yahya ibn Mahmud al Wasiti, published in Bagdad in 1237).

An observatory, late sixteenth century. Study of the sciences, particularly astronomy, was far more advanced in the Muslim than the Christian world. Caliphs supported the building of observatories and every major mosque had its own astronomer.

(*Above*) Reforming the monasteries was crucial to the establishment of Church power through moral authority. In this late thirteenth-century manuscript an abbey cellarer tests his wine.
(*Right*) Cluny Abbey, founded in 910, was the fountainhead of the monastic reform movement.

The Holy Roman emperor Henry IV begs for Pope Gregory VII's forgiveness at Canossa in 1077.

Abu Bakr, commander of the Almoravids from 1056 until his death in 1087. The Almoravid dynasty and their successors the Almohads were by the standards of Muslim rulers exceptionally intolerant. Under their brand of hardline traditionalist Islam, Jews and Christians were persecuted and forced into exile.

Peter the Hermit, one of the leaders of the First Crusade involved in the Rhineland Massacres of Jews in 1096.

Saladin's benign treatment of Jerusalem's inhabitants when he conquered the city in 1187 was in marked contrast to the massacre perpetrated by the crusaders in 1099. Portrait of Saladin (Salah al-Din Yusuf ibn Ayyub) probably by his contemporary ibn al-Razaz al-Jazari (1136–1206).

The earliest surviving caricature of Jews scribbled by a clerk of the English exchequer on a roll of parchment in 1233.

The Mongols' ruler Mahmud Ghazan Khan (*centre*) converted to Islam in 1295. A scholar on the left reads the Quran. But the Sunni scholar Ibn Taymiyya declared Mongols were not true Muslims. His fatwas are still cited by today's Islamic terrorists

Between 1347 and 1351 the Black Death or plague killed more than 25 million people in Europe. In the Islamic world, plague killed more than 17 million people. The response to this catastrophe was strikingly different in the Islamic and Christian worlds.

Jews in Christian Europe were blamed for causing the Black Death. They were rounded up in their thousands and executed. The worst atrocity occurred in Strasbourg, Germany, on 14 February 1349, where about 2,000 Jews were burned alive and the rest were expelled from the city.

Ferdinand II of Aragon and Isabella I of Castile presided over the creation of Catholic Spain. They established the Inquisition in 1483, expelled all Jews from their kingdoms in 1492 and all Muslims in 1609. Anonymous portrait of Ferdinand and Isabella of Spain, *c.* 1469.

The friar Tómas de Torquemada, Spain's first Grand Inquisitor, appointed by Ferdinand and Isabella in 1483.

The horrors of the Catholic Inquisition have been exaggerated but its autos-da-fé, when sentences of the guilty were announced, could be spectacularly fearsome. Three years after the Madrid auto-da-fé in 1680, the artist Francisco Ricci packed all the events of the day into this oil painting.

The conquest of Granada by Ferdinand and Isabella in 1492 signalled the end of Muslim rule in Spain.

every horn they possess: 'Peal sixty thousand clarions high, / The hills re-echo, the vales reply… / 'Tis the Emperor's advance, / We hear the trumpets resound of France.'

By the end of the fourteenth century the Crusaders' red cross had become part of the iconography of St George. Allegedly a Roman soldier martyred for his Christian faith by the emperor Diocletian at the beginning of the fourth century, George was adopted by England as its patron saint.

Religion and nationhood – the two most powerful ways of creating a community, and the two most powerful tools of enemy-making. The Crusades had invoked both, indeed had reinforced the links between religion and nation. The Church used the Crusades to build up its own position and therefore deliberately fanned the flames of religious hatred. That hatred had initially been directed against the Muslims in al-Andalus and outside the borders of western Europe, but inevitably it had spilled over to encompass that other group of monotheists, the Jews. In what was becoming a self-consciously Christian Europe, there was no place for non-Christians. The Church had set the dreadful ball of Jewish persecution rolling.

CHAPTER 8

THE MONEYLENDER

'The Jews of Lincoln stole a boy of eight years of age, whose name was Hugh; and, having shut him up in a room quite out of the way, where they fed him on milk and other childish nourishment, they sent to almost all the cities of England where the Jews lived, and summoned some of their sect from each city to be present at a sacrifice to take place at Lincoln.'

– Matthew Paris, *English history*, *c.*1253

'Our first foe, Serpent Satan, who has
Made in the Jew's heart his wasps' nest'

– Geoffrey Chaucer, 'The Prioress's Tale', 1387–1400

IN 1144 THE MUTILATED body of a ten-year-old skinner's apprentice was found in a wood near Norwich, one of the largest towns in England. The murder remained a mystery for several years, until a monk at the nearby monastery declared he had found the culprits – Jews. They had, he said, tortured and crucified the young boy William as part of an annual ritual sacrifice to demonstrate their hatred and contempt of Christ.

Over the following decades and centuries Jews in England and continental Europe were periodically subjected to 'blood libels', accused of torturing and murdering Christian children for ritual purposes. After Norwich it was the turn of Jews in Gloucester in 1168, Jews of Bury St Edmunds in 1181, Jews of Bristol in 1183 and Jews in France, Austria, the Rhineland and Spain. The murdered boys were, like young William of Norwich, transformed into saints and martyrs and objects of pilgrimage – much to the profit of the monks and priests who housed their relics.

In 1182 Philip Augustus, the King of France, expelled all Jews from his kingdom on the grounds that they had murdered Christian children. In reality the king had borrowed so much money from them and taxed them so heavily that they could no longer finance his campaigns against the English (the English owned more territory in France than Philip himself did), or his grand construction projects in Paris, such as the building of Notre-Dame Cathedral. He had milked them dry and had no intention of repaying his debts. But Jews had been so financially useful that in 1198 Philip Augustus allowed some Jews to return and resume their banking business, though under strict royal control so as to ensure large profits for himself.

Blood libels against Jews reached their heyday in the fifteenth century but continued into the sixteenth century and then subsided. During that time only three popes, out of fifty-three, publicly declared their opposition to blood libels. One European ruler, however, deserves honourable mention. The thirteenth-century King of Germany and Sicily, Frederick II, was so sceptical of the blood libel that he held a Europe-wide council to determine the truth. The council decided that there was no basis to such allegations. Sadly, it had little effect. Accusations of ritual murder proliferated again at the end of the nineteenth and beginning of the twentieth centuries in Russia, Germany and Austria–Hungary. And for the first time they were made against Jews in the Muslim world (see Chapter 20). They are still being made today in Russia and in the Middle East.

Ever since Pope Urban II had launched his Crusade in 1095, Europe had been taking on an increasingly aggressive Christian identity. After the First Crusade, 'anti-Semitism', a word that was not actually coined until the nineteenth century, became the backdrop of Jews' daily life in Europe. Christians were claiming Europe for themselves. Jews were excluded from this assertive imagined identity, all the more so as they were confined to one of the least popular, but in a growing economy most necessary, professions – lending money.

Thanks to centuries of urban living and a network of close relationships with Jewish business communities around the world, Jews had been extremely useful to a northern Europe which was only beginning to develop a commercial life and the cities that went with it. But as northern European Christians began to acquire the trading and financial skills which had formerly been the almost exclusive preserve of Jews, Christian merchants wanted to squeeze Jews out. Merchant and craft guilds insisted that every member should take a Christian oath, which meant that Jews were effectively barred from most trade and artisanal professions.

Losing access to other ways of using their financial skills, Jews increasingly turned to moneylending. The ability to borrow money was essential for a growing economy, for building a stone bridge across the river Thames or a royal castle, for improving an estate or raising an army to go on crusade. Everyone, from king to feudal baron to aspirational city dweller, at some point felt the need to borrow money.

At the best of times, the moneylender is unlikely to be loved by the borrower. The Church gave the Christian borrowers a good religious underpinning for their dislike and demonized the profession to which Jews were being increasingly restricted. Yahweh had condemned usury but only between fellow Jews: 'Unto a stranger thou mayest lend upon usury,' he had told Moses, 'but unto thy brother thou shalt not lend upon usury' (Deuteronomy 23:20). Jesus had exhorted his followers to 'Lend, hoping for nothing again [in return]' (Luke 6:35). By the twelfth century the Church had turned usury into a sin. The relatively neutral term 'usury', meaning the lending of money at interest, had become far more condemnatory: 'usury' now meant the lending of money at *extortionate* rates of interest. In 1139, the Church condemned 'the ferocious greed of usurers'; in 1179 it declared that all Christian usurers would be excommunicated: they would be unable to receive Communion or be given a Christian burial – terrifying deprivations for any Christian.

Christians were still able to borrow, but they had been given free licence to hate their creditors. Jews thus found themselves to be the potential focus of multiple hatreds. They were not just 'Christ-killers' but grasping moneylenders; as the only visible minority they were subject to all the resentments so often felt by a majority towards minorities, compounded by the fact that they were living in a society which was experiencing a triumphalist sense of itself as Christian.

Of course, not all Jews were moneylenders. Jews still worked as goldsmiths, merchants and importers, especially of wine, and Italian Jews in England were renowned as fencing and dancing masters. Nonetheless, by the end of the twelfth century the Jews' major occupation was moneylending, or its poor relation pawnbroking, and as far as Christians were concerned, to be a Jew was to be a moneylender.

On 3 September 1189 crowds gathered outside the gates of Westminster Palace. They were trying to catch a glimpse of their new king, Richard I, the unloved son of Henry II. Amongst the crowd were a delegation of wealthy Jews from York in the north of England. They had come bearing valuable gifts to honour the new king at his coronation feast but had been refused entry. Their presence would have jarred with the whole image of England that Richard wanted to project. Richard 'the Lionheart', Christian king of a Christian nation, was preparing to go on crusade to recapture Jerusalem from the magnanimous Saladin.

Jews were, of course, the major financiers of the Crusade, although the party from York were left to jostle with the rest of the gawping crowd at the entrance to the banqueting hall. Several of them, however, managed to slip through the doors, much to the fury of the crowd which rapidly turned into a mob. According to the chronicler William of Newburgh, 'At first they beat them viciously with their fists, but as they became more enraged they used sticks and stones. The Jews fled; but some were caught and beaten to death, while others were trampled to death.'

Benedict, one of the wealthiest Jews in England, and the foremost moneylender in York, was viciously attacked. He saved himself by agreeing to be baptized as 'William' at the nearby Church of the Innocents. But it was only a temporary reprieve. 'William' died later from his injuries. Neither Jewish nor Christian cemetery would accept his body for burial. His forced conversion had anyway done nothing to appease the mob.

They had heard what William of Newburgh called a 'gratifying rumour'; the king had ordered the extermination of all Jews. The rumour spread from Westminster downriver to the city of London, home to the largest community of Jews in England, though that was not saying much; there were about 400 Jewish men, women and children out of a population of about 18,000 Londoners.

King Richard was informed of the riot during his banquet. But he sent too few men to quell it, and their heart was probably not in it anyway. Faced with an intimidating mob, they withdrew. Rioting continued through the night and into the morning, by which time the mob had turned from attacking the Jews bodily to attacking their homes and belongings: 'A surging mob surrounded their homes and laid siege to them from mid-afternoon until sunset,' William of Newburgh reported. 'The Jews were either burned to death in their homes or, when they tried to escape, were slain with swords.'

In all about thirty Jews died, but no serious measures were taken to hunt down and punish the perpetrators. The riot had been too popular: the Jews of England, like their fellow Jews in France, found themselves to be targets of the combined hostility of the people, the Church which had preached anti-Semitism since Christianity's inception, and a king who havered between protecting them and throwing them to the wolves to appease the Church and the mob. Jews in England had in fact been under royal protection since the beginning of the twelfth century, but for the Jews it was a double-edged sword. They were protected by the king because they and their possessions were declared to be his property. No one was allowed to harm Jews when it was in his interests to protect them and their businesses; but when it was not, they could be sold or thrown away – as property. Jews were totally dependent on the king's favour.

The coronation riots against the Jews in 1189 did not stop with London. Disastrously for the Jews, preparations for the Third Crusade were in full swing. Christian assertiveness was therefore at its most belligerent. Violence against Jews broke out in the twenty or so towns of England where they had established small communities, numbering no more than a hundred or so individuals. In the port town of Lynn (today's

King's Lynn in Norfolk) almost every Jew living there was butchered or burned to death; a few days later in Norwich, infamous for the murder of the young apprentice William in 1144, Jews were massacred, though some found refuge in the royal castle. At Stamford, in Lincolnshire, the Crusaders gathered at the local Lent Fair in early March 1190, and were, according to William of Newburgh,

> ... indignant that the enemies of the cross of Christ, who lived there, should possess so much, while they themselves had so little for the expenses of so great a journey. Thinking, therefore, that they [the Crusaders] would render service unto Christ by attacking His enemies, whose goods they desired to possess, they boldly rushed upon them.

Nothing could better sum up the poisonous combination of economic resentment given a patina of righteousness by the Church, which lay behind the violence inflicted on the Jews. Looting out of greed was criminal and sinful; looting in the name of God was praiseworthy. No Christian onlooker stepped in to protect the Jews who, as in all the other attacks across England, were either killed or found protection in the local royal castle.

The combination of religious and economic hatred proved to be at its most lethal in York. On a stormy night in the first week of March 1190 fire broke out in the city. William of Newburgh puts the responsibility squarely on 'certain persons of higher rank [members of the Percy, Faulconbridge and Darrel families] who owed large sums' to the moneylenders. Deliberately started or not, the debtors took advantage of the fire to take revenge on the people they perceived as stealing their land and possessions. Led by one such landowner, Richard, rightly called Mala-Bestia or Malebisse (the Evil Beast), a mob headed for the home of Benedict, the Jewish financier who had died from his injuries in the coronation riots. Although his son managed to escape, Benedict's wife and daughters were in his magnificent palatial home when the mob forced their way in and murdered them, then stole all that they could and burned the house down.

'Those men can by no means be excused,' wrote William of Newburgh – but, he added, the Jewish 'impious usurers' had been 'lifting themselves up imprudently against Christ … they had inflicted many sufferings upon the Christians.' The Jews, in other words, had been asking for it.

The rioting and looting continued. Most Jews took advantage of the governor of York Castle's offer to find shelter behind its protective walls. But they made a fatal, though perfectly understandable, mistake. The governor had to leave the castle on an errand. When he tried to return, they refused to let him back in. They dared not trust him. Who can blame them? Why would the local authorities not share the general prejudices against Jews?

Barred entry to his castle, the governor sought the help of the sheriff of the county, John Marshall, who ordered the castle to be attacked and the Jews expelled. Troops surrounded the castle. They were joined by a crowd of urban and country poor, local priests and Crusader recruits led by a white-coated friar screaming 'Down with the enemies of Christ!' The friar, however, was the only Christian casualty of the two-day siege. He was crushed by a stone hurled down by the Jews from the castle battlements. For several days the Jews held off the besiegers with stones. But on 16 March, the Christian troops brought in siege machines. The Jews realized that defeat was inevitable. Their rabbi, who had come to York from Joigny in France because of York's reputation as a centre of Jewish learning, called on them to face their death heroically in the manner of the Jews of Masada.*

Joceus, a wealthy moneylender, was the first to follow the rabbi's advice, slitting the throats of his wife Anna and of his two young sons. Other fathers followed suit, and then offered their own throats to be cut by the rabbi who ended the mass suicide by killing himself. About sixty Jewish men, women and children died. At dawn the following day, those Jews who had refused to participate in the self-slaughter stood on the castle battlements and promised they would accept baptism if they were

* At the end of the Jewish War against the Romans in 73 CE, 960 Jews are said to have committed mass suicide on the rocky promontory of Masada at the edge of the Judaean Desert rather than surrender to the besieging Romans.

allowed to leave the castle safely. Below them the triumphant Christians agreed. The castle gates were opened and the exhausted and despairing Jews emerged. They were promptly murdered.

The probable inciters of the massacre immediately set off for the white-plastered York Minster. There they compelled the terrified sacristans to hand over those 'evidences of detestable avarice, the bonds acknowledging their debts to the Jews' (cathedrals and churches often agreed to be safety-deposit boxes for Jews' precious documents – a sign that not all Church–Jewish relations were antagonistic). The bonds were burned on the Minster's floor, the flames lighting up stories from the Old and New Testaments, lavishly depicted in brilliant reds, whites and blacks on the walls.

The 'conspirators', as William of Newburgh called them, had achieved their purpose. They were free of debt – at the cost of 150 lives, virtually the whole of the Jewish community of York. A day later, on Palm Sunday, fifty-seven Jews were killed in Bury St Edmunds in Suffolk.

King Richard was still in Normandy when news of the massacre at York reached him. He was, it seems, enraged and sent troops to the city. The chancellor, William Longchamp, Bishop of Ely, was ordered to hold an enquiry. But the baronial ringleaders had been warned in advance and several had already fled to Scotland while others had left on crusade; the good citizens of York, when questioned, said they had been powerless to prevent the rampages of the mob. William Longchamp dismissed the sheriff of York and the constable of York Castle, fined fifty prominent townsmen, and confiscated the estates of seven fugitives, though these were subsequently restored. Otherwise, the people of York went unpunished. Richard was extremely lenient to the malefactors, as he had been with the London coronation rioters. No doubt for the same reason: he could not afford to risk the hostility of most of his subjects. Persecution of the Jews was far too popular.

Of course, there were times of common humanity, when Christians and Jews treated each other as fellow humans, friends, businessmen and businesswomen (Jewish women ran businesses on their own account and had a correspondingly far higher judicial and social status than Christian women). They travelled and even drank together and no doubt performed many small acts of kindness towards each other, such as this one which has been passed down to us through the centuries. One Saturday in London, a boatman on the river Thames stole a sun canopy from a riverside garden. The canopy belonged to a rabbi, but it was the Sabbath and Jewish law determined that the rabbi could not chase the thief. No such law restricted his gentile neighbour, however, who retrieved it for him.

Within ten years of the York massacre, Jews had returned to the city. But they must always have lived with the uneasy awareness that hatred against them could erupt at any time; at best they were only ever a tolerated minority in a world of potential enemies.

Undoubtedly Muslim Almoravid and Almohad treatment of Jews and Christians was no better, as we saw in the last chapter. But they strayed particularly far from Islam's usual record of tolerance. For the most part the Eastern Islamic world saw nothing comparable to the expulsions, massacres and vitriol poured on the Jews of Europe.

Muslims did not hate Jews on theological grounds as the Christians did. The Quran explicitly says that the Jews did not kill Jesus, while the Gospel of Matthew holds them responsible (see Chapter 1); Muhammad had stressed from the beginning that Jews and Christians were fellow People of the Book, albeit misguided ones. Islam's whole attitude to these religious minorities was based on that fact – it was why Muhammad usually taxed them rather than killed them as he did the pagans.

Muslim hostility to Jews was based more on the usual attitude of the dominant to the subordinate and found its expression not so much in murdering them as in emphasizing their inferiority by enforcing the regulations set out in the Pact of Umar more rigorously. But the advantage of having a so-called pact was that at least Jews knew the deal. The pact could be more or less strictly enforced; new regulations were, however, almost never added to it. On the whole, Jews in the Islamic world were not subjected to the sudden intolerant whims of their rulers as European Jews were.

*

By the eleventh century there were almost no pagans left in western Europe, except in northern Scandinavia and the lands east of the Baltic Sea; they had all been converted to Christianity despite the frequent survival of furtive pagan practices. Jews in western Europe therefore bore the full brunt of being a religious minority, whereas in the Islamic world they shared that burden with Christians of many denominations, as well as with Zoroastrians. Furthermore, Jews were not newcomers in the East, as they were in northern Europe. They were already well established in the cities of the former Byzantine and Persian empires by the time the Muslims conquered them in the seventh and eighth centuries. By the twelfth century 7,000 Jews were living in Egypt's original Muslim city of Fustat and its neighbouring capital Cairo, a number which though inevitably exaggerated, dwarfs primitive little London's population of 400 Jews.

But more importantly, Islam's and Christianity's fundamentally different attitude to trade, wealth-creation and the city profoundly affected their attitudes to Jews. Muslims had been involved in city life and trade since the birth of Islam in the seventh century; Muhammad himself was a trader and his first wife Khadija had been a wealthy merchant who funded his preaching life. He came from Mecca. Admittedly Mecca was a primitive small town compared to the great trading cities of Alexandria, or Baghdad, although it was nonetheless an important stopping place on the north–south trading route. But though Christianity took off in the cities, its founder and the stories that he told, the images of him that every Christian saw in their churches and manuscripts, the morals that every Christian learned, were rural and portrayed the suspicions of the rural towards the urban, the peasant to the trader. Christ was a shepherd, a fisherman of souls, but above all he was poor and lauded poverty over wealth, or at least he saw wealth as a potential hindrance to goodness. The poor man would enter heaven more easily than the rich one. Christianity was imbued with a suspicion and disapproval of wealth and money-making. Of course it came to terms with both – it could not have survived had it not – but as with its attitude to authority and to war, Christianity's relationship to wealth was and still is deeply ambivalent. It is an impediment, but it is also, as Weber pointed out in his analysis of the causal connections between some Protestantisms and capitalism, the proof of God's favour.

In Islam, the wealthier Muslim has a duty to give to the less well off. Zakat, charity, is one of the Five Pillars of Islam. But the idea of wealth as being morally questionable is absent. True, the Quran bans lending at interest (*riba*), and unlike Judaism has no get-out clause which allows usury as long as it is not with co-religionists.* But Islam shares with Judaism a far less ambivalent attitude to wealth than Christianity. Islamic law, like the Judaic equivalent, is filled with detailed instructions about contracts and borrowing, reflecting the concerns of the scholars who compiled the sharia. Like the rabbis, they were not priestly professionals set apart from the world but had to make their own living *in* the world. Many of them were merchants or were certainly involved with the trading world. Naturally they were sympathetic to the needs of business and made sure that the ban on *riba* could be easily circumvented by clever legal fictions such as disguising loans as capital investments.

Nor were the Jews of the Muslim world confined to usury. Indeed, it was Christians, not Jews, who were considered the stereotypical men of money in the Muslim Middle East. Though Jews were excluded from the army because they were forbidden to bear arms, they were employed as government officials to an extent far beyond their proportion in the general population, and were involved in every aspect of economic life. In marked contrast to the Jews of northern Europe, Jews of the Islamic world were involved in most of the same crafts and businesses as Muslims. They were often in partnership with Muslims, wrote in Arabic and transported their merchandise – flax, pearls, pepper, soap, silk, copper, tin – in ships owned by Muslims. They lent money to Muslims, as Muslims also lent money to them. Jews were considered equals economically even if they were not considered to be so religiously; in Europe, by contrast, Jews were virtually shut off from the Christian economic world.

* 'Allah permitteth trading and forbiddeth usury' (Quran 2:275).

*

In December 1192 Richard the lionhearted Crusader was captured by his fellow Crusader, Leopold V, Duke of Austria, and held for ransom. The Third Crusade, on which Richard had embarked shortly after his coronation, had been a disaster: it had failed to win back Jerusalem from Saladin and had ended with the rulers of Christendom – amongst them King Richard himself, King Philip II of France, who according to some historians was his lover, King Tancred of Sicily and Leopold V of Austria – quarrelling amongst themselves. The Holy Roman emperor, Frederick of Barbarossa, had been an early casualty – he had drowned en route to Jerusalem. But his son Henry VI took charge of King Richard's kidnap. He needed the ransom money and demanded 150,000 marks, a vast sum equivalent to about twice the annual income of the English Crown at the time.

Richard's brother John and King Philip of France did not help matters by offering to pay the emperor almost all of the ransom to keep Richard exactly where he was – a prisoner, albeit a comfortably housed one. It took Richard's mother Eleanor of Aquitaine a year to raise the ransom money for his release. Inevitably, it was the 'King's Jews' in England on whom the financial burden fell most heavily.

By now the kings of France and England had abandoned all pretence of arranging loans with the Jews which would be repaid; instead Jews were simply taxed exorbitantly. On his death a wealthy Jew forfeited at least a third of his estate to the Crown, and the Crown could in principle confiscate all his property. Jews were the king's chattels or those of the lord to whom they were given. That meant he could do with them as he pleased. It was understood that Jews must pay, and pay heavily, for the right to exist in England and if they did not pay up, they would forfeit their right to protection and be expelled.

In 1193, a year after Richard had been kidnapped, Saladin died, worn out by fighting. For centuries his memory remained largely ignored in the Muslim world. Since the Muslims were the victors in all but the first of the nine wars they fought against the Christian Crusaders, Saladin's reconquest of Jerusalem was not that remarkable. He in fact owes his mythical status to European Christian historians, poets and novelists. The authors of the *chansons de geste*, the popular French epics, in the twelfth and thirteenth centuries, Dante in the following century, the eighteenth-century historian Edward Gibbon, and nineteenth-century British novelist Walter Scott, all turned Saladin into the exemplar of chivalry. He was considered superior to his adversary, the tall, beautiful Richard the Lionheart, who beheaded about 3,000 Muslim hostages along with their wives and children without a qualm, though he had promised Saladin they would be protected.

It was above all Kaiser Wilhelm of Germany who resurrected Saladin in Muslim eyes. In 1898, the Kaiser and his entourage dressed up as Crusader knights and rode into Jerusalem; one of the gates to the city was knocked down and the moat filled in so that they could do so. It was part of an elaborate tour of the Middle East organized by Thomas Cook, who also took part in the charade. The Kaiser went on to Damascus where he laid a silken banner on the neglected tomb of Saladin and paid for a sparkling new mausoleum in his honour.[1]

Today the Crusades are seen as the turning point in relations between Muslims and Christians, casting the Christians for ever after as the aggressors intent on conquering Muslim lands. But at the time Muslims in the Islamic world regarded the Mongols as a far greater threat than the Crusaders.

Richard the Lionheart and his fellow Crusaders had failed to retake Jerusalem from Saladin. Nonetheless, despite the Third Crusade's failure, the Church was profiting from its aggressive stance. And it was learning the value of finding enemies not just outside Christianity in the Muslim and the Jew, but within Christianity itself, in the form of the heretic, the leper and the homosexual, as we shall see in the next chapter.

CHAPTER 9

ENEMIES WITHIN: THE HERETIC, THE LEPER, THE SODOMITE AND THE JEW

'There is one Universal Church of the faithful, outside of which there is absolutely no salvation.'

– Fourth Lateran Council, 1215

IN 1212 THOMAS OF Herdington, Radulfus, known only as 'son of Nicholas Esquire', and Robert, a cleric from London, left England on a secret mission to Morocco. They bore a letter from King John in which he promised that 'he was fully prepared to hand over himself and his kingdom' to the caliph, and 'would not merely relinquish the Christian faith, which he considered vain, but would adhere faithfully to the law of Muhammad' – if the caliph would only back him against his many enemies.[1]

King John had been excommunicated by Pope Innocent III in 1209 for refusing to accept the pope's appointment of Stephen Langton as Archbishop of Canterbury. The excommunication put the king in a particularly dangerous position because it absolved his rebellious barons from their oath of allegiance to him – in effect they had the blessing of the pope to rebel. It also gave an ever-threatening France the perfect justification to invade. In addition, the pope had placed England under an interdict. Priests were only permitted to baptize children or administer 'the penance of the dying' (the last rites); but no one was allowed a Christian burial. As a result, every church in England was shut. Every church bell – the background music of everyday life, that rang the time for every parish of England in town or country – was silenced.

As recounted by the chronicler Matthew Paris, Muhammad al-Nasir, fourth caliph of the Almohad dynasty, the fundamentalist Muslims who now ruled North Africa and what remained of al-Andalus, was sitting reading on his throne when the envoys were ushered in. After an interpreter had translated King John's letter, the caliph closed his book, turned to the envoys and spoke.

> I have been reading a book written by a learned Greek Christian by name of Paul, whose manner and words have given me much pleasure. One thing, however, displeases me, namely that he did not remain in the faith in which he was born, but with inconstancy flew over to another one like a fugitive. And now I say the same thing of your English king who in a waxen [soft] and unsteady way is sliding away after abandoning the most holy and universal faith of the Christians in which he was born … if I were an infidel I would choose that faith above all others, and would embrace it wholeheartedly.[2]

Could these really be the words of an Almohad? Or were they put into his mouth by Matthew Paris? I like to believe Matthew Paris. After all, he may well have got the whole story from the horse's mouth since one of the three envoys, Robert of London, was a patron of Matthew's own abbey at St Albans.

If we stick with the chronicler, the caliph then grilled the envoys on the state of England. Thomas of Herdington at once painted a rosy picture of the 'queen of islands', prosperous and well ruled, at which al-Nasir rightly asked why, if that was the case, 'any king possessing such a prosperous and loyal kingdom … wished of his own accord to ruin his own principality, and to turn a free into a tributary state, to pass it from himself to a stranger'. Robert of London then privately confessed to the caliph the true state of affairs, that John was in fact 'a tyrant rather than a king … the oppressor of his own people … a lion to his own subjects, a lamb to foreigners and rebels … who by his greed had lost the Duchy of Normandy'.

The envoys were sent packing. England never did convert to Islam. A year later in 1213 King John capitulated to the pope. He humbly accepted Pope Innocent's appointment of Stephen Langton as Archbishop of Canterbury. The king also became a vassal of the pope and as such agreed to make him an annual payment of 700 marks sterling for England, and 300 for Ireland.

No pope would ever again be so powerful as the small, dark, autocratic and irascible Innocent III, whose only endearing trait was that he was a beautiful singer and composer of songs. Innocent was head of Europe's most powerful institution, prepared to fight the Holy Roman emperor and every monarch in Europe, including the King of England. Rulers fell like ninepins before his excommunications – the Holy Roman emperor, Otto IV (King John's nephew), because he was threatening to take over the Papal States in Italy, Alfonso II of Portugal, Leo II of Armenia, and Raymond VI Count of Toulouse in southern France (King John's brother-in-law), because he was not tough enough on heretics; Innocent excommunicated them all.

Fiercely aggressive in his assertion of Church power, Innocent had called for a Crusade to recapture Jerusalem. It had ended disastrously with the sacking of Constantinople by Crusader armies in 1204. Undaunted, Innocent called for a further Crusade (the fifth thus far) in 1213. It too ended in failure in 1221.

Innocent was equally ruthless towards those he considered his enemies within Europe, namely Christian heretics. The heretic, of course, is in the eye of the beholder; as far as Innocent III was concerned, that meant any individual or group that he considered to be an opponent of the Church or to be undermining its authority.

In 1198 Innocent authorized his bishops to eliminate the 'contagion' of heresy, telling them 'if necessary, you may cause the princes and people to suppress them with the sword'. Ten years later he called on King Philip II of France to head a Crusade against one of the most popular heretical movements in southern Europe. Philip naturally agreed. It was a chance to crush their joint enemy the Cathars (also called Albigensians because the city of Albi in southern France had so many Cathar adherents). The heartland of Catharism was in southern France where King Philip was fighting both King John of England, who ruled the vast territory of Aquitaine, and the local magnates who ruled as virtual kings in Languedoc. If not dedicated Cathars themselves – and some were – the nobles certainly gave their support and protection to the Cathars, as did King John. The Albigensian Crusade was as much a war of France against England, and a war of independence between nobles and the French king, as it was a religious war to stamp out the Church's enemies.

Even though Church and State had become two separate, sometimes antagonistic, institutions, their interests were still so intertwined that to oppose one was usually to oppose the other. When it came to heresy, religion and politics were impossible to disentangle. As well as being a critic of the orthodox religious authority, the heretic is, almost inevitably, a critic of the political authority that maintains it; the heretic is, therefore, also an enemy of State. Heresy is just another name for sedition. Jesus, after all, was both condemned for blasphemy – heresies, being 'untruths', are blasphemies – by the Sanhedrin, the Jewish ruling council, and condemned for sedition by the Roman authorities.

The Cathars, from the Greek *katharoi*, pure, presented themselves as the real inheritors of Christ. The 'Church of Satan', as they called the Catholic Church, had lost any resemblance to the early Apostolic Church. They, the Cathars, were embodying the true Church stripped of its false hierarchy, its institutional trappings, its buildings and its wealth and corruption. The Cathars did away with all the sacraments except baptism, and did away with the priests who administered them. Instead the Cathars had their *perfecti*. These were women as well as men devoted to prayer. Distinguished by their black or dark blue robes and in the case of the men by their flowing beards and long hair, they lived in single-sex, celibate communities. Cathars believed that all matter was evil, including the body and therefore sex. That, however, led them to an unexpected conclusion. Since celibacy could only be expected of the *perfecti*, and the ordinary Cathar was inevitably going to indulge in sex, better by far to commit acts of sodomy. Heterosexual sex was much more sinful because it resulted in the creation of beings, of matter. The *perfecti* preached in the villages of southern France, Italy, Spain and the Rhineland, but they preached in pairs so they could keep a watchful eye on each other. Any transgressions – even if it was failing to clean off all traces of meat from the bowl of food they were given – and they were expelled from the *perfecti*.

By 1200 Catharism was firmly established in many parts of southern Europe, an alternative Church which stood as a constant rebuke to its wealthy over-mighty opponent. Catharism attracted the poor and disaffected, as well as merchants and traders who were happy to embrace a form of Christianity which did not condemn usury. But what made Catharism so particularly dangerous was that it attracted the mighty local lords fighting for independence from the French king.

The Crusade against the Cathars was, of course, brutal. The tone of the campaign was set from the start in July 1209 when Crusaders massacred the entire population of the town of Béziers, near Narbonne. Asked by one of his soldiers how they were to distinguish between Cathar heretics and orthodox Catholics, the commander of the campaign, the papal legate Abbot Arnaud Amalric, allegedly replied, 'Kill them all; God will know his own'. Almaric estimated that the Crusaders killed 20,000 people in this 'divine vengeance miraculously raged' against Bézier's Cathars.

The Crusaders went on to terrorize the region in an attempt to cow it into submission. At Bram they gouged out the eyes and cut off the ears, noses and lips of the hundred men who had unsuccessfully tried to defend the town. Only their leader was left with one good eye so that he could lead them out of Bram.

In 1215, riding high on his success, Pope Innocent III summoned 1,200 cardinals, archbishops, bishops, abbots, princes and nobles from around Europe to Rome. It was the same year that the pope declared the Magna Carta forced on King John by his barons to be 'illegal, unjust' and predicted that it would be 'null, and void of all validity for ever'.[3]

In the marble coolness of his Lateran Palace, while Rome sweated in the August heat, the little dark-haired pope sat on his throne, the pope-emperor of Christendom. Under his guiding hand the Fourth Lateran Council drew up a list of regulations: they were the manifesto of a Church triumphant, determined to impose a uniformity of view on its members. 'There is one Universal Church of the faithful, outside of which there is absolutely no salvation,' declared the council in tones worthy of the emperor Theodosius.

The 'extermination of the heretics', as Canon 3 of the Fourth Lateran Council put it, was an imperative. Henceforth the Church would be systematically and relentlessly hunting down the heretic. Every archbishop or bishop had to make the rounds of his diocese each year to search out heretics; neighbour must inform on neighbour if he or she was suspected of heresy or of differing from 'the common way in law and morals'. Any bishop or archbishop who was not deemed vigilant enough in confounding 'heretical depravity' would be stripped of their office. On top of that, the council emphasized that it was the duty of secular authority to punish heretics at the Church's request. The king himself was subject to this duty. If he proved insufficiently eager to punish the heretics, he would be excommunicated as Raymond Count of Toulouse had been in 1208; if he failed to act within a year, the pope would 'declare the ruler's vassals absolved from their allegiance and may offer the territory to be ruled by Catholics, who on the extermination of the heretics may possess it without hindrance and preserve it in the purity of faith'. It was an astonishing declaration of Church power.

On 16 January 1205, Pope Innocent had sent an official letter to King Philip II complaining of the privileged status that the king accorded to 'sons of the crucifiers'. It was no more than the complaint that had been levelled by Agobard against Louis the Pious and by al-Jahiz against the caliph al-Mutawakkil in the ninth century: the tolerated were being over-tolerated. They had crossed that tortuously invisible, ever-shifting boundary which the tolerator erects against the tolerated: Jews were becoming the equals of Christians and not accepting their inferior status. In particular the pope attacked the practice of moneylending, which turned upside down the normal power relationships between Christians and Jews. But he also complained that Jews had built new synagogues, one of which was taller than the neighbouring church, in an echo of the Pact of Umar; that they had Christian servants, in violation of Church law; and that they openly mocked Christians. At the end of the letter he exhorted the king to 'turn against these blasphemers that the punishment of some should be a source of fear to all'.[4]

The Lateran Council reissued the Church's centuries-old prohibition against Jews holding public office. The ban was explicitly extended to include 'pagans', meaning Muslims, since 'it is quite absurd that any who blaspheme against Christ should have power over Christians' (Muslims of course were equally adamant that no *dhimmi* should be superior to a Muslim). No Jew was allowed to walk in public during the last three days of Holy Week and on Easter Sunday. On usury, however, the council was relatively silent. This was no more than a hard-headed acceptance of reality. Pope Innocent himself borrowed money at interest, and so did churches. As he conceded in a letter to the Bishop of Arras, if all the churches of Arras had obeyed the laws against usury, they would all have closed down. The Fourth Lateran Council therefore refrained from repeating the condemnations of usury made by its predecessors, going no further than a conveniently vague ban on 'heavy and immoderate usury'.

The council did, however, introduce a new and humiliating regulation. Innocent III was an enthusiastic adherent of the doctrine of 'perpetual servitude'. The Jews must realize, he wrote, that their 'guilt has consigned them to Perpetual Servitude'. Jews must be kept in a subservient condition in order to increase devotion to Jesus by reminding the Christian faithful of his sufferings and death. It was therefore the Church and State's duty to subjugate the Jews. Henceforth Jews and 'Saracens' (that is Muslims, who were still a presence in Reconquista Spain, Sicily and Italy's great trading cities on the Mediterranean) must wear distinctive clothing. They would thus 'be marked off in the eyes of the public from other peoples' and Christians would be protected against 'accidental commingling' and 'polluting' sexual contact.

This regulation, so specifically designed to exclude and humiliate, may well have been inspired by the Muslims' Pact of Umar which stipulated that *dhimmis* 'must not attempt to resemble the Muslims in any way with regard to their dress', though it was only periodically enforced with much harshness. In the ninth century the caliph al-Mutawakkil had ordered all Jews to dress entirely in yellow or at least wear two yellow patches on their cloaks (see Chapter 5). In the twelfth century the Almohads had introduced the requirement that Jews must dress in the Muslim fashion of mourning, in dark blue or black. And in 1212, the current Almohad ruler, Muhammad al-Nasir who had turned down King John's offer to convert, had decreed that Jews must wear yellow cloaks and turbans. It was a reassertion of superiority after the devastating defeat inflicted on him in al-Andalus by the Christian kings of Spain at the Battle of Las Navas de Tolosa.

On 16 July 1216, Pope Innocent died in Perugia. Three months later his vassal, King John of England, at war both with his barons and with a French invasion force that had landed in Kent, died of dysentery. 'Foul as it is, Hell itself is made fouler by the presence of John,' was Matthew Paris's epitaph. As far as the Jews of England were concerned, John's son Henry III was even fouler. His reign initiated the beginning of the end for them in England. And their fate was no better across the Channel.

In 1233 Henry III ordered that all Jews should be expelled from the kingdom if they could not financially benefit the king, while at the same making it ever more impossible for them to do so. Henry limited the rate of interest to two pence a week, forbade crown tenants from borrowing money from Jews on the security of their estates – the risk of losing their estates to the Jews was too great; Jews were not allowed to charge Crusaders interest on their loans or even on loans to 'virtual' Crusaders who gave the king money rather than going on crusade themselves.

Two years later the king commanded England's twenty-one Jewish communities to make a 'gift' of 3,000 marks to pay the expenses of his brother Richard, the Earl of Cornwall, when he went on crusade. There were only about 3,000 Jews in the whole of England. Five years later the demand went up to 20,000 marks, equivalent to about one third of the property owned by Jews in England. In 1244 he demanded 60,000 marks, on the grounds that Jews had been guilty of a ritual murder (blood libels were always useful to the king; see Chapter 8). Any Jew who was unable to pay up was imprisoned in the Tower of London along with his wife and children.[5] Henry exacted, in effect stole, yet more money from individual wealthy Jews – Licoricia, the widow of an Oxford financier, had to 'make a gift' of £2,500; Moses of Hereford, £3,000; Aaron of York, the wealthiest of them all, was a regular target of the king's rapacity. Over the course of seven years he was, he told Matthew Paris, forced to pay 30,000 marks in silver and 400 in gold.

Henry was, in theory, heavily indebted to the Jews. So he did the logical thing: he mortgaged (today we might say 'securitized') the Jewish communities in England to his brother Richard. In return, the king would receive a loan of 5,000 marks, to be paid by the Jews in instalments over two years; Richard later mortgaged the Jews to Henry's son Edward who in turn mortgaged them to French moneylenders.

In 1233 a clerk of the English exchequer at Westminster whiled away his time by doodling on the upper margin of a roll of parchment where he was listing the tax payments made by the Jews of Norwich. It is the earliest surviving caricature of the money-grasping, hook-nosed Jew.

The doodler has made sure that the viewer will be in no doubt who his targets are. At the top and clearly labelled is 'Isaac of Norwich'. Isaac was one of the richest Jews in England and certainly the richest Jew in Norwich, one of the largest and most important towns in England. Merchant, rabbi and physician, he was chief moneylender to the king. Whole districts of Norwich owed him money and he was consequently deeply unpopular with its Christian inhabitants. Their loathing was given the blessing of Pandulf, Bishop of Norwich, who declared that he wanted to see all Jews thrown out of the country to 'beyond the seas'. In the monk's doodle, Isaac is depicted as three-faced, and wearing a crown, a deliberate reference to the Antichrist who was traditionally portrayed as three-faced and wearing a crown.

Below Isaac is a horned devil who is touching the long noses of the figures on each side of him. One is labelled Mosse (Moses) Mokke, an associate of Isaac's though of a shadier character – he was involved in an assault case and later hanged for coin clipping; the other is labelled Avegaye, probably Mosse Mokke's wife Abigail, who was well known in Norwich as a usurer. To Abigail's right are three more horned devils. The association of Jews, money and the Devil could not be plainer.

The Lateran Council had insisted that Jews should look physically distinguishable from Christians by their clothes. Increasingly Christian art was driving that message home. A grotesquely over-physicalized image of the Jew with huge hooked nose and beard, usually red, was beginning to appear in sculptures, wall paintings and manuscripts. Before the eleventh century there had been no attempt in Christian art to make Jews visually distinctive.[6] By the mid twelfth century, Jews were being depicted as the despicable enemy that the Church was trampling underfoot.

The Church's triumph over Judaism was embodied in the new Gothic cathedrals that were springing skywards in the cities of northern Europe. Miracles of technology, their massive weight of stone no longer borne on squat, elephantine pillars but on slim, soaring columns, these airy, light-filled structures were visible for miles around. No Christian who saw the vast building sites, heard the clink of the stonemason's hammer or craned their neck to look up at the towers of Notre-Dame or Strasbourg Cathedral (in today's north-eastern France) could doubt the power of God and his representative on earth, the pope.

On either side of the entrance to these two cathedrals stands a large sculpted figure of a woman. One is crowned and cradles a chalice in one hand, a tall cross in the other. She stands contrapposto, looking with cool confidence at the other woman who has turned away in shame with head cast down, the graceful curve of her body transformed into an abject admission of defeat and shame. She is blindfolded, her sceptre of authority is broken and the Tablets of the Law are slipping from her left hand. It is the triumph of Ecclesia over Synagoga. Synagoga is a cowed, humiliated figure, stripped of her crown and blindfolded because she refused to see the truth of Christianity. Triumphant

Ecclesia and defeated Synagoga became familiar figures, carved on the facades not just of Notre-Dame and Strasbourg Cathedral but on dozens of cathedrals and churches. Over the decades the images of Synagoga got nastier. By the fifteenth century Synagoga rides a pig or is ridden by a devil.

The Jews' physical loathsomeness was a reflection of their inward spiritual loathsomeness. Apart from their long, hooked noses, they were horribly misshapen and sprouted tiny devil's horns and tails. If churchgoers had good enough eyesight they might glimpse the grotesque figure of a Jew sucking at a pig's udders carved into the capitals of the graceful Gothic columns that bore up their new church. Jews were also equated with lepers. With their eroded noses, damaged eyes, the sores that covered their faces, their gangrenous limbs that smelt of putrefying flesh, lepers were amongst the most shunned and feared inhabitants of the medieval world. Leprosy, an infection that spread by prolonged physical contact, was the plague of the rapidly growing new cities of the twelfth and thirteenth centuries. The medievals thought it was divine punishment for sexual promiscuity. Sexual depravity, disease and heresy were all bound up together. Not just Jews but every group that the Church singled out as heretical were also branded as sexually depraved.

Heretics were regularly accused of indulging in wild sexual orgies, even though one of the most notable heresies, Catharism, explicitly lauded chastity. Sex in the eyes of the Church was an act that could only be 'justified' by its outcome: a child. Desiring sex for sex's sake was the prompting of the Devil. It was no coincidence that the new Church hostility to homosexuality arose at the time of the First Crusade, when Crusader propagandists, eager to whip up hostility against the Muslims, began to demonize Muslim men for their homosexual predilections.* Although sharia law considers homosexuality to be a crime, the celebration of male beauty and the homoerotic had been a constant of Arabic

* 'Homosexual' is actually an anachronism. For Christians in the Middle Ages there was no such person as a homosexual, only people who performed acts of sodomy whether with a woman or with a man.

literature and poetry since at least the late eighth century, as in ancient Greek and Roman times.*

Muslims were 'sunk, dead, and buried in the filth of obscene desire', said the Crusader-preacher, Jacques de Vitry.[7] Homosexuality in the Christian world thus became associated with the vile enemy of the Church, the Muslims, and the Church's Christian enemies, the heretics. The common French word *bougre* for heretics, since their doctrines were thought to be of eastern (Bulgarian) origin, came to apply to any homosexual male, hence the English word for gay men 'bugger'. By the middle of the thirteenth century, sodomy had become not just a sin in the eyes of the Church but a crime in the eyes of the State punishable by death; how many people actually suffered the death penalty is unclear. According to John Boswell, the historian of religion and homosexuality, there are extremely few recorded instances of capital punishment for the simple crime of sodomy.

Heretics, lepers, Jews, homosexuals, and of course witches, were working in league with the Devil to infect, have sex with and entice Christians away from the true Church and destroy the Christian world. That medieval belief that the Jews were in league with the Devil lives on today in the secularized form of a worldwide conspiracy of Jews, notoriously in *The Protocols of the Elders of Zion*, and most recently in the wild accusation that Jews were behind the 9/11 Muslim terrorist attacks against the United States in 2001.

---

* As in the Bible, explicit condemnation of homosexual activity is actually quite rare in the Quran. Homosexuality is mentioned twice with reference to the story of Sodom and Gomorrah, when Lot condemns his people for practising an 'outrage' because they 'lust after men rather than women' (see Quran 7:80–81 and 26:165–166). No punishment is ever specified in the Quran, but in formulating sharia, the schools of law determined on the basis of the Quran and the hadiths that homosexual activity should be regarded as a crime; they differ only on whether it merits the death penalty or a less drastic punishment. In the Old Testament, Leviticus pronounces that 'if a man lies with a man … they must be put to death'. Homosexuality is not mentioned in the Gospels, but it is condemned by Paul who refers to 'males with males, committing what is shameful' and in the only reference to lesbianism in the Bible to women changing the 'natural use into that which is against nature'.

In 1227 Cathar heretics and the rebel nobles of Languedoc admitted defeat and surrendered. The Albigensian Crusade was over. It had taken twenty years and the lives of thousands of men, women and children – Catholics as well as Cathars, since many Catholics had sided with their Cathar neighbours against the Crusaders. Regional independence was more important to them than religious affiliation.

The pope and the King of France had won. But the Church continued to hunt down the Cathar heretics, with the aid of its new foot soldiers the Dominican friars, and their new instrument for imposing Church uniformity, the inquisition. Dressed in their white habit and black cloak and hood, these 'inquisitors of heretical depravity' ran their tribunals on scrupulously legal lines. 'We do not proceed to the condemnation of anyone without clear and evident proof or without his own confession,' declared the *Manual for Inquisitors at Carcassonne*, a city in the Languedoc Cathar territory of southern France.[8]

Once they agreed to 'recant sincerely and unfeignedly', convicted heretics were either imprisoned or given traditional penances, which ranged from fasting, to going on pilgrimage or crusade, to having to wear two large yellow crosses on their clothing. The King of France declared that any Cathar who had refused to recant after one year would have all their goods confiscated; it proved to be such a fruitful source of income that the inquisition tribunals extended their inquiries to the dead so that their goods too could be appropriated in the event of their being found guilty. Unrepentant living *perfecti* who refused to recant were burned at the stake; the few who recanted were, however, well treated.

On the whole the inquisition was not the bloody, murderous thing that it has become in popular imagination (see Chapter 12). It hardly had to use violence. The very arrival in the local town of the inquisitors, the fear of being subjected to their inquisitorial examination, the fact that torture was allowed as long as no blood was shed, was weapon enough. By the 1270s the Cathars had virtually disappeared from western Europe. The Dominicans turned their attention to other heretics, to homosexuals and to Jewish converts to Christianity who were suspected of not being true converts.

In June 1242 the people of Paris gathered in what is now the Place de l'Hôtel de Ville, close to the brand-new fortress of the Louvre. In the centre of the square were piled about 10,000 parchment copies of the Talmud and other Jewish religious works. The Talmud had been found guilty of blasphemy at a trial convened by King Louis IX of France. French rabbis acted as lawyers for the defence; the prosecutor was a Jew turned Franciscan friar, Nicholas Donin. The Talmud was sentenced to be burned at the stake. Copies were impounded from Jews all over France and brought in twenty-four oxcarts, the largest means of land transport in the medieval world, to their place of execution. As Christian crowds (the Jews of the city had sensibly shut themselves away) jostled for a glimpse of this spectacular display of Christian supremacy, the executioner set fire to the pyre of treasured manuscripts. It took two days for the fire to consume the work of untold hours of laborious copying (the Talmud consisted of about 2,000,000 words).

For all People of the Book, the burning of their holy text was a shocking sign of contempt and an ominous statement of intent. Short of burning people to death, burning their sacred book was the next best thing and for that reason was a practice adopted not just by Christians, but by Muslims and Jews themselves.

Some years earlier, in 1234, the Dominicans (as ever, leading the charge against heresy, hence their soubriquet, *domini canes*, 'hounds of the Lord') had burned the works of Maimonides. The Dominicans may well have been acting at the request of traditionalist French rabbis. If so, the rabbis would have come to bitterly regret the example they had set. The Talmud would become the most burned book in history.

King Louis, whose Christian zealotry earned him a sainthood after his death in 1290, was determined to advertise his, and therefore France's, Christian credentials. Apart from burning the Talmud, he made sure that France finally complied with the Fourth Lateran Council and ordered that all Jews wear 'a circle of felt or yellow cloth, stitched upon the outer garment in front and in back' and that 'its area must be the size of a palm'. He also led two Crusades, both of which ended disastrously.

*

The punitive measures of Europe were no different than those inflicted on Jews by the Almohads in North Africa and what remained of al-Andalus (see Chapter 7). The Almohads, too, had burned books, forced Jews to wear distinguishing clothes, forbidden the building of new synagogues, and banned Jews from any office which made them superior to Muslims.

By the middle of the thirteenth century, Christian Spain had driven the Almohads out of al-Andalus and back to Morocco from where they slowly lost their empire. The new Christian rulers of al-Andalus were, however, as harsh towards Muslims, Jews and heretics as the Almohads had been towards *dhimmis*. Many Muslims were expelled; those that remained were heavily taxed and forbidden from publicly practising their faith. The muezzins, whose chant from every minaret had called Muslims to prayer five times a day, were silenced. These were the foundation stones that would pave the way for the final expulsion of Islam from Spain in 1609.

Europe's Jews were also caught in a downward spiral: confined to usury, squeezed ever more mercilessly for money by the monarch, hated ever more viciously by anyone in debt to them, scapegoat for all the ills and disruptions of a rapidly growing economy, outsiders in countries that were using the outsider to create a unified nation, and targets of a Church high on its own power and determined to extend it.

Church and State exaggerated if not created the enemy within as part of their jockeying for power. The Islamic world, however, had no need to manufacture an enemy within; it was about to confront a truly frightful enemy without.

CHAPTER 10

THE MONGOLS AND THE 'CLOSING OF THE DOOR'

'Purity is the enemy of change.'

– Mary Douglas, *Purity and Danger: An Analysis of Concepts of Pollution and Taboo*, 1966

'Everyone who is with them [Mongols] in the state over which they rule has to be regarded as belonging to the most evil class of men. He is either an atheist (zindiq) and hypocrite who does not believe in the essence of the religion of Islam ... or he belongs to that worst class of all people who are the people of the bid'a [heretical innovations].'

– Ibn Taymiyya, Fatwa against the Mongols, *c*.1300–1317[1]

'When I lead my army against Baghdad in anger, whether you hide in heaven or in earth, I will bring you down from the spinning spheres; I will toss you in the air like a lion. I will leave no one alive in your realm.'[2]

The caliph of Baghdad should have listened to this message sent to him by Hulagu Khan, grandson of Genghis Khan.* The Mongols were always as good as their savage word. Mongol forces the size of large cities, accompanied by herds of horses numbering in their tens of thousands, some said hundreds of thousands, obliterated every city that refused to surrender to them, leaving nothing but a pyramid of skulls behind.

---

* 'Khan' means 'commander' or 'chief'.

In November 1257 they were at the gates of Baghdad, one of the world's greatest cities at the time. Muslim envoys had sent desperate appeals to Louis IX of France and King Henry III of England begging for help against 'a monstrous and inhuman race of men'. Mongol tribesmen had burst forth from the steppes of Central Asia only fifty or so years earlier and had gone on to conquer most of China, Russia, Turkey, Iran, Poland and Hungary and threaten Austria and Germany. In speed and extent of conquest, the Mongols had no rivals. Their empire was over twice the size of the Islamic Empire; only the British Empire would ever be larger. But the Mongols were unique in the scale of their savagery.

Baghdad's pleas for help were ignored. On the contrary, in 1251, Louis IX of France sought a deal with the Mongols against the Muslims. It was not the first time that Louis and the Mongols had sought a military alliance. Pope Innocent IV had also entered into negotiations, but they had always broken off when the Mongols demanded that the pope and France become their vassals.

In 1251, however, Louis was fresh from the failure of his Crusade (the seventh) in which he had been held to ransom by Muslim forces in Egypt. He sent his envoys on a year-long journey to Karakorum. Set in the boundless pasture lands of Mongolia, the town had been founded by Genghis Khan in around 1218 as a military base. An envoy from an earlier papal mission in 1245 had been struck with both admiration and disgust for the Mongols. On the one hand 'there are neither thieves nor robbers of great riches to be found, and therefore the tabernacles and carts of them that have any treasures are not strengthened with locks or bars,' the Dominican Giovanni da Pian del Carpine commented approvingly in what is the earliest description of Mongolia by a western European. But on the other hand: 'They are unmannerly also and uncleanly... Drunkenness is honourable among them, and when any of them hath taken more drink then his stomach can well bear, he casts it up [vomits] and falls to drinking again... They eat dogs, wolves, foxes and horses, and, when in difficulty, they eat human flesh.'[3]

When Louis' envoys arrived, Karakorum was a thriving cosmopolitan town of tradesmen, artisans and ambassadors from China, Russia,

Central Asia and France. Never mind the table manners, it was religiously tolerant, as cosmopolitan towns tend to be. 'There are there [sic] twelve idol temples of different nations, two mahummeries [mosques] in which is cried the law of Machomet, and one church of Christians in the extreme end of the city,' William of Rubruck, a Franciscan missionary friar, wrote in his report to Louis IX.[4] A silversmith from Paris had designed a silver tree for the courtyard of the Khan's great palace. Whenever a mechanical angel at the top of the tree blew a silver trumpet, wine and fermented mare's milk gushed out of the mouths of four gold serpents that wound around the tree. William himself took part in a debate between Christians, Muslims and Buddhists called by the khan to determine which religion was correct. Christianity, according to William anyway, won.

But the Mongols turned down Louis' offer of an alliance and again demanded that he become their vassal and pay an annual tribute in gold and silver. The envoys departed.

The Mongols did not need the help of Christian Europe to attack Baghdad. They surrounded the city in their thousands and hacked down groves of feathery date palms to use as battering rams against its walls. On 5 February 1258, they smashed their way into the city and embarked on a seventeen-day orgy of rape, murder and destruction. The caliph himself was wrapped in a carpet and trampled to death – a sign of respect had the poor caliph but known it, since Mongols considered the shedding of royal blood deeply shameful.[5]

Baghdad, the jewel not just of the Islamic but of the whole civilized world, its thousands of manuscripts, its mosques and palaces, its canal walkways and markets, was smashed and burned to the ground. The Mongols claimed they slaughtered 200,000 out of a population of around 1 million. Only the Christians were spared – Hulagu Khan's mother was a Christian, as was his favourite wife, many of his advisers and indeed about one third of the Mongol forces. The Christian inhabitants of Baghdad had tended to welcome the Mongols as enemies of the Muslims, and some Christians even took part in the frenzy of killing and destruction. They may not have lived in fear of their lives under the Muslims, but they could never escape their *dhimmi* status. The Christians were doing no more than they and the Jews had done when faced with Arab invaders in the eighth and ninth centuries. They welcomed the new invaders in the hope of getting better treatment, of being not just tolerated but treated equally.

After a couple of weeks the great storm cloud of men, horses and cattle, along with wagonloads of pilfered treasures, pulled out of Baghdad leaving behind a city reduced to smoking ruins, which stank of rotting corpses. The Mongols headed for Syria and Egypt. But in 1260 their implacable advance west was finally halted at Ain Jalut north of Jerusalem by an Egyptian army led by Baibars. Tall and strong as a giant, with one blue eye and one eye clouded by a cataract, Baibars has become for the Islamic world what Charles Martel, victor of the Battle of Poitiers in 732, became for Christendom. Martel is credited with halting the Muslim conquest of Europe, Baibars with preventing the Mongol takeover of the Islamic world. As a result, Baibars (the name means 'great panther', has become the hero of Islamic myth, far eclipsing Saladin. In Muslim eyes Saladin had only defeated the Crusaders, and they had been no more than annoying flies that periodically had to be swatted. Baibars, on the other hand, defeated not just the Crusaders (his army had captured Louis IX) but also a far more devastating enemy. The Mongols never did advance beyond Syria and Egypt. They continued to rule a vast empire ranging from China to eastern Europe, but its territories were in constant rebellion and it finally disintegrated in the mid fourteenth century. Baibars followed up his victory by assassinating his sultan and usurping the throne to become the fourth of the Mamluk sultans.*

Despite Baibars' victory, the confidence of the Islamic world had been shattered. Not just by the Mongol conquests, but by the Christians' conquests in al-Andalus. As a result, Sunni Islam took on a harsher, more inflexible form and became increasingly intolerant of its religious

* In 1250 mamluk slave soldiers had overthrown the Ayyubid dynasty founded by Saladin and seized control of Syria and Egypt. The Mamluk Sultanate ruled until the Ottoman conquest of Egypt in 1517.

minorities – whether Muslim Shiites or non-Muslims. It was one way of asserting Sunni Islam in the face of the battering it had received.

At the forefront of this crusade for orthodoxy was the Syrian jurist Ibn Taymiyya. When Ibn Taymiyya was six, the Mongols destroyed his home town of Harran (on the borders of modern Syria and Turkey), forcing him, his three brothers and his father to flee south to Damascus. That experience had repercussions which are still with us today. It turned Ibn Taymiyya into a passionate traditionalist. He had seen Islam almost annihilated. The only way to defend and strengthen it, he believed, was to adhere strictly to the Quran and sunna. Traditionalism, and its more extreme form, fundamentalism, are the natural children of a religion or ideology that feels under threat.

By 1290, Ibn Taymiyya, aged twenty-nine, had succeeded his father as head of a Hanbali madrasa in Damascus. He was preaching to enraptured crowds at the Umayyad Mosque (built on the site of the Church of St John which Christians had once shared with Muslims; see Chapter 3). Muslims must return to the true Islam, stripped of its innovations, he told them. It was the failure to follow strictly the practices laid out in the Quran and the sunna that had led to Islam's weakness. Ibn Taymiyya condemned *bid'a*, that is, any innovation in Muslim belief or practice that was established after Muhammad and the *Salaf* (the first three generations of Muslims). The Prophet himself had condemned *bid'a*: 'the worst things are those that are novelties, every novelty is an innovation [*bid'a*], every innovation is an error and every error leads to Hell-fire,' one hadith has the Prophet saying.

Islam and Judaism have an inbuilt tendency to traditionalism. Both religions are based on holy books that are considered to be the verbatim words of God. Though within Judaism this is now a belief held only by the Orthodox and ultra-Orthodox, pre-modern Jews believed that the Torah, the first five books of the Hebrew Bible, are God's words as recorded by Moses; the rest of their holy book contains the words of humans. But for Muslims, the whole of their Quran is the recorded word of God. Since God's word is immutable, it makes the essential adaptation of God's law to changing circumstances a fraught one. Most especially this was and is a problem for Sunni Muslims who believe that the Quran is itself divine, not created by God, but eternal and uncreated as God himself. Belief in the uncreated nature of the Quran was the test of faith put to Muslims and so strongly defended by Ibn Hanbal during the inquisition in the ninth century (see Chapter 4). Christian scripture is different. Christians may see parts of the Old Testament as the literal word of God, but the New Testament is not the word of God transmitted through his mouthpiece Jesus; the Gospels, in fact, constitute a sort of biography based on the memories of four of his all-too-human, and therefore flawed, followers. This makes interpretation of the Christian scriptures a more fluid and permissible act.

The crowds loved Ibn Taymiyya, this broad-shouldered, fiery, charismatic preacher whose eyes were like 'eloquent tongues'. They loved his ready solutions to the terrible travails they had undergone, his total conviction that their enemies were God's enemies also. Muslims, he believed, must fight for their faith. For Ibn Taymiyya jihad was at the heart of Islam. God gave not just his permission but insisted that it was the *duty* of every good Muslim to defend Islam against its enemies. And those enemies were everywhere, as much within as without Islam; not just Christians and Jews, but Muslim infidels – any Muslim who deviated even slightly from the orthodoxy. It is why Ibn Taymiyya is considered to be, along with Ibn Hanbal and Ibn Abd al-Wahhab, the architect of a literalist and rigid form of Islam, the Salafiyya movement, and the source of inspiration for today's jihadists.

But Ibn Taymiyya's views were far more complex than that. As a traditionalist, he believed that Islam must return to its roots in the practices and sayings of Muhamad and the *Salaf*, hence the Salafiyya movement. Yet though he firmly opposed *bid'a*, Ibn Taymiyya was critical of *taqlid*, the unquestioning acceptance of and conformity to the legal decisions made by jurists of the seventh to tenth centuries. There was a growing tendency amongst jurists to believe that all the important questions of law and theology had been settled and that Muslim jurists should no longer practise *ijtihad* (independent reasoning). Ibn Taymiyya, however, insisted on the importance of *ijtihad*. The jurist should make his legal judgement according to his own understanding of the divine principles revealed in the Quran and sunna, not because it conformed to judgements made by humans in earlier centuries working under very different circumstances.

Ibn Taymiyya was called on to make his own legal judgement in 1293. Feeling against Christians was riding high.* Some did indeed collude with the Mongols. But though some Christians also fought alongside Muslims against the Mongols and indeed against the Crusaders, their loyalty was always doubted. The Christians within the Muslims' midst were always suspect as fifth columnists, allies both of the Mongols and of the Crusaders. Christians were held responsible for the fires that burned down parts of Fustat (in modern-day Cairo) in 1264. They were the spies of 'the un-eyelashed Tartars', as the mid-thirteenth-century government official Ghazi Ibn al-Wasiti called the Mongols. 'By God they are the source of all misfortune and treason,' thundered one Muslim preacher.[6] 'It is because of them that strangers beset us... And major secrets will leak out to the enemy through them.' They suffered from discrimination and mob violence in a way that they had almost never done before. It was significant that the proportion of Christians in the Muslim world declined sharply during the period of the Crusades and Mongol invasions. Having been the majority in the Fertile Crescent (modern-day southern Iraq, Syria, Lebanon, Jordan, Israel and northern Egypt) Christians became a minority. Jews suffered far less because they posed less of a political or religious threat: they had no rival empire with which to ally themselves, although the violence and discrimination directed primarily against Christians often spilled over on to Jews, especially in areas where there were no Christians.

Christians were already loathed for their role as tax collectors – a not surprisingly unpopular job which the authorities deliberately allocated to Christians and Jews rather than to Muslims. But the authorities also employed Christians as secretaries/scribes and in other administrative roles and the *dhimmi* regulations had been so little enforced that wealthy Christians were resented for visibly flaunting their superiority over Muslims. Like the Jews of Europe, Christians in the Islamic world

* Eastern Christianity was composed of nine different confessions, amongst them the Copts, numerically dominant in Egypt, the Maronites, the Armenians and the Syrian Orthodox.

had become the object of a whole cluster of suspicions, resentments and religious hatred. They were potential traitors working with either the Mongol or the Crusader enemy; they were milking the Muslims for their taxes; they were lording it over the Muslims when they should be the Muslims' inferiors; and they were infidels.

Attacks on Christians increased. In 1293 a wealthy Copt tax collector, sporting a turban, dressed in sumptuous clothes and riding a horse – looking in fact like a wealthy Muslim rather than a humble *dhimmi* – was dragging one of his Muslim debtors on a rope through the streets of Cairo. The sight of this brazen display of Coptic domination incensed the passersby, the shopkeepers and the men playing backgammon. They set upon the Copt and killed him, and then went off to kill what Copts they could find and loot and burn down their houses. It was the first serious mob violence that Copts had experienced.

That same year Muslims accused a Christian cleric in Damascus, in Syria, of insulting the Prophet. Ibn Taymiyya, Damascus's hard-line populist, was asked to give his legal verdict, his fatwa. His verdict was that the cleric must be put to death since under sharia law blasphemy was considered to merit the death penalty (see Chapter 5).

But Ibn Taymiyya's fatwa was ignored. Instead of executing the Christian cleric, the Syrian governor saved his life by persuading him to convert to Islam. The authorities still needed *dhimmis* as government administrators. Ibn Taymiyya and his many supporters protested outside the governor's palace. The protest turned into a riot and the cleric was beaten up. Ibn Taymiyya was imprisoned for his role in the affair. Though his fatwa was ignored at the time, it would have huge significance for modern times: today's jihadists cite it to justify the killing of anyone who insults the Prophet Muhammad.

Over the course of his life, Ibn Taymiyya was imprisoned a further five times in Cairo, Alexandria and Damascus, often on the instigation of the ulema, who considered some of his views to be blasphemous and heretical. Traditionalist and leading Hanbali scholar though he was, Ibn Taymiyya's zealotry was always going to lead him to overstep the mark set by the religious and by the secular authorities. And he took the people with him into the dangerous realms of public unrest, whether it was protesting against the leniency of the governor of Syria towards a Christian blasphemer, rioting against Christians, or smashing up wine shops in Damascus.

But Ibn Taymiyya was no political rebel. On the contrary, he followed his master Ibn Hanbal and indeed the Sunni line that political authority must be obeyed. He believed State power was essential for upholding and enforcing sharia and the *umma*, the Muslim community. As Ibn Hanbal himself had said: the rebel 'has broken the unity of the Muslims and opposed the tradition coming from God's Messenger'. A good Muslim must obey the ruler – except when that ruler was no longer following the Quranic obligation of 'order what is right, forbid what is wrong' (3:110). Who was to decide that was another matter.

Ibn Taymiyya claimed that the authorities were endangering the restoration of true Islam by being too lax in enforcing the Pact of Umar. He was deeply concerned that close proximity to Jews and Christians would contaminate Muslims; they could be corrupted even by sharing food, dressing similarly or living too closely to *dhimmis*. There should, Ibn Taymiyya argued, be a clear distinction between the 'loyalists of Allah' and the 'loyalists of the devil', the disbelievers. The demand to erect strong barriers between 'us' and 'them' was nothing new amongst Muslims, or Christians, as we have seen. At times of crisis there was a particular need to close ranks against the enemy – which was why in 1301 the authorities announced harsh regulations against *dhimmis*. All churches were closed and all *dhimmis* were ordered to wear identifying coloured turbans – blue for Christians, yellow for Jews. From then on *dhimmis'* lives became increasingly restricted. Sunni Islam, with Ibn Taymiyya leading the way, was battening down the hatches in the face of the multiple assaults it had received.

If the authorities did not love Ibn Taymiyya – he was too much of a populist and too stern a zealot for that – they found that their aims and Ibn Taymiyya's often dovetailed perfectly. Especially when it came to the Mongol invaders whom Baibars had repulsed in 1260.

Despite Baibars' victory, the Mongols were still trying to capture Syria. In 1300 they hammered on Damascus's walls for the third time. Islamic law condemns all warfare that does not qualify as jihad, and jihad against fellow Muslims is forbidden. But in 1295 the Mongols' ruler Ghazan Khan had converted to Islam, as had most of his soldiers. War against them was therefore hard for the Syrian Muslim authorities to justify religiously and reports were reaching them that troops were refusing to fight the new converts. Ibn Taymiyya came to the rescue.

In three fatwas he declared that it was lawful to wage jihad against Mongols on the grounds that they still stuck to their 'man-made laws' (their traditional tribal code) and many of their pagan customs. After his conversion, Ghazan Khan had never even given up drinking, persuaded by his advisers that there need be no contradiction between being a good Muslim and a good hard drinker. Furthermore, Mongols were showing themselves to be the enemy of Sunni Islam and favouring Shiism. In Iran, invading Mongols were destroying Sunni madrasas and libraries and virtually wiping out the Sunni ulema, forcing most Sunni scholars to flee.

Islam is much less prone than Christianity to label its co-religionists as heretics, though it does do so. Islam has no central institution or legal body authorized to define what is and is not orthodox and to excommunicate those it considers to be *kafirs* (unbelievers or apostates). But Sunni attitudes were hardening. In the eyes of traditionalists like Ibn Taymiyya, Shiism was a heresy. The Shiites followed legal innovations (*bid'a*), which had no basis in the Quran or the sunna. They were also polytheists since they revered not just Allah but imams and saints too.

Ibn Taymiyya never actually declared the Mongols to be *kafirs*, and scholars disagree as to whether he believed heretics like the Shiites should be sentenced to death.[7] But as far as he was concerned, the Shiites were 'more heretical yet than Jews and Christians'. In this, he did not differ much from senior clerics within the Catholic Church, men like the Abbot of Cluny, Peter the Venerable, who ranked the struggle against the Cathars, the 'false Christians', higher than that against the heathen who did not know God. As the thirteenth-century Church's greatest theologian, Thomas Aquinas, argued, and few would have disagreed with him:

> ... heresy is a sin which merits not only excommunication but also death, for it is worse to corrupt the Faith which is the life of the soul than to issue counterfeit coins which minister to the secular life. Since counterfeiters are justly killed by princes as enemies of the common good, so heretics also deserve the same punishment.[8]

By heretic, Aquinas meant Catholics who deliberately chose to adhere to beliefs which they knew contradicted the Catholic faith. He did not include Muslims or Jews on the grounds that you cannot condemn someone for doing something you do not agree with, if they have followed the dictates of their conscience.

According to Ibn Taymiyya, Mongols were both apostates and heretics. And the penalty for apostasy was death. The boundaries are inevitably blurred between the apostate who rejects his or her religion, the heretic who propounds beliefs different to those accepted by the majority or orthodox community, and the blasphemer who performs or speaks an impiety against God. The Quran condemns all three but as we have seen is not specific about punishment (see Chapter 5). From the seventh century on, however, it was generally agreed by jurists that apostasy/blasphemy deserved the death penalty on the basis of the hadith in which Muhammad said: 'Whoever changes his religion, kill him.'

The apostate, by rejecting Islam, was committing a sin for which he or she would be sent to hell but was also committing the crime of treason by undermining the social and political order, which was underpinned by Islam. Ibn Taymiyya's opposition to Shiism was perfectly in tune with the sultan, as well as the people. For Sunni rulers, Shiites were the enemy – not just the Mongol invaders but their Shiite sympathizers who were potential or actual rebels against Sunni rule.

Ibn Taymiyya's popular support increased further in 1303 when Mongol forces occupied Damascus. Most of its inhabitants, along with the military, fled the city. Ibn Taymiyya, however, remained to become one of the leaders of the resistance. He spurred on the governor to fight, negotiated with the Mongols for the release of Syrian Muslim – and *dhimmi* – prisoners, and organized military reinforcements from Cairo. The Mongols were driven out of Damascus and all Syria.

But Ibn Taymiyya's huge popularity with the people did not help endear him to his fellow jurists, nor did his character. Not even Ibn Taymiyya's religious adversaries doubted his 'asceticism, piety, and religiosity … his selfless championship of the truth, his adherence to the path of our forebears, his pursuit of perfection'. But they thoroughly disliked his bad-tempered self-righteousness. 'How long will you look at the motes in the eye of your brother, forgetting the stumps in your own?' asked a critic, possibly Ibn Taymiyya's close disciple, the hadith scholar and historian al-Dhahabi. 'How long will you praise yourself and your prattling phrases while disparaging the "*ulema*" and pursuing other people's weaknesses?' And so it came about that Ibn Taymiyya the heretic-hunter was himself found guilty of blasphemy by the *qadi* in 1326.

But even when Ibn Taymiyya was being marched to the Damascus Citadel, he could not resist stopping before two men playing backgammon outside a blacksmith's shop and kicking their board over: the sharia forbade gambling and for Ibn Taymiyya backgammon was inseparable from gambling. He died in the Citadel two years later at the age of sixty-five. Thousands of mourners turned out to watch his funeral procession.

Eight centuries after his death jihadists now look to Ibn Taymiyya for much of their inspiration. In preaching jihad against the Mongols, Ibn Taymiyya had made a distinction between the true and the false Muslim. Two centuries earlier, the Almoravids (and later the Almohads) had done the same. They had conquered their fellow Muslims in al-Andalus at the end of the eleventh century armed with a fatwa declaring that the Andalusian Sunni rulers were too decadent to be called Muslims. In later life Ibn Taymiyya would express outright disapproval of what came to be called *takfir* (declaring a Muslim to be an apostate), but his fatwas have been understood by jihadists as doing exactly that. In principle, according to Sunnis, only the ulema as a group can pronounce *takfir* and even then only under strict conditions. Ibn Taymiyya, however, had taken upon himself the right to practise *takfir*, rather as the Kharijites had done in the seventh century (see Chapter 2). Certainly that is how the ultra-traditionalist Muhammad Ibn Abd al-Wahhab in the eighteenth century and today's extremists interpret Ibn Taymiyya's fatwas. Such an interpretation gives jihadists, as it gave Ibn Abd al-Wahhab, a precedent for declaring any Muslim or group of Muslims to be apostates whose beliefs or practices deviate from their own view of what is the true Islam. And it gives them the licence to kill. Jihadists believe they have a duty to wage jihad against anyone they consider to be an apostate.

Ibn Taymiyya is today associated with the time when Islam, in the face of the traumas it had undergone, retreated into traditionalism. But that is not the full picture. In terms of legal thought he was and is often considered to be an innovator. He believed it was essential that the jurist exercise his own independent reasoning, *ijtihad*. Nonetheless, his condemnation of *bid'a* confirmed the traditionalist route that Sunni Islam had already set out on. Any innovation in belief or practice was in a sense to say that God's word was not enough. Since Ibn Hanbal, Sunni Islam had favoured *taqlid*, 'imitation' or 'adherence', over *ijtihad*; by condemning *bid'a* Ibn Taymiyya gave Islam a further nudge in that direction. Sunni Islam became a harsher more intolerant religion under his tutelage. But the door was never firmly closed against speculation; as in Judaism, it was disguised in the form of commentary on pre-existing legal rulings.[9]

Ibn Taymiyya had played upon fears of the Mongols together with suspicions and resentments of the *dhimmis* to foster an increasing loyalty to Sunnism; its corollary was a growing belief amongst Sunnis that any creed or sect which was not Sunni was Islam's enemy. The relatively tolerant Islamic world of the Middle East in which *dhimmis* and Muslims lived, worked and socialized together was disappearing. Progressively over the fourteenth century, *dhimmis* were segregated and regarded with contempt.

But the *dhimmis*' experience, harsher and more humiliating though it had become, did not compare to the level of persecution that was being meted out to the Jews of northern Europe. Nor did the *dhimmis* ever find that at a stroke of the ruler's pen, they could lose their homes, their belongings and their wealth as the Jews of England did under Edward I.

On 18 July 1290 King Edward ordered all Jews in England to leave the country. They had until 1 November, the Feast of All Saints, to do so; Jews who remained in the country after that date faced execution.

Edward I's expulsion probably came as no terrible surprise to the 2,000 or so Jews living in England. The writing had been on the wall for a long time. Since the first blood libel levelled at English Jews in 1144 (see Chapter 8), they had been subjected to increasing levels of persecution and mob violence. They had been expelled from about twenty cities, including Marlborough, Gloucester, Worcester and Cambridge; they had been massacred in London, Winchester, Canterbury and other cities during the civil war between Simon de Montfort and King Henry III in the 1260s when those in debt to Jewish moneylenders had taken their revenge. Synagogues had been closed down; England had applied the Church councils' anti-Jewish rulings more enthusiastically than any other country in Europe; nowhere was the requirement for Jews to wear a distinguishing badge more rigorously enforced. Jews had been taxed mercilessly. The Statute of the Jewry in 1275 forbade any lending of money at interest. In 1287 all the Jews of England had been suddenly arrested and thrown into prison: they were not released until they had paid a fine of 20,000 marks.[10]

It was not that Edward did not still desperately need money, more that he and his father, Henry III, and his grandfather John who had flirted with Islam, had taxed the Jewish communities of England so heavily and had borrowed from them so regularly without ever paying interest, that the Jews had almost no more money left to give. Besides, despite the rulings of the Church, there were Christian usurers aplenty by the mid thirteenth century. The Lombards from Italy and the Cahorsins from France were notorious for the ploys by which they circumvented the Church ban on Christian usurers, disguising interest as payment for possible loss, injury or delay. Edward no longer needed to rely on Jews for loans.

Edward's actual decree of expulsion has been lost. But he clearly wanted it organized in a legal, orderly fashion. The sheriffs were told that no one should 'injure, harm, damage, or grieve' Jews in the three months that were allotted for them to pack up and leave.

They took what they could – precious mementoes, cash, jewellery, the scrolls of the Torah – shut the doors of their homes for the last time and headed for the coast. Edward had ordered that the poor should be allowed to travel at cheap rates, and that the port authorities should ensure all the exiles had a safe passage across the sea. This was not always the case.

In October, a ship carrying some of London's poorest Jews grounded on a sandbank at Queenborough, at the mouth of the Thames. The captain invited his passengers to disembark while they waited for the tide to rise. But when the tide rose, he refused to let them back on board, yelling as the ship sailed off that they 'ought to cry unto Moses, by whose conduct their fathers passed through the Red Sea'.[11] The Jews all drowned. King Edward, however, was told of the incident and captain and crew were hanged. But October was the stormiest time of the year to sail anyway, and many ships carrying Jews went down on the crossing to northern France.

Back in England their deserted homes and tenements, their cemeteries and synagogues, were looted by local townspeople, or appropriated by the Crown. Hugh of Kendal was appointed to oversee the sale of Jewish properties. The total value from the nineteen towns where Jews had lived came to £1,835. 13s. 4d. of which about £100 went on stained-glass windows for Westminster Abbey and on completing Henry III's tomb there. Not a single voice, Church or secular, seems to have been raised in protest at the expulsion. On the contrary, it was greeted with delight.

A grateful Parliament gave Edward a £100,000 tax grant, the largest tax grant made by any medieval English Parliament. It seemed to his Christian subjects a fine price to pay for getting rid of the Jews. After 200 years Jews had all but vanished from England. The only Jews that remained were those who had converted to Christianity, or who practised their own religion in secret, or had been granted a special licence to visit England. Otherwise, as far as most English were concerned, their country had become a purely Christian one.

They would not knowingly set eyes on Jews in their cities and towns for another 300-plus years, when Oliver Cromwell permitted Jews to resettle in 1656.

As for the Jews who had been expelled, those who had hoped to make a new life for themselves in France managed to live there for only sixteen years before the French king, Philip the Fair, followed King Edward I of England's example and expelled them. Equally heavily in debt and under heavy financial pressure Philip ordered all France's Jews (about 125,000) to leave the country in 1306; all their property was sold at public auction.

But nine years later the new King of France, Louis X, realized his father had made a bad financial mistake. Moneylenders might be disliked, but they were essential. And Christian usurers proved to be no better, and often worse, in terms of the interest they exacted. Louis permitted Jews to return, just as his predecessor King Philip Augustus had done in 1198, though they had to pay to do so on a twelve-year 'lease'. Jews were expelled again in 1394.

Poland, alone in Europe, extended a welcome to the communities of Jews that were being expelled from elsewhere. Since the Rhineland massacres perpetrated during the First Crusade in 1098, and the persecutions and forced conversions inflicted on Jews in Prague in the late eleventh and early twelfth centuries, large numbers of Jews had found refuge in Poland. Their numbers only increased in the twelfth and thirteenth centuries as Jews in western Europe were treated ever more savagely and driven out from England, France, Germany, Italy and Spain. Poland was in the main a backward agricultural economy of feudal lords and peasants. The princes recognized the economic contribution that Jewish merchants and financiers could make, especially after the Mongol invasion of 1241 which had ravaged Poland economically and decimated its population. Poland's princes in fact outdid each other in encouraging Jews to settle in their own rather than a rival's territory.

In 1264, the Polish Prince Boleslaw the Pious issued the General Charter of Jewish Liberties, known as the Statute of Kalisz. It was an unprecedented document in medieval Europe that treated Jews as legally equal to Christians,* that fined Christians if they did not come to the aid of their neighbouring Jews, that protected equally the interests of the Jewish creditor and the Christian debtor, that forbade accusations of blood libel and threatened the Christian accuser with the death penalty if he was found to have made a false accusation.

The Church, however, did all it could to prevent their emancipation. A Church council was held in 1266 in the city of Breslau (Wroclaw), which had been rebuilt after its destruction during the Mongol invasion a little more than twenty years earlier. Because, said the council, Poland is 'a new plantation on the soil of Christianity, there is reason to fear that her Christian population will fall an easy prey to the influence of the superstitions and evil habits of the Jews living among them'. It therefore declared that Jews in city or village should live apart 'separated from the general dwelling place of the Christians by a hedge, wall, or ditch'.[12] Jews should lock themselves in their houses while Church processions went through the streets, and they should wear a special hat with a horn-like shield to distinguish them from Christians. In 1279 the Church declared that Jews also had to wear a red cloth badge on their chest, while Muslims had to wear a saffron-coloured badge. Christians were forbidden under penalty of excommunication to invite Jews to eat and drink with them or take part in joint festivities. Over the next one hundred or so years, the Church in Poland continued to push for a degrading separation of Jews from Christians. Poland's rulers, however, ignored the Church, just as the Carolingian Louis the Pious had done over 400 years earlier (see Chapter 5); Jews were too useful in the complex task of earthly government.

But the Christianization of Europe was accelerating. It was becoming part and parcel of a growing sense of nationhood and the consequent need that each nation felt to assert its superiority over the other by claiming its own special relationship with God. 'God would never have honoured this land in the same way as he did Israel … if it were not that He had

* The Statute of Kalisz, the General Charter of Jewish Liberties in Poland, issued in 1264, recognized Jews as legally equal to Christians.

chosen it as His heritage,' the chancellor of England told Parliament in 1376. There is heavy historical irony in the observation that Moses and Yahweh showed Christian Europe the way to creating a cohesive nation; it would be that process of binding a disparate group into one with a special destiny which would so often be the source of the persecution of the Jews.

And then in 1347 the world was turned upside and, in the words of the fourteenth-century German chronicler Jakob von Königshofen, 'Death went from one end of the earth to the other.'[13] Christian Europe blamed the Jews; the Islamic world did not.

CHAPTER 11

THE BLACK DEATH: AN EXPERIMENT IN TOLERANCE

'In the matter of this plague the Jews throughout the world were reviled and accused in all lands of having caused it … and for this reason the Jews were burnt all the way from the Mediterranean into Germany.'

– Jakob von Königshofen, chronicler of Strasbourg, 'The Cremation of Strasbourg Jewry, St. Valentine's Day, February 14, 1349'

'This plague is for the Muslims a martyrdom and a reward, and for the disbelievers a punishment and a rebuke… If the liar disputes the matter of infection and tries to find an explanation, I say that the Prophet, on him be peace, said: who infected the first?'

– Ibn al-Wardi, fourteenth-century historian, on the divine source of plague, *Risala an-Naba' 'an al-Waba* (*News of the Pestilence*), 1348

EARLY IN OCTOBER 1347, twelve trading ships crept into the harbour of Messina in Sicily. To the townsmen and women gathered at the dock, expecting to hear the shouts of relieved sailors, and to see the bustle of men ready to stand on firm ground at last after their long journey from the Crimea across the Black Sea and the Mediterranean, the ships were unaccountably silent. The reason was soon obvious – the ships' crews were either dead or dying, their noses and the tips of their fingers covered in black blotches. The terrified authorities at once ordered the death ships out of the harbour. But it was too late. The plague had landed in Messina – partly thanks to the townspeople who had looted the defenceless fleet.

By early 1348 the plague, which may well have originated in China and India, had rampaged through Italy and was sweeping across Spain and southern France; by the spring it had reached Paris, where the monks of Saint-Denis recorded that 800 Parisians were dying every day; by May it had reached Weymouth in south-west England; by late summer of 1348 about 290 people were dying in London every day; by the autumn it was decimating towns and villages in Switzerland and Germany and was spreading north to Scandinavia. In the course of four years from about 1347 to 1351, the Black Death, as it came to be known, killed over 25 million people in Europe, about a quarter to a half of its population.

A different strain of the plague hit Islamdom and killed at least 75 million people, about a third of its population. The plague-struck world became an appalling laboratory for testing how Islamdom and Christendom behaved when put under the same cataclysmic pressures. Christendom did not fare well.

The Black Death in its commonest form in western Europe, the bubonic plague, started with a headache and a high fever; within a day, hard, painful swellings (buboes) began appearing on neck, arms and inner thighs, ranging from the size of an egg to the size of an apple. Soon the buboes began to ooze pus and blood. Within a week the victim was usually dead from massive internal bleeding and probably blood poisoning.

No one was certain of the cause or the solution. Some believed it was spread by contagion and counselled flight or avoidance of all contact with any one or any thing. In the desperate attempt to shut themselves away in safety, 'brothers abandoned brothers, uncles their nephews, sisters their brothers, and in many cases wives deserted their husbands', wrote Boccaccio in his introduction to *The Decameron* which was inspired by his own experience of the plague in his home city of Florence. 'But even worse,' he added, 'and almost incredible, was the fact that fathers and mothers refused to nurse and assist their own children, as though they did not belong to them.'[1] Within a couple of months of the plague's arrival in 1348, 60 per cent of Florence's population had died from the plague.

'Many dropped dead in the open streets, both by day and by night,' Boccaccio wrote, 'whilst a great many others, though dying in their own houses, drew their neighbours' attention to the fact more by the smell of their rotting corpses than by any other means.'[2] Every hour more corpses were brought to Florence's cemeteries until there was no space left and huge trenches had to be dug into which hundreds of bodies were thrown.

In the face of such terror, people responded in contradictory ways. There was a mass outbreak of piety and superstition. But equally there was a breakdown in moral order: Christians shook their fist at God and acted with the terrified defiant lawlessness of people who believed the end of the world, or at least their place in it, was nigh. As Boccaccio noted, many Florentines,

> … maintained that an infallible way of warding off this appalling evil was to drink heavily, enjoy life to the full, go round singing and merry-making, gratify all of one's cravings whenever the opportunity offered, and shrug the whole thing off as one enormous joke … they would visit one tavern after another, drinking all day and night to immoderate excess … people behaved as though their days were numbered, and treated their belongings and their own persons with abandon. Hence most houses had become common property, and any passing stranger could make himself at home as naturally as though he were the rightful owner.[3]

Other Christians were in no doubt that the plague was God's punishment for humanity's sins. Christians must purify themselves to regain God's favour – hence the spectacular rise of movements like the Flagellants, groups of pilgrims who paraded the streets whipping themselves with heavy leather straps studded with sharp pieces of metal until they bled.

But though some Christians might see the plague as punishment for their sins, on the whole it was far easier to put the blame on others. The Church and the Crusades had encouraged Europe to identify itself as Christian. In the face of the catastrophe that was afflicting the world, Christendom found its scapegoat in the Jews, the 'sons of the crucifiers', thereby conveniently forgetting that Jews too were dying in the epidemic. Since the authorities had no solutions to offer the terrified, grieving people whose friends and family were dying all around them, they were only too happy to divert the blame away from themselves – indeed they positively encouraged it. Between 1348 and 1351 thousands of Jews in Germany, Spain, southern France and the Low Countries (today's Netherlands and Belgium) were rounded up in city squares, or their synagogues, and butchered. Jews in Europe would not experience such slaughter again until the Holocaust of the twentieth century.

It started with a report from the Alpine town of Chambéry. The local rabbi, a man called Peyret, was said to be handing out little leather bags of poison to Jewish travellers, especially traders, with instructions that they should empty them into wells and fountains throughout the cities of Europe. It was clear that Jews were deliberately conspiring to kill Christendom. The authorities rounded up a number of Jews living on the shores of Lake Geneva. Amongst them was Agimet, a Jewish merchant. Having been 'put to the torture a little', Agimet confessed that he had indeed been given a leather pouch of poison whose contents he had poured into wells, cisterns and public fountains on his travels to the cities of Venice, Apulia in southern Italy and Toulouse in southern France.

Copies of Agimet's and other confessions were passed to the authorities throughout Switzerland and down the Rhine to Germany and France. Jews in towns and hamlets were tortured into confessions and massacred. In January 1349, 600 Jewish men and women in Basel were herded into a wooden barn and burned to death. In February it was the turn of the Jews in Strasbourg in today's France; in August the Jewish communities in Cologne and Mainz were slaughtered.

Although chroniclers like Jakob von Königshofen, writing a generation after the massacre, are keen to blame such atrocities on the urban mob and the peasantry, it was the elites – the city councils run by merchants and craftsmen, the great lords and dukes who ruled cities and territories, and the Holy Roman emperor himself – who arrested Jews, initiated the tortures, presided over the confessions and 'trials' and organized the massacres. The Prince-bishop of Basel, the Bishop of Strasbourg, and other senior clergymen all supported the massacres.

Of course, the mob who took part in the massacres was happy to vent all its terror, grief and bewilderment on the Jews. 'They were burnt in many cities,' records Königshofen, 'and wherever they were expelled they were caught by the peasants and stabbed to death or drowned.'[4] In Königshofen's home city of Strasbourg, before the first tell-tale signs of sweating and vomiting and the first bodies had even started appearing on the streets, about 2,000 Jews were rounded up and burned to death as a pre-emptive measure. About 16,000 of Strasbourg's Christian citizens in fact died of the plague. The council appropriated most of the Jews' possessions, and some of the spoils were handed over to the cathedral. Jews were slaughtered in Nuremberg, Frankfurt, Cologne and Hanover; 'in some cities the Jews themselves set fire to their houses and cremated themselves', so great was their fear of what awaited them, according to Königshofen.[5]

Jews were not the only scapegoats. Outsiders of any sort, whether they were beggars, lepers or foreigners, were also targeted. But Jews were the most obvious scapegoats, even though the pope himself tried to protect them. Clement VI issued two papal bulls in 1348 condemning the conspiracy theory that Jews were poisoning Christians – anyone who believed that was, he said, 'seduced by that liar, the Devil'. Besides, the pope argued, Jews were also dying of the plague though admittedly their mortality rate was lower. That in itself was a matter of suspicion for Christians, though it had a perfectly natural explanation: the Jews' religion required them to be cleaner, and their relatively isolated existence in Jewish communities prevented the epidemic from spreading as swiftly as it did amongst Christians. Pope Clement urged the clergy to protect Jews, but clergy and people were against him. The Flagellants, the pilgrims who whipped themselves as penance for their plague-inducing sins, were particularly enthusiastic supporters and proponents of massacring the Jews.

In the autumn of 1347, about the same time that it got its tentacles into Sicily, the Black Death arrived in the Egyptian port city of Alexandria. From there it spread through the Mamluk Sultanate, east through

Palestine, north through Lebanon and Syria and south to Mecca and Yemen.

'Cities and buildings were laid waste, roads and way signs were obliterated, settlements and mansions became empty, dynasties and tribes grew weak,' wrote Ibn Khaldun, the fourteenth-century philosopher-historian of nomadic conquest and decline (see Chapter 7). For Ibn Khaldun, whose parents were killed in Tunis by the Black Death, 'the entire inhabited world changed... It was as if the voice of existence in the world had called out for oblivion and restriction, and the world had responded to its call.'[6]

One of the forms the plague took in the Islamic world was even more terrifying than the bubonic plague, because of the speed with which it killed. The pneumonic plague was transmitted by particles in the air – people caught it just by breathing, it did not need to be spread by rats or fleas. Death was not completely inevitable with the bubonic plague. But with the pneumonic plague it was. From the time the victim started coughing up blood to the time they collapsed and died was usually a matter of a couple of hours. Bodies lay abandoned under palm trees, in gardens, streets and markets or were laid on makeshift biers, sometimes two to three corpses sharing a plank, ladder or basket. There were so many funeral processions that mourners jostled each other for space in the streets of Cairo.

Despite the fact that Islam was much more advanced medically than western Europe, and that Islam's requirement of washing before prayers meant that, as was the case with Jews, the epidemic spread less easily than amongst Christians, about a third of the population of the Islamic world died.[7]

But what was so strikingly different from the Christian response to the plague was that Muslims never turned on Jews and Christians as savagely as Christians turned on Jews. In the autumn of 1348, the plague was mowing down about 300 Londoners every day compared to about 1,000 people in the Syrian city of Damascus. In response, the Mamluk authorities made a joint appeal to Jews, Christians and Muslims to fast and pray for three days. As result, Damascus became a multi-faith city of prayer and fasting. On the fourth day, before morning prayers, Jews, Christians and Muslims together marched barefoot through streets of densely packed unpainted wooden houses, past marble-floored palaces, and out of the city gates.

'The entire population of the city joined in the exodus, male and female, small and large,' noted the Moroccan traveller Ibn Battuta, whose account of his travels, set down in 1354, is as famous in the Muslim world as that of his near contemporary Marco Polo's is in the Western world. 'The Jews went out with their Book of the Law and the Christians with their Gospel, their women and children with them; the whole concourse of them in tears and humble supplications, imploring the favour of God through His Books and His Prophets.'[8] Outside the city they walked through an oasis of pleasure gardens and orchards, a miracle of lushness in a semi-desert landscape, the air thick with the scent of ripening fruit. After two miles the pilgrims reached the Mosque of the Footprint where they spent the day chanting and praying together. But notwithstanding such a united appeal to God by all three monotheisms, by the time the epidemic had run its course in the spring of 1349, 400,000 Syrians had died from the plague, about 30 per cent of Syria's population.

As passersby collapsed and died in the streets, and unburied bodies lay rotting in silent houses, pious Muslims, like pious Christians, sought to explain the breakdown of their world in the face of a remorseless, swift and inexplicable disease. And they explained it in the only way they could – in terms of God's will. As in Christendom so in the Islamic world the plague led to a mass outbreak of piety and superstition. The Christians, however, viewed the Black Death as God's punishment for human sinfulness, which every human had inherited since Adam and Eve defied God and tasted the fruit from the tree of knowledge of good and evil. But Islam, like Judaism, does not share the Christian doctrine of original sin. In Islam, misery and evil do not arise from human sin which only God's mercy can expunge. The question of guilt and responsibility for the plague did not really arise.

For Muslims, the Black Death was ordained by a God whose reasons could not be fathomed by humans; but remarkably, from the Christian point of view, Muslims also saw the plague as God's reward. The believer who died from the plague would receive the same heavenly rewards as the believer who died fighting a holy war – both were martyrs. Death by jihad or death by plague were equally meritorious in the eyes of God. Plague as God's blessing rather than plague as God's punishment. Such a belief, fatalistic in its acceptance that the disease was part of a divinely ordained plan which would ultimately reward the faithful, tempered the natural response to the terrifyingly inexplicable, which is to find someone to blame and then exterminate them.

In Muslim eyes, the plague, like famine and drought, was quite literally an act of God, rather than caused by human sinfulness. Therefore there was nothing to be done but behave as a good Muslim should and do what could be done to preserve the community. Muhammad himself was said to have prohibited flight from a plague-infected community. But many Muslims disobeyed the prohibition. It was, of course, hard for anyone, however devout, to accept such a terrifying disease as a blessing, and the plague was in fact often seen as God's punishment on a Muslim world that had strayed too far from its religion. In Syria, plague was blamed on Muslims who drank wine, and offenders were lashed as punishment.

Dhimmis also suffered. There were outbreaks of mob violence when Christians in particular were attacked and their churches destroyed; Copts were burned to death. Feeling increasingly vulnerable, they disguised themselves as Jews in order to avoid being attacked. Their degradation increased as the authorities responded to popular and religious pressure for a strict enforcement of Muslim laws and the Pact of Umar. In 1354 the Mamluk government announced that Christian and Jewish doctors could no longer treat Muslims.

It was indicative of the times that a mid-fourteenth-century guide to the collection of the *jizya* emphasized that 'the *dhimmi* has to be made to feel that he is an inferior person when he pays'. The emir receiving the *jizya* had to sit on a high throne. 'The *dhimmi* appears before him, offering the poll tax on his open palm. The emir takes it so that his hand is on top and the *dhimmi*'s below. Then the emir gives him a blow on the neck, and one who stands before the emir drives him roughly away.' It was a spectacle designed to demonstrate the *dhimmis*' position in the Islamic world for the satisfaction of Muslims. 'The public is admitted to see this show,' the guidelines make a point of saying.

The number of conversions to Islam increased – a sure sign that it was becoming more and more uncomfortable for *dhimmis* to retain their own faith. The authorities, however, always suspected that the conversions were not genuine and only done for the sake of keeping a government position. Orders were published that even if a Jew or Christian had turned Muslim, he was not to be given a government job. Any convert to Islam was to be watched, to make sure that he observed the five daily prayers and the Friday prayer. Converts could only bequeath their possessions to members of their family who had similarly left their previous faith for Islam. Humiliation, yes, but not death. The bonds of human kindness never seem to have broken down so completely as they did in Christendom.

By 1350 the plague had virtually run its course in Europe (it took longer in the Middle East and Asia). In the Rhineland, home to the largest Jewish communities in Europe, Jews had been virtually wiped out, slaughtered by their Christian neighbours as well as by the plague itself.

Of those Jews that survived, many opted to move eastwards to the slightly more hospitable cities of Poland where it is clear from the absence of Jewish accounts of massacres that they escaped relatively unscathed. Poland was simply continuing its policy, begun in the late eleventh century, of encouraging Jews to settle. But that policy was now adopted not just by Poland but by Austria, Hungary, Bohemia and Lithuania, who all wanted to take advantage of Jewish wealth, trading networks, credit and financial expertise. Eastern Europe welcomed Jews with the semi-open arms that western Europe's rulers had once extended to Jews in the eleventh century, promising them benevolent treatment, autonomy and no restrictions on the interest rates moneylenders could charge. By the middle of the sixteenth century, about three quarters of the world's Jews are thought to have been living in Poland. By the beginning of the seventeenth century, there were no overtly practising Jews or Muslims left in Spain.

CHAPTER 12

INQUISITIONS AND EXPULSIONS

'There is now no one in the city who is not a Christian.'

– Cardinal Francisco Jiménez de Cisneros,
Grand Inquisitor of Spain 1507–1517

If ever a man was associated with intolerance it is the late-fifteenth-century Spanish friar Tómas de Torquemada, the Grand Inquisitor. For us today he is the brutal face of the Spanish Inquisition, and of the Catholic Church. His name conjures up images of priests in white habits and black cloaks torturing their victims into confessions of heresy, of flames lighting up the public squares of Spain as the 'heretics' were burned alive in elaborate mass executions presided over by crimson-robed cardinals. But that picture is in part the creation of sixteenth-century Protestants and after them Enlightenment thinkers for whom the inquisition, especially the Spanish Inquisition, became the symbol of Catholic religious and intellectual intolerance.

The fact is that the Inquisition has been, as it were, much maligned, at least when put in the context of the harshness of the times. True, the Inquisition tortured its victims. But then the state authorities used torture (the strappado and water torture in Spain and the Holy Roman Empire, the rack and the thumbscrew in England) on most suspected criminals – whether their crime was religious or not. True, the heretics who refused to recant after they had been convicted by the Inquisition, and they were always urged to do so, were handed over to the state and 'relaxed', that is, consigned to the most painful of all executions, slow burning to death. But then petty criminals, from thieves to forgers, were also executed.

The Spanish Inquisition is rightly considered to be far nastier than its counterpart inquisitorial courts set up in France and Italy. But estimates vary as to how many victims the Spanish Inquisition claimed over the following 300 years. Between about 1530, when the Inquisition was also hunting Protestants and Moriscos (Muslim converts to Christianity), and 1834 when the Catholic Church formally abolished the Inquisition, the numbers who died at the stake are put at anything from less than 1,000 to 32,000, including those from Spain's empire in the Americas and in the Spanish-held Netherlands.[1] Professor Henry Kamen, one of the first contemporary scholars to argue that the bloodthirsty nature of the Spanish Inquisition has been greatly exaggerated, argues that of the 44,674 people hauled up before the Spanish inquisitorial courts a maximum of 3,000 were actually convicted as heretics, and many of those were executed only symbolically – a straw dummy was burned instead of the person.[2]

Perhaps the reason the Spanish Inquisition was so comparatively restrained in inflicting the death penalty was that its fearsome reputation was sufficient to enforce Catholicism across Spain without actually having to kill too many people. Fear of torture, of losing all your property, of imprisonment, whipping, being sent to work as a galley slave on the royal fleet and in the worst-case scenario death itself, were good reasons to give up any wayward beliefs, assuming that the suspect even held them and was not simply the unfortunate object of a malicious accusation.

Nevertheless, if the Inquisition was less savage in reality than in imagination, it still represented the aggressive spirit of the Church determined to assert its supremacy with the threat of brute power if not its actual execution. And nowhere was this more so than in Reconquista Spain. In the late fifteenth century all that was left of Muslim al-Andalus was the Kingdom of Granada. But 'Spain' as an entity, rather than a collection of disparate Christian kingdoms, did not yet exist. Despite the marriage in 1469 of King Ferdinand II of Aragon and Queen Isabella

I of Castile, which united the two most powerful Christian kingdoms on the Iberian peninsula, 'Spain' still had to be created. Ferdinand and Isabella embarked on its creation with the help of the Church, in the shape of their political adviser and Isabella's confessor, Torquemada. Together they would create a Spain united by its Christian identity.

But unity, as this book has shown, is bought at the cost of those excluded from the magic circle of the unified. The insider is made so by defining the outsider. A Spain united by its Christianity could not include Jews or Muslims. Their Catholic Majesties Ferdinand and Isabella and the Church killed off all prospects that Christian Spain would follow in the steps of its more tolerant Islamic predecessors.

Feelings against Muslims were already running high. Christian Spain was fighting the last vestiges of Muslim rule in al-Andalus. Furthermore in 1453 the new rising power in the Islamic world, the Ottoman Turks, had conquered Constantinople. The city had been all that remained of the Christian Byzantine Empire. It had been the last outpost of Christianity in the Near East; it now belonged to the Muslims under its new name of Istanbul.

Muslims who lived under Christian rule were still allowed to practise their religion openly, but the persecution of Jews in Reconquista Spain escalated; persecution of Muslims would come a little later. In 1391, mobs in Seville, incited by their archdeacon, Ferrand Martinez, killed 4,000 Jews. Anti-Jewish violence erupted across Spain. About one third of Spain's Jews (estimates of their total population vary between 200,000 and 800,000) were murdered; another third were forcibly converted. After that time, anti-Jewish edicts multiplied. Jews who had previously lived in the same neighbourhoods as Christians, though many had preferred to live in their own communities, were forced to live in a fixed area segregated from Christians – a ghetto in all but name (see Chapter 14); they were excluded from public office; in some towns they were forbidden to sell food; fines were levied against them for failing to pay their respects to religious processions. As a result Jews converted to Christianity in their tens of thousands over and above those who had been forced to do so. Between 1400 and 1490 about half the Jewish population of

Spain is thought to have converted.[3] How many of the *conversos* continued to practise their former religion in private is unclear. Certainly 'Old Christians' suspected the 'New Christians' of faking their conversions solely to obtain the privileges to which Christians were entitled. Jews who outwardly converted to Christianity but who continued to practise Judaism in private were common enough, or thought to be so, that they were collectively known by Christians as Marranos, a deliberately insulting word (meaning filthy or pig). To this day there are still 'Marranos' living in Spain.

It was because *conversos* were suspected of still being Jews at heart, ready to undermine Christian Spain, that Ferdinand and Isabella got permission from Pope Sixtus IV to establish an inquisition. Church courts would interrogate the *conversos* and uncover their true beliefs, by torture if necessary. In 1483 Torquemada was appointed Grand Inquisitor.

The Spanish Inquisition was at its most frenzied during his fifteen-year rule. About 2,000 men and women were burned to death; many died in prison as they awaited trial or were cowed or tortured into recanting. No doubt Torquemada, 'the most accursed man in the world' according to one Jewish doctor, was particularly zealous in rooting out 'fake' converts because he himself came from a family of Jewish *conversos*.

The inquisition of Jews was on the whole hugely popular amongst Christians. The courts also examined those suspected of practising sodomy, polygamy and witchcraft. But it was Jews who comprised nearly all of the Spanish Inquisition's victims until the mid sixteenth century when the Moriscos became its second major target.

When the Inquisition tribunal made up of clergymen – two to three inquisitors who were trained lawyers or theologians, a defence counsellor whose role was to advise the accused, a judge and clerks – arrived in a city, their first task was to round up suspects. After Sunday Mass the inquisitor would stand up and read the 'Edict of Grace'. The edict urged the congregation to present themselves and 'relieve their consciences' by confessing their heresies. Heretics were given an added inducement to reveal themselves with the guarantee that if they did so within thirty to forty days, they would not be severely punished. Most pernicious of all, the edict called on those who suspected anyone of harbouring heretical beliefs to tell the tribunal of their suspicions. It was a signal for neighbour to denounce neighbour, and many did so whether out of genuine concern for their neighbour's soul, or out of spite. Neighbours could be denounced for being seen to smile at the mention of the Virgin Mary, or for eating bacon and onions having forgotten it was a day of abstinence. The Inquisition relied on informants, but then so did every secular judicial system in Europe.

The fear of being denounced was sufficient to induce thousands to denounce themselves. In the year 1486, 2,400 confessed in the city of Toledo alone. As for the accused, when the tribunal deemed there was sufficient evidence, they were imprisoned, their children sometimes left to starve on the streets, their possessions, including pots, pans and old clothes, taken away to be sold at auction. If they did not freely confess, they were tortured, the details of their torment scrupulously noted down by a secretary, such as this one who in 1568 observed a poor woman stripped and bound, accused of not eating pork and of changing her linen on Saturdays.

> She was ordered to be placed on the rack. She said: 'Señores, why will you not tell me what I have to say? Señor, put me on the ground – have I not said that I did it all?' She was told to talk. She said: 'I don't remember – take me away – I did what the witnesses say.' She was told to tell in detail what the witnesses said. She said: 'Señor, as I have told you, I do not know for certain. I have said that I did all that the witnesses say. Señores, release me, for I do not remember.'

Pressed again and again to talk, the poor woman could only cry: 'Señores, for God's sake have mercy on me… Do you not see how these people are killing me? I did it – for God's sake let me go!'[4]

Eager to show how fair the Inquisition was, the accused who confessed under torture had to confirm their confession the following day as proof that the confession was not just extracted under duress but was true.

Once they had been found guilty, a date was fixed for the auto-da-fé, a formal announcement of the sentence passed by the Inquisition (from the Latin *actus de fide*, literally 'act of faith'). The autos-da-fé could be semi-private ceremonies in a church, or – and these are the ones with which the Spanish Inquisition is forever associated – spectacular day-long events. During the sixteenth century, they became increasingly elaborate and therefore expensive, and for that reason they were held infrequently (Granada, for instance, held fifteen autos-da-fé between 1549 and 1593, one every three years). But those that were held were unforgettable. Thousands attended these great spectacles.

The day began at dawn with prayers and Mass. It was followed by a military-style procession of the inquisitors, the black and white robed friars, and civic dignitaries on horseback, dragging the heretics by ropes tied round their necks. Crowds thronged the streets and jeered as the barefoot men and women, holding candles and wearing Ku Klux Klan-like tall paper hats on which were written the details of their crimes, filed by. Those condemned to die were sometimes gagged to prevent them crying out. Bringing up the rear was the Grand Inquisitor dressed in purple. The procession entered the plaza; the 'reconciled', those who had confessed their loyalty to Judaism or heresy, mounted a wooden platform specially erected for the auto-da-fé. On a separate wooden stage opposite, the inquisitors 'stood up and began to call each one by name, saying, "Is X here?" The penitent raised his candle and said, "Yes",' recalled a witness to one auto-da-fé of 750 men and women held on a February Sunday in Toledo in 1486.

> There in public they read all the things in which he had Judaized. When this was over they were publicly allotted penance and ordered to go in procession for six Fridays, disciplining their body with scourges of hemp cord, barebacked, unshod and bareheaded; and they were to fast for those six Fridays.[5]

They were also banned from public office, and forbidden to wear 'silk or scarlet or coloured cloths or gold or silver or pearls or coral or any jewels'.

Apart from doing public penance the 'reconciled' might be physically beaten, fined or exiled. But those who refused to recant were led out of the city on donkeys to be 'relaxed' as night fell. At this last moment, the recalcitrant were given one more chance. If they showed 'some token of repentance', they were 'mercifully' strangled before the flames had a chance to roast them alive.

The public auto-da-fé was designed to instil fear and awe. No one who witnessed such an event could fail to understand the might of the Church and the dire consequences of a failure to conform to its beliefs and practices.

In 1492 Islam lost its last tenuous foothold in Spain. Ferdinand and Isabella's soldiers completed their conquest of the Emirate of Granada, in the foothills of the Sierra Nevada mountains of southern Spain. A vast silver cross was erected on the tallest tower of Granada's Alhambra Palace, which had been one of the architectural wonders of al-Andalus. The Christian Reconquista of Spain was complete.

That same year Queen Isabella appointed as her new confessor a 56-year-old Franciscan friar, Francisco Jiménez de Cisneros. Like his 72-year-old predecessor Torquemada, Cisneros was completely in tune with his monarchs' desire to unify Spain by asserting its Christian identity. Tall and slim, with an angular face, aquiline nose and deep-set eyes, Cisneros had all the markings of the unyielding ascetic. 'He avoids human contact and prefers the solitude of the forests,' noted Pietro Martire, a contemporary of Cisneros and observer of the royal court. 'He walks barefoot through the silent woods, dressed in sackcloth, content with little, sleeping on straw. In private he punishes his flesh with vigils and castigations.'[6]

Not long after his appointment as confessor, a royal decree was posted and read out in every city, town and village of Spain and in the Kingdom of Sicily, which was under direct Spanish rule:

> We order all Jews and Jewesses of whatever age they may be, who live, reside, and exist in our said kingdoms and lordships ... that by the end of the month of July next of the present year [1492], they depart from all of these our said realms and lordships, along with their sons and daughters, menservants and maidservants, Jewish familiars, those who are great as well as the lesser folk, of whatever age they may be, and they shall not dare to return to those places, nor to reside in them, nor to live in any part of them, neither temporarily on the way to somewhere else nor in any other manner, under pain [sic] that if they do not perform and comply with this command and should be found in our said kingdom and lordships and should in any manner live in them, they incur the penalty of death and the confiscation of all their possessions by our Chamber of Finance.

As Christopher Columbus noted in his diary, the order came 'the same month in which their Majesties [Ferdinand and Isabella] ... gave me the order to undertake with sufficient men my expedition of discovery to the Indies'. Isabella ordered that the 'Indians', as the conquered inhabitants were called, should be Christianized and therefore should be treated as equal to Christian subjects in Spain, in marked contrast to the recalcitrant non-Christian Jews. But Columbus and the Spanish settlers notoriously ignored her order; Indians were enslaved and treated in the subhuman fashion that slaves usually are.

The Jews were to be expelled, announced Ferdinand and Isabella 'so that there will not be any place where they further offend our holy faith, and corrupt those whom God has until now most desired to preserve'. It was no more than what the Protestant reformer Martin Luther would later advocate in 1543. According to the Edict of Expulsion, or Alhambra Decree as it is also known, Jews could either convert or leave Spain. Their Catholic Majesties were as punctilious as Edward I had been when he expelled the Jews of England in 1290 (see Chapter 10). In the three months' grace that was given to them before they were exiled, Spain's Jews were told that they 'may travel and be safe, they may enter, sell, trade, and alienate all their movable and rooted possessions and dispose of them freely and at their will' – at knockdown prices of course, since they had so little time in which to sell their homes, land, livestock and businesses. The monarchs' guarantee of protection did not anyway amount to much. Convinced that Jews had swallowed their gold and diamonds for safekeeping, robbers stabbed them to death in order to extract their valuables from their stomachs.

There are thought to have been between 250,000 and 800,000 Jews in 1490s Spain; some historians even put the number as high as 1 million. Of those, about half converted. The other half preferred exile. Many thousands died of famine and plague on their journey in search of a new homeland. Most of Europe did not want them; France, which had expelled Jews in 1394, now expelled them from Provence, a territory which had just been incorporated into the French kingdom.

Spanish and Italian ship captains treated the expelled Jews as brutally as English sea captains had done, charging them vast sums for their passage, only to rob or abandon them to drown at sea. According to an Italian Jew writing in 1495, just three years after the expulsion, 120,000 Jews (the numbers may be exaggerated) paid the King of Portugal 'one ducat for every soul, and the fourth part of all the merchandize they had carried thither' for a safe haven.[7] Six months later the king reneged on the deal. He enslaved the adults and banished 700 children to a remote island, São Tomé, off the coast of Africa, where they all died. In Europe only Poland continued its record of tolerance towards the Jews.

Many Jews made for Morocco. Only twenty-seven years earlier in 1465 Muslims had massacred the Jews in Morocco's main city of Fez during a revolt against the sultan. The new sultan, however, offered a home to the exiled Jews. But once arrived they found neither accommodation nor much welcome. They were attacked by gangs and were forced to camp in the fields surrounding the city. Possibly as many as 20,000 Jews died from disease and hunger.

After such hardships in exile, many Jews gave up, returned to Spain and converted – even if it was only a token conversion – joining the thousands of Jews who had from the start preferred conversion to exile.

For Jews in Europe, whether converts or still practising, Christendom had once again shown its ugly face. It was made all the uglier by contrast with the tolerant age – perhaps becoming ever more golden in retrospect, but golden nonetheless – that their ancestors were said to have enjoyed when Muslims ruled al-Andalus. And it was yet again the Muslim world that now proved itself the more tolerant.

The Ottoman emperor Sultan Bayezid II, ruler of what was becoming the most powerful state in the world, extended a formal invitation to the Sephardim, as Jews from Spain were called (Sefarad is the Hebrew name for Spain). He offered them tax remissions, and laid on ships to transport them to the cities of Salonica (Thessaloniki in today's Greece) and Smyrna (in modern Turkey). Since the Ottomans' welcome to Sephardic Jews was for economic rather than humanitarian reasons, their benign attitude had its limits, however. Existing Jewish and Christian communities within the empire were forcibly resettled in areas where they were thought to be needed, in Greece and Turkey and in other parts of the Balkans such as Bosnia and Serbia.

Spain's loss was the Ottoman Empire's gain. Sephardim were welcomed, though not necessarily by the indigenous Jewish communities, for their skill in banking, tax farming and commerce. They were also valued for their knowledge of how to manufacture gunpowder and artillery – technology which the Ottomans urgently needed in their battle against their Christian enemies on one side and their Muslim enemies, the Safavids of Iran, on the other. Indeed Sultan Bayezid marvelled at the stupidity of the Spanish monarchs for failing to appreciate how useful Jews were. 'How can you call Ferdinand of Aragon a wise king?' he asked. 'The same Ferdinand who impoverished his own land and enriched ours?'[8]

Though Islam's mathematicians and scientists far outstripped Christendom's – they had, for instance, developed an approximation of pi which Europe's mathematicians took another two centuries to arrive at – Sephardic Jews brought with them new skills, new technologies and new medical knowledge from Europe which were harbingers, had the

Ottomans but known it, of the coming dominance of Christian Europe and the stagnation and decline of the Ottoman Empire. Their expertise in textile manufacturing made Ottoman carpets the must-have item for every wealthy home from Sweden to Poland. They were skilled in the new printing press technology. The Ottomans, however, forbade printing in Turkish or Arabic characters thanks to the objections of the calligraphers/scribes and ulema, who were concerned to protect their respective monopolies on the creation of books and the understanding of the Quran. The ban was not lifted until the eighteenth century. Who knows how much intellectual creativity was stifled as a result.

But in comparison to Christendom, the Ottoman Empire was a model of tolerance and would be used in later centuries to shame Christendom. Even Christian visitors to the Ottoman Empire were impressed. By the early part of the fifteenth century, the Turks' reputation for tolerance towards Jews was well established. Isaac Zarfati, who had been born in Germany but became Chief Rabbi of Edirne in today's north-west Turkey, wrote to his fellow Jews in Europe, urging them to escape 'the tyrannical laws, the compulsory baptisms and the banishments':

> Turkey is a land wherein nothing is lacking, and where, if you will, all shall yet be well with you. Is it not better for you to live under Muslims than under Christians? Here every man may dwell at peace under his own vine and fig tree. Here you are allowed to wear the most precious garments. In Christendom, on the contrary, you dare not even venture to clothe your children in red or in blue, according to our taste, without exposing them to the insult of being beaten black and blue, or kicked green and red, and therefore are ye condemned to go about meanly clad in sad coloured raiment.[9]

Seven years after Jews had been forced to convert or leave the Iberian Peninsula, it was the turn of the Muslims of Granada, which was now part of Ferdinand and Isabella's Kingdom of Castile. Muslims no longer belonged in a Spain which was uniting around its Christian identity. In

1499, Cisneros – as Isabella's confessor and political adviser the most powerful Catholic in Spain – accompanied the court of the Spanish Inquisition to Granada. There he ordered that all its Muslims should be forcibly converted and its Arabic manuscripts publicly burned. At least 5,000 precious manuscripts went up in flames; only medicinal treatises were exempted. The wonders of Muslim Granada's intellectual achievements were reduced to ashes.

Cisneros had destroyed any prospect of Christian and Muslim co-existence. Muslims broke out in revolt and assassinated one of Cisneros' agents. It was the excuse Ferdinand and Isabella needed to break the treaty made when they conquered Granada in 1492. Under the terms of the treaty, they had promised Granada's Muslims that they would be allowed to follow their own religious and social customs, preserve their mosques and religious institutions, and speak their own Arabic tongue. But in 1502 Islam was officially banned in Granada and in the whole of the Kingdom of Castile. 'There is now no one in the city who is not a Christian, and all the mosques are churches,' Cisneros reported triumphantly.

In a ghastly repetition of the fate of Spain's Jews, around 300,000 Muslims in Castile (there were probably between 500,000 and 600,000 Muslims in Spain, of which about half lived in the Kingdom of Castile) were now forced to 'choose' between conversion and exile. Thousands emigrated to North Africa. The majority, however, agreed to be baptized, though many converted in name only. Those Muslims, who were desperately trying to cling on to their home while not rejecting their Muslim faith, were given succour by a North African jurist. In 1504 Ahmad ibn Abu Jum'ah issued a fatwa specifically instructing Moriscos, Spanish Muslims who had converted to Christianity, on how to practise Islam in secret. The fatwa allowed them to eat pork, drink wine, marry their daughters to Christians. When obliged to do something that violated Islamic law, Moriscos were told to 'abhor it in your hearts, so that you would do otherwise, if you were able'. Moriscos could even curse Muhammad publicly so long as they loved him in their hearts. Maimonides had offered the same religious leniency to Jews who converted to Islam so as to escape Almohad persecution in the late twelfth century (see Chapter 7). He was opposed by most rabbis just as Ahmad ibn Abu Jum'ah was opposed by most jurists. Nonetheless the fatwa was followed for over a century by generations of Moriscos.

Increasing numbers of Moriscos were, however, suspected of secretly maintaining their Muslim faith and were subjected to the Inquisition. If anything, Spanish Christian hostility to Muslims in al-Andalus was even greater than it had been to Jews.

In the light of the West's global dominance from at least the eighteenth century on, it is easy to forget that until then Islamdom, not Christendom, was the dominant global power, economically and intellectually. The Ottoman Empire had become all the more menacing after its conquest of Constantinople in 1453 which brought to an end the Byzantine Empire and with it the last remnants of Christian rule in the Middle East. But in 1571, Don Juan of Austria, half-brother of King Philip II of Spain, scored a notable victory against the Ottomans. At the Battle of Lepanto he led a combined Catholic fleet of Spanish, Venetian, Papal and Maltese galleys to its first naval victory over the Ottomans. Cervantes, author of one of the classics of Western literature, *Don Quixote*, was badly wounded in the battle and lost a hand. The Catholic Church still celebrates the victory as the feast day of Our Lady of the Rosary.

Christian Spain celebrated with vindictive triumphalism. Moriscos were banned from public office and forbidden to speak Arabic or wear any form of distinctive dress. They were vilified as traitors and heretics still secretly loyal to the Ottoman Empire and Islam. For some time churchmen had been arguing that Moriscos should be expelled from Spain. Foremost amongst them was one of the most powerful men in Spain, the 79-year-old Archbishop of Valencia, Juan de Ribera. Like many churchmen, Ribera had also considered enslaving or castrating Moriscos, but expulsion was the kindest option and it was welcomed by the Spanish king, Philip III (Philip II's son) and his Christian subjects. A display of Spanish Catholic dominance was naturally appealing but so was Ribera's argument that the Moriscos' impounded wealth would boost the royal coffers.

On 11 September 1609 an order from King Philip III was read out to the Moriscos of Valencia, where they formed the majority of the peasantry. They were to pack their bags and leave Spain in order to ensure the 'conservation and security' of the realm. After the Moriscos of Valencia, it was the turn of the Moriscos of every city in Spain to receive their expulsion orders. From September 1609 to August 1610 an estimated quarter of a million to 1 million human beings were driven from their homes, leaving untilled fields, half deserted villages and towns, vandalized mosques and bathhouses behind them.

One in six of those expelled are thought to have died on their way to a new home. Thousands ended their days as galley slaves; others sold their children into slavery in exchange for bread. Many who survived the journey arrived at their destination starving and destitute; farmers had forced them to pay for sitting in the shade of a tree or drinking from a river; they had been robbed of all their possessions. The majority headed across the Mediterranean to the Barbary Coast of North Africa. Some of them would become the redoubtable Barbary pirates (or Corsairs), preying on Christian ships, in part to make a living but also in revenge for their expulsion from Spain.

By early 1614 Spain had truly become a Catholic country. Scarcely a Muslim or Morisco remained to bear witness to the glories that had been al-Andalus. Juan de Ribera, the man most associated with the expulsion, was canonized in 1960.

For the Church the expulsion marked a rare victory at a time when it was waging war against the greatest enemy it had ever yet encountered – an enemy from within its own Christian ranks. It was as though, having become accustomed to the fortifying presence of an enemy – either within or on its doorstep – the European order found and created its best and most lasting enemy yet: itself, through schism.

Western Europe descended to a level of intolerance that would spark off over a hundred years of war and leave Europe with millions dead, its cities and villages in ruins.

CHAPTER 13

THE REFORMATION'S WAR AGAINST THE CATHOLIC CHURCH

'Whoever contends that punishing heretics and blasphemers is wrong is himself guilty of blasphemy.'

– Calvin, *Defensio Orthodoxae Fidei*, 1554

'To kill a man is not to protect a doctrine, but it is to kill a man.'

– Castellio, *Contra libellum Calvini* [Against Calvin's Booklet], 1555

Augsburg, southern Germany, court records 1524: A Protestant glazier, Bartholomew Nussfelder, objected to the Catholic ritual of blessing the water in the baptismal font and told the monk to bless the water in German rather than Latin 'so that we can understand it too'. When the monk refused, Nussfelder shouted at the monk to get out of the church 'for you are turning us away from the Gospel truth that they preach to us every day. You're keeping us from it.'[1] Nussberger then grabbed the devotional book the monk was reading and threw it into the font, while Protestant women in the Church yelled that 'someone should throw the monk in the holy water too'.

Augsburg, court records 1527: a Catholic serving girl outraged Protestants taking Communion in St George's Church by snatching up a piece of the Communion bread with her mouth and shouting, 'Ei, you cursed Lord's supper, choke it down alone, and you can shit it out alone.'

A shoemaker and his servant crept into the churchyard and cloisters of Augsburg's cathedral and threw cow's blood over the funerary plaques in the churchyard and cloister which was 'decorated with figures, crucifixes ... Our Dear Lady Mary and images of the saints'.

The records are littered with such accounts of quarrels breaking out between Catholics and the new Protestants. The court clerks were careful to note down in each instance whether the information was extracted from witnesses 'without torture' or 'with torture' and if with torture, whether it was 'with weights' or 'without weights'. These 'new Protestants' were Christian critics of the Catholic Church who followed the teachings of the monk Martin Luther. They only began to call themselves Protestants in 1529 when Lutheran princes within the Holy Roman Empire formally protested at the empire's decision to treat Lutherans as 'heretics'.

In Augsburg's narrow alleyways, alongside its canals, in its squares where fountains splashed with running water, along the broad cobbled street lined with the new Renaissance palaces of the city's merchants and bankers, neighbours were playing out on a petty scale the profound and irrevocable splintering of Christendom. Once every inhabitant of the Western Christian world had been by default a Catholic. Now throughout the towns and villages of Europe, from England, Scotland, Sweden, to the Low Countries (Holland and Belgium), France and the Holy Roman Empire, a fissure had opened up between Catholics and Protestants. States too were dividing along confessional lines between those governed by Protestant and those by Catholic rulers. And Protestantism itself was breaking up into rival denominations ranging from the more moderate, conservative Lutherans, to the more radical followers of Huldrych Zwingli and of John Calvin, to the even more radical Anabaptists.*

---

* Anabaptists believed in adult baptism and that Christianity had to return to its New Testament roots; that meant a complete separation of Church and State which precluded any involvement in civil government or military action. Anabaptists are the spiritual forebears of the Baptists, the Quakers, the Amish, the Hutterites and the Mennonites.

Friends, neighbours, trading partners, customers and servants had become 'heretics' to each other. That, of course, did not always mean they had become enemies, or if they had theoretically, that relations turned really nasty. It was inconceivable for many to break the relationships of a lifetime for the sake of what still seemed to be religious differences that could be resolved. Cross-confessional marriages were fairly common; Protestants and Catholics still drank together even if religious disputes did break out. Many neighbours made their 'ad hoc arrangements', their 'private treaties of internal toleration', as the Reformation historian Norman Jones described them. Life still had to be lived. Lutheran goldsmiths, engravers, printers and painters even produced objects for Catholic worship and devotion.

And compromises did emerge. The entangled and complicated systems devised to enable Catholics and Protestants to live together in relative peace were testimony to how serious each community felt the divide to be. The *schuilkerk* (the Dutch word for clandestine church) allowed Catholics, Lutherans, Mennonites and even Jews to practise their faith more or less freely, as long as they did not advertise the fact. Places of worship were built to look like private homes; in some cases services did indeed take place at home – in Protestant-ruled England and Scotland for instance Mass was held in private chapels built by the Catholic gentry. The most complicated arrangement was the simultaneum, the shared use of a church by both Lutherans and Catholics. It often involved a division of the Church building and an elaborate timetable specifying when each faith was to hold its services. In Alsace (in today's north-eastern France) there was even a trimultaneum, with a Catholic, Lutheran and Calvinist congregation sharing one church.

Periodically, though, the smell of singed flesh rose up from the market places and public squares of Europe's towns as 'heretics' (whether Catholic or Protestant depended on what branch of Christianity the ruler espoused), were burned to death. Crowds screamed abuse and hurled excrement at the condemned bound on their stakes. In England's city of Exeter, onlookers threw sticks and branches into the fire to encourage the flames licking at the 'whoreson heretic'. Unwittingly they were thereby doing the victim a favour; the larger the fire, the more likely it was that the victim would die from carbon monoxide poisoning rather than from the unbelievable pain of extensive burns in the far longer drawn out agony of a smaller fire. Between the mid sixteenth and the mid seventeenth century about 5,000 men and women, Catholics, Protestants and Anabaptists, were executed by their fellow Christians, notably in England, France and the Low Countries (today's Holland and Belgium) – a surprisingly small number perhaps, until it is added to the 11 million or more who were killed in the so-called 'wars of religion', the series of conflicts which engulfed the whole of Europe from Italy through central Europe to Scandinavia during this period.

The 'wars of religion', beginning with the revolt of German peasants in 1525, and ending with the English civil wars of 1642–51, were characterized by the participants as religious, but they were more than that. Essentially, they were a battle for power between the old and the new world order, between a world where authority rested in the Church and in the landed feudal aristocracy, and a new world of urban merchant power and self-determination. This struggle is what gave the Reformation and the 'wars of religion' their particular ferocity.

The religious issues at stake were indeed of life and death importance to Christians – questions of doctrinal truths and the very nature of the Christian God they should believe in. But the choice between being Catholic or being on the side of the Church's critics, the 'protesters' or Protestants, also involved making a fundamental choice between political loyalty and rebellion. In the Holy Roman Empire the Catholic emperor was ranged against Protestant princes and city councils like Augsburg's, fighting for their independence from imperial rule. Protestantism and the birth of the nation and nationalism went hand in hand. And of course it was in both Catholic and Protestant rulers' interests to ratchet up hostility to the other. Intolerance was the natural response to the enemy.

Paradoxically, it was the very strength of the Catholic Church as an institution, an institution which had no counterpart in the Muslim world, that proved its downfall. It became too rich and sleek, more concerned with maintaining itself than in upholding the original intentions and values of Christianity itself.

That was the substance of the monk Martin Luther's list of ninety-five points on which he disagreed with the Church (too many, I'm afraid, for him to have been able to attach them to Wittenberg's cathedral door in 1517, popular tradition notwithstanding).

Luther was pursuing the objectives shared by all fundamentalists. Like the Sunni Muslims, Ibn Hanbal and Ibn Taymiyya (see Chapters 4 and 10), Luther wanted to rid his religion of all its false accretions and corruptions and return it to its fundamentals from which it had so lamentably strayed. In his eyes, the institution of the Church had become too worldly. Furthermore, contrary to Christ's intentions, it had taken upon itself the role of having exclusive access to God. True Christians needed no priestly elite to mediate between themselves and their God, Luther argued. It was the Word of God, as revealed in the Bible, that was the supreme authority in all matters of doctrine and practice, not the pope – the Antichrist as Luther and his followers called him – and his priests.

The Protestant reformers' bid to dethrone the pope and the Church, to take religion out of the hands of the Church and its elite body of religious professionals, and return it to where it belonged, the 'priesthood of all believers', was perfectly suited to the changing political and economic circumstances of sixteenth-century Europe. It found a welcome hearing amongst a rising merchant class who were beginning to assert their power against a landed aristocracy; and it was attractive to a peasantry that was also fighting to escape from the feudal stranglehold of their aristocratic landlords.

In what would be the largest popular revolt against the old order that Europe would ever see until the French Revolution, German peasants, inspired by the principles of the reformers, rose up against Church and feudal lord alike, demanding the abolition of serfdom, the right to elect and dismiss their priests and a reduction in the tithes – the tax on their crops which the Church exacted from the peasants.

Luther – like Ibn Taymiyya, a respecter of authority as long as it was in what he considered to be the right hands – was in fact so appalled by this threat to social order, that he sided with the nobles and condemned the peasants as 'faithless, perjured, disobedient, rebellious, murderers, robbers, and blasphemers' in his diatribe 'Against the Rioting Peasants' of 1525.

Luther, though excommunicated by the Church and expelled from the Holy Roman Empire by Charles V, had conceived of himself as a reformer, not a revolutionary. He had condemned the peasants' revolt which was put down in 1525 and had cost between 100,000 and 300,000 peasants' and farmers' lives. Nevertheless he and his fellow reformers contributed to a revolution, whether wittingly or not. Their beliefs were invoked by merchants, peasants and all those struggling to assert their power against the old order.

Protestantism also informed the battles of the motley collection of 300-odd duchies, principalities and imperial cities ruled by secular as well as ecclesiastical princes who were fighting to liberate themselves from the Holy Roman Empire and the pope.

For many of these mini-statelets, Protestantism, which was so opposed to the imperial authority of the Church, also meant liberation from the Catholic emperor, Charles V. In theory, Charles, scion of the Habsburgs, the ugliest dynasty ever to reign in Europe, was astonishingly powerful. He ruled the Holy Roman Empire and the Spanish Empire, which was growing fat on the vast hoards of gold and silver plundered from its conquests in the Americas. But he was surrounded by enemies. France, England and much of Protestant Europe were determined to put a stop to the most powerful monarch in Europe. As a result they sided with the Protestant breakaway principalities within the Holy Roman Empire and also with Charles's external enemy, the Ottomans, with whom they periodically attempted to create an alliance. Negotiations always came to nothing, however – each side considering the other to be demanding too much.

As far as Charles V was concerned, and those rulers within the empire who supported him, every prince's 'defection' to Luther was a signal of revolt. Indeed, throughout the sixteenth and seventeenth centuries, Protestantism, for Catholics, meant revolt. In 1531 Charles V ordered that all Lutheran princes and cities must renounce their new faith and return to the Catholic fold. Furthermore, they had to restore all Church and monastic property which they had seized – a serious matter since the revenue generated from such property was considerable; so was the tax revenue that would be lost with the reinstatement of Catholicism since Catholic clergy were exempt from taxes.

In 1537, only twenty years after Luther had written his ninety-five theses, the council which ruled Augsburg, the scene of so many petty but bitter interfaith squabbles, was taken over by Protestants. The old Catholic patrician elite, who were loyal to their Catholic emperor Charles V, had been powerless to resist the pressure from the newly turned Protestant merchants, weavers and goldsmiths.

Augsburg was witness to the astonishing speed with which the Protestant movement was winning converts. From the middling merchant to the weaver who lived crammed into one of the city's narrow alleys with his wife, children, maid and journeymen, the majority of the city had turned Protestant in just two decades. The speed of the conversion to Protestantism was in part due to the new technology of printing. Before Gutenberg and his printing press, news of Luther's 'heresy' would have circulated slowly. But only three years after Luther had written his ninety-five theses, Europe's printing presses had produced about 300,000 copies of his works, which were avidly read and passionately debated amongst the newly literate urban classes. This was in marked contrast to the Ottoman Empire, where printing was very tightly restricted and literacy rates very low (see Chapter 15).

Hans Welser, member of one of the richest merchant-financier families of Augsburg, had become a fervent follower of the Swiss Protestant reformer Huldrych Zwingli. In 1537 Welser was elected as one of the city's two mayors. Coins of the time show him sporting a long full beard and wearing the customary flat bonnet. He was 'a brash young man who would make a better military office than mayor', according to the brewer

Georg Siedler. Admittedly, Siedler would not have been best pleased with Welser's decree that craftsmen should not waste their money on drink during the week.[2] It was one of the many measures that Welser would introduce so that the city could become a city modelled along true Christian lines – or what he believed those were.

Immediately on obtaining office, the new mayor ordered workmen to 'tear down all the altars, paintings, panels, lamps, and more in all the churches in the city'. Protestants were just as austere as traditionalist Sunni Muslims in condemning images: images were idolatrous. Westerners who were rightly appalled at the Taliban's destruction of the magnificent Buddhas in Afghanistan in March 2001 should remember the destruction wrought by fundamentalist Protestants in the sixteenth and seventeenth centuries.

Protestants in Augsburg stripped the churches of their sensuous trappings. Their brightly coloured, verging on the garish, frescoes disappeared under whitewash, statues were smashed or removed. On the orders of the council 'all Roman Catholic holidays were denounced from the pulpits and only Christmas, New Year and Annunciation Day were to be celebrated'.[3] All Catholic clerics were dismissed, Mass was prohibited and monasteries were dissolved. Church property was taken over by the council. The economic incentive for turning Protestant should not be underestimated; those patricians who stuck to their Catholic faith were frozen out of the means of acquiring wealth and exercising power. The Church had brandished the sword of intolerance against Jews, Muslims, and heretics/critics in order to increase its own authority and power. Now Protestants did the same against Catholics.

In 1541 the council decreed that the people of Augsburg

> . . . will until further notice hold no dance, whether at weddings, engagements, or otherwise. There will be no courting with string instruments, singing, piping, or drummings in the streets whether during processions to Church or otherwise. And everyone should also refrain from all cheering, yelling and screaming, and from indecent or shameful songs, gestures, and talk, on the streets and

> inside ... likewise, all musicians, waffle sellers, acrobats, and ridiculous, wanton comedians or dancers should stay out of the inns and guildhalls...

The council further reiterated its previous ordinances banning 'blasphemy, vanity, usury ... idleness, going for walks and gambling during the sermon'.[4] It was clear that in following the precepts of the Bible, all Augsburg's citizens must eschew the sensuous pleasures that the Church of Rome so tolerantly allowed its laypeople.

Catholics suspected of leaving the city in order to attend Mass in adjacent territories which remained loyal to the Catholic Church could be arrested and interrogated. Augsburg required all its citizens to take an oath of citizenship in which they swore to admonish 'fraternally and modestly' anyone whom they observed committing a sin, and to report them to the magistrates if they did not improve their ways.[5] No behaviour was beyond the reach of the Zwinglian council. Augsburg was the sort of theocratic state that Dunstan, the archbishop-leader of the Witan in tenth-century England, and the Sunni Muslim Ibn Taymiyya in fourteenth-century Damascus, could only have dreamed of.

In fact, reformers, like the Zwinglians in Augsburg, and Calvin a hundred miles away in the Swiss city of Geneva, wanted to create societies akin to Islam's ideal model of the state, which had been established by Muhammad in Medina. The political state run according to religious principles under a religious leader is the model that Muslim countries today such as Iran and Saudi Arabia emulate and that Islamic fundamentalists everywhere are determined to establish.

Paradoxically, although Protestantism is credited with effecting the final separation of Church and State, its more radical leaders wanted to knit the religious and the political back together again, with, of course, the religious controlling the political. By dethroning the pope and his priests and depriving them of their roles as sole spokesmen for God, the duty of being a Christian fell more heavily on every individual. It was up to ordinary Christians, not religious professionals, to infuse the world with Christianity. And that required participation in the world, not a withdrawal from it into a life of monkish asceticism and prayers. Calvin's Geneva, Zwinglian Augsburg, even Puritan England, were precisely attempts to weld the religious and political worlds back together, to establish a 'city on a hill', a theocratic state truly modelled along Christian lines.

In 1536 the city of Geneva had revolted against its Catholic prince-bishop and turned Protestant. In the cantons of Switzerland, as in the rest of Europe, Protestantism was harnessed to the struggle for independence from Catholic religious and political rule. Protestants took control of Geneva's council and expelled the bishop and most of the Catholic clergy, monks and nuns. The council invited John Calvin, one of the most eminent and brilliant Protestant theologians of his time, to draw up the laws for their Protestant city. He had broken with the Catholic Church in 1533 and been forced to flee his native France where the Catholic king had embarked on a virulent campaign to eliminate the growing numbers of French Protestants.

Calvin was a lawyer and self-taught theologian. Small and frail but intransigent and irascible, he stares out from Titian's portrait of him, his wide, dark eyes fixed on the world beyond, a gaunt, unforgiving ascetic. Under Calvin's control Geneva became 'the most perfect school of Christ on earth since the days of the apostles', according to his disciple John Knox, the founding father of Presbyterianism/Calvinism in Scotland. But to create the perfect Christian city meant, as in Augsburg, exerting a tight control over the behaviour of Geneva's citizens and cracking down on anyone who deviated or was even suspected of deviating from the religious path set by Calvin.

The city council banned dancing, card playing, expensive clothes and heavy drinking. Fines were levied for non-attendance at Sunday church services, or for not remaining in church to hear the sermon. A court composed of Calvinist pastors met every Thursday to correct the beliefs and behaviour of any citizen deemed to have strayed from the correct Christian path. During the course of Calvin's fifteen-year rule, up to seven per cent of the adult population of Geneva were 'denounced' each year by a neighbour, a passerby or a customer (Zwinglian Augsburg had also encouraged informants) and hauled before the court where they could be fined – or perhaps worse, excommunicated, deprived of partaking in the Lord's Supper. A butcher who could only say his prayers in Latin (a sure sign of a Catholic), women who still venerated the Virgin Mary or prayed to the saints or were seen dancing, a barber who shaved a 'papal crown' (a tonsure) on the head of a priest, a tradesman who sold rosaries and a Protestant who married a Catholic were all brought before the court and punished.[6]

Not surprisingly, there was some opposition to 'these fucking renegade priests' as a placard stuck on a church pulpit called the Calvinists.[7] But attempts to overturn Calvinist rule in Geneva failed; the ringleaders of what was seen as an attempted coup on the city council were decapitated. Calvin became more powerful than ever.

In 1553 he consigned Michael Servetus (Miguel Serveto) to the flames. Calvin, pre-eminent opponent of the Catholic Church, had allied himself with his erstwhile persecutors, the King of France, Henry II, and the Grand Inquisitor of France, the Dominican friar Matthieu D'Ory. They were at one in their determination to rid the world of Michael Servetus – a Spanish theologian, physician and scientist, and possibly a Marrano, a Christian convert from Judaism. Servetus had denied one of the most fundamental tenets of Christianity. The Trinitarian God was, he said, 'a Cerberus with three heads' (Cerberus is the three-headed dog in Greek mythology that guards the gates of the underworld). Servetus had published anonymously in France what was considered a shocking blasphemy. But Calvin provided the Inquisition with proof of the author's identity by giving them some of the increasingly furious letters that he and Servetus had written to each other. Servetus escaped from France and headed for Naples. Unwisely, he stopped off in Geneva, where he was arrested. Calvin himself drew up the charges of grave heresy and blasphemy. Servetus was condemned by the court to be burned at the stake.

To add to his ordeal, while in prison awaiting his death, Servetus was visited by his insufferably self-righteous and self-absorbed persecutor Calvin. Having failed to convince Servetus of his blasphemous errors, Calvin wrote:

> I reminded him gently how I spared no effort … to win him to Our Lord even to the point of hazarding my own life [a reference

> to the letters the two men had exchanged and which Calvin had handed over to the Inquisition]… Then afterwards, saying that I put aside everything that concerned me personally I prayed him to devote his efforts to asking pardon of the Son of God whom he had disfigured with his fantasies.[8]

After which, his conscience clear, Calvin bade Servetus farewell. Calvin further demonstrated his capacity for mercy by suggesting Servetus should be beheaded, a less agonizing way to die than death by burning. Servetus was burned alive, however, along with his book, on 27 October 1553.

He was in fact the only person to be burned as a heretic under Calvin's rule. But all the leading reformers approved of Servetus's execution and wrote to Calvin to congratulate him; so did several Catholics. Luther had died seven years earlier but Philip Melanchthon, who succeeded Luther as intellectual leader of the Lutheran Reformation, called it 'a pious example, which deserved to be remembered to all posterity'. The State had inflicted the death penalty on those denying the doctrine of the Trinity since at least the time of the Christian Roman emperor Justinian in the sixth century. Western Europe assumed that it was the monarch's duty to enforce religious uniformity and persecute the heretic, as long as the heretic was the 'right' heretic. As Calvin said, 'Those who would spare heretics and blasphemers are themselves blasphemers … devotion to God's honour should be preferred to all human concerns and as often as His glory is at stake we should expunge from memory our mutual humanity.'[9] In handing over Servetus to the authorities for execution, Calvin was doing what was right; to tolerate Servetus would have been considered morally wrong.

But voices of criticism soon began to be heard. Sebastian Castellio, a French Protestant theologian and former close friend and protégé of Calvin's, was bitterly opposed to the burning of Servetus. It was Castellio who launched the debate on religious toleration which would be pursued through the sixteenth, seventeenth and eighteenth centuries by Milton, Locke, Pierre Bayle and Voltaire amongst others.

Castellio used the same argument for tolerance that al-Ghazali, considered to be one of Sunni Islam's greatest philosophers and theologians, had used at the end of the eleventh century: heresy was in the eye of the beholder. Since it was impossible to prove which among contradictory beliefs was the true one, 'I can discover no more than this', Castellio wrote, 'that we regard those as heretics with whom we disagree.'[10] For that reason alone, the death penalty should never be imposed.

Such an argument would fulfil all his critics' worst fears: it set Christendom along a path from which it could never return. Truth had once been unproblematic: it was what a higher authority declared was the case, consigning any contradictory claims to the bin of heresy. Now tolerationists were questioning whether we could ever be sure what the truth was. That scepticism would soon be applied to the very existence of God himself.

It was in fact Luther and Protestant reformers, including Calvin, who had themselves let the cat of tolerance out of the bag. They believed that the word of God as laid down in the Bible must be at the heart of Christianity, not the Church with all its rituals and its presumption of being God's interpreter. The reformers, however, like all fundamentalist traditionalists, had taken it for granted that the meaning of holy scripture was clear and self-evident. But the Bible, like the Quran, was susceptible to many interpretations and was by no means transparent. Taking control out of the hands of the Church and democratizing it led inexorably to an explosion of groups all claiming that they alone were privy to God's truths. Of course, Luther, like Calvin, was convinced that his 'side' would prevail because its truth would be recognized. But nonetheless, since they had both put a primacy on the individual's own relationship with God, it was hard to see why the individual who arrived at a different conclusion to Luther or Calvin should be burned to death.

Castellio argued that the death penalty should never be imposed because it was impossible to say who was a heretic. Luther had originally argued for toleration on the grounds that the State could not force people to believe against their own conscience, and therefore could not impose religious uniformity. In 1523 Luther wrote:

> As little as another can go to hell or heaven for me, so little can he believe or disbelieve for me. Since, then, belief or unbelief is a matter of every one's conscience, and since this is no lessening of the secular power, the latter should be content and attend to its own affairs and permit men to believe one thing or another, as they are able and willing, and constrain no one by force.[11]

But the German Peasants' War in 1525, which was fought in the name of Protestant principles and had threatened the entire feudal and Church system, had profoundly shocked Luther. When the Protestant ruler Philip of Hesse (in today's central Germany) asked the Lutherans for their advice on whether Anabaptists should be burned to death, Luther still proclaimed loudly for tolerance. 'Let everyone believe what he likes. If he is wrong he will have punishment enough in hellfire,' Luther wrote in 1527.[12] But he made two vital qualifications to this declaration of tolerance. Anabaptists should be sentenced to death if they were guilty of blasphemy or sedition. Luther's definition of blasphemy and sedition were very broad. In effect all heresy was seditious and blasphemous since it was a threat to both the political and the religious order. Religious pluralism meant dissension and, at its worst, treason, since to oppose the ruler's religion was to oppose the ruler. 'Although it seems cruel to punish them [Anabaptists] with the sword, it is crueller that they condemn the ministry of the Word and have no well-grounded doctrine and suppress the truth and in this way seek to subvert the civil order,' Luther wrote in a memorandum in 1531. Luther was to be even harsher in his attitude towards Jews (see next chapter). Philip of Hesse proved, however, to be far more tolerant than the Lutherans. Despite Luther's advice, and an imperial decree announcing that Anabaptists should be punished by death, no Anabaptist ever suffered the death penalty during his rule.*

Although some Christians were beginning to question whether heretics deserved the death penalty, the majority of Christians in the sixteenth

---

* This was the case even after radical Anabaptists had briefly taken over the town of Münster by force in 1534 and declared polygyny to be the ideal form of marriage.

century – both Catholic and Protestant – did not believe in religious tolerance, let alone religious pluralism. But that is what Protestant reformers had set in motion and that is what the Catholic Holy Roman Empire had to come to terms with.

War broke out in 1546 between the Catholic emperor Charles V and an alliance of Protestant princes and city states including Augsburg. The emperor's fight against these rebellious territories meant re-imposing his rule, which of course meant re-imposing Catholicism. The religious and the political did not always strictly map on to each other, however: Catholic France, despite its persecution of Huguenots (Calvinists), supported the Protestant league within the Holy Roman Empire for political reasons: to stop Charles V from becoming the dominant power in Europe.

But in 1555, after eleven years of fighting, Charles finally recognized that he was not strong enough to defeat the Lutheran princes and impose his Catholicism on the empire. Protestantism and the drive for independence had established themselves too firmly. Religious concessions on the part of the Catholic Holy Roman emperor were at the heart of the Peace of Augsburg, the settlement which put a temporary end to the wars.

The Peace of Augsburg allowed the rulers of states within the Holy Roman Empire to determine the religion – Lutheran or Catholic – of their own territories. In the sixty-five free imperial cities, both Lutherans and Catholics were free to practise their religions – a genuine religious pluralism. By recognizing that there was a choice that could be made between Lutheranism and Catholicism, the greatest Catholic ruler in Europe had publicly declared the defeat of the Catholic Church. The Church was no longer the universal voice of Christendom; it had lost its monopoly. Protestantism, or at least Lutheranism, was officially accepted as a Christian alternative to Catholicism. Calvinists were not included in the treaty, nor were any of the other more radical forms of Protestantism; the Anabaptists were, of course, completely beyond the pale for both Catholics and Protestants who, except for Philip of Hesse, persecuted them ruthlessly.

The Peace of Augsburg, guided as it was by the doctrine of *cuius regio, euius religio* (literally 'whose realm, his religion'), was certainly not a doctrine of religious freedom and pluralism. The citizens of each state had to adopt the religion of their rulers. Dissenters who would not subscribe to their ruler's religion were allowed to leave the territory. But if they stayed they could be banned from practising their own religion and banished, whipped or even executed. The Peace still acted within the framework of religious uniformity – but uniformity was now restricted to each separate territory rather than to the empire as a whole.

It was perhaps not surprising that the Church sought to reassert itself. In 1555, the year that the Peace of Augsburg officially ended the Catholic Church's monopoly over Western Christendom, the year that Calvin was at the height of his power in Geneva, the pope walled off a small area of Rome on the banks of the Tiber and forced the city's 2,000 Jews to live there. The Catholic Church had given its blessing to the ghetto.

CHAPTER 14

THE GHETTO

'They have surrounded us in with walls which are entirely shut in. Thus, no man can go forth to have any sort of intercourse with our neighbours...

Moreover, the Gentiles are changed against us from sweet to bitter, saying that it is forbidden for them to give us any assistance or domesticity or to help us in any way.'

– Petition from the Jews of Cori in Italy, *c.*1561[1]

ALMOST AS SOON AS he became pope in 1555, Paul IV, a grim old man of seventy-nine, issued a papal bull. Whatever tolerance the Church had previously extended to Jews was over, 'since it is absurd' (*cum nimis absurdum*), he declared, to allow Jews the ample toleration they had hitherto enjoyed – their 'own guilt has consigned them to perpetual servitude'.

The *Cum Nimis Absurdum* bull perfectly expressed the Church's new Counter-Reformation belligerence – its hard-line attitude towards Jews was part and parcel of a determination to assert and define itself against its Protestant enemies. That self-assertion was embodied in the new order of Jesuits, 'the soldiers of God', who were founding schools around Europe to instil the Catholic message and sailing to India and the Spanish Americas to convert the heathens; it was embodied too in the autos-da-fé, the processions and incense, and in the magnificent, swirling, luxuriant baroque architecture of its churches, which sought to contrast all the sensuous splendour of Catholicism with the austerity and joylessness of Protestantism.

The Church was fighting to preserve its dominance, even its very existence. Feeling vulnerable, it became that much more hostile to those it had always seen as its competitors and opponents, the Jews. Nowhere more so than in the Papal States which the pope himself ruled, but which were fighting to free themselves from papal rule and were simultaneously being fought over by Catholic France and the Catholic Holy Roman emperor.

Pope Paul's bull laid out how he would treat Jews in his Papal States, and how secular Catholic rulers elsewhere should treat Jews. It renewed all the Church's previous anti-Jewish rulings: Jews should wear distinguishing clothing (yellow hats for men, kerchiefs for women); they should not be allowed to employ Christian servants; Christians and Jews should not socialize with each other. But the bull went much further. In effect it deprived Jewish communities in the Papal States of all their rights. Jews were forbidden to own property; no more than one synagogue was permitted in each Papal State (in Rome alone nine synagogues were destroyed); Jews could only work as traders in second-hand clothing and food. And *Cum Nimis Absurdum* made one further pronouncement: Jews in the cities of the Papal States would now be separated by a wall from Christians. Pope Paul recommended that all secular rulers who had not already expelled Jews from their cities should do the same. He immediately commissioned ghetto walls to be built in Rome, and in his other states, where war did not prevent it. Jews had to pay for the construction.

The perception of the Jew as enemy which had always stained Christianity was only inflamed by the increasing focus on Christian doctrine made inevitable by the Reformation. In pre-Reformation Europe rulers and ruled were on the whole simply Christians, that is Catholics; it was a sine qua non and did not need thinking about. Now they had to choose between different types of Christianity, a choice which was intimately bound up with political questions of loyalty to a state. As Christian doctrinal correctness took on ever more salience, so also rose the importance of demarcating the other, the Jew. Jews across sixteenth-century Europe were forced to pack up their possessions and either move behind the newly constructed walls of the ghetto or leave Europe for good for the more tolerant Ottoman Empire.*

That Jews might sully the 'purity' of Christians had been a fear voiced by the Church for centuries. There was nothing new for either Muslims or Christians in the association of the enemy with the unclean, the filthy. To make the enemy physically repulsive is a sure way to incite a visceral feeling of loathing. Jews had been depicted as physically grotesque since at least the thirteenth century (see Chapter 9). Since 1179 it had been official Church policy that Jews and Christians should live in separate communities and not mix socially. And on the whole Jews, like all vulnerable minorities, preferred to live within their own communities. But the ghetto was different. Jews had no choice in the matter: they were forcibly made to live there. Between sunset and sunrise the ghetto's gates, which gave Jews access to the Christian world outside, were locked. And so Christians could sleep soundly, dreaming only of their purity. The Roman ghetto was not abolished until 1870, when the Kingdom of Italy took Rome away from the pope. But the ghetto would take on its most unbearable form in the twentieth century under the Nazis.

The walled ghetto was not, however, a papal innovation. Jews in Spain had been forced to live in segregated areas in the fifteenth century (see Chapter 12), as had Jews in Germany. Pope Paul was, in fact, following the example set by Venice, the greatest entrepôt city in Europe. Venice's Jewish population had swelled rapidly thanks to the numbers expelled from Spain in 1492 and the influx of Jewish refugees from war-torn northern Italy. In 1516 the authorities established a walled quarter near Venice's iron foundry (hence the name 'ghetto', from *gettare*, to pour or to cast), where Jews were compelled to live.

The ghetto was useful for any Christian ruler, Catholic or Protestant.

---

* Jews were not the only victims of the fatal alliance between faith and politics; Muslims were too. During the sixteenth century when the central European territories of Slavonia and Croatia were being fought over by the Holy Roman and Ottoman Empires, about 130,000 Muslims were forcibly driven to Ottoman-controlled Bosnia and Herzegovina with the Catholic Church's blessing.

It gave them total control of 'their' Jews and it satisfied Christian merchants and craftsmen who feared and resented their Jewish rivals.

The man who probably did more damage to Jews than any other religious Christian leader in history was the reformer incarnate, Martin Luther. He was, as the Luther historian Martin Brecht points out, one of the 'Church fathers' of anti-Semitism.[2] Luther had initially been certain that Jews would become 'Lutherans' (rather as Muhammad had been certain Jews would become Muslims). But when it became clear to Luther that the Jews were not convinced, he turned on these 'poisonous envenomed worms' in his viciously anti-Semitic work, 'On the Jews and Their Lies', written in 1543. 'We are at fault in not slaying them,' he wrote. '[They are] full of the devil's faeces ... which they wallow in like swine.' Luther urged Christians to set fire to synagogues and Jewish schools, destroy their houses, confiscate their holy books, forbid rabbis to teach, abolish safe conduct for Jews on the highways since they had no business to be in the countryside, deprive them of all their gold and silver and prohibit usury or expel them from the country. All this was 'to be done in honour of our Lord and of Christendom, so that God might see that we are Christians'. Four hundred years later the Nazi party displayed Luther's pamphlet 'On the Jews and Their Lies' during Nuremberg rallies. Hitler called Luther a great warrior, a true statesman and a great reformer. Himmler was also an admirer.

Under the promptings of Luther and Lutheran clergy, some of Germany's new Protestant converts, including the rulers of Saxony, Hanover and Brandenburg, had expelled Jews from their cities. In Protestant Frankfurt Jews were confined in a ghetto outside the city walls.

The concept of the ghetto began benignly enough. It owed its origins to the desire, or at least the alleged desire, of the Christian authorities to protect Jews from the 'insolence of the people'. That was certainly what Bishop Rüdiger Huzmann claimed when he created a separate walled area for Jews in the German city of Speyer in 1084 after a series of massacres in neighbouring towns. And that was the reason given by other towns in Germany and in south-western France who followed the bishop's example.

In the sixteenth century, however, prompted by Pope Paul IV, the ghetto became a prison rather than a defensive fortress. Its aim was not so much to protect as to ostracize. The ghetto gates might be locked to keep the Christian mobs out, but they were also locked to keep Jews in. On Sundays, Easter week and Christian holy days, Jews were often forbidden to leave the ghetto at any time – though this was again said to be for their own safety as these were the times when anti-Jewish passions were at their most intense. In Augsburg, Jews had been pushed outside the city walls. Any Jew who wanted to enter the city to do business or go shopping had to get written permission from the city authorities. Even then Jews had to be escorted by a guard who would take them only to the places approved in their note of written permission, after which they had to be immediately escorted out of the city.[3] By contrast, Jews in Prague also lived behind gates, but they had voluntarily chosen to do so and not been forcibly resettled; equally significantly they were not confined to an area with rigid boundaries.

One of the nastiest effects of the ghetto was the overcrowding and disease that came with it. The authorities usually refused to allow the ghetto to expand, even though the Jewish population increased. Houses became more and more cramped and dimly lit as they were subdivided, or had extra storeys added to them. 'Four to eight Christians would take up the space occupied by twenty Jews', according to the Venetian nobleman Paolo Loredan who had escaped the humiliations of being a Jew by converting to Catholicism.[4] In the same area of Rome where Catholics had once lived in roomy palaces, Jewish families were now forced to live in back-to-back houses shut off from all light, sharing a single room. By 1580 about 3,500 Roman Jews were crammed into an area of seven acres, consisting of two main streets, several small streets and alleyways, and a few meagre piazzas. Shortage of housing meant that Jews were paying three times as much rent as Christians living in similar conditions. The ghetto was a dark place of disease, with no gardens, no greenery and no space. When the Tiber flooded, as it did every year, the ghetto on its banks became a plague-ridden swamp.[5] Not surprisingly, ghettoes rapidly deteriorated into slums.

But the ghetto did have some benefits for Jews, even if they were unintended. Within their enclosed world, Jews could live relatively autonomously and relatively safe from the hostility, the insults and violence which always threatened them in the Christian world. For many the ghetto did not just ostracize them but kept them together as a culturally and religiously distinct community; it prevented them from melting away into the Christian world. The establishment of a ghetto meant that the state had at least recognized the existence of a Jewish community in the city and was not going to summarily expel them; after all, the reason England, France, Spain and much of the Holy Roman Empire did not have ghettoes was because there were no Jews to put there: they had all been expelled.

Nor were the boundaries between Jews and Christians completely impermeable. Jewish–Christian intellectual debate still continued. Christians often worked in the ghetto, as artisans, water carriers, street sweepers or servants and labourers – for one thing they could work on the Sabbath when Jews were forbidden to do so. Passover matzos were made by Christian bakers, Jewish soothsayers might have Christian clients, and because the authorities recognized that Jewish doctors still had Christian patients, the regulation stipulating that all Jews must wear distinguishing yellow headgear was waived so that Jewish doctors who left the ghetto at night to attend to their Christian patients would not be singled out for attack by Christians.[6]

In many ways the ghetto gave physical form to toleration at its worst: its presence meant for Jews that they were allowed to live in the Christian world, its walls gave them some sort of protection from persecution. But the price was degradation.

In the Islamic world, the ghetto did not exist except in Yemen and North Africa, outside the Ottoman Empire. Indicatively, Jews there occupied very much the same position as Jews in Christian Europe. In Morocco, the Jewish population, its numbers boosted by the Sephardic Jews expelled from Spain and Portugal at the end of the fifteenth century, were the only visible non-Muslim minority – the Almohads had persecuted Christians out of existence in the twelfth century. As a result Jews were the sole focus of all the suspicions and loathing that can so easily and so usefully be whipped up against the outsider (though some Sephardic Jews did occupy senior government positions). In 1438 the mellah of Fez with its walls and gateway had been established on the same grounds as Christian ghettoes had originally been, to protect Jews from attack. Not that it did protect them. In 1465, Muslim mobs in Fez slaughtered thousands of Jews because a Jewish vizier had allegedly treated a Muslim woman insultingly. In 1555, six months after Pope Paul IV had given his official blessing to the ghetto, Morocco established its second mellah in Marrakesh, at the foot of the High Atlas Mountains. A third was created in 1682. By the early 1900s, most Moroccan towns contained one.

But as with Europe's walled areas for Jews which morphed from asylum to prison, so the mellahs too became places of isolation and humiliation. Many Jews preferred to convert to Islam rather than be moved there. The mellah did, however, differ from the ghetto in two significant ways: the ulema never formally approved of its creation (though they may have done so tacitly), while the Church, under the leadership of the pope, gave its formal blessing to the ghetto. And Morocco's mellahs were an exception in the Islamic world; in the Christian world, life in the ghetto became the norm for Europe's Jews.

In 1561 all the Jewish communities of Italy received a letter inviting them to join a new Jewish colony at Tiberias on the Sea of Galilee in what is now Israel and was then part of the Ottoman Empire; moreover, free transport across the Mediterranean would be laid on. The letter was issued by Joseph Nasi (formerly Don Juan Mendez), a Sephardic Jew expelled from Portugal who had become a senior adviser to the Ottoman sultan.

Joseph Nasi came from a wealthy Jewish. His aunt Gracia was an independent businesswoman with a banking house and trading company and was probably the richest Jewish woman in Europe. In his native Portugal, the family had taken the name Mendez and converted to Christianity. But as Marranos (Jewish converts to Christianity), and therefore potentially 'false Christians', they fell under the suspicious gaze of the Inquisition launched by Ferdinand and Isabella in 1483. Indeed, the Mendez family had continued to practise secretly as Jews. They were forced to flee and were pursued through Europe by the Inquisition. In 1555, the year that Rome's ghetto walls were built, Doña Gracia Mendez and her nephew set sail from Venice for Istanbul, capital of the Ottoman Empire, the most powerful and probably best administered empire in the world. In comparison to Christendom, it was a model of tolerance. It was, as Rabbi Samuel ben Moses de Medina, prominent leader and scholar in Salonica, said, a realm 'wide open without a wall'.

Free from fears of the Inquisition, Don Juan Mendez 'came out' as Joseph Nasi and openly practised his Judaism. He developed a thriving import and export business. Together aunt and nephew used their wealth, charm (Gracia Nasi was renowned for her beauty) and acumen to wield great influence at the Ottoman court. Gracia Nasi had already established an escape network which enabled hundreds of *conversos* to flee the Inquisition in Spain and Portugal. In 1558 she acquired from Suleiman I ('the Magnificent') the lease of the Tiberias region in Galilee.

The Nasis dreamed, as the Zionists of the nineteenth century would do, of turning Tiberias into a Jewish state. When she had been in Venice, Gracia Nasi tried to buy an island from the Venetian authorities so that she could set up such a haven in Europe, but the authorities had refused. The Ottomans, however, saw Nasis' plan as an opportunity to repopulate a desolate part of the empire with a people whom the Ottomans had already specifically welcomed as refugees from Europe. In 1561, Joseph Nasi was given authority to rule Tiberias and the surrounding area. Hundreds of Jews in Italy accepted his invitation to settle there and left on the ships he provided. Three years later, work on repairing Tiberias's city walls began. Ruins were cleared; an ancient synagogue was reopened. Jews began moving into abandoned houses and repairing them. And quarrels inevitably broke out – two rabbis even punched each other over their rights of ownership.[7]

To make Tiberias economically viable, Nasi tried to set up a wool and silk industry, importing wool from Spain and organizing the planting of mulberry trees on which silkworms feed. Travellers described a transformed city, surrounded by strong city walls, filled with the scents of date palms, orange trees and pine trees. 'The habitations of the wilderness have been turned to a garden of Eden, and the parched soil like to the vineyard of the Lord,' wrote one Christian visitor.[8]

Gracia died in Istanbul in 1569. Today she is more honoured than her nephew. New York City designated a Dona Gracia Day in June 2010, Turkey has a commemorative stamp in tribute to her and the study of her life now forms part of Israel's school curriculum. But Tiberias was never as popular as the Nasis had hoped. It may also have lost the support of the sultan who began to fear the dangers of a separate Jewish state within the empire. By the mid seventeenth century Tiberias was again semi-abandoned, only to be revived again a century later, when it became a centre for Jewish learning.

Elsewhere in the Ottoman Empire, however, from Salonica to Cairo, Istanbul and Baghdad, Jews from Europe swelled the pre-existing Jewish communities who did not always greet them with welcome arms, though the sultan did.

Descended from the chief of a small Turkish tribe, the Ottoman sultans had, in the space of a little over 200 years, become the 'terror of the world', as an English diplomat called them. That their empire was already beginning its slow decline would only be discernible to later historians. At the time the Ottoman Empire towered over Christendom militarily, economically and culturally.

From Istanbul, formerly the great capital of Byzantium, Sultan Suleiman I ruled an empire of 20 to 30 million people. Tall and wiry, and dressed in a black silk kaftan, Suleiman held court in the vast magnificence of Topkapi Palace, overlooking the Bosphorus where hundreds of ferries criss-crossed the water. In the city itself, narrow streets of red-roofed houses wound up and down the countless hills. Men gathered in coffee houses which had become all the rage in Istanbul (the fashion would not hit England for another century), while, sequestered in their homes, Muslim women peered out from behind latticed balconies shielded from the male gaze. When they ventured out, they dressed like the men in kaftans, with long baggy trousers, their nails tinted red with henna, a black veil covering all but their eyes, which were ringed with kohl.

Minarets and domes dominated the city skyline. It was in fact with tribute money paid by the Habsburg emperor Charles V that Sultan Suleiman I commissioned the building of the Suleymaniye Mosque in Istanbul. Mimar Sinan, perhaps the greatest of all the Ottoman architects, began work on this glorious monument to Islam in 1550, the same time that Michelangelo was designing his glorious monument to Catholicism, St Peter's in Rome. (Michelangelo was in fact invited, along with Leonardo da Vinci, to submit plans for a bridge across the Bosphorus in Istanbul, but neither was ever commissioned.)

Islamic art and architecture were blossoming as never before, but not so Islamic thought and scholarship. Islam's religious scholars tended to frown on speculation. It was dangerously close to blasphemy since it led to new religious ideas and practices (*bid'a*). In effect the philosopher was saying he knew better than God, whereas his task should be to understand God's intentions as set out in the Quran and sunna. Speculation was permitted in some circumstances, but only as a last resort.

It is not surprising, then, that the ulema disapproved of the printing press. It was the technology that in Christendom was proving to be the greatest propagator of new ideas, with all the potential for subversion that went with them. Thanks to the printing press, the ideas of Luther and his fellow critics of the Catholic Church spread with astonishing speed. In the Ottoman Empire, printing in Arabic or Turkish characters was banned on pain of death in 1483, on the grounds that it 'would defile the holy script'.[9] Although printing in other languages was allowed, printing secular works in Arabic was not legally permitted until 1727.

And yet despite this traditionalism, what struck the traveller or Jewish refugee from Europe was the astonishing multi-ethnic-religious-linguistic-cultural mix of the Ottoman Empire's cities. Until the sixteenth century non-Muslims outnumbered Muslims in the Ottoman

Empire. But even when Suleiman became sultan in 1520, Istanbul was more diverse, ethnically and religiously, than London is today; 42 per cent of the population were non-Muslims. Almost the same was true of many of the empire's great cities – of Aleppo in Syria, Jerusalem in Palestine, of Salonica in today's Greece. There were Greek, Armenian and Syrian Orthodox Christians, Egyptian Copts, Sunnis, Shiites, Druzes, Jews, Tartars, Serbs, Arabs, Iranians, Kurds, Berbers, Nubians, Slavs, Bulgars, Hungarians, Georgians and of course Turks drawn from every corner of the empire. They all had their synagogues, mosques and churches, they all bought and sold in the bazaars, and joined the same trade guilds (by contrast, Jews were excluded from the Christian guilds of Europe), though these were usually headed by a Muslim. Muslims still lived amongst Jews. In the Jewish neighbourhood of Fustat (now part of Cairo), at least half the houses were inhabited by Muslims.

On the whole, however, each group tended to live in their own separate quarters, often behind walls and gates. These cities within a city had some degree of freedom to raise their own taxes, educate their children and have their own religious courts. In some ways they resembled the ghettoes of Europe – except that while religious and ethnic communities in the Ottoman Empire might ghettoize themselves, they were never forcibly segregated as the Jews of Christendom were.

The Ottoman city accepted religious difference – how could it not? The empire, after all, spanned southern and eastern Europe, Asia, Africa and the Middle East, with all the diversity of religions, lifestyles, forms of governance and cultures that entailed. Like all empires it had to tolerate difference if it was to keep control of its disparate peoples and above all extract their taxes. In essence, Jews and Christians in all their sectarian varieties lived as they had always done since Arabs first conquered the Roman/Byzantine and Persian empires in the eighth century. Jews and Christians were *dhimmis*, free to practise their religion as long as they paid their taxes and agreed to their inferior position.

The resulting system of semi-autonomous communities, later called millets, created a very different type of city to the European one and this had a crucial impact on Jews and other religious minorities. The Ottoman city was an agglomeration of different communities which were allowed to be different; there was no attempt to create a single uniform entity as there was in Christendom. To adopt the terms of a later age, the Ottomans ruled their minorities according to a multicultural model. Different communities were expected and allowed to maintain their own separate religious and cultural life, within certain well-defined limits, of course. Christian Europe, on the other hand, followed an assimilationist model where everyone must belong to a single uniform entity, or risk being excluded from it. The Ottoman 'federal' city was the natural product of an empire, and Jews could live there far more easily than in the unitary mono-religious European city.

But the Reformation had destroyed Christian uniformity. Catholicism was no longer the default position of every ruler and subject in Christendom. Now there were choices to be made between different brands of Christianity. The principle of *cuius regio, eius religio* (whose realm, his religion) by which the 1555 Peace of Augsburg had temporarily settled the wars in the Holy Roman Empire, therefore became of enormous significance.

Heresy and treason, the religious and political faces of subversion, had been linked since Jesus was tried by the Jewish religious court for blasphemy and by the Romans for sedition. In the sixteenth and seventeenth centuries affiliation to Protestantism or Catholicism became a marker of political loyalty. That was the case in England, as much as in the Holy Roman Empire and France. In the space of thirty years England lurched from a bastardized form of Catholicism under Henry VIII to a radical Protestantism under his son Edward, back to Catholicism under his daughter Mary and to a more moderate Protestantism under his other daughter Elizabeth. Of all of them, the Catholic 'Bloody Mary' burned the most heretics. But it was not surprising that each monarch wanted to impose an act of uniformity, forcing their subjects to adhere to one set of beliefs and practices and detecting potential treason in adherence to any other.

In Catholic France, the Huguenots, followers of Calvin, were the objects of virulent political suspicion.* Despite the fact that Huguenots were forbidden to meet together and Calvinist pastors from Geneva had to be smuggled into France, Calvinism had proved unstoppable. By the middle of the sixteenth century nearly 2 million people were Huguenots, that is, about one tenth of the French population. As far as French Catholics generally were concerned, the sheer number of Huguenots was threatening the stability of the state. In the eyes of the ruling Valois royal family, who were Catholics, to be a Huguenot was to be a supporter of their rivals for the throne, the Bourbons, who had turned Protestant.

Civil war, or the 'French Wars of Religion' as they have been called, broke out in 1562 and lasted off and on for thirty-six years. In all some 2 to 3 million died, the casualties of violence or its attendant famine and disease. Amongst the dead were the thousands of Huguenots slaughtered throughout France by Catholic mobs on St Bartholomew's Day, 1572. Historians estimate that anywhere between 5,000 and 20,000 men, women and children were killed.

By 1589 the Huguenots/Bourbons and the Catholics/Valois had fought themselves to a stalemate. Neither side had been able to win outright; Huguenots still controlled the south and west of the country, Catholics most of the rest. But in 1589 the Catholic Valois king, Henry III, was assassinated. The Huguenot Bourbon Henry of Navarre was next in line to the throne. Politics came before religious conviction. Henry of Navarre, one of the foremost Protestants in France, converted to Catholicism and was crowned king. Paris, as he famously said, was worth a Mass.

But Henry remained deeply sympathetic to the Huguenots, as was clear in the Edict of Nantes which brought the civil wars to a close in 1598. France faced the same stalemate as the Holy Roman Empire

---

* There are several explanations for the origins of the Huguenots' name. One of the most convincing is that they were named after the legendary ghost of Huguet. At night Huguet was said to haunt the city of Tours in central France, just as Calvin's followers haunted the cities where they congregated, since they were forced to meet clandestinely at night-time.

had done in 1555. The Peace of Augsburg had attempted to settle that stalemate between Protestant and Catholic rulers by allowing each to determine the religion of their own territory. But *cuius regio, eius religio* was still based on the assumption, questioned by only a few, that uniformity of religion was essential to stable government. The ruler should allow only one religion to prevail and prohibit any alternatives, or the state would descend into dissension and chaos. The Edict of Nantes in 1598 went much further. It abandoned the principle of religious uniformity and recognized that France could no longer outlaw Protestants but must accommodate them *within* the Catholic state of France.

The edict did not provide for religious equality between Catholics and Huguenots, but it was a step in that direction. And as always with such advances, it was dictated by political necessity. Under the new dispensation, Catholicism was still to be the religion of the state. But Huguenots were no longer to be considered heretics liable to execution. They could practise their faith, although only in private, and not at all in Paris, and they could even practise their faith publicly in certain legally approved towns. Huguenots were now able to hold office, engage in trade, attend schools and universities, and inherit property. Most significantly, the Edict of Nantes formally recognized the de facto reality that Huguenots controlled a virtual state in the south and west of France where they outnumbered Catholics. Huguenots were allowed to hold nearly 200 fortified towns, including La Rochelle in south-west France; more extraordinary still, the king was to pay for garrisoning about half of those towns.

Such remarkable toleration was of course resisted by Catholics. And few on either side of the religious divide considered it to be any more than a temporary measure. Necessity had dictated a limited acceptance of religious pluralism in France, but only until *une roi, une foi, une loi* (one king, one faith, one law) could be restored. As indeed it was. But not before the whole of continental Europe had been caught up in the bloodbath of the Thirty Years' War – which would force Christendom to rethink its attitude to tolerance.

CHAPTER 15

THE RELIGIOUS WARS OF EUROPE

'François I, most Christian, will unite with Mussulmans against Charles V, most Catholic. François I will give money to the Lutherans of Germany to support them in their revolt against the emperor; but … he will start by having Lutherans burned at home. For political reasons he pays them in Saxony; for political reasons he burns them in Paris.'

– Voltaire, *Philosophical Dictionary*, 1764

IN 1632, HANS DOBEL, a peasant-farmer living in the German village of Vinsberg, set down in his diary a 'Register of everything that happened in the year'. It is the record of a bewildered man caught up in the ever-shifting boundaries of a war. Villages, towns and local castles changed hands every week, sometimes every day; thousands of soldiers carved their way through Dobel's province of Franconia and stripped it bare.

In the course of thirty years between 1618 and 1649, 8 million people died in central Europe, most of them German. The war's consequences were felt as far away as Africa, Peru and Mexico, where Spain's newly conquered peoples sweated and died in silver mines to pay for its involvement in the war.

The Thirty Years' War was seen at the time as yet another, albeit the most lethal, of the religious wars that had been ripping Europe apart for almost a century. Like all religious wars, it was of course far more than a battle between religious doctrines. It was a battle for power. Under the Augsburg treaty of 1555, the Holy Roman emperor, Charles V, had recognized that he could no longer impose Catholicism on the whole of his empire and conceded to Lutheran princes in his empire the freedom to rule their lands as Protestant states. By granting these rulers such religious freedom, the Peace of Augsburg had thereby also recognized their political freedom to rule their own states as they chose rather than as the emperor chose.

But in 1618 Ferdinand II had tried to re-impose Catholicism on the whole of his empire. Such a violation of the Peace of Augsburg was an attack on the Protestant princes' political as well as their religious autonomy. But it was in the name of defending their religion that they called on the Protestant powers of Europe to come to their aid. And it was in the name of protecting Protestantism that Protestant England, Scotland, Sweden, Denmark and the Dutch provinces that were fighting for independence from Catholic Spain's imperial rule, responded. Similarly, it was in the name of restoring Catholic hegemony in Europe that the Papal States and the Spanish Empire came to the aid of the Holy Roman emperor and his loyal Catholic states within the empire. In reality the European powers were fighting for control over Europe – whether to further or to thwart the Catholic Habsburgs who dominated Europe: one branch of the family ruled Spain, with its vast empire, while another ruled the Holy Roman Empire.

It was symptomatic of how political the religious wars really were, that Catholic France fought on the side of the Protestant states of Germany and the rest of Europe's Protestant states. France was far more fearful of being encircled by the Catholic Habsburg emperors of Spain and the Holy Roman Empire than it was of Protestant doctrines. Catholic France and Protestant England made alliances with the Ottoman sultan, Suleiman I, as a counterweight to the Catholic powers; while the Catholic states sought alliances with the Ottomans' Muslim rivals, the Safavids in Iran.

Useful political alliances aside, the belligerents nonetheless went to war under the banner of fighting for God, a far better rallying call than a fight for power and self-interest. The Swedish king, Gustavus Adolphus, invaded the empire in 1635 to further his own imperial ambitions, though he did so under the title of 'Protestant Godly Warrior'. Spain and some of the Catholic princedoms in the Holy Roman Empire, such as Bavaria, justified their engagement in the war by describing it as a crusade, a fight to repulse the heretics.

In religion's name, armies of around 5,000 cavalry, 9,000 foot soldiers and up to 2,000 wagons, not including artillery, criss-crossed the Holy Roman Empire.[1] During 1632, the year that Dobel was writing his diary, total troop numbers in Germany reached 250,000.[2] As their pay was almost always in arrears, the troops, mostly mercenaries, resorted to pillaging in order to feed themselves and their hungry families who travelled with them. Pillaging was the regular resort of poorly paid seventeenth-century armies, as it had been for the crusading armies (see Chapter 7). Often feeble with hunger, they inflicted starvation on the local peasants by stealing their cattle and crops. It was so common and so necessary during the Thirty Years' War that the soldiers, sometimes barefoot because they hadn't the money for shoes and stockings, had even developed their own language: 'a goose is called a straw brush and catching is called interrogation, so that to interrogate a straw brush is to catch a goose,' one soldier noted in his diary.[3] Sometimes the whole encampment of soldiers would go pillaging – the women and children running through the fields, stealing apples, pears and beans, or breaking into houses to steal bedlinen, dresses, in one case even a taffeta ball gown. Armies on both sides demanded contributions from the villages they descended on. Sometimes they would ransom a wealthy local farmer or the prior of the local monastery. At their most appalling, the soldiers raped the women in the villages or towns where they were quartered.

While Hans Dobel struggled to pursue his daily life, he noted the following in his diary: the local town is captured; the local commander is killed and several soldiers shot and wounded; cavalrymen steal twenty-five horses from a local village, kidnap villagers and demand a ransom – which is paid; imperial soldiers invade a local town and demand meat, wine and fifty loaves of bread every day. Swedish troops, enemies of the

Catholic imperial army, advance and demand to be billeted; they steal twenty-four horses and shoot a pheasant. The local gamekeeper gets married and Dobel's wife attends the party. The district overseer orders the village to pay money plus corn to pay for the billeted soldiers. Dobel is threshing corn when the imperial army ride through the village; the troops set fire to local villages whose wooden fences erected to keep out wild animals could not keep out the soldiers; imperial horsemen arrive and stay for fourteen days and are 'given' bread and corn. The gatekeeper of the local town is shot in the thigh and dies six days later. Three hundred Swedish horsemen steal the bailiff's cows, slaughter some pigs and steal a pair of Hans Dobel's boots and two shirts.[4]

Dobel wrote his diary for eight months. On Saturday 8 September 1632, he recorded the burial of his godfather. That was the last entry. Maybe he was one of the countless victims of the war.

In a war composed mostly of sieges rather than battles it was the poor bloody civilians who suffered disproportionately. Wagonloads of refugees from their own bombarded and looted homes sought protection in other villages and cities; the resulting overcrowding made pestilence, which always threatened in the summer months, far more virulent. In times of siege, the starving inhabitants ate cats and dogs, drank their own urine when water ran out and even resorted to cannibalism, if some reports are to be believed.*

It was not just the townspeople and peasant-farmers like Hans Dobel who were the victims of war. So too were the men and women on the margins of society – the unmarried, the crippled, the eccentric, the slightly mad, the 'different'. They were seen as the source of social disorder, working in league with the Devil to turn the world upside down. In just one year alone, 1629, the town of Eichstatt, Upper Bavaria, burned to death 274 people condemned as witches and another fifty were burned in the neighbouring duchy of Palatinate-Neuburg. The same witch-hunting frenzy swept over England during the civil wars of the 1640s.

* Cannibalism is often used by chroniclers almost as a rhetorical device to emphasize just how dire circumstances were, so such reports cannot be entirely relied upon.

Perhaps the only group that benefited from the Thirty Years' War were Jews. Surprising, given that they were always scapegoated for any of Europe's calamities. During the sixteenth century, armed with the poisonous religious justifications provided by Luther and with the blessing of the Catholic Church, the authorities had ghettoized Jews or expelled them from most of the larger principalities and major cities in Germany.

However, during the course of the Thirty Years' War Jews were admitted or re-admitted to territories from which they had been excluded. The Holy Roman emperor Ferdinand II had once been almost as hostile to Jews as he now was to rebel Protestant princes, but he was forced to rely on massive loans, in particular from the Jewish financier Jacob Bassevi, to maintain an army powerful enough to confront his Protestant rebels and foreign foes. Even the provision of horses – and armies needed tens of thousands of them – was a problem handed over to central Europe's Jewish merchants who were expert horse dealers. In return, stringent trade restrictions previously inflicted on them were lifted, and instead they were granted trade concessions.

The Lutheran Swedish king, Gustavus Aldophus, had always barred Jews from his territories. But now that he was invading the Holy Roman Empire, he too needed cash. He also needed the sheer logistical know-how to move and supply hundreds and thousands of men around central Europe. Jewish merchants and financiers were now considered so vital to Sweden's military success that Swedish troops were under strict instructions not to loot or attack any Jewish community that lay in their path.

During the decades of the war, Jews moved into abandoned villages and towns across central Europe. New Jewish communities were established, old ones expanded. Taking advantage of the complete collapse of the economy, they traded in grain, wine, cloth and other markets from which they had previously been excluded.

By 1648, when the Peace of Westphalia put an end to fighting in central Europe, Germany had been decimated. About a quarter to a half of the German population had died, though more were killed by the famine and epidemics of bubonic plague, typhus and dysentery which accompanied the wars, than by war itself. The worst-hit areas had become deserted landscapes of burned-out farmhouses, empty villages and unploughed fields; packs of wild pigs were destroying untended crops; the population of rats had exploded; wolves roamed Bavaria; not a cat or a dog was to be seen because they had all been eaten.[5]

The exhausted belligerents saw religion as lying at the root not just of the Thirty Years' War but of the century-long wars and civil wars that had and still were bedevilling Europe. 'The grievances of the one and the other religion [Protestant and Catholic] ... have been for the most part the cause and occasion of the present war,' declared the treaty that was concluded between Sweden and the Holy Roman Empire. It was one of a number of treaties that made up the Peace of Westphalia.

The Peace was designed to solve the two-fold but interconnected nature of the Thirty Years' War – the conflict within the Holy Roman Empire between the emperor and the princes opposed to him – and the wider struggle for control of Europe between the European powers who had all been drawn into the empire's conflicts.

It was in the peace terms concluded by then Catholic Holy Roman emperor Ferdinand III and his rebel Protestant princes that the relationship between State and religion underwent a shift which would be momentous for European attitudes to religious tolerance. The signatories in effect secularized politics.

The Peace of Augsburg in 1555 had tried to resolve the conflicts of the Holy Roman Empire by legalizing the de facto practice of *cuius regio, eius religio*. It had given Protestant princes the freedom to determine the religion of their principalities. Those who then found themselves on the wrong side of the religious divide were forbidden to worship openly, but they were allowed to leave and find a new home under a prince who espoused their own confession. France's Edict of Nantes had gone a step further in 1598, bringing an end to civil war by allowing Huguenots and Catholics to co-exist in the same territory. The Peace of Westphalia went even further. The prince would still determine the religion of his principality, but any of his subjects who espoused a different confession, whether Catholic, Lutheran or Calvinist, would be allowed to practise openly. Calvinism, along with Lutheranism, was now included as a confession to be recognized and tolerated – more radical brands of Protestantism were not and nor, of course, was Judaism. But as far as most Christians were concerned, the choice of which type of mainstream Christianity to follow had now become their own affair, not the State's. Those who did not adhere to the faith of their ruler were, it is true, made to feel their minority status – they could not, for instance, hold public processions, or summon their followers by ringing bells, though even that stricture was not always obeyed – but nonetheless, they were free to practise their faith without fear of persecution.

The Peace of Westphalia changed the rules of the game. It put into legal terms what had become the new reality of Europe. Europe had become both politically and religiously pluralist. Every signatory had to tolerate all three confessions: Catholic, Lutheran and Calvinist. If he did not then another ruler was entitled to declare war on him. Intolerance had become a legitimate cause for war.

The universalist, supra-nationalist model of religious and political governance, of Catholic Church and empire, had gone for ever. Under the treaty the Spanish Empire formally recognized the independence of the Protestant Dutch provinces who had been fighting for independence for eighty years. In the peace arrangements negotiated between the Holy Roman emperor Ferdinand III and his rebel Protestant princes, their states were recognized as having quasi-independent status. The Holy Roman Empire had become a federation of states whose representatives would meet regularly at the imperial diet (parliament) to determine matters affecting the empire as a whole.

Recognizing how much peace in the Holy Roman Empire was dependent on religious toleration, the Peace of Westphalia stipulated that there should be no backtracking 'irrespective of the objection or protest of anyone within or without the Empire, at any time whatsoever; all such objections are by virtue of the present provisions declared null and void'. This was above all directed at the pope. Pope Innocent X of course loathed the peace terms, knowing full well what their implications were for Catholicism – perhaps even suspecting the consequences of the Peace for the survival of God himself.

He had sent his papal nuncio to the negotiations but papal objections had been ignored by the other delegates. Religious toleration was considered to be too important to the peace settlement to be jeopardized by the pope's inevitable religious partisanship. But in November 1648, six months after the treaty had been signed, Pope Innocent retaliated. In a papal bull he declared the Peace of Westphalia to be 'null, void, invalid, iniquitous, unjust, damnable, reprobate, inane, empty of meaning and effect for all time', words which almost exactly replicated those with which Pope Innocent III had condemned the Magna Carta in 1215 (see Chapter 9).

The pope understood full well that the Peace of Westphalia was a disaster for the Catholic Church. Europe's secular powers had declared that the Church could no longer even claim to speak for all Christendom but had to take its place amongst other Christian sects. The Counter-Reformation had failed. After 1648 the papacy ceased to be a great European power. The pope would be increasingly sidelined by heads of state, even Catholic ones.[6]

Not just the pope but religion itself was being sidelined. Religious affiliation was still a clear marker of political affiliation, and religion was still being used to inflame political passions in the English civil wars of the 1640s which were in full flood when the Peace of Westphalia was signed. But by the eighteenth century religion was no longer used as a justification for war and had ceased to play a significant role in international alignments.

Intolerance had led to the Church's undoing. The creation of the enemy had become an essential way by which the Church had boosted its popularity and power. And rulers had also benefited. Their subjects had been united by defining themselves against an out-group that was loathed by God and moreover made a useful scapegoat in times of trouble. Jews, Muslims, lax priests, Cathars – all had served their purpose well. But the Church's reliance on an enemy had gone too far. The Church had created one, the Protestant, who could not be beaten, and, moreover, who had turned the Church's weapon of enemy-making against itself.

After a century of bloodshed all sides had had enough. The final casualty was God. The slow withdrawal of God from the political arena began with the Peace of Westphalia. Rulers could no longer legally impose their religion on all of their subjects. Catholics and Protestants had to live together. Did tolerance require a religious neutrality that came perilously close to religious indifference? It was what the opponents of toleration in the Islamic world, as in Christendom, always feared.

CHAPTER 16

SUNNIS VS SHIITES

'The pious will take on the responsibility of governing and administering the country, in accordance with the Qur'anic verse, "My servants, the righteous, shall inherit the earth".'

– Constitution of the Islamic Republic of Iran, 1979

'The Glorious Qur'an and the Sunna contain all the laws and ordinances man needs in order to attain happiness and the perfection of his state.'

– *Islamic Government*, Ayatollah Khomeini, 1970

If only the Islamic world had also had its bloodbath, there would be no clash of civilizations today. If Islamdom had had its St Bartholomew's Day massacre, its rapes and sieges, burnings at the stake and inquisitions, it too could have separated Mosque and State, and the Muslim world would have learned not just to accept tolerance as an unfortunate necessity but to love it as the Christian West finally did.

Caricatured though it might be, readers will nonetheless recognize this argument in the works of Samuel Huntington, Roger Scruton, Bernard Lewis or Ayaan Hirsi Ali, to name but a few.[1] The Muslim world, they argue, lacked its Westphalian moment when, for the sake of peace, religion and politics became truly separated. The Peace of Westphalia marked the final parting of the ways between the Muslim and Christian worlds when religion in the West retired to the interior world of the individual, leaving the State to rule supreme over the political world.

But such a view fails to understand that the Peace of Westphalia should more accurately be seen not as the triumph of the State over religion but as the defeat of one state, the Catholic Church, by another, the sovereign national state. Early Christians had developed the institution of the Church in order to protect themselves from the Roman state. But the unintended result was that over the centuries the institution had become too powerful. It had itself become a State.

Islam, on the other hand, never had the need to establish a strong independent religious institution to protect itself from a sometimes oppressive State. And yet between the sixteenth and mid seventeenth centuries, at almost exactly the same time that Christian Europe was enduring its 'wars of religion', the Islamic world was enduring its own conflicts where religion and politics also mapped on to each other as they did throughout the pre-modern world and often still do. In Islam's case the political battle was played out against Islam's major schism between Sunni and Shia.

The Sunni Ottoman Empire was fighting the rising new Shiite Iranian Empire to the east, ruled by the Safavids. Whereas in Christendom political loyalties were signalled according to which side of the major Christian schism you belonged, in the Islamic Middle East loyalty to one or the other empire was signalled by whether you were Shiite or Sunni.

The wars between the Safavids and the Ottomans, however, were never so cataclysmic as the Protestant–Catholic ones. Islam's wars involved neither a fight for independence, identity and nationhood, nor a fight against a mighty religious institution. Its wars were a straight two-way political fight between two empires battling for control of the fertile plains of what is now Iraq. The Protestant–Catholic wars, on the other hand, were part of the fight to the death between the old and new world order.

Europe's wars were a continent-wide civil war, as small territories sought to break away from empire and the Church. They were battles by the landed aristocracy to rule their own territories. The landed aristocracy were the third element (along with King and Church) in the triangulation of power which, as Weber pointed out, was a distinctive feature of Christian Europe (see Chapters 5 and 6). That triangulation was absent from the Ottoman world.

From Carolingian times onwards, Europe had been forced to reward its soldiers with land because it had been too poor to recompense them in any other way. The soldiers had turned into landholders who eventually became powerful enough to threaten their rulers. The Ottoman world on the other hand had never developed a feudal system with its landed elite because it had been rich enough to import slaves and train them up into privileged, well-educated soldiers and administrators. And while mamluks (slave soldiers) did become powerful enough to threaten their rulers, in the absence of a feudal system their battle with the sultan was for the administrative apparatus of the state, not for rule over a chunk of land which they owned. In Europe, on the other hand, the soldier-lord fought to make his own local territory a state which he could rule independently of his more powerful overlord, king or emperor. The feudal system was always going to foster fissiparous tendencies.

In the first half of the sixteenth century the Ottoman Empire's sultan Suleiman the Magnificent was the most powerful monarch in the world. He was far mightier than his contemporaries Henry VIII and even the Holy Roman emperor Charles V who ruled a large part of Europe as well as Spain's new empire in the Americas. Suleiman, however, did not attempt to impose religious uniformity on his subjects in the way that Christian rulers were attempting to do in Europe.

Periodically Shiites in the Sunni Ottoman Empire and Sunnis in the Shiite Safavid Empire were suspected of siding with the enemy. Indeed they often were, and the whole community suffered persecution and massacre as a result. But on the whole the Sunni Ottoman emperors were tolerant, verging on the indifferent, to other faiths. The emperor considered himself to be more sultan (political ruler) than caliph (head of the community of Muslims). He presided over an astonishing diversity of religions, ethnicities, languages and cultures. As we have seen throughout this book, tolerance tends to be the default position of an empire which contains a variety of different ethnic-religious groups: it is the cheapest, most efficient way to prevent unrest and keep the taxes rolling in.

While professing his commitment to Islam and sharia, the emperor allowed Christians and Jews an astonishing degree of autonomy to run their own religious and educational affairs, even raise their own taxes. The semi-independence of the millets (from the Arabic *milla*, meaning religious community) would be formally organized in the early nineteenth century. Tolerance did not of course mean equality; the *dhimmis'* lot was almost always to be treated as inferior, to a greater or lesser degree. But the emperor usually only cranked up the intolerance levels when he felt himself to be vulnerable.

Of the Sunni and Shia empires the latter was the more intolerant. The Shia Safavid Empire resembled Christendom in its insistence on imposing religious uniformity and its consequent intolerance of religious difference. Safavid Iran would witness the development of a religious hierocratic institution which in its power and independence had much in common with the Catholic Church; indeed the ulema would exceed the Church in power. Essentially, Iran would do in reverse the journey that Church and State made in Europe in the Middle Ages – the Catholic Church ended up being dominated by the State: the shah would end up being dominated by the Shiite ulema.

The Safavids owed their rise to power to a combination of religious and political leadership. Originally tribesmen like the Ottomans, the family became the hereditary leaders of a particular brand of Islam, a mixture of Shiism and Sufism which was adopted by tribesmen in northern Iran. Since the eleventh century, tribes from Central Asia had been settling in Iran and parts of what is now Turkey and vying with each other for land. As leaders of what had become known in their honour as the Safaviyeh religious order, the Safavids led their religious-warrior followers to victory after victory. By 1501 Ismail, then head of the order, was in control of most of Iran and posing a real threat to the Ottoman Empire.

That year Ismail declared himself to be the Mahdi or the Mahdi's precursor (it is not clear which). In Islam the Mahdi is the messianic figure who will return at the end of the world to vanquish evil. Shiites merged the figure of the Mahdi with the last of the rightful imams who,

Shiites believe, had been forced, thanks to Sunni persecution, to disappear from the world and go into occultation (see Chapter 2).

Since the tenth century, however, Shiism had been divided over which imam went into hiding, the nature of his authority and functions, and what authority Shiite jurists had in his absence; this division and its accompanying divergence of beliefs continues to the present day. What has come to be known as Twelver Shiism (because it believes that the twelfth legitimate imam to succeed Muhammad went into occultation) now predominates.

Calling himself 'the just, the perfect Imam' and 'Jesus, son of Mary', Shah Ismail set about imposing Twelver Shiism – or at least his particular brand of it which included belief in the semi-divine nature of Ismail himself – on Iran. In his person Ismail united secular and religious rule as Muhammad had always intended and as the Sunnis had, in the eyes of Shiites, so conspicuously failed to do. The Safavid vision would lay the foundations for the theocratic institutions that are so important in Iran's politics today.

'If the people utter one word of protest, I will draw the sword and leave not one of them alive,' Shah Ismail was alleged to have said of his predominantly Sunni subjects. But his persecutory fervour was a rarity amongst Muslim rulers. Only a fellow Shiite, the Fatimid imam-caliph al-Hakim who ruled Egypt in the early eleventh century, could compare. Al-Hakim had conducted a merciless campaign of persecution against the *dhimmis*. He was unique, however, amongst Fatimid caliphs who were renowned for their tolerance, and besides, many modern historians have excused him on the grounds of insanity. Furthermore, al-Hakim rescinded his persecution after nine years, while Ismail never ceased to persecute Sunnis throughout his twenty-three-year reign.

With the same ferocity with which Augsburg's Zwinglian rulers had authorized the stripping or tearing down of Catholic churches, Ismail destroyed Sunni mosques. The Sunni ulema were presented with the usual choices of the persecuted: conversion, exile or death. A few chose death, but many fled to the Ottoman Empire or the Mughal Empire in India.

The Shiite–Sunni schism had become a salient feature in the contest between Ottoman and Safavid empires. Shah Ismail was an insecure ruler of a newly developing empire, locked in an almost constant war over territory with his mighty Sunni neighbours, the Ottomans. No doubt that fuelled his religious intolerance, while the Ottomans, for their part, shed their tolerance in the face of the rising threat of the Safavid Empire. Thousands of Turkic tribesmen living in the contested territories on the borders between the two empires had flocked to Ismail's banner and rebelled against Ottoman rule. The Qizilbash, as the Ottomans called Safavid sympathizers, suffered mass deportations to areas of the empire remote from Safavid influence.* They were imprisoned, sentenced to forced labour as oarsmen on Ottoman galleys, or were massacred – some reports, admittedly by the Qizilbash themselves, put the number killed as high as 40,000.

In 1512, the Ottoman sultan Selim I had in fact asked for a fatwa on the permissibility of killing Qizilbash/Shiites. An eminent religious scholar, Hamza Saru Görez, duly delivered his fatwa: the Qizilbash, he said, were 'worse than the unbelievers [Christian and Jews]'. They were infidels and pagans. 'It is any Muslim's duty to destroy such a population. The holy martyr Muslims who die in this connection will achieve the highest paradise.'[2]

Despite this religious blessing, however, the Ottomans still preferred to follow the imperial policy of tolerance when they felt safe enough to do so. In 1534 when Selim I's son, Suleiman the Magnificent, recaptured the city of Baghdad from Shah Ismail, he continued to endow Shiite shrines and even paid the salaries of Shiite as well as Sunni clergy. Why alienate the Shiites of Baghdad and force them back into the arms of their erstwhile Safavid rulers?

For over 600 years the Ottomans had dealt with the diversity of their empire by exercising a pragmatic tolerance towards their religious communities; the Safavids, on the other hand, sought to establish control

---

* Qizilbash means redhead. The Qizilbash wore turbans wound around a bright red cap with a tall red cone in its centre made of twelve pleats to signify their adherence to Twelver Shiism.

over their new empire by imposing religious uniformity. But Iran had few Shiite scholars, and they were ill qualified to set Iran on the correct religious footing and convert its people, most of whom were Sunni, to Twelver Shiism. Ismail turned to well-respected Shiite scholars from within the Ottoman Empire. Many, prompted by a mixture of frustration at the limited opportunities open to them under Ottoman rule, and religious fervour, took up Ismail's invitation. They did not agree with his strange brand of Sufism and Shiism, nor with his claim to be the Mahdi (or his deputy). Nonetheless, they were happy to emerge from the quietist shadows under which they had lived in the Ottoman Empire and co-operate with Ismail in the creation of a Shiite state.

Amongst them was the scholar al-Karaki, whom Ismail appointed to oversee the spread of Shiism in eastern Iran. He attacked Sunnism from the pulpit of every mosque in which he preached. He made cursing of the first three caliphs (whom Sunnis revere and Shia regard as illegitimate) a religious duty. Anyone who failed to curse might be put to death on the spot.[3] One European traveller described the heaps of smouldering bones scattered in the streets and squares of Iran's cities. About 5,000 Sunnis were reported to have been killed – whether as traitors or heretics or both is unclear.[4]

Al-Karaki was a staunch and loyal supporter of the regime. He gave Shah Ismail the legitimacy which, as brand-new conqueror of a divided land who fully intended to expand his territory further, Ismail certainly needed. Al-Karaki's unswerving support was well rewarded with vast endowments of arable land and villages.

In 1514 the Safavid Empire was severely defeated by the Ottomans at Chaldiran in north-western Iran. Ismail withdrew into his palace and sought solace in alcohol. By the time his ten-year-old son Tahmasp succeeded to the throne, Iran had descended into civil war. It took ten years for Tahmasp to regain control of his empire, and even then his grip on it was extremely shaky.

The backing of al-Karaki and the ulema was even more crucial to Tahmasp than it had been to his father. Tahmasp sought to encourage their loyalty with yet more land, exemptions from taxes and promotions to administrative and religious positions. In doing so he was also trying to control the local Iranian nobility who were in a battle for power with the Qizilbash tribal chiefs.

The Safavids were weaker than the Ottomans and were forced to operate a more feudal system. They had to reward the Qizilbash chiefs, who had fought for Shah Ismail when he was founding his empire, with land and prominent government positions; in return the Qizilbash provided troops on demand. The old Iranian nobility, on the other hand, was fighting to retain its own elite position against both the chiefs and the new religious elite. Until the coming of al-Karaki and the other Shiite scholars and jurists, they had been in charge of religious administration, notably by managing religious endowments. Tahmasp however was transferring the nobility's religious authority and the wealth and power that went with it to the Shiite scholars. The result was the creation of a financially independent wealthy institution which in time would become a rival to the State; Christian rulers, starting with the emperor Constantine in the fourth century, had done the same when they boosted the material fortunes of the Church in the hopes of creating a reliable ally.

Shah Tahmasp was as eager to eliminate potential sources of opposition as al-Karaki was to enforce Shiism and stamp out any competing source of religious authority. Together the two sought to impose an austere moral regime that Augsburg and Geneva would have been proud of. Tahmasp closed down taverns, brothels, gambling houses and opium dens; he forbade shaving* and any poetry or music which did not praise Ali and the imams; he set up quasi-vigilante units within his army charged with sniffing out any hints of Sunni activity and with enforcing the practice initiated by al-Karaki of ritually cursing the first three caliphs. Al-Karaki himself would roam city streets with the vigilantes, shouting out his curses.[5] Indeed he enforced religious observances with such rigour that he was known as 'the inventor of Shi'ite religion'.[6] He wrote works denouncing Sunnism, encouraged the faithful to publicly humiliate Sufi leaders,

* Although the Quran says nothing specifically about facial hair, Muhammad is believed to have worn a beard, and scholars cite the hadith 'Cut the moustache and let the beard grow; be different from the mushrikeen' (al-Bukhaari 5442; Muslim 382).

provided simple guides to Shiite doctrinal and legal works, and organized the appointment of a prayer leader in every Iranian village and city.

And yet Tahmasp was no ascetic. A shocked Flemish ambassador described him as 'leading the life of a mere voluptuary' and neglecting his duties; 'he never leaves his harem, where he divides his time between dallying with his favourites and forecasting the future by means of lots'.[7] Tahmasp and his courtiers wore clothes of unparalleled richness: white silk turbans which ended with a flourish in a fan-shaped cockade, silk and velvet robes in brilliant blues, greens and reds, embroidered in gold weave with a profusion of animals, birds and flowers. The women, with delicate veils covering their long plaits, wore similar clothes to the men – loose baggy trousers under brilliantly coloured robes. But the women's finery was rarely visible since when they went out, they wore an all-enveloping white chador along with a white veil or black horsehair visor.

Al-Karaki was soon strong enough to challenge the Safavids' particular brand of Sufi-Shiism which made them divine in the eyes of many of their followers. Despite the Safavid imam's claim to be the occulted imam who had chosen to make himself visible, al-Karaki, like most of the ulema, believed that the true imam was still in occultation, hidden from earthly view. But al-Karaki claimed that he, al-Karaki and his most learned fellow jurists (*mujtahids*) were so knowledgeable about Islamic law that they were able to act as the deputies of the occulted imam. Until the imam made himself visible, they could make legal judgements and interpret tradition on his behalf, using their own rational opinions, *ijtihad*, when necessary. Interestingly, al-Karaki thus gave his blessing to *ijtihad*, a practice which had been considered questionable by many Sunni and Shiite jurists. Al-Karaki's claim that *mujtahids* could be the deputies of the occulted imam gave them extraordinary authority. It made their judgements infallible. At the top of the *mujtahid* hierarchy would be the ayatollahs, a title which became famous in the Western world when Ayatollah Khomeini presided over the Iranian Revolution in 1978.

In 1532 al-Karaki became the religious ruler of Iran. Shah Tahmasp recognized him as 'the Deputy of the Imam'.[8] Without declaring it in so many words, the shah had in theory relinquished his claim to religious authority, although in practice his association with divinity would never leave him or his successors. Viziers and ambassadors allowed into the shah's presence continued to prostrate themselves three times, and then only the most senior were permitted to kiss his hand; otherwise they had to kiss the hem of his kaftan or the tip of his hanging sleeve, retiring backwards out of the room, so that they would never turn their back on the shah's majesty. Anthony Jenkinson, the representative of the English Muscovy Company, described having to wear special shoes when he arrived at the shah's court in Qazvin, north-western Iran, on 2 November 1562. The shoes were to prevent Jenkinson, an infidel, from sullying the floor on which the shah walked.[9] It was perhaps a sign of al-Karaki's power that he suffered no ill effects from agreeing with the Sunni ruler of the Ottoman Empire, the Safavids' greatest enemy, that such signs of veneration were un-Islamic, since prostration is only permissible to God.

Tahmasp certainly recognized al-Karaki's religious supremacy. He ordered all provincial governors and officials of the realm to consider him as 'their guide and leader, offer him obedience and submission in all affairs, carry out what he orders and refrain from what he forbids'. Al-Karaki was also given the power of appointing and dismissing religious and military officials throughout the country; he even issued a set of instructions as to how governors should administer their provinces.

Unsurprisingly, al-Karaki's new powers aroused intense opposition both amongst the nobles, who saw themselves being supplanted, and also amongst some of the ulema. They were shocked at the claim he made for himself and his fellow *mujtahids* that they were the deputies of the occulted imam, and objected profoundly to the position he had assumed as the voice of Shiism in Iran. It was a position akin to the pope's as head of the Catholic Church, with the additional asset of infallibility that the pope would not give himself until the nineteenth century. Resentment against al-Karaki was so intense that a letter charging him with obscene attacks on Shah Tahmasp was circulated at court. Al-Karaki was, however, exonerated.

He had transformed the nature of the ulema's role and their status in Iranian society. They were evolving into a religious elite, headed by the most learned and pious among them. Their religious rulings partook of the infallibility of the occulted imam. Their wealth and influence at court, thanks to the shah's promotions and endowments, their reputation for learning, their control over the systematization of Twelver Shiism, were transforming the ulema into a quasi-independent hierarchical institution distinct from the State and not dissimilar from the Catholic Church.

It took the religious scholar Muhammad Baqir Majlisi, however, to turn Iran into a theocracy around a century later. In 1687 Majlisi was appointed by Shah Suleiman I as the Shaykh al-Islam, the religious leader of Isfahan. Isfahan was becoming one of the most breathtakingly beautiful cities in the world but, more importantly, it was the new capital city of the Safavids. Majlisi had thus become the foremost religious authority in the empire. He was to become the most powerful figure in Iran and one of the most influential Shiite theologians that has ever lived. Majlisi's admirers call him the renewer of Islam and the greatest scholar of his age; his critics vilify him as a fanatic and ruthless oppressor of minorities.

Under Majlisi, the ulema consolidated their power. They believed that the State must be directed by the Mosque and that the shah's duty was to obey the *mujtahid*. No doubt it helped that Suleiman, notable for his pale white skin and dyed black hair and beard, was in no position to exert his own authority. Iran had again been riven by rebellion following a series of earthquakes and epidemics and a succession of devastating raids by Cossack forces from southern Russia. Suleiman preferred to retreat back to the harem where he was reared and rely on the ulema to give him the authority he so desperately needed.

Majlisi rejected al-Karaki's use of *ijtihad* and was determined that a literal-based Shiism should prevail. The Quran and the hadiths would answer every question. Shiites, like Sunnis, had their battles between the traditionalists and the rationalists; Majlisi was with the traditionalists. For him, the seeking of knowledge was 'a waste of one's life' which would 'lead to apostasy and heresy'. Majlisi, a Shiite equivalent of Ibn Hanbal or Ibn Taymiyya, opposed everything that he considered to be an innovation – *bid'a*.

How much Majlisi actively persecuted 'infidels' is unclear. He is thought to have been responsible for the forced conversion of about 70,000 Sunnis and non-Muslims, though, as always in the history of persecution, this was more for political than religious reasons.[10] In the light of severe political and economic problems, areas populated by Sunnis, such as Kandahar in today's Afghanistan, rose up against Safavid rule. Sunnis were the enemy – and besides, they made a useful scapegoat for the ills of the empire.

Majlisi also condemned any of the ulema who had Sufi sympathies. Under his prompting, the shah banned Sufis from Isfahan, suppressed Sufi brotherhoods and destroyed their shrines. In addition, he prohibited the consumption of any alcohol. About 6,000 bottles of wine owned by the Safavid royalty were publicly destroyed. The shah took up drinking again, however, after his eunuchs and royal princes convinced him of the health benefits of wine.

But Majlisi's puritanism did not dent his popularity amongst ordinary Muslims. Indeed he set out to popularize Shiism. He introduced highly charged emotional public rituals. Most important was the commemoration of the death of Imam Husayn (the son of Ali) murdered, as Shiite clerics made sure to point out, by the Sunni Umayyads in 680. Neighbourhood groups, young and old, rich and poor, competed to outdo each other in their veneration of Husayn. According to the seventeenth-century Ottoman travel writer known as Evliya Çelebi, 'Hundreds of professional barbers circulate … with razors in their hands [and] those wishing to demonstrate their love for Husayn … have the barbers slash their arms and breasts, shedding so much blood that the verdant green ground turns tulip red.'[11]

A weak shah had needed the ulema to give him the authority he lacked. Majlisi had exploited this imbalance of power to ensure the triumph of the religious. The ulema were developing into a religious, landed and political aristocracy owning large tracts of land and intermarrying with merchants and the secular landed aristocracy. But while the Shiite scholar was turning Iran into a theocracy, in an outlying colony of Western Christendom, a Protestant was laying the foundations for secularism.

CHAPTER 17

THE PURITAN WHO FOUGHT THE PURITANS

'Every sect saith, Oh! Give me liberty. But give him it, and to his power he will not yield it to anybody else.'

– Oliver Cromwell, Lord Protector of England, speech at the opening of Parliament, 4 September 1654

'The liberty that I contend for is more than toleration. The very idea of toleration is despicable; it supposes that some have a pre-eminence above the rest, to grant indulgence; whereas all should be equally free, Jews, Turks, Pagans and Christians.'

– John Leland, *The Virginia Chronicle*, 1790

IN DECEMBER 1630 THE Calvinist clergyman Roger Williams and his wife Mary boarded the *Lyon* at Bristol along with twenty other passengers, and set sail for the newest of North America's colonies, Massachusetts Bay. It was 3,000-odd miles away. But the ship made good going and weighed anchor two months later on 5 February 1631 near today's Boston.[1]

Williams was amongst the thousands of Puritans leaving England to escape an increasingly persecutory government. To be a Puritan was to be both religiously and politically suspect.* As a critic of the current state

* 'Puritan' is a slippery term. In essence it refers to Protestants who were critical of the compromise Protestantism that Elizabeth I had established in England in 1559 in an attempt to placate moderate and radical Protestants, as well as Catholics. Puritans (Calvinists counted among their number though not the more authority-minded Lutherans) believed the Church of England, headed by the monarch, still retained too many Catholic elements and was not reformed enough. The more radical amongst them, collectively known as the dissenters or non-conformists which included the Quakers, Baptists, and later the Methodists, believed that they should split from the English Church rather than remaining and reforming it from within.

of the Church of England, the Puritan was implicitly if not explicitly criticizing the authority of the monarch himself who was the head of the church. 'No bishop, no king,' as James I observed. And how prescient he was. His son Charles I would be beheaded by Puritan Parliamentarians who had combined opposition to Charles's authoritarian rule with opposition to the authoritarian rule of the Church of England and its hierarchy of bishops.

Under James, Puritans who refused to worship in accordance with the prayers and rituals set down in the Book of Common Prayer and clergymen who refused to wear vestments, which in Puritan eyes smacked of Catholicism, risked heavy fines, loss of their jobs, imprisonment, or even execution (only two heretics were actually executed during James's reign).

Intra-faith antagonisms, which had been bedevilling continental Europe as much as they had been England, only intensified. Neighbour denounced neighbour, priest or pastor to the authorities for being too Catholic, or too radically Protestant, and not conforming to the act of uniformity which laid down the minimum requirements of belief and practice that every subject was required to follow. Of course individual acts of cross-confessional kindness co-existed alongside acts of betrayal or violence: the entire body of constables and churchwardens of one Yorkshire parish was imprisoned for refusing to certify what kind of education the children of local Catholic recusants were receiving; Lincolnshire villagers payed the debts of a Quaker who had been imprisoned for non-payment of tithes.

Between 1629 and 1640, 80,000 people left their homes, livelihoods, neighbours and country to start a new life in the Netherlands, the West Indies (where the English had just taken possession of Barbados and Jamaica and were importing slaves to work the sugar cane plantations) or North America. Roger Williams and his wife were amongst them.

Five years after his arrival the General Court of the Massachusetts Bay Colony found Williams guilty of sedition and heresy, spreading 'diverse, new and dangerous opinions', and ordered his banishment, threatening him with execution if he ever returned.

The fact that the New England Puritans had journeyed thousands of miles to an unknown land in order to escape discrimination if not outright persecution, did not turn them into religious tolerationists. Almost inevitably religiously fervent – it was after all the strength of their religious commitment that had forced them to take this leap into the unknown – they wanted to establish a community which approximated more nearly to what they believed God had envisaged, that is, one where the principles of their own sect prevailed. They were not revolutionaries. They believed, as virtually every Christian (and Muslim) did, that society must be founded on God's laws, and that it was the duty of every ruler to uphold those laws. New England Puritans were not opposed to an established Church, as long as it was their type of Church.

They certainly did not believe in toleration. On the contrary, men like John Winthrop, governor of Massachusetts Bay Colony, and John Cotton, one of its most prominent pastors, believed it was the duty of the ruler to root out heretics and other troublemakers who threatened their godly society. As Winthrop pointed out in 1637: 'If we are bound to keep off whatsoever appears to tend to our ruin or damage, then we may lawfully refuse to receive such whose dispositions suit not with ours and whose society (we know) will be hurtful to us.'[2] Jews were forbidden to live in Massachusetts. In 1647 the colony prohibited any Jesuit priest from entering under pain of banishment or execution. Anglicans (Protestants who supported the beliefs and organization of the Church of England with its bishops and the English monarch at its head) were forbidden to build churches or hold services within the colony. The Massachusetts Bay Colony would soon be the most active of the New England persecutors of Quakers and would execute four of the most troublesome of them between 1659 and 1661; in 1662, however, the newly restored Charles II would order Massachusetts to end its Quaker persecutions.

Roger Williams had shocked, scandalized and offended the colony authorities on many grounds. He had questioned the very legality of the colony, condemning Charles I for 'stealing' the Indians' land without their permission and with no compensation. Williams was learning some of the Indians' languages and culture. English colonization was, according to him, 'a sin of unjust usurpation upon others' possessions'. A brave voice of criticism, and not entirely unique. The Dominican Francisco de Vitoria, a professor at the University of Salamanca, was similarly critical of Spain: discovery alone, he said, gave Spaniards no more right to American territory than the Indians would have acquired had they 'discovered' Spain.[3]

But Williams' criticisms were more shocking yet. He dared to criticize the whole idea of the 'city upon a hill', the dream that had inspired not just the governor of the Massachusetts Bay Colony, but so many thousands of Puritans. Calvin himself had dreamed of creating such a city in Geneva. He believed that the State should not interfere in religious matters, but he did believe that it was the State's duty to obey the Church, to ban heresy and impose a true Christian way of life.

Williams, however, believed in a complete separation between Church and State. He was fiercely opposed to an established Church. All attempts by the State to dictate the practice of a religion, he said, was 'rape of the soul' which 'stinks in the nostrils of God'. And he spoke of the 'oceans of blood' shed as a result of trying to command conformity. About ten years later Europe's powers would reluctantly come to a similar conclusion when they signed the Peace of Westphalia.

It was because the Boston Church was in his opinion 'unseparated' that Williams turned down their offer to become its minister when he first arrived in the Massachusetts Bay Colony in 1631. Williams argued for a 'hedge or wall of Separation between the Garden of the Church and the Wildernes [sic] of the world'. Over a century and a half later, in 1802, Thomas Jefferson would take up Williams' metaphor when he praised the First Amendment of the American Constitution for 'building a wall of separation between Church & State'.

Williams is one of the unsung heroes of religious freedom and pluralism. He blazed the trail that would be followed by Locke nearly fifty years later, and then by Jefferson, Madison and their fellow writers of the bible of liberalism and toleration: the American Declaration of Independence and the United States Constitution.

Williams was one of the first white settlers to argue for Indian rights. In Rhode Island, the colony he founded, he supported a bill proposing that 'blacke mankinde' could not be enslaved for more than ten years. It was not abolition, admittedly, and the bill was never enacted. But Williams should not be forced into a modern liberal mould. He was a tolerationist of his times, more radical than most certainly, but not the liberal that many today would like to make him. He believed entirely in the literal truth of the Bible; his God was harsh and intolerant. It was not up to the State to impose religion on its subjects, but it was certainly up to God and his angels. With all the relish of the intolerant, Williams looked forward to the time 'when the world is ripe in sin, in the sins of Antichristianism' – in other words Catholicism. Then, said Williams, 'those holy and mighty officers and executioners, the angels, with their sharp and cutting sickles of eternal vengeance, shall down with them, and bundle them up for the everlasting burnings'.

To his critics, he was a zealous troublemaker. According to the pastor John Cotton, Williams was 'determined to be purer than anyone else, his church more "separate" than anyone else's, his allegiance to the New Testament more nearly perfect than that of other faithful Christians. And he would never listen to any reasonings that did not spring out of his own brain.' He was, in short, an extremist. 'If he spots a sore on a man's leg, he immediately calls for an amputation,' Cotton remarked sourly.[4]

What most Puritan colonists desired was little different from the Church–State governance they had left behind in England: they still wanted religious uniformity and an established Church, though of course one which was in their hands. In 1635 Williams appeared three times before the Massachusetts court to answer for his 'erroneous' and 'dangerous' opinions.

A sheriff was ordered to arrest him and put him on a ship back to England. But Williams was tipped off by friends and he fled, leaving his wife and their two young children behind. It was a harsh New England winter, and a blizzard was raging when Williams made his escape. For fourteen weeks he wandered through the deep snow, and would have starved or frozen to death had it not been for the kindness of the Wampanoag Indians who offered him food and shelter during the long winter months.

In the springtime of 1636 Williams bought some land near Narragansett Bay (part of what is now Rhode Island) from the local Indians. 'Having, of a sense of God's merciful providence unto me in my distress, called the place PROVIDENCE,' he wrote, 'I desired it might be for a shelter for persons distressed for conscience.' In the first months the settlement was tiny, consisting of Williams himself, his wife, his two small children, plus twelve followers from Salem in the Massachusetts Bay Colony, where Williams had been preaching before he fled. But by 1640, forty families had settled in Providence.

To his credit, Williams really did try to construct a society according to his ideals. The first thing he did was to divide up the land that he had acquired from the Indians into equal strips and share them with his fellow settlers, his own narrow strip being no larger than the others'; in the main, Williams would support his family – soon to be four sons and two daughters – by his Indian trading post south of Providence. But good man that he was, he refused to sell weapons or strong alcohol to the Indians, though they would have been highly profitable.

Under the 'constitution' of Williams' new settlement, each head of household was to sign a covenant, or agreement, that would bind them to come together 'with free and joint consent' and 'to promise each unto other' that they would all abide by whatever the majority decided to do. Williams was to have one vote, just like everyone else. When new arrivals came, they too would be obliged to sign this agreement.

'I infer', he wrote, 'that the sovereign, original, and foundation of civil power lies in the people.' The governments they establish 'have no more power, nor for no longer time, than the civil power or people consenting and agreeing shall betrust [sic] them with'.[5] Government came from the people; it arose from a covenant, a voluntary agreement. Williams was setting out to establish the sort of contractual state that his successors Locke and Rousseau could only theorize. Locke did in fact look to the

North American Indians' style of governance as a model. Maybe his precursor Williams had too.

In essence Williams was making the same revolutionary claim that radical Parliamentarians were making in England: the authority of the ruler did not come from God but from the people. Opposition or support for the divine right of kings was at the conceptual heart of the civil wars that were about to burst out in England. Charles I believed that since his right to rule derived from God, his subjects had no right to make demands or overrule him. Radical Parliamentarians believed that since it was the people who gave Charles the right to rule, they were entitled to make demands on the king or withdraw their loyalty.

In a far less radical way, most Puritan settlers agreed with Williams' contractual view of government. They were embarked on the very creation of their new societies. They could see for themselves how magistrates' authority could not be imposed. Policies had to be agreed on, if their new and fragile communities were not to fall apart in disagreements. But their contractual community was to be far more limited than that envisaged by Roger Williams. It was to be a community of those who shared the same religious beliefs. In Massachusetts, only the 'saints', the self-selected 'godly' who believed they had the power of saving grace in their hearts, were qualified to be Church members. And only Church members were allowed to vote. They would elect a godly ruler, that is; one who would follow God's laws. In their version of sovereignty, the people, the Church members, selected their rulers but were then obligated to follow them (at least for one year, since elections for the governor and other magistrates were held annually), just as rulers were obligated to follow God. Had the Puritan settlers but seen it, the contractual view of government would eventually lead to God's dethronement.

Williams' model contractual society differed from that of his fellow settlers in one crucial way: government was to be only in 'civil things' and liberty of conscience was guaranteed 'provided it not be directly repugnant to the government or laws established'.[6] While Massachusetts' civil magistrates vigorously maintained a religious uniformity on which they thought the solidarity and very survival of the

The Reformers Martin Luther (*top left*) and John Calvin (*top right*).

In 1555 the Holy Roman emperor Charles V was forced to concede that the Catholic Church had lost its monopoly over Western Christendom. Under the terms of the Peace of Augsburg, which put a stop to the wars within the empire between Catholic and Protestant states, he officially recognised Protestantism.

(*Above left*) Michael Servetus, burned at the stake for heresy in 1553 in Calvin's Geneva. Though Calvin's responsibility for Servetus's execution was applauded by most Protestant reformers, it launched the argument for religious tolerance. (*Above right*) Beatrice de Luna/Gracia Nasi, and independent businesswoman and one of the wealthiest Jewish women in Europe. In 1561 she and her nephew, Joseph Nasi, founded a homeland for Jewish refugees in Tiberias, Palestine.

(*Above left*) Suleiman the Magnificent. When he became ruler of the Ottoman empire in 1520 about 42 per cent of Istanbul's population were non-Muslims. (*Above right*) Shah Ismail I, founder of the Safavid Dynasty which ruled the Iranian empire from 1501 to 1736, made Shiism the state religion of Iran in 1501.

The Thirty Years' War between 1618 and 1649 killed more than 8 million people in central Europe. It was one of the many wars between Catholic and Protestant states that tore Europe apart for over a century.

The Peace of Westphalia, 1648, which ended Europe's wars of religion, including the Thirty Years' War, is considered to mark the beginnings of the secularization of Europe and the parting of the ways between Islamdom and Christendom.

(*Above left*) The Puritan Roger Williams, pioneer of religious liberty. In 1636 Williams founded the colony of Providence (Rhode Island), the first polity in the modern world where freedom of conscience was guaranteed.
(*Above right*) Muhammad Baqir Majlisi, renowned Twelver Shiite cleric, was appointed *Sheikh ul-Islam* (religious leader) of Isfahan in 1687. He turned Iran into a theocracy.

The French Enlightenment: François-Marie Arouet (*above left*),who took the nom de plume Voltaire, and Jean-Jacques Rousseau (*above right*).

Robespierre was determined to destroy the Catholic Church but still thought religion was essential for the wellbeing of the individual and society. He inaugurated his own religion, the cult of the Supreme Being, in 1794.

Napoleon, the 'Enlightenment on horseback', invaded Egypt in 1798.

The hunchbacked figure on the left, the Jewish German philosopher Moses Mendelssohn, plays chess with his close friend, the writer Christian Gotthold Ephraim Lessing. Mendelssohn was a leading advocate of Jewish cultural and social assimilation.

Mendelssohn's daughter Brendel took assimilation to the point feared by many Jews. She Christianized her name to Dorothea, married a Christian – the poet, critic and philosopher Friedrich Schlegel – and converted to Christianity in 1804.

(*Above left*) The French Jewish officer Captain Dreyfus's false conviction for treason in 1894 revealed the anti-Semitism at the heart of the Catholic Church in France and the French establishment. (*Above right*) Theodor Herzl had been the assimilated Jew personified. The Dreyfus Affair, however, convinced him that Jews must have a nation of their own because they would never be accepted in Europe.

While Mustafa Kemal Atatürk (*above left*), elected first president of Turkey on 29 October 1923, enforced a radical programme of secularization, Hassan al-Banna (*above right*) thought the Muslim world needed to become more not less Islamic. One of the founding fathers of Islamism, he is a major influence on today's jihadi movements.

The three pashas (pasha was the title given to high-ranking officials) who ruled the Ottoman Empire during the First World War and were responsible for the Armenian Genocide. Cemal Pasha (*left*), Enver Pasha (*right*), Talaat Pasha (*standing*). Nazi Germany explicitly looked to their treatment of the Armenians as a model for how to 'solve' the 'Jewish question'.

Pope Pius XII (*centre*): did he appease the Nazis? the Reichskonkordat, the 'Concordat between the Holy See and the German Reich', was signed on 20 July 1933. The treaty guaranteed the rights of the Catholic Church in Germany and is still in force today.

colony depended, Williams' constitution breathes not a single mention of the word God. The Constitution of the United States, drawn up in 1787, would make the same glaring omission. It was no part of the remit of the rulers of Providence to build a city on a hill, enforce one type of religious belief or interfere in what its citizens chose to believe. Williams had indeed built a wall of separation between Church and State with which his fellow settlers in Providence unanimously agreed. How Williams would have reacted if they had disagreed with his draft constitution, we will never know.

The new settlement at Providence (Rhode Island) did not initially prove a success, no doubt to the satisfaction of Williams' opponents. They had predicted that social order would disintegrate without an established Church – and it seemed to be doing so. In the absence of an established religion Rhode Islanders found it difficult 'to find a common ground upon which to base their civil deliberations'. Dissension was rife, to the extent that some inhabitants even petitioned Massachusetts for aid.[7] That seemed to be proof enough that toleration set neighbour against neighbour and worked against a sense of unity and common purpose essential for the welfare of the colony.

Toleration was indeed the downfall of the Catholics who founded the colony of Maryland in 1632, around the same time as Providence.* Most of New England banned Catholics, as did Virginia. The Catholic founders of Maryland, however, turned the other cheek and allowed in Anglicans. By 1701 Anglicans had become the dominant presence in the colony and voted to make the Church of England the established church of Maryland. Over the course of the eighteenth century Maryland Catholics were first barred from public office (though some Catholics did continue to hold government positions), then disenfranchised.[8]

But Rhode Island, though it seemed to be disintegrating, was still considered to be sufficiently threatening that its neighbouring New England colonies – Massachusetts, Connecticut and Plymouth – formed

* Although some historians like to think the colony was named after the Mother of Jesus, it was actually named for Queen Henrietta Maria, the Catholic wife of King Charles I who granted Maryland its charter.

a military alliance against it. In part this was to counter Rhode Island's own alliance with the Narragansett Indians, the most powerful Indian tribe in southern New England, with whom Williams had extremely good relations. But it was also to put an end to Williams' 'lively experiment' in religious freedom. In response to this threat, Rhode Islanders sent Williams to England in 1643 to secure its legal recognition and a patent for his colony.

In England, Williams found that war had broken out between the Royalists and Parliamentarians. As in the rest of Europe, what type of Christianity you espoused crudely signified which side you were on politically. Defenders of King Charles I's authoritarian rule were usually on the quasi-Catholic authoritarian end of the Protestant spectrum; they tended to be Anglicans, supporters of the Church of England with its episcopalian rule of bishops. As far as Parliamentarians were concerned, to be a Royalist was to be a Catholic hell-bent on enslaving the people. As far as Royalists were concerned, to be a Parliamentarian was to be a Puritan hell-bent on overturning the social order upheld by King Charles I and his archbishop, Laud. Of course, it was not as simple as that: Presbyterians/Calvinists, for instance, were committed Parliamentarians.* They were dedicated to reforming the Church of England and abolishing its government by bishops, and were bitterly opposed to Charles I's authoritarian rule. But they were so appalled by Charles's execution that a chasm opened up between them and the Puritan 'regicide' Oliver Cromwell and his more radical Puritans.

For nine years English men and women went through, on a smaller scale, the terrors, poverty, disease and hunger that the Thirty Years' War

* Calvin is considered to be the founding father of Presbyterianism. It is both a theology based on his works and a particular type of church organization modelled on his city state Geneva. Theologically, Presbyterianism emphasizes predestination, faith by grace rather than good works, and the authority of scripture. Administratively, it is anti-episcopalian, and believes that church affairs should be run not by bishops but by elders, laypeople (usually men) elected by their congregation. Calvin's disciple John Knox, a former Catholic priest, brought Presbyterianism to Scotland in the 1560s.

was inflicting on the peoples of central Europe. In what seemed like the end times, when the king was put on trial and executed in 1649 for being 'a tyrant, traitor, murderer and public enemy to the good of this nation', when social order was turned on its head, the nature of political and religious authority was being fundamentally re-examined by a radical few. But it was Roger Williams, in England to secure his patent for Providence, who pioneered the way.

In 1644, five years before King Charles was beheaded, a 400-page tome written by Williams was published. It was called *The Bloudy Tenent [tenet] of Persecution, for Cause of Conscience: discussed in a Conference between Truth and Peace* – and was universally condemned. Luckily for Williams, he had already secured his patent legally recognizing Providence's right to exist, thanks in large part to the enormous popularity of his earlier book, *A Key Into the Language of America*, published in 1643. Part dictionary, part guide to Indian culture, it was unique at the time for treating Indians not as savages but as peoples who were as civilized as Europeans, if not more so. Two years later, Parliament ordered that copies of *The Bloudy Tenent* should be burned by the public hangman.

Williams had antagonized every shade of Protestant in England and New England, except the most radical. He had become a friend of Cromwell, a committed Puritan who would soon be one of the signatories to the king's death warrant and rule the country as Lord Protector. But even Cromwell opposed the book. Williams was overturning all pre-existing assumptions about the State's relationship with religion.

It had gone virtually unquestioned by ruler and subject alike that the ruler should seek to impose the religion he followed on all of his subjects and punish those who deviated. Even Castellio, who had condemned the burning of Servetus in Geneva under Calvin's aegis, had not questioned the idea that the State should punish the heretic; he only questioned whether heretics should incur the death penalty. When, four years after *The Bloudy Tenent*, Europe's powers signed the Peace of Westphalia in 1648, they acknowledged that they must allow some sort of religious pluralism. But they certainly did not think that such toleration was a good thing in itself. On the contrary, it was a recipe for moral and political disorder. Since Augustine, tolerance had been considered to be morally wrong: it allowed the misguided to pursue their way to eternal damnation. During the Reformation, when sects began to multiply and a choice of sect had to be made, intolerance increasingly came to be seen as a sign of religious commitment. Tolerance was unholy.

But Williams, meticulously citing example after example from the Bible, argued that holy scripture specifically condemned intolerance. *The Bloudy Tenent* was his theoretical justification for his settlement at Providence. In the book's preface Williams asked the reader to imagine what religion Jesus would have endorsed if he had been in London in 1644. Every reader, wrote Williams, will have assumed that Jesus would have chosen theirs. Williams then went on to ask his readers what weapons they thought Jesus would have used to ensure that that religion was followed by everyone in England. The answer, of course, was none. Jesus had used no force to spread his own message, only love. 'Inforced uniformity', said Williams, 'is the greatest occasion of civill Warre, ravishing of conscience, persecution of Christ Jesus in his servants and of the hypocrisie and destruction of millions of souls.'

Williams was declaring intolerance to be un-Christian. Furthermore, his view of tolerance extended way beyond that which even those in favour of toleration were espousing. He was arguing that if the Bible forbade intolerance, then all heretics – blasphemers, Catholics, Jews, Muslims, even atheists, must be tolerated.

Neither John Milton, who had published his call for freedom of speech *Areopagitica* a year earlier in 1643, nor one of the greatest of all the advocates of religious freedom, the Anglican John Locke, ever dreamed of extending toleration so far. Locke, writing about forty years later, explicitly excluded Catholics and atheists. Atheists could not be trusted, because since they denied divine authority and therefore lacked fear of divine punishment, they undermined the social order: any oaths of loyalty which they took would carry no conviction. Catholics could also not be trusted because they were members of a Church beholden to a foreign prince, the pope. With his sword of excommunication, the pope could depose rulers he deemed heretics, and authorize their subjects to rebel. Though Locke would later argue that Jews and Muslims should be tolerated, few contemporaries of Williams would have included Jews under the sheltering umbrella of tolerance. Notable exceptions were Cromwell, the Baptists and the Levellers, a radical political faction that was a prominent voice during the Civil Wars. (The Levellers, led by 'Liberty John', John Lilburne, even believed in the equality of women and men.)[9]

But Oliver Cromwell condemned as blasphemous Williams' belief that the State had no right to punish heretics. So did Parliament, which was dominated by Presbyterians who had suffered persecution themselves. Radical toleration had limited appeal within the Puritan movement. The majority remained wedded to the idea of some sort of State–Church union where it was the magistrate's role to suppress heresy. Indeed, the same year that *The Bloudy Tenent* came out in England, Parliament was so alarmed by what it called the plague of 'erroneous opinions, ruinating schisms, and damnable heresies' infecting England that it forbade preaching except under licence from Parliament; it also passed strict rules for the observance of Sunday, with no games or sports, no trade or travel. Puritans did not, however, deny themselves all pleasure: they were great users of, and proselytizers for, marijuana or 'Spanish tobacco' as it was called.[10]

But by the time the hangman was burning his books, in August 1644, Williams had set sail for Providence, bearing with him the charter guaranteeing its survival. The charter said not a word about religious worship.

Providence became the first polity in the modern world where Church and State were actually separated, where freedom of conscience was guaranteed, and where government was by majority vote. In severing the link between Church and State, Williams paved the way for religious minorities to be accepted in a religiously pluralist state, not just tolerated, as they would be under the Peace of Westphalia. Every individual would be free to follow their own conscience. The ruler's duty was simply to ensure their subjects could do so. 'Soul libertie', freedom of conscience, Williams argued, was a God-given right as much as the right to life itself.

It is with the language of rights that religious toleration becomes something more than a reluctant permission by the State for minority religious communities to practise what were perceived as their wrong-headed and evil beliefs. Toleration granted by the ruler becomes religious liberty demanded by the citizen (not subject). 'By nature we are the sons of Adam and from him have legitimately a natural property, right and freedom,' argued the Leveller Richard Overton in his pamphlet *An Arrow Against all Tyrants*, published in 1646 a year after Williams' *Bloudy Tenent.* Overton is one of the unacknowledged heroes of the fight for religious liberty. He followed Williams in taking the debate on tolerance into new territory.

The case against religious intolerance was mounting up. It was contrary to Christ's teachings; it was the cause of too much bloodshed; it was counter-productive since, although intolerance can force people to *abandon* their religious practices, it cannot force people into *adopting* certain beliefs – belief has to be freely embraced or it does not constitute true belief; and finally freedom of belief, of conscience, was a right.

The idea of natural rights was ineluctably tied to the Europe-wide battle over authority. As far as one can pin down this impossibly vague concept, 'natural rights' spring from the idea of what it is to be fully human. For seventeenth- and eighteenth-century believers in rights, it was not possible to be fully human unless you were a free, independent agent, free to live, think and have possessions which could not be taken away from you. Once members of a society are seen as having rights, the whole relationship between ruler and ruled changes. The ruler's legitimacy no longer depends on the authority bestowed by God, the 'divine right' of kings, it depends on the people. They give their consent to be ruled but are entitled to withdraw it if the monarch fails to protect them or deprives them of their rights. 'Ask not what your people can do for you,' Williams and Overton were in effect telling rulers, 'but what you can do for your people'. The two men were beginning to forge links between toleration, separation of Church and

State, rights and democracy, which have become standard thinking in the West today. As we will see, most proponents of the idea of natural rights at the time did not seem unduly worried that their definition of what it meant to be human excluded slaves, people of colour and women.

In the eighteenth century, Muslim modernists would insist that it was one of Islam's greatest philosopher-theologians, al-Ghazali, who had pioneered the concept of natural rights back in the eleventh century. Al-Ghazali defined what he considered to be the 'five necessities' essential for human well-being. These were: the preservation of religion (that is, Islam), life, progeny, intellect and property. They are remarkably similar to Locke's 'natural rights' formulated in the late seventeenth century: 'Life, Liberty [in the seventeenth-century sense of the concrete ability to do whatever you wanted with yourself and your property] and Property.' And Locke's rights are in essence those listed in America's Declaration of Independence of 1776 and France's Declaration of the Rights of Man and of the Citizen (see Chapters 18 and 19).

But, of course, there is one crucial difference between al-Ghazali's five necessities and the Western versions: in the latter the word 'religion' does not appear. The concept of the necessities was al-Ghazali's solution to the problem of how religious judges should make a ruling when the Quran and sunna were unclear or had nothing to say on the matter. In such cases, a ruling should be determined by whether it was or was not in line with the five necessities. Al-Ghazali, of course, conceived of the necessities within the context of God's authority and his law. It was because of the primacy of God's authority that al-Ghazali believed that Muslims who held views that violated central elements of the Muslim creed should be sentenced to death for apostasy. Locke, however, believed that religious *freedom*, within certain limits, was essential. What were God-given necessities for al-Ghazali were God-given rights for Locke, which every citizen was entitled to demand and which every ruler had to protect or else lose their right to rule.

But in 1646 a rights-based way of thinking was too dangerously revolutionary even for the Parliamentarians who rebelled against Charles's rule. Overton was imprisoned. Parliament went on to declare that the denial of the Trinity and the divinity of Jesus was punishable by death. No one was ever executed, however.

Three years later in 1649, on a cold January afternoon, King Charles I was beheaded, to the disbelief and outrage of many Parliamentarians. In the new republican regime that followed, English men and women were given an unprecedented measure of religious freedom. Parliament, on the promptings of Cromwell and his army, repealed Elizabeth I's Act of Uniformity of 1558 which had made it a legal requirement to attend Church of England services at least once a week.

Freed from this constraint, in an atmosphere where all authority was being questioned, the radicalism incipient in Protestantism found its full voice. Religious and political sects sprang up like mushrooms, some breathtaking in their revolutionary behaviour and views.

A group called the Ranters believed that Jesus was just a man. Everyone could enjoy the same spiritual wisdom and authority that he had possessed, they claimed. They did not need to obey the spiritual rules and moral conventions that he had inspired, but could create their own rules. As radical politically as they were religiously, Ranters believed that property was theft, and governance a tyranny. Quakers did not believe in the authority of the Bible, but in the authority of personal revelation and experience. Fiercely egalitarian and anti-authoritarian, Quakers refused to doff their hats to their social 'superiors', nor would they swear oaths on the Bible because they did not believe that it had more spiritual authority than the individual. Fifth Monarchists believed that Charles I's execution heralded the imminent return of Christ, who would establish his kingdom in England where he would rule with his saints for 1,000 years. Muggletonians were said to run naked through the streets to advertise their sect, though sects were always vilified with accusations of revelling in nakedness and orgies.

The new government was silent on rites, ceremonies and sacraments. But Cromwell, Lord Protector of England, Wales, Scotland and Ireland, had inherited a country that was still riven over how it should be ruled politically and religiously. He was critical of those who would not be satisfied 'unless they can put their finger upon their brethren's consciences, to pinch them there'.[11] But unlike Williams and the radicals, he still believed that the State should punish blasphemers and heretics – who they actually *were*, was, as always, the problem. Toleration should not 'be stretched so farr as to countenance them who denie the divinity of our Saviour, or to bolster up any blasphemous opinions contrary to the fundamentall verities of religion' he said, when approving the imprisonment of John Biddle for denying the deity of Christ. Toleration was to be withheld from the ungodly and the followers of false religions. And Catholics were certainly outside the pale of toleration.

Cromwell was notoriously savage against the Catholics during his conquest of Ireland. In 1649 he had ordered, or at least turned a blind eye to, the massacre by his troops of the combined English Royalist and Catholic Irish troops who were defending the towns of Drogheda and Wexford. On the heels of these massacres, Cromwell would ban the practice of Catholicism, execute priests and confiscate land owned by Catholics.

But his ordering of, or complicity in, the Irish massacres was largely for political not religious reasons: the Irish Catholics were the Parliamentarians' enemies, allies of the English Royalists. In 1641 they had rebelled against English Protestant rule and behaved as savagely as Cromwell's troops would do, massacring about 3,000 English and Scottish settlers in Ireland. Cromwell's troops in turn massacred about 5,000 Catholic soldiers and civilians in Drogheda and Wexford.

Cromwell has, however, been hailed for his policy on Jews. In 1655 Rabbi Menasseh ben Israel arrived in England from Calvinist Holland, one of the most tolerant places in Europe.* Menasseh was famous across Europe for his writings and speeches on behalf of persecuted Jews. In his home city of Amsterdam, where he was a friend of Rembrandt (who lived

* Holland was just one province amongst the seven provinces that made up the Dutch Republic (the United Provinces of the Netherlands) which had broken away from Spain. But as it was the most important of the provinces, its name was used synecdochically.

in the Jewish quarter), his superb oratory had attracted crowds of gentiles. Charles I's wife, the Catholic Henrietta Maria, had been amongst those who crowded into his synagogue to hear him speak.

Only a handful of openly practising Jews had lived in England since their official expulsion in 1290. After the expulsion of Jews from Spain in 1492, a few Sephardic Jews had made their way to England, but they had come in the guise of Marranos (converts to Christianity) and did not dare reveal their true religious identity. Henry VIII had, however, employed a few Jewish musicians at court, along with several Jewish scholars to help him with biblical niceties in the argument for annulling his marriage to Catherine of Aragon.

Menasseh shared with many Puritans, including Cromwell, a belief that was common in those turbulent times: that the end of the world was nigh and the Messiah's arrival on earth was imminent. Menasseh's mission in England was to convince Cromwell and Parliament that England must provide Jews with a refuge from persecution until the Messiah's arrival. Since Puritans were convinced that the conversion of Jews was a precondition of the Messiah's coming, many, including Cromwell, were prepared to re-admit Jews to England – they would not, after all, remain Jews for long.

But Cromwell also looked favourably on Menasseh's request because he wanted to attract wealthy Jews to help in the economic recovery of a war-torn England. Perhaps inevitably, the petition aroused all the fears and prejudices – economic and religious – that the Jews' presence in Europe had always aroused. Merchants warned that Jews would take over English trade; clergymen protested that it would be blasphemous to allow Jews to practise their faith openly. Rumours spread that Jews had made an offer of half a million pounds to buy St Paul's Cathedral and turn it into a synagogue. But Cromwell finally got his council of state to agree to a nicety of wording by which, although Jews would not be formally admitted into the country, Jews in England would no longer be considered illegal. It is perhaps indicative of how inflammatory the issue was that the records of that day's council deliberations, 25 June 1655, have been torn out of the Council Book. In 1664, England's newly restored king, Charles II, son of Charles I, formally legalized the Jews' position. They were permitted to live in England and to worship publicly 'so long as they demeane themselves peaceably & quietly with due obedience to his Majesty's Laws'.

On the whole it was the Catholics who then replaced Jews as the scapegoats to be blamed for every disaster. Catholics, especially 'those sons of division, the Society of Jesuits', were everywhere seeking to destroy Protestantism in England. It was the 'Treachery and malice of the Papists' that were responsible for the fire of London in 1666, according to the monument erected in memory of 'that most Dreadfull Burning of this Protestant City' which still stands in the City of London today.

In the Restoration England of the 1660s, traumatized by years of what many felt had been religious and political anarchy, intolerance became the order of the day. Charles II was prepared to give Jews 'legal permission' to live in England. But he re-imposed a religious uniformity on his Christian subjects with a harshness which exceeded his father's.

Anyone who refused to take Communion in the Anglican Church and who would not swear an oath declaring that they did not believe in the Catholic doctrine of transubstantiation (that the Communion bread and wine were literally transformed into the body and blood of Christ) was to be excluded from public office. Unless they were prepared to deny their own faiths, Catholics, Jews and many Puritans were excluded from office, from Parliament and from university. About 2,000 clergymen lost their jobs. Protestant dissenters, non-conformists as they were called, who refused to take the oath, were forbidden to hold meetings of more than five people. Thousands of dissenters were put in jail, the Quaker John Bunyan among them. None were executed, but they were subjected to heavy fines or had their scant but precious possessions taken away from them: their Bible, pewter dish or warming pan, their cows or sheep. A great wave of dissenters left England for Calvinist Holland or North America. But Quakers found they were as persecuted as they had been in England; some North American colonies like Connecticut refused to accept them and Massachusetts even executed four Quakers. Their views were too subversive, both religiously and politically.

Huguenots from France joined the migration in 1685. Louis XIV had revoked the Edict of Nantes which had given Huguenots some measure of freedom to worship and they had become outlaws once again. Despite being forbidden to emigrate, between 1685 and 1760 about 100,000 Huguenots escaped to Russia, South Africa and the North American colonies. Up to 80,000 Huguenots fled to England, Wales and Scotland where such a wave of immigrants had never before been witnessed.* Between 75,000 and 100,000 Huguenots settled in Holland, where Locke was then living. Their plight prompted him to write *A Letter Concerning Toleration* in 1689, one of the seventeenth century's most influential arguments in favour of religious toleration.

For Locke the free exercise of religion – as long as it did not disrupt the social order – was a God-given right. The attempt to impose religious uniformity only resulted in persecution and the century-long wars which had devastated continental Europe and England. Like Williams before him, Locke argued for a total separation between Church and State. But unlike Williams, Locke did not argue for separation on the grounds of protecting religion from corruption by the State but on the grounds that it was the State's role to protect the *rights* of the people, not their souls. The fate of their soul was a matter between each individual and their god.

Only thirty years earlier Thomas Hobbes, simultaneously one of the most admired and loathed thinkers of his time, had come to the completely opposite conclusion. Hobbes had lived through England's Civil Wars. He believed that it was religious differences – the failure to impose religious uniformity – that was to blame for the wars. His answer, propounded in 1651 in his famous work *Leviathan*, as to how to prevent such conflict ever occurring again, was absolutist rule. The ruler must be head of Church as well as of State and impose religious uniformity.

On the one hand an acceptance of pluralism, on the other a determination to reimpose uniformity at all costs. The signatories to the Peace of Westphalia had reluctantly taken the pluralist route. But that experiment

---

* 'Refugee', from the French *réfugier*, to take refuge, was coined in England at this time to refer to the Huguenot immigrants seeking asylum.

soon broke down and was replaced by an authoritarianism which was adopted by monarch after monarch across Europe: Peter the Great of Russia, Charles XI of Sweden, Frederick William ruler of Brandenburg-Prussia, which was becoming one of the most powerful states in the Holy Roman Empire, and Louis XIV of France. All of them broke free from the restraints of their parliaments and ruled as autocrats in the interests of stability; pluralism of power and beliefs was too dangerous – though Frederick William, an autocrat politically, did welcome immigrants of most Christian denominations. Peter the Great determinedly set his face against the more tolerant attitude to Jews exhibited by England. He maintained a hostility to Jews which the Russian Orthodox Church, like its Catholic counterpart in Europe, had always espoused. When asked about admitting Jews into the empire, the Tsar answered: 'I prefer to see in our midst nations professing Mohammedanism and paganism rather than Jews. They are rogues and cheats. It is my endeavour to eradicate evil, not to multiply it.'[12]

In 1683 Roger Williams died thinking himself to be a defeated man. War had broken out between colonists and Indians. Williams, though in his seventies, was elected captain of Providence's militia, but they failed to protect Providence and it was burned down. Fifty years after his death, Williams' house had collapsed into the cellar and the location of his grave had been forgotten. But his ideas lived on, though perhaps not in the ways he had hoped.

In 1697 a twenty-year-old Edinburgh medical student, Thomas Aikenhead, was found guilty of mocking the doctrine of the Trinity and was hanged for blasphemy. He was the last person to be executed for blasphemy in Britain. Daniel Defoe, spy and author of *Robinson Crusoe*, applauded the execution, despite being a passionate supporter of extending religious tolerance to Protestant dissenters like himself.

But though neither Williams nor Locke, a devout Anglican, nor Defoe, intended it, religion was being pushed offstage. Church and State were being separated. The State was becoming a secular state, its function to guarantee the rights of its people, including their freedom to follow their own chosen religious beliefs and practices. Locke argued that that right should be extended even to those with erroneous beliefs such as Jews and Muslims, though not, of course, to atheists or Catholics.

Such pluralism, however, requires an official neutrality on the part of the ruler, whatever his or her own religious proclivities. Opponents of religious tolerance prophesied that it would herald the death of God. And to some extent they were right.

CHAPTER 18

AMERICA WRITES GOD OUT OF THE CONSTITUTION

'I do not believe in the creed professed by the Jewish Church, by the Roman Church, by the Greek Church, by the Turkish Church, by the Protestant Church, nor by any church that I know of. My own mind is my own church.'

– Thomas Paine, *The Age of Reason*, 1794

'It does me no injury for my neighbor to say there are twenty gods, or no God... Constraint may make him worse by making him a hypocrite, but it will never make him a truer man.'

– Thomas Jefferson, *Notes on the State of Virginia*, 1785

'WHERE A PEOPLE ARE gathered together the word of God requires that to maintain the peace and union of such a people there should be an orderly and decent Government established according to God ... to maintain and preserve the liberty and purity of the Gospel of our Lord Jesus which we now profess.'

So reads the preamble to Connecticut's constitution drawn up by its Puritan settlers in 1639. One hundred and fifty years later, in 1789, the descendants of Puritan settlers were putting their signatures to a constitution for the United States of America in which the word 'God' is not even mentioned. The preamble to the constitution defined the aim of government as being 'to establish Justice, insure domestic Tranquility, provide for the common defence, promote the general Welfare, and secure the Blessings of Liberty.' It was the same year that revolution broke out in France and the country was de-Christianized.

Christianity is still considered to play a far more prominent role in the United States today than it does in most of secularized western Europe. Yet it was the first nation to declare itself a specifically non-religious state, 'not in any sense founded on the Christian religion' according to the Treaty of Tripoli which America signed with Libya in 1797. And almost to a man its Founding Fathers did not believe in the divinity of Christ.* George Washington, who led the colonies' victorious war for independence from Britain, was 'not a professing Christian'. The tall, red-haired, badly dressed Jefferson, who wrote the Declaration of Independence in 1776, justifying the colonies' revolt against English rule, described himself as 'Christian, in the only sense in which [Jesus] wished any one to be; sincerely attached to his doctrines, in preference to all others; ascribing to himself every human excellence; and believing he never claimed any other'.[1] The diminutive Madison, a bad orator but the intellectual powerhouse behind the Constitution, declared that 'It is the duty of every man to render to the Creator such homage and such only as he believes to be acceptable to Him'. And vain, hot-tempered John Adams who would throw his wig on the floor and stamp on it in a fit of temper, said his religion could be 'contained in just four short words, "Be just and good."'

These men, the future presidents of the country, were the sons and grandsons of men and women whose religious commitment had driven them thousands of miles across the ocean to start a new life in unknown territory. But the colonies set up in the seventeenth century had shed

* 'Founding Fathers' usually refers to the men who had the most significant role in shaping the United States, that is, in conducting the War of Independence against Britain and drafting the Declaration of Independence and the Constitution. Most prominent were John Adams, Benjamin Franklin, Alexander Hamilton, John Jay, Thomas Jefferson, James Madison and George Washington. The English-born Thomas Paine is admitted to the pantheon of Founding Fathers thanks to his extraordinarily influential and popular writings in support of the American, and French, Revolutions.

much of their religious fervour by the time the Founding Fathers created the United States. The Massachusetts Bay Colony's first governor, John Winthrop, had dreamed of creating a 'city upon a hill'. He had expelled Roger Williams in 1635 and a few years later the Puritan midwife Anne Hutchinson for their 'heretical views'. In 1659 Massachusetts and Connecticut were deeply opposed to Williams' tolerant policy towards Quakers in neighbouring Providence/Rhode Island. Massachusetts and Connecticut threatened to force Providence to expel its Quakers by imposing a trade embargo. But after pressure from their merchants, they withdrew the threat. The embargo would have damaged Massachusetts' trade. The needs of the market took precedence over the needs of God. In the fiercely Anglican state of Virginia, merchants supported the plea by dissenters, the critics of Anglicanism, to have their own meeting houses. If the dissenters were forbidden there was the risk that they might move to another more tolerant state and take their business elsewhere. Virginia would be the loser economically. That was the problem with freedom of movement: people could, and would, vote with their feet.

Limited tolerance had become a practical necessity in Europe by 1648, but it was even more essential in the colonies. Settlers in a particular colony may have been bound together initially by a shared religious vision of what their society should be, but that vision inevitably faded and lost its intensity before the practical requirements of attracting people to their colony, and not a rival one. Spiritual correctness gave way to pragmatism. Colonies needed colonists and tolerance was a good way of attracting people. Merchants began to push for less religiously exclusive regimes: an open market in goods required an open market in beliefs.

The Scottish economist and philosopher Adam Smith in fact explicitly made the connection between an open market in faith as well as in trade. In *The Wealth of Nations*, published in 1776, the same year as the Declaration of Independence, Smith compared the established Church in England to a monopoly. The established monopoly Church, he argued, would never flourish because it was protected from competition and therefore would never need to improve itself. But in a free and open market where men and women had a choice of contending faiths, each religion would be forced to improve itself in the endless competition for souls. Furthermore, in a free market religion would not only prosper but also ensure some measure of peace. Whereas Hobbes thought there could be religious tranquillity only if there was a monopoly Church protected by the coercive powers of the State, Smith thought, along with Voltaire and an increasing number of thinkers, that religious uniformity was a recipe for violence. Europe's recent wars of religion were the only proof they needed.

This newly discovered link between free trade and free religion worked to the benefit not just of Christians, but of Jews as well. As Hasia Diner, professor of American Jewish History, has noted, 'Since trade made the colonies and Jews made trade, European antipathy toward Jews as the rejecters of the Gospel weakened.'[2]

In September 1654 a small group of Jews landed in the sea port of New Amsterdam (soon to become New York when it was taken over from the Dutch by the English). The Jews were refugees from the city of Recife in Brazil. As part of Europe's commercially fuelled land grab of other parts of the world, the Portuguese had just seized Recife from the Dutch. Fearful that the Portuguese would prove as cruelly anti-Jewish as their Iberian forefathers had been in the late fifteenth century (see Chapter 12), a party of Jews set sail for a new home.

New Amsterdam was the capital of New Netherland, the colony owned by the Dutch West India Company. The company had initially made its profits from the Spanish galleons captured by the Dutch in their war for independence from Spain. But the Peace of Westphalia in 1648 had virtually put an end to that trade. The company had switched to the less risky and more profitable trade of supplying enslaved West Africans for domestic and agricultural work on the plantations in South America, in the British- and French- occupied West Indies and in the southern colonies of North America.

At the time when the Jews arrived, New Amsterdam had a population of about 800 men, women and children. About 600 of them were European and Christian – Lutherans, Calvinists, even Baptists and Catholics from Scandinavia, Germany, France and England. They owned the other 200 or so inhabitants, the West African slaves, though some slaves were allowed to earn wages and own property.[3] New Amsterdam was in the process of becoming the sort of town that settlers from Europe might have recognized. It was crammed with windmills, taverns and warehouses; its winding lanes, stinking of leaking privies, were beginning to be replaced by straight cobbled streets; residents had just been forbidden to throw their rubbish on to the streets and had been ordered to clean the bit of the thoroughfare in front of their home. A speed limit had been imposed on wagons and carts. Wealthy merchants, in their lace coats and silk and velvet breeches, strolled the new streets with their wives dressed in the latest European fashion. Their new brick and stone two-storey houses, with steep gabled roofs in the Dutch style and neatly trimmed gardens of tulips and roses, were taking their place alongside the thatched one-roomed wooden homes of the soldiers, sailors, craftsmen, apprentices and minor officials. A fort protected the inhabitants from incursions by Indians or the expansionist aims of neighbouring colonies.

But if the Jews had hoped that the colony of New Netherland would live up to its mother country's tolerance towards Jews, they were sadly disappointed. The colony's governor, Peter Stuyvesant, was a deeply committed Calvinist, determined to maintain the dominant position of his Dutch Reformed Church in the colony. Its charter stipulated that 'no other religion shall be publicly admitted in New Netherland except the Reformed'. Catholics were still the enemy. After eighty years fighting the Catholic Spanish Empire, Holland's independence had only recently been recognized by the Peace of Westphalia. Catholics were treated with extreme suspicion and heavily discriminated against, starved of Catholic priests, banned from worshipping in public and banned from public office. Stuyvesant, a veteran of the Dutch–Spanish wars in which he had had one leg blown off by a cannonball, was equally opposed to Catholicism in his colony.

But by the standards of most of Christian Europe and the Christian colonies of North America, Holland was extraordinarily tolerant of most

Christian sects and of Jews, so long as they did not worship in public. In the great trading city of Amsterdam, Lutherans and Jews were exempted even from that condition. Tolerance was after all conducive to the trade interests of the merchant elite that ruled the city, and the Sephardic Jewish community there, one of the richest in Europe, included many wealthy merchants. In the early 1670s they would build the largest synagogue in the world, a sign of their unusual confidence in a European city.

Stuyvesant and his Calvinist pastors, however, were not prepared to be so tolerant to the four Jewish couples, their thirteen children, and the two widows who now landed in New Amsterdam after fleeing Recife. The Jews, he said, were 'hateful enemies and blasphemers of the name of Christ'. Determined not to let them stay, he told New Amsterdam's owners who had appointed him governor, 'These people have no other God than the mammon of unrighteousness, and no other aim than to get possession of Christian property'.[4] But Jews back in Amsterdam interceded. They pointed out to the Dutch West India Company how loyal and economically beneficial Jews had been to the Netherlands. Besides which, they said, 'many of the Jewish nation were principal shareholders in the Company'. It was a convincing argument. The company ordered Stuyvesant to let the Jews 'live and stay'.[5] They would be the founders of the first Jewish community in North America. In 1657 they were granted full citizenship and allowed to worship in a private house, though Stuyvesant would not allow them to build a synagogue.

A boatload of Quakers were not so fortunate. Persecuted in Holland, as they also were in most of North America's colonies, Stuyvesant was hardly going to make them welcome in his New Netherland colony. In 1656 he declared that anyone found harbouring a Quaker would be fined or imprisoned. But in 1682 Quakers would at last find their place of greatest safety, Pennsylvania. Its founder, the English Quaker William Penn, guaranteed freedom of religion not just to Quakers but to Jews, Catholics, Huguenots, Lutherans, Mennonites and Amish. Penn drew the line, however, at atheists. He also subjected the settlers in his 'Holy Experiment' to a strict regime: they were forbidden to swear, lie, get drunk or indulge in the evils of gambling, theatre-going, masques, cockfighting or bear-baiting. And Jews, though they were free to worship, could not vote or hold public office.

Small handfuls of Jews continued to arrive in North America. By the end of the eighteenth century about 2,000 Jews had made their homes in the colonies. That was out of a total population in the colonies of 2.5 million. They met a mixed reception. In some of the New England colonies, Jews did not have the right of residence, let alone the right to build synagogues. For the first time, however, Jews found they were not the most despised people in society, as they had been in Europe. In the colonies of North America that dreadful privilege went to black Africans. Jews suffered disadvantages but no more than any other white Christian minority sect. They owned and trafficked in slaves just as their white Christian neighbours did. By virtue of their non-blackness Jews shared a kind of equality with white gentiles, giving them a status that had been almost impossible for them to achieve in Europe.

Jews, at least Jewish males, were implicitly included in the magnificent assertion of man's equality with which Thomas Jefferson justified rebellion against British rule in 1776: 'We hold these truths to be self-evident [that is, derived from reason], that all men are created equal, that they are endowed by their Creator with certain unalienable Rights, that among these are Life, Liberty and the pursuit of Happiness.' In that one sentence, Thomas Jefferson, congressman for Virginia, shunted God sideways and put 'man' at the centre of the universe. The Declaration of Independence sums up what standard Western opinion considers to be the fruits of Enlightenment thinking: the turn from blind faith to all-seeing reason, from the tyranny of authority to the liberty of equality, democracy and freedom of thought.

The people, the ruled, had taken over sovereignty from the erstwhile sovereign. It was now the duty of the ruler to protect the rights of their citizens, not the duty of the subject to obey their ruler – that duty was now conditional. No country had conceived of itself in this way before, but then no country had constructed itself before – certainly not at a time when ideas of rights, and doubts about religious uniformity and intolerance were in the air. Jefferson was giving pithy and eloquent expression to ideas that had been simmering in the minds of the more radical thinkers since the seventeenth century. Those ideas were now to become the founding principles of a nation.

Jefferson justified the rebellion of thirteen North American colonies on the grounds of natural rights. It was because King George III had violated the rights of his American subjects that they were no longer bound to be loyal to him. He had, according to the reasoning of the Declaration, fundamentally misunderstood the nature of government and of the people he ruled. They were free citizens with rights, not just subjects who only had duties of obedience to their ruler; his rule depended on their consent and he had forfeited that consent by violating their rights. The Declaration was adopted by the rebellious colonies in August of 1789 one month after Jefferson had watched Parisian crowds storm the Bastille, the symbol of French monarchical tyranny, and liberate its seven prisoners.

The Declaration can still stir the heart today, but only if one can ignore the unignorable. By 'men' Jefferson did not include the 600 black Africans he owned over the course of his lifetime who worked for him as domestic servants or agricultural labourers on his 5,000-acre plantation at Monticello, in Virginia. Of those slaves, only the children he fathered with his slave Sally Hemings were granted their freedom. When Jefferson claimed that 'all men are equal' what he meant was not humankind but white, reasonably wealthy Christian males (though Jews slipped under the radar). Black African slaves, North American Indians and women were not included.

In his original draft of the Declaration, Jefferson had in fact condemned Britain's role in the slave trade, which he called a 'great political and moral evil'. But the paragraph was excluded from the final Declaration. Jefferson did not want to antagonize slave-trading colonies in the north (including Roger Williams' Rhode Island which by 1744 had become a major player in the global slave trade) nor slave-owning colonies in the south, Virginia, of course, amongst them. But he clearly did not believe in racial equality: 'blacks … are inferior to the whites in the endowments both of body and mind,' he claimed. Such an 'unfortunate difference of colour, and perhaps of faculty is a powerful obstacle to the emancipation of these people'.[6] In a twisted piece of logic Jefferson went on to argue that because slavery had so poisoned the relations between black and white Americans, emancipation would lead to bloodshed as former slaves sought revenge: 'Justice is in one scale, and self-preservation in the other,' he wrote. Self-preservation of the white-skinned won.*

Jefferson was not unique in his failure to see the appalling contradiction between his declaration that all men are created equal and that liberty was one of their 'unalienable rights', and his ownership of people. Many of his fellow Founding Fathers, including George Washington, were also slave owners. John Adams and the English-born Thomas Paine were the exceptions. Adams was the only non-slaveholder among the early presidents of the United States. Benjamin Franklin had been the owner of two slaves, whom, in what he thought was a good political joke, he had 'named' George and King, and the newspaper he owned, the *Pennsylvania Gazette*, regularly ran notices involving the sale or purchase of slaves. But in 1785, after returning from his posting in Paris, where his brilliant diplomacy had brought France over to the American rebels' side, he joined North America's small abolitionist movement. Franklin – statesman, philosopher, scientist, the Edison of his day, signatory to the Declaration of Independence and the United States Constitution – freed his two slaves. On the other hand, Jefferson's protégé and fellow Virginian James Madison, the most brilliant and influential of the Founding Fathers and an ardent fighter for liberty, kept hundreds of slaves on his plantation in Montpelier.

---

* The Islamic world too depended on slaves. The Quran accepts the institution of slavery, just as the Bible does, though the Quran does proclaim that to free a slave was one of the most praiseworthy of acts, which would be rewarded in heaven. Yet sharing this iniquitous system though they did, the Islamic world did use their slaves in one significantly different way. Slaves in the Islamic world were not just used for hard labour, as miners or agricultural and domestic labourers, they were also, as we have seen, trained up to be a military and administrative elite. For those so selected, to be a slave was to be privileged. Part of the deal was that they had to convert to Islam, but for most the conversion was well worth it.

Madison and Jefferson must have made a strange pair. Jefferson at 6'2" was 'a tall straight-bodied man as ever you see', according to one of his slaves. Bespectacled and unpowdered, his critics thought he deliberately dressed unostentatiously in order to parade his anti-aristocratic republican virtue (rather as the Jacobins did in France). Jefferson appeared before the appalled British minister Anthony Merry 'not merely in undress, but actually standing in slippers down at the heels, and both pantaloons, coat and under-clothes indicative of utter slovenliness and indifference to appearances.' By contrast, Madison was just over five foot (he would be the smallest president the United States has ever had). He was a simple dresser but, like Robespierre, a vain one, perhaps to compensate for his nose scarred by frostbite and his receding hairline, which he tried to conceal by combing his powdered hair forward. Madison suffered from epileptic-like fits which might well have been psychosomatic. Though physically such opposites Jefferson and Madison were, however, united in their vision of what a just society should be.

In 1787, four years after the North American rebels had won their revolutionary war, their European Union-style confederation was falling apart in the face of interstate conflict. The states agreed that they needed a new constitution which would keep them together. Madison became its driving force; Jefferson, though one of its guiding spirits, was physically out of the picture. As American ambassador in Paris, he was living through the first heady days of the French Revolution. One of his tasks was to help his friend, the Marquis de Lafayette, French hero of the American revolutionary war, draw up the Declaration of the Rights of Man and of the Citizen. Passed in 1789, it would be France's version of Jefferson's Declaration of Independence. It too restricts 'man' to white, male property-holders. Revolutionary France continued to be a major slave-holding and slave-trading empire, though the Declaration proclaimed that 'Men are born free and equal in rights.'

Only Robespierre, responsible for the bloodiest, most ruthless years of the Revolution, condemned the Declaration as 'the destruction of equality'. Under his reign of terror, slaves in the French colonies were emancipated, though their emancipation was due more to the rebellion of the slaves themselves and to political necessity than to being the logical outcome of Robespierre's and the Jacobins' principles.

North America, however, remained a slave society. Working by candlelight late into the night Madison was concerned only to hammer out a constitution that at least nine of the thirteen states could agree on. That meant not antagonizing the slave states. The problem was that the number of people in each state would determine the number of delegates each state could send to the House of Representatives. The northern states were not major slave owners though the eastern seaboard was a huge beneficiary of slave trading. They argued that since slaves would have no vote, their numbers should not affect the number of representatives the slave-owning states could elect. Were slaves people? In which case their actual numbers should count. Or were they property? In which case, the number of slaves a white landholder owned was immaterial. The answer Madison came up with was enshrined in Article I, Section 2, Clause 3 of the Constitution, otherwise known as the 'Three-Fifths Compromise'. According to the compromise, 'other Persons', that is to say slaves, should be counted as three fifths of 'free persons'; native Americans were not counted at all; and though white women were not allowed to vote, they got smuggled in as full persons. The clause was not repealed until 1868.

While slaves saw no improvement in their circumstances under the new constitutional federal arrangements, religious minorities were to be major beneficiaries. Since every state, with or without its established Church, contained different religions, and since no one denomination had an overall majority in the confederation, it was clearly best to keep religion out of the Constitution. No mention was made of what role if any government should have in religious affairs. States who were reluctant to put their signature to the Constitution due to this omission were persuaded to sign with the promise that the question of religious freedom would be dealt with later.

James Madison, now a member of the newly created House of Representatives, was selected to deal with the issue along with drafting other additions to the Constitution. The first of his ten amendments was perhaps the nearest to Madison's heart, consisting of just one sentence: 'Congress shall make no law respecting an establishment of religion or prohibiting the free exercise thereof, or abridging the freedom of speech or of the press, or the right of the people peaceably to assemble and to petition the government for a redress of grievances.' With this sentence, as revolutionary as the Declaration of Independence's one-sentence assertion of 'unalienable rights', the United States of America became the first country in the world to explicitly make religious intolerance illegal.

Although drafted by Madison, the First Amendment was also hugely important to Jefferson. Jefferson was fiercely anticlerical and deeply committed to the cause of religious liberty. Though thousands of miles away in Paris, he kept in close touch with the progress of the First Amendment through his correspondence with Madison. Over the four months that it was intermittently discussed, the House of Representatives voiced few objections to Madison's draft. Peter Sylvester from New York 'feared it might be thought to abolish religion altogether'; Benjamin Huntington from Connecticut similarly feared 'that the words might be taken in such latitude as to be extremely hurtful to the cause of religion'. But most congressmen agreed with Daniel Carroll from Maryland who 'thought it would tend more towards conciliating the minds of the people to the government than almost any other opinion he heard proposed'.[7]

The amendment was ratified in 1791, a few months before the death of Muhammad Ibn Abd al-Wahhab, founder of the Wahhabi movement, which would become one of Islam's most fundamentalist and puritanical movements (see Chapter 21). Jefferson, of course, was delighted with the First Amendment. He was, he said, filled with 'sovereign reverence' for 'that act of the whole American people which declared that their legislature should "make no law respecting an establishment of religion, or prohibiting the free exercise thereof", thus building a wall of separation between Church & State'. With that phrase Jefferson paid homage to Roger Williams, the founding father of religious liberty in the American colonies (see Chapter 17). A divorce had finally been effected between what Thomas Paine called 'the adulterous connection of church and state'.

But it was George Washington, first president of this new creature produced by the Constitution, the United States, who summed up most succinctly the radical shift that the State had undergone in terms of toleration. 'It is now no more that toleration is spoken of, as if it was by the indulgence of one class of people that another enjoyed the exercise of their inherent natural rights,' he wrote in a letter to the Jews of Newport, Rhode Island. Jews were seeking reassurance that the right of freedom of religion would apply to them as well as to all denominations of Christians. 'All possess alike liberty of conscience,' Washington declared. That included 'The Children of the Stock of Abraham... [who] shall sit in safety under his own vine and fig tree' – a reference to the Hebrew scriptures 'But they shall sit every man under his vine and under his fig tree', which notably ends 'and none shall make them afraid' (Micah 4:4).

The United States now had a constitution which forbade an established religion, forbade religious discrimination by the State and which did not even mention the word 'God'. But the fact that the United States was forbidden to impose religious uniformity and on the contrary was required to protect freedom of religion did not mean that at a stroke America had become a 'godless' secular nation. It was not then and still is not now. The Declaration of Independence, after all, founded though it was on the ostensibly rationalist principles of rights, had still proclaimed that 'all men are... endowed by their Creator' with those 'unalienable Rights'.

Almost all of the Founding Fathers would have called themselves Christians. But almost all of them were Christians of a very different type from their Puritan ancestors. These late-eighteenth-century Americans were Enlightenment Christians, 'deists', as they were called. They still believed in God, but in a new type of God and a new type of Christianity shorn of all but its fundamentals and uniting religion and reason. Deism and separation of Church and State were seen as joint solutions to the problems of religious conflict which had bedevilled Europe and to a less violent extent the North American colonies. If Christianity could be reduced to its essentials, then all Christians could agree. For Benjamin Franklin, philosopher and scientist as well as statesman, those essentials were a creator God, the immortality of the soul and 'that all crime will be punished, and virtue rewarded, either here or hereafter'.[8] The rest, he argued, the detailed doctrines, types of worship and service, were 'without any tendency to inspire, promote, or confirm morality, [and] served principally to divide us and make us unfriendly to one another'. Franklin, whose ancestors had been persecuted for their Protestant faith in England under the Catholic Mary Tudor, was himself wonderfully religiously promiscuous: he owned a pew in the Episcopal church in his home city of Pennsylvania, built a meeting house there for the English Methodist evangelist, George Whitefield, and contributed to the building of the city's first Jewish synagogue.

Deism's creed, according to Paine, Franklin's protégé and fellow Founding Father,

> … is pure, and sublimely simple. It believes in God, and there it rests. It honours Reason as the choicest gift of God to man, and the faculty by which he is enabled to contemplate the power, wisdom, and goodness of the Creator displayed in the creation… it avoids all presumptuous beliefs, and rejects, as the fabulous inventions of men, all books pretending to revelation.[9]

And therein lay the problem.

The trouble with a Christianity based on reason is that it is no longer Christianity and no longer a religion. A monotheistic religion is based on faith and obedience to a superior authority. Deism does not rule out God, but it does rule out the miraculous and those doctrines which contravene the laws of reason. For deists, there can be no Trinity, no Resurrection, and therefore, of course, no divine Christ. For Paine, Christ was no more than 'a virtuous and an amiable man' and God was not to be found in the Bible or the teachings of the Church but in 'free rational enquiry'. Deism was the Enlightenment's way of uniting religion with reason. But that way led to scepticism and eventually to atheism, as Paine showed all too clearly in his book that shocked America in 1794, *The Age of Reason*. 'Christian theory', he wrote, 'is little else than the idolatry of the ancient mythologies, accommodated to the purposes of power and revenue.'[10] Hitherto the darling of America, though thanks to his irascibility he lost friends as quickly as he made them, Paine's book sales plummeted.

Nonetheless, radical though he was, even Paine believed in some sort of God. So did Voltaire and Rousseau, the two men who more than any others are associated with the Enlightenment, much though they disliked each other and differed in every way. Rousseau was a rarity amongst the French intellectuals of the Enlightenment: he came from a humble background and had worked in his youth as a footman and a clerk. Voltaire, on the other hand, was a member of the upper bourgeoisie. His real name was François-Marie Arouet; 'Voltaire' was a nom de plume. He was fundamentally suspicious of the people, the 'mob' as he called them. Rousseau, by contrast, was fundamentally optimistic about the innate goodness of humanity. But his views in *The Social Contract*, published in 1762, would lend themselves to a more frightening authoritarianism than Voltaire could ever have envisaged.

Rousseau was exasperatingly self-righteous and prickly. He presented to the world an image of unimpeachable saintliness – for which, much to Voltaire's irritation, he was idolized. But he abandoned his five children to an orphanage so as not to be distracted from his work, admitted in his own *Confessions* that he had loved being spanked and had lived in a *ménage à trois*. Rousseau, however, was a far more fervent and sincere believer than his fellow deist Voltaire. 'All the subtleties of metaphysics will never make me doubt for one moment the immortality of the soul and a beneficent providence. I feel it, I believe it, I want it, I hope for it, and I will defend it to my dying breath,' Rousseau told Voltaire in 1756.[11]

Religion for Voltaire was a much less passionate, needy affair. On seeing the sun rise over the Jura Mountains, he is alleged to have thrown himself on the ground and, in a parody of Rousseau, exclaimed 'I believe, I believe in you! Powerful God, I believe!'; then getting back on his feet, drily added, 'As for monsieur the Son, and madame his Mother, that's a different story.'[12] Voltaire's God, unlike Rousseau's, was not so much beneficent as reasonable: 'a supreme intelligence, an immense power, an admirable order' and his religion boiled down to two simple maxims: 'There is a God, and one must be just.'

From Voltaire and Rousseau to Thomas Paine and the Founding Fathers across the Atlantic, the men we think of as representing the Enlightenment were united in their opposition to an established Church. But they were equally united in believing that religion itself, even their form of rational religion, was essential to a good society. Religion to them was necessary, not because it was the truth ordained by God and the way to salvation, but because it was the way to create good citizens. And in a republican society, which was governed by consent rather than authority, it was especially necessary to have virtuous citizens.

The link between civic virtue and religion went virtually unquestioned. Voltaire is alleged to have told his mistress, 'Whatever you do, don't tell the servants there is no God or they'll steal the silver.' Franklin believed that all religions helped to fortify the personal self-discipline and morality required for self-governance and democracy. He told his daughter Sarah to attend church every Sunday, but that he did not care which one she chose to attend. He himself admitted that he 'seldom attended any public worship', but nonetheless still 'had an opinion of its propriety, and of its utility when rightly conducted'.[13] Robespierre, at the height of the Terror when heads were falling like ninepins, agreed. Though he was determined to persecute the Catholic Church out of existence, he was equally determined to put another religion in its place. But this one would ultimately be a religion of nationalism.

CHAPTER 19

ROBESPIERRE'S NEW RELIGION

'Atheism is aristocratic.'

– Robespierre, Address to the National Convention, 21 November 1793

'If the existence of God and the immortality of the soul were nothing but dreams, they would still be the most beautiful conceptions of the human spirit.'

– Robespierre, Address to the National Convention, May 1794

'Who commissioned you to announce to the people that God does not exist?'

– Robespierre, Address to the National Convention, May 1794

At precisely nine o'clock on a July morning in 1794, when the Reign of Terror was at its height, a procession set off from the newly renamed Promenade of Liberty in Châlons-sur-Marne (now Châlons-en-Champagne), a town set in the rolling Champagne countryside of north-eastern France.[1]

Heading the procession was a detachment of cavalry waving a banner which read 'Reason guides us and enlightens us'. Behind them marched the cannoneers, the artillerymen who fired the cannons; their banner read: 'Death to the Tyrants'. Next, a cart loaded with broken chains carried six prisoners of war; behind the cart, more contingents of soldiers walked arm in arm, singing hymns to liberty, accompanied by drummers and military bands. Their banners proclaimed 'We will exterminate the despots' and 'Unity is our strength'. Bands of Châlons' citizens followed, each contingent waving its slogans of revolutionary virtue: 'Respect old age' borne by an old man and woman; 'The virtuous mother will produce defenders for the *Patrie*' fluttered from a cart drawn by two white horses in which a young mother nursed her baby; 'The *Patrie* adopts us, we are eager to serve it' was held aloft before children bearing baskets of fruit and flowers; 'Austere Morals will strengthen the Republic' was carried by forty women dressed in white, with large tricolour ribbons tied round their heads.*

Pacing behind them were members of the town's Surveillance Committee – the henchmen of the Terror launched by Robespierre in March 1793. The committees were responsible for drawing up and arresting avowed or even possible enemies of the Revolution. Who constituted an enemy, or 'suspect' as he or she was called, was so terrifyingly loose that by the time Châlons-sur-Marne's Surveillance Committee members were parading through the town as many as 50,000 people had been guillotined in a little over a year. The Committee's banners were suitably menacing: one simply depicted the image of a finger on the lips, another bore the inscription 'Our institution purges Society of a multiple of suspect people'.

They were followed by three sections representing *liberté, égalité, fraternité* (a phrase first used by Robespierre in a speech to the National Assembly in 1790). Their banners called on the onlookers to 'Honour the Plough', 'Respect Conjugal Love', and declared that 'Our blood will never cease to flow for the safety of the *Patrie*'.

Finally a cart pulled by four donkeys with mitres on their heads carried the emblems of the *Ancien Régime* that the Revolution was pledged to destroy in the name of *liberté, égalité* and *fraternité*: armorial bearings

* The Paris militia, who had been at the forefront of the storming of the Bastille in 1789, wore a cockade of blue and red ribbons, the colours of Paris. Later, white, the colour of France, was added. The tricolour flag, which was adopted in 1790 and combined the three colours was therefore a symbol both of the Revolution and of the unity of the nation.

representing feudalism, the Catholic Church's trappings of copes, mitres and chasubles, and a man dressed as a pope flanked by two 'cardinals'. On the back and front of the cart, two billboards were attached: 'Prejudices pass away' read one, 'Reason is eternal' read the other.

At the steps of the city hall, the procession burst out singing the Marseillaise. The 'pope' and his 'cardinals' were ceremonially attacked and chained to the cart of liberty while all the accoutrements of the old order, the Catholic vestments and armorial bearings, were burned. Privilege and superstition having been destroyed, a litter bearing the Goddess of Reason led the procession on. She was followed by two nymphs carrying the tricolour flag and the Declaration of the Rights of Man and of the Citizen, which had been drawn up with the help of Jefferson in 1789. The procession ended at the Romanesque-Gothic Church of Notre-Dame. A military band played hymns to Reason, to Liberty, to hatred of tyrants and to sacred love of the *Patrie*. The church was 'rechristened' as the Temple of Reason.

Parades like this lauding the civic virtues of motherhood, family values, love of country – with all their chilling foretastes of Nazi rallies – were taking place all over urban France. The Jacobins even instituted 'battalions of hope' for France's seven- to twelve-year-old boys. Dressed in the uniform of the national guard, the boys were taught to recite passages from the Declaration of the Rights of Man and of the Citizen and were drilled and trained up to be young soldiers of the Revolution, a more benign version of the Hitler Youth. *La Patrie*, or *Le Peuple* which was often considered the same thing, was taking over from God as the new religion. In the name of the people, in the name of *égalité*, thousands were being killed as they had once been in the name of God. Yet in the name of *égalité* the Revolution also emancipated thousands of Jews and black slaves.

Both France and America justified their revolutions on the notion of the rights which every 'man' possessed. Thomas Jefferson's 1776 Declaration of Independence listed life, liberty and the pursuit of happiness as 'man's' fundamental rights, while France's 1789 Declaration of the Rights of Man and of the Citizen listed liberty, property, security and resistance to oppression.

The Founding Fathers wanted freedom from British rule, but they had no desire to remake society. They were rebels not revolutionaries. What they were fighting for was the freedom to run their own affairs and tax themselves, and the freedom to worship according to their own lights. The fact that the North American colonies had been founded in the main by men who may have had different religious affiliations but who were all escaping from religious persecution, was a foundational experience for the creators of the United States: religious freedom was integral to the government they envisaged.

France, by contrast, had its real revolutionaries who took control of the country. They wanted to undo a system that had developed over centuries in which the Catholic Church, the monarchy and the aristocracy were equally implicated in the oppression of the people, the non-aristocrats. The French Declaration insisted that 'No one shall be disquieted on account of his opinions, including his religious views.' Nonetheless, French revolutionaries were prepared to sacrifice that principle and persecute the Catholic Church as part of their 'resistance to oppression' in a way that the Founding Fathers could not have countenanced.

But the French revolutionaries faced up, at least partially, to the logical implications of their Declaration of the Rights of Man. Since everyone had the same rights by virtue of being a 'man' how could it be right that some men were deprived of them? How could Jews be? How could slaves? (Whether women, too, had rights was not even considered.) Jefferson and some of his fellow slave-owning signatories of the earlier Declaration of Independence in 1776 also recognized the uncomfortable inconsistency of their position, but they preferred to shelve the problem. The most radical of France's revolutionaries did not.

During the first heady months of the Revolution in the late summer of 1789, the revolutionaries frenziedly tore down brick after brick of the *Ancien Régime*. As delegates to the National Assembly, the parliamentary body which had been created in June, they declared that it 'hereby completely abolishes the feudal system'; almost incoherent with delight, they nationalized Church property, turned Catholic clergy into salaried State officials and announced that henceforth clergy were to be elected by citizens, including Protestants and Jews, rather than by the Church itself.

In August 1789, leaders of the 500-strong Jewish community in Paris petitioned the National Assembly for the same political and civil liberties as French Christians living under the new political regime.[2] In *Ancien Régime* Paris, Jews had had to apply for a licence in order to live in the city and that could be withdrawn by the authorities, who made regular visits to report on them. Note that Paris's Jews were not asking for greater tolerance but for equality. The Paris petition was followed by a similar petition from the 5,000 Jews of Bordeaux. Jews in Alsace, in the east of France, demanded no more than better treatment. Of the 30,000 Jews in France, Alsatian Jews were the third and largest group, numbering about 25,000. They were also the most persecuted. Alsatian Jews were forbidden to live in towns, they were confined to moneylending as a profession and the loans and interest they charged were usually irrecoverable by law.

The Jews' demands met with fierce opposition especially from the clergy and the nobility. They were appalled at the idea that if emancipated, Jews might be elected to positions of authority over a country which was 99 per cent Christian. Abbé Maury, an eloquent defender of the *Ancien Régime*, deployed the argument that would become a mainstay for anti-emancipationists in the following century. 'Jews have traversed seventeen centuries and not mixed with other nations', he declared; they were 'not a sect but a nation'. How could Jews be trusted, since they did not consider themselves part of the country in which they lived? The liberal Parisian nobleman Comte de Clermont-Tonnerre's answer was that Jews 'should be denied everything as a nation, but granted everything as individuals… The existence of a nation within a nation is unacceptable to our country.' Every Jew, he said, 'must individually become a citizen; if they do not want this, they must inform us and we shall then be compelled to expel them'. Jews must, in other words, assimilate. The Comte had spelt out what has been, in some form or other, France's attitude to immigrants and minorities ever since. Jews must shed their Jewish particularism and 'universalize' themselves; they must become part of the *Patrie* and see themselves not as Jews but as French. This was equality with coercive strings attached. It was a step up from the inferiority of the *dhimma*, true, but emancipation would be, in some ways, still a form of toleration.

Talleyrand, Bishop of Autun, a master of the art of survival during the terrifying political swings of the Revolution, was one of the few members of the Catholic hierarchy to support emancipation. He joined Robespierre, Mirabeau and all those inspired by Enlightenment principles or the desire to bring down the insolent and mighty Catholic Church, the oppressors of Jews. 'The Revolution, which has made the recovery of their rights possible for all Frenchmen, cannot be the agent of their loss to any such citizens,' Talleyrand declared.

Two years of wrangling ensued. When the vote was finally called, passions were so high that bishops were leaping out of their seats and other delegates were shouting so loudly that a recall was necessary. The result was only declared after a delegate put his hand over the mouth of one of the most vociferous opponents of emancipation, Jean-François Rewbell, leader of the Alsace deputies. The motion in favour of emancipation was carried by 373 votes to 225 on 28 September 1791. Two months later Louis XVI, still surviving as monarch though a hamstrung one, put his signature to a decree announcing that all France's 40,000 Jews were now officially equal with every other citizen in France; 'any man who swears a civic oath, and commits to fulfil all the duties that the constitution imposes has a right to all the advantages it ensures,' the decree announced.

France had become the second nation in the world, after Poland over 500 years earlier, to emancipate Jews (see Chapter 10). In England, under George II, Parliament had passed a bill in 1753 which allowed foreign Jews to 'be naturalized by Parliament, without receiving the Sacrament of the Lord's Supper'. But the bill was greeted with such public outcry that it had been almost immediately withdrawn. In America, despite the First Amendment's disestablishment of all religions, several states such as Maryland and New Hampshire continued to require public office holders to take an oath on the Bible which effectively precluded Jews from holding office.

But though France may have been 'our Palestine, its mountains are our Zion, its rivers our Jordan … it is the water of liberty', according to a jubilant writer to the newspaper *La Chronique de Paris*, nothing much changed for Jews after their emancipation. The national guard refused to enlist them, they were still subject to hostility and attacks, and most continued in their former occupations. Napoleon, however, carried on from where the National Assembly left off. For the brief time that he ruled an empire, Jews across Europe were liberated from their ghettoes and from the restrictions on their rights to property, worship and occupation (see Chapter 20).

The French revolutionaries, the more radical of them anyway, were not, however, prepared to tolerate those they perceived to be the enemies of the Revolution. By 1792 revolutionary France was under serious attack from both within and without its borders. France was at war with Austria which was threatening to invade France in support of Louis XVI. Pope Pius VI had declared, with perfect justification, that the Revolution was an attempt 'to annihilate the Catholic Religion and, with her, the obedience owed to Kings'. Equality and liberty, he declared in 1791, were 'no more than imaginary dreams and senseless words'. Unlike divinity and promises of an afterlife, we might add. Louis XVI himself was a rallying point for resistance to the Revolution until, in January 1793, he was beheaded and the radical Jacobins came to power a few months later, with Robespierre at their head. Under the banner of defending the Revolution from its enemies, anyone even suspected of counter-revolutionary tendencies was sacrificed.

Revolution and the guillotine were essential partners for Robespierre and the more extremist of his fellow Jacobins. Robespierre, the implacable, neatly dressed and neatly coiffured lawyer, whose green-tinted spectacles matched his green eyes, whose name is synonymous with the Reign of Terror, had argued for the abolition of the death penalty in the early days of the Revolution. But circumstances had changed for the 'seagreen Incorruptible', as Thomas Carlyle called him in his wonderful novelistic history of the French Revolution, published in 1837. The survival of the Revolution was now at stake, and any means were justified to preserve it. Living a celibate life as lodger in the house of a master carpenter and his family, Robespierre was passionate only in defence of the Revolution. 'Revolutionary government owes to all good citizens the fullest protection the state can afford; to the enemies of the people it owes nothing but death,' he declared in a speech to the Committee of Public Safety on 25 December 1793. From June 1793 to the end of July 1794, when Robespierre himself was guillotined, an estimated 17,000 to 50,000 'enemies of the people' were executed and between 200,000 and 500,000 were imprisoned.

For Robespierre *liberté*, *égalité*, *fraternité* were the three foundation stones of the Revolution.* But the greatest of these was *égalité*. Which was why Robespierre extended an unheard of tolerance to those who were the most discriminated against in society.

Throughout his political life Robespierre opposed black slavery as being fundamentally inconsistent with the principle of equality. Sadly, he did not apply the same logic to women. Like the Founding Fathers, Robespierre and his fellow revolutionaries considered women to be outside the pale of 'man' whose rights they had so eloquently propounded in their Declaration of the Rights of Man and of the Citizen in 1789. It took the playwright and intellectual Olympe de Gouges, bastard daughter of a butcher, to issue her own Declaration of the Rights of Woman and of the Citizeness in 1791. 'Women are born free and remain equal to men in rights,' it proclaimed. 'The only limit to the exercise of the natural rights of woman is the perpetual tyranny that man opposes to it.' The 'de Gouges woman' was brought before the Revolutionary Tribunal's public prosecutor Antoine Quentin Fouquier-Tinville and guillotined in November 1793, though more because she opposed Robespierre's Reign

* While *liberté* and *égalité* were rights, *fraternité* was a moral obligation. *Fraternité* was a far more 'advanced' version of tolerance since it required not just 'putting up with' others, including the dislikeable, but acknowledging them, religious minorities included, as brothers – though not, of course, sisters.

of Terror than because of her support for women's rights. French women had to wait until 1946 to acquire the rights she had fought for.

Four months after her execution, on 16 Pluviôse (4 February 1794),* the National Convention (formerly the National Assembly), under Robespierre's guiding hand, declared 'the abolition of Negro slavery in all the colonies'. Furthermore, 'all men, without distinction of colour, residing in the colonies, are French citizens and will enjoy all the rights assured by the constitution'. Abraham Lincoln would not proclaim the emancipation of 3 million slaves in the southern states of America for another seventy years.

Of course, it was not principled revolutionaries in Paris, but slaves themselves who procured their emancipation. The Declaration of the Rights of Man and of the Citizen had said nothing about the abolition of slavery; it was as blind to the issue of slaves as America's Declaration of Independence. Post revolution, the French economy continued to be heavily reliant on slave labour. But in 1791 slaves in France's Caribbean colony of Saint-Domingue, now Haiti, rose in revolt led by the charismatic ex-slave and Jacobin, Toussaint Louverture. Over the next couple of years they burned and destroyed hundreds of sugar, coffee and cotton/indigo plantations. Saint-Domingue was perhaps the most profitable of any European colony, supplying most of the world's sugar. France could not afford to antagonize the slaves, especially when in 1793 Spain and Britain invaded the colony. How, anyway, could the deputies of the National Convention resist Toussaint Louverture when he appealed to the Revolution's own principles and declared: 'I want Liberty and Equality to reign in Saint-Domingue'? As Danton, one of the leading figures of the National Convention before Robespierre had him executed, told the delegates when the slaves' emancipation was ratified: 'Until now

* The destruction of the *Ancien Régime* extended to abolishing the old Gregorian calendar with its religious references and creating a new Republican calendar. The months were given new names principally based on what the weather was like in Paris at that time of year. So, for instance, the month which according to the new system began at the end of January, was called Pluviôse, from the French *pluvieux*, rainy, and the month beginning in what had formerly been late October was Brumaire, from the French *brume*, mist.

our decrees of liberty have been selfish, and only for ourselves. But today we proclaim it to the universe, and generations to come will glory in this decree; we are proclaiming universal liberty.'

Sadly this state of affairs did not last, and the slaves of the French colonies, freed by the National Convention in 1794, were re-enslaved by Napoleon. After his *coup d'état* in 1799, Napoleon restored slavery everywhere – everywhere, that is, except Saint-Domingue, which would become the world's first black republic in 1804, though Dessalines, Haiti's leader, soon proclaimed himself emperor.

French radicals were prepared to tolerate black slaves in a way that the Founding Fathers could not do, but unlike the Founding Fathers, the Jacobins were happy to persecute Catholics. Even though freedom of worship was included as one of the rights specified in the French Declaration of the Rights of Man and of the Citizen, that right could not be extended to Catholics. The Church was the enemy of the Revolution and all that the revolutionaries were fighting for. In 1793 the National Convention launched a virulent 'de-Christianization' programme. On 21 October that year it decreed that all nonjuring priests (priests who refused to take an oath of allegiance to revolutionary France) and anyone who harboured them were liable to be executed on sight. Only a small percentage of these 'refractory priests' were actually guillotined, but many were interned in chains on prison ships where the appalling conditions killed them instead.

Foot soldiers of the revolutionary army were dispatched from Paris to oversee the de-Christianization. The more enthusiastic of them shot cannonballs at church steeples – a lazy way of dislodging the church bells which were then carted off, along with silver chalices, candlesticks and plate. The precious metals were melted down and turned into weapons for the war against the Austro-Hungarian Empire. In the diocese of Châlons-sur-Marne, scene of the civic parade, churches were stripped of 3,300 kilos of silver and 276 tons of bronze; in the department of Doubs wooden crucifixes and statues were destroyed in a great bonfire over eighty feet tall.[3] Towns, squares and streets lost their Christian names.

Saint-Tropez became Héraclée, but many communes simply dropped the prefix 'Saint' and replaced it with Mont or Font.[4] Catholicism was being eradicated from the face of France. Nor was Judaism immune from the anti-religious zealots, despite the Jews' emancipation in 1789: synagogues and other Jewish properties were nationalized and silver from synagogues was taken to feed the depleted French treasury.

In 1789 France's population of 28 million had been almost entirely Catholic. By 1794 most of its 40,000 churches were closed. Catholicism was no longer to be seen or heard. The sound of church bells, the sight of religious processions, the shrines and crosses that had marked every crossroads, had disappeared. About 30,000 priests had fled the country, leaving France so depleted of priests that laymen and women had taken over their work, celebrating Mass – 'white Masses', they were called – burying the dead, baptizing children and teaching them the fundamentals of the Catholic faith.

But like the Founding Fathers, even the most virulent opponents of the Church recognized the essential role that religion played in inculcating the moral values which created good subjects and united them together. The revolutionaries wanted to destroy the Catholic Church, but they still wanted the social glue that religion provided so effectively. They were, however, split as to what kind of religion it should be. On the one side were the extreme radicals, led by the firebrand journalist Jacques Hébert, who prided himself on being the voice of the sans-culottes, the urban working classes, and was a wholehearted champion of the Reign of Terror. Hébert and his supporters, ardent atheists and savagely anti-Catholic, wanted a religion without God. Their Cult of Reason substituted worship of the abstract concept of Reason, of the people, of the *Patrie*, for worship of God. Where they did not close down churches and turn them into warehouses and stables, they transformed them into Temples of Reason, inscribing their walls with the words *liberté, égalité* and *fraternité*. Châlons-sur-Marne's church of Notre-Dame became one such temple but so, most notably, did Paris's Notre-Dame Cathedral.

Robespierre was, however, horrified by the Hébertistes' atheism. To do what Joseph Fouché, one of the creators of the Cult of Reason, did

– to order that the phrase 'Death is an eternal sleep' be written over cemetery gates – was to deprive the people of all solace. 'Who commissioned you to announce to the people that God does not exist?' Robespierre thundered. 'How does it help a man if you persuade him that blind force presides over his destiny, and strikes at random, now at the virtuous, now at the criminal?... will the idea of annihilation inspire him with purer and higher sentiments than that of immortality?... if the existence of God and the immortality of the soul were nothing but dreams, they would still be the most beautiful conceptions of the human spirit.'[5]

For Robespierre, atheism was an enemy of the Revolution. So, therefore, were its propounders, who conveniently also happened to be part of a faction more extreme than Robespierre's own. Robespierre denounced them as traitors to the revolutionary cause. In March 1794 Jacques Hébert, fainting with fright, submitted to the guillotine, as he had once insisted so many 'enemies of the Revolution' should do.

But although Robespierre was implacably opposed to the Church, he, like America's Founding Fathers, believed in God – an Enlightenment god, a god of reason, but nevertheless a god. Like all rulers, he understood the invaluable function that religion performed for the State, its potential for swaying the hearts of people. France, he believed, still needed God, but a new type of god, and Robespierre, virtually single-handedly, created him. 'Catholicism being burned out, and Reason-worship guillotined, was there not need of one?' as Thomas Carlyle put it.[6]

Robespierre's Supreme Being was a god who was fully behind the Revolution, who 'sees at this moment a whole nation, grappling with all the oppressions of the human race ... who has given it the mission it has undertaken and the strength to accomplish it'. Rather than the authority-loving, docile subject that the Christian god created, Robespierre's radicalized god would create the kind of citizen that revolutionary France required. His 'immortal hand, engraving on the heart of man the code of justice and equality, has written there the death sentence of tyrant', declared Robespierre, who clearly knew the Supreme Being's intentions well. But this god was also a nationalist who 'silences the most imperious and tender passions before the sublime love of the fatherland'; the nation was the new object of worship. Intolerance, the loathing of the enemy, did not disappear with the disappearance of the Christian god; it would simply be transferred to nationalism. The intolerance unleashed by a religion of the nation would result in the worst of the industrial slaughters of the twentieth century.

On 7 May 1794 Robespierre's Cult of the Supreme Being was made the established religion of France in a decree drawn up by Robespierre and agreed to by the National Convention. 'The French people recognize the existence of the Supreme Being and the immortality of the soul,' the decree told the French people, not all of whom agreed. Catholic saint's days which had sprinkled the year with festivals were deleted from the new Republican calendar and replaced by festivals to celebrate 'the human race; the French people; the benefactors of mankind; the martyrs of freedom; liberty and equality; the Republic; the liberty of the world; patriotism; hatred of tyrants and traitors; truth; justice; modesty; glory and immortality; friendship; temperance; courage; good faith; heroism; impartiality; Stoicism; love; conjugal fidelity; fatherly affection; mother-love; filial piety; childhood; youth; manhood; old age; misfortune; agriculture; industry; our ancestors; posterity; happiness'. These festivals, dedicated to creating model citizens prepared to lay down their life for France, were to be held according to the new calendar on successive *decadis* – that is, every tenth day, which had been declared the new day of rest; the Christian Sunday, which from time immemorial had been the day of rest, was abolished.

On 8 June 1794 the whole of Paris turned out to celebrate the first festival of the Cult of the Supreme Being. It was designed by Robespierre's friend the painter Jacques-Louis David. Thousands gathered in the Tuileries gardens. Magnificent in sky-blue coat, white silk waistcoat and black silk breeches, Robespierre 'the seagreen Pontiff' (Carlyle's words, again), appeared before them and set a flaming torch to a vast papier mâché statue of Atheism and Anarchy. To the amazement of the crowds, out of the flames emerged a towering statue of Wisdom. The crowds then moved to the Champs de Mars where a huge mountain symbolizing Nature had been built. The deputies filed up to its summit and sat under a tree of liberty, while bands struck up, cannons were fired and the park echoed to cries of '*Vive la République*'.[7]

How much the cult really reflected Robespierre's personal religious beliefs, how much Robespierre was trying to preserve the Revolution by creating a religion to go with it, and how much the cult was his self-serving attempt to boost his own political position is unclear. Certainly his enemies thought it was the latter. 'Look at the bugger,' Jacques-Alexis Thuriot, one of Robespierre's more outspoken opponents, was overheard saying. 'It's not enough for him to be in charge, he has to be God.'

Robespierre was certainly at the height of his power. Two days after the great festival, the Committee of Public Safety passed the *loi de la Grande Terreur*, the law of the Great Terror. The counter-revolutionary enemies of the Revolution who could be tried and sentenced to death by the Revolutionary Tribunal were now to include anyone considered to be 'slandering patriotism' or 'seeking to inspire discouragement'. All citizens were ordered to denounce and bring to justice anyone they suspected of such counter-revolutionary tendencies. A guilty sentence was almost guaranteed since witnesses or council for the defence were now banned. The number of executions rose almost immediately from an average of five a day to seventeen and then twenty-six a day. A little over a month after the law was passed, one of the victims was Robespierre himself. His Reign of Terror and accompanying dictatorial powers had gone too far. The 'axe of the nation', as Robespierre had called the guillotine, fell on him on 24 July 1794.

Robespierre's Cult of the Supreme Being died soon after. In 1802 it was officially banned by Napoleon who restored Catholicism to France. Churches were re-consecrated and church bells once again rang out from villages and towns. Laypeople had their Sundays fully restored to them, along with their priests, who had returned from exile or emerged from hiding and were now triumphing over the jurors, the priests who had sworn an oath of loyalty to the Revolution. In some parishes feeling against the jurors was so strong that they were forced to scrape clean the tongues of those to whom they had given Communion.[8] The Catholic Church, it seemed, was back. Except that it had lost its power. Napoleon, a deist like Robespierre, was not prepared to return the Church to the independence and wealth it had enjoyed before the Revolution. The State would keep the Church firmly under its control.

By the early years of the nineteenth century, the religious landscape of Christendom had changed irrevocably. The newly constituted American State had withdrawn itself from the religious realm and allowed each religious community to worship as they saw fit. France, though it had tried and failed to eliminate Catholicism entirely, now controlled the Church, and protected freedom of worship.

The principles of liberty, fraternity and equality that lay at the heart of the idea of natural rights had driven the moral argument beyond tolerating the other to embracing him (and perhaps her). They had in theory broken down the barriers between 'us' and 'them' by recognizing everyone's common humanity. Instead of tolerating the other, you embraced them as your fellow human. It was Christianity in its secular form. Except that not everyone counted as human. The principles of liberty, fraternity and equality were only selectively applied, to slaves in the French Empire but not in the American; to Jews in the French Empire but not in some American states; to men but not to women. France's enlightened rulers prided themselves on eliminating the terrible intolerances provoked by the desire for religious uniformity. They were guilty, however, of seeking to impose a new type of uniformity which would have equally lethal consequences, the uniformity of nationalism. But, blind to these defects, certain of the moral and intellectual superiority of European Enlightenment thought, Napoleon invaded the Islamic world in 1798 bringing an army of Enlightenment thinkers with him.

CHAPTER 20

IBN ABD AL-WAHHAB VS THE ISLAMIC ENLIGHTENMENT

'In political matters we shall defer entirely to the advice of Europe. In religious matters we need all our liberty. Religion is the basis of our laws. It is the principle of our government; His Majesty the Sultan can no more touch it than we can.'

– Grand Vizier Sadik Rifat Pasha to Stratford Canning,
British Ambassador to the Ottoman Empire, 1844

'The Muslim religion would on no account permit the development of the mind.'

– Jean-Baptiste Joseph Fourier, mathematician and physicist,
Description de l'Égypte, 1809–1822

'IN THE NAME OF God, the Merciful, the Compassionate. There is no God but God. He has no son and no companion in his sovereignty. On behalf of France, which was built on the foundations of freedom and equality – the commander in chief of the French armies, Bonaparte, informs the inhabitants of Egypt … that I came to you only to restore your rights to you from the hand of the oppressors.'

With these words 'the Enlightenment on horseback', as Napoleon was called, announced his invasion of the Ottoman Empire's province of Egypt in 1798. About sixty years earlier an unknown cleric from a lawless backwater in Arabia had begun preaching a new and stringent form of Islam. Muhammad Ibn Abd al-Wahhab, a contemporary of Kant's, preached the message of fundamentalists everywhere: his religion had become debased and needed to return to its basics.

Napoleon's Enlightenment versus Ibn Abd al-Wahhab's unenlightened fundamentalism. For the West it is the clash of civilizations epitomized: the tolerance of the Christian West cherishing progress, liberty, equality and fraternity versus rigid intolerant Islam mired in slavish obedience to an outdated religion. While the proponents of this view have some truth on their side, they nevertheless fail to acknowledge the paradox in Napoleon's Enlightenment position. He was waving the banner of equality while at the same time heralding the Western world's conquest of the Islamic world. Only four years after his invasion of Egypt, the enlightened Napoleon would reintroduce slavery in the French colonies. Although a supporter of the emancipation of Jews, he would issue the 'Infamous Decree' in 1808 which restricted French Jews' economic activity and their rights to settle where they pleased on the pretext of integrating Jews more fully into French society.

For many Muslims the Enlightenment meant not equality but humiliation at the hands of European powers who were convinced of the superiority of their own culture. The result would be a Muslim backlash against *dhimmis* and the enlistment of Islam in the battle against Europe.

But it was not the puritanical Ibn Abd al-Wahhab who led the way. Ibn Abd al-Wahhab was a peripheral figure in the late eighteenth century. Now a byword for intolerance, he was then an anomaly in Islam, his message only attracting notice in a poor and neglected area of Arabia. Ibn Abd al-Wahhab was born and spent most of his life in Najd, what is now central Saudi Arabia. A land of warring tribes, sandstorms and lawlessness, Najd was so lacking in resources that it was ignored by the Ottomans who controlled the holy cities of Mecca and Medina to the west; Najd was even ignored by the voracious Europeans, anxious to exploit whatever trading opportunity they could find. A series of droughts and plagues of locusts had made the tribal conflict for pasture land to graze their sheep, goats, horses and camels particularly violent, and forced many nomads to settle in the oasis towns.

Nomads, and even the settled Arabs cultivating their crops and date farms, had developed their own hybrid Islam, a combination of traditional customs – worship of trees, the wearing of amulets and talismans – and a somewhat lax observance of sharia. In some of the larger settlements there were, however, certain families who had become the guardians of Islamic law, *qadis* dispensing justice and fatwas on townsmen and villagers. Ibn Abd al-Wahhab belonged to one such family. Like most of Najd's *qadis*, they belonged to the Hanbali school, the most literal and least speculative of the Sunni schools of law (see Chapter 4). But to the dismay of his father, and the outright hostility of his brother, Ibn Abd al-Wahhab was a far severer traditionalist than they were. For Ibn Abd al-Wahhab, Najd's lax Islamic behaviour was an outrage that would lead to hell. Muslims must be returned, by force if necessary, to the true path.

He began to preach, calling for strict adherence to the fundamental tenet of Islam, the oneness of God (*tawhid*). Ibn Abd al-Wahhab's pure monotheism excluded worshipping or praying to any thing or person other than God. He believed that the Shiites' 'saint-worship' of the martyr Ali and his descendants as interceders with God was a form of polytheism (*shirk*). It was akin to the Sufis' veneration of their spiritual leaders and to the worst excesses of his fellow Sunnis in Najd.

Ibn Abd al-Wahhab had taken the late thirteenth–early fourteenth-century scholar Ibn Taymiyya's ideas to their extreme in his strict literalism, his hostility to intellectualism, his downgrading of the authority of the ulema, his insistence that every Muslim should understand the Quran for himself, and that the good Muslim must seek out and pursue the heretic in order to keep Islam pure. Ibn Abd al-Wahhab had in fact much in common with Luther, Calvin and the Protestant reformers. He too did not believe that a specialized religious clergy was needed as intermediary or interpreter between the believer and their God. He too wanted to purge his religion of all its later accretions and innovations and return it to its original purity based on the word of God as revealed in scripture. He too urged all believers to read the texts for themselves and not rely on the clerical elite. But he was in no way politically egalitarian and his writings show little interest in social justice. Like the Protestant reformers, he refused to allow the comforting props of religion, such as the appeal to saints. He focussed on God's power rather than God's goodness. He believed that true Muslims should be totally submissive to God, and to whatever earthly ruler they were subject to, as long as that ruler conformed to the standard Sunni dictum to command the good and forbid the evil (as determined, of course, by Ibn Abd al-Wahhab).

What was shocking to most of the ulema, including his own brother and father, however, was that Ibn Abd al-Wahhab had assumed the right, properly belonging to a consensus of the ulema, and then only under specific conditions, to *takfir* (to denounce Muslims as apostates or infidels). He condemned not just those nomad Muslims who worshipped stones and trees as well as Allah, but Shiism and Sufism for *bid'a*, heretical innovations, and for *shirk*, polytheism. Shiites and Sufis venerated holy men whom they considered to be intermediaries between humankind and God. Essentially, anyone who did not follow Ibn Abd al-Wahhab's fundamentalist type of Islam, who, like the Shiites and Sufis, followed traditions that had emerged after the first generation of Islam, was an apostate or an infidel (*kafir*) and it was therefore legitimate to kill them. In addition, any who did not *takfir* a disbeliever were themselves disbelievers.

Ibn Abd al-Wahhab believed he was following the precedent set by his ideological mentor: Ibn Taymiyya had also assumed the right to *takfir* (though this is disputed by some scholars) when he argued in his writings that Shiites were heretics and pronounced his fatwa that the Mongols were non-Muslims (see Chapter 10). Ibn Abd al-Wahhab's assumption of that right was, of course, consistent with his belief that the ulema were no more qualified than the ordinary pious Muslim to make judgements on the basis of their understanding of the Quran; indeed, he went further and thought that religious scholars were often wrong. But as far as the ulema were concerned, Ibn Abd al-Wahhab was assuming an authority for which he was not qualified. This was not simply pique at his questioning of *their* authority, but a serious concern that one man, and a not particularly learned one at that, as Ibn Abd al-Wahhab himself would have been the first to admit, should take it upon himself to rule on what was and was not Islamic, on who was and was not an apostate or infidel.

Eminent Hanbali scholars who were contemporaries of Ibn Abd al-Wahhab condemned his teachings. Amongst them was Sulayman ibn Suhaym who urged scholars to refute Ibn Abd al-Wahhab on the grounds that he was ignorant and fermenting hatred and enmity. Scholars of all four schools agreed. Ibn Abd al-Wahhab's brother Sulayman, who was now a *qadi*, declared him to be an ill-educated fanatic; Muhammad in turn condemned his brother as an atheist and enemy of religion, and as one of those corrupt members of the ulema who exploited the idolatry of ordinary Muslims for his own gain.

In 1743 Ibn Abd al-Wahhab was forced out of his home town. Clerics in Mecca from all four schools had called on the authorities to expel him. Several even demanded that he should be killed.[1] Ibn Abd al-Wahhab's attempts at puritanical reform, including destroying the tomb of one of the Companions of the Prophet and having a woman stoned to death for adultery, had gone too far. He was escorted by guards to the small town of al-Diriyah which was under the rule of Muhammad Ibn Saud. Ibn Saud was a not very important ruler of a not very important settlement, but he was ambitious and had expansionist dreams.

The two men had the good sense to recognize what each could do for the other – what in fact politics and religion have always done for each other since the earliest societies: Ibn Abd al-Wahhab could spread his religious message and ensure its enforcement thanks to the expansionist aims and coercive power that Ibn Saud possessed as ruler, and Ibn Saud could benefit from the religious legitimacy which Ibn Abd al-Wahhab's zeal and increasing number of supporters gave him. In 1744 they exchanged vows of allegiance. Together they set out to conquer Arabia and unite its diverse principalities under the Saudi family and the Wahhabi faith. That pact between the house of Saud and the descendants of Ibn Abd al-Wahhab has continued to this day.

Ibn Abd al-Wahhab set to work wielding his mighty sword of *takfir*. The pronouncement of *takfir* was far deadlier than Christian excommunication. For a Muslim, to be declared an infidel was not only to be consigned to damnation in the next world, but also to face loss of all your property and death in this world. Ibn Abd al-Wahhab believed that if the proclaimed infidel was offered the chance to repent but refused, it was legitimate to kill him. The polytheist, as defined by Ibn Abd al-Wahhab, whether Sufi mystic, Shiite venerator of the martyrs, lax Sunni or Sunni tree-worshipper, had flouted one of the Five Pillars of Islam: that there is only one God. God ordered jihad by word and deed against unbelievers and it was, therefore, the duty of the true Muslim, that is, Ibn Abd al-Wahhab's followers, to wage war against every infidel who refused to change their ways.

'A person's Islam is not sound even if he practises *tawhid* of God [belief in absolute monotheism] and deserts polytheism unless he is hostile to polytheists and declares to them his hostility and hatred,' he wrote.[2] Ibn Abd al-Wahhab was, in fact, far more forgiving of one of his followers who indulged in drink or committed other transgressions, than he was of anyone who did not display enmity to those he deemed to be polytheists. Any of Ibn Abd al-Wahhab's disciples who found themselves in the unfortunate position of living in a community which Ibn Abd al-Wahhab had pronounced polytheistic had to leave their home, their livelihood and their friends, and make a new life in a community which Ibn Abd al-Wahhab had not condemned. He did, however, make sure that such refugees would be provided for.[3]

The practice of *takfir* was an extraordinarily effective weapon in the Saud–Wahhabi conquest of Arabia. Ibn Abd al-Wahhab pronounced as infidels not just the rulers of all the multifarious mini-principalities of central Arabia, but everyone that was under their control. *Takfir* turned a fight for territory into a holy war just as the notion of crusade had done for Christians. Ibn Abd al-Wahhab's brand of Islam made for perfect soldiers. It stressed the duty of total obedience to the one and only God, and through him to the Saud ruler who would ensure the establishment of a regime of godliness on earth. It emphasized the necessity of loyalty to fellow believers which must override all tribal allegiances. Obedient and united, buoyed up by the certainty that God was on their side and that paradise awaited them for waging jihad, Ibn Abd al-Wahhab's followers conquered most of central and northern Arabia.

In a succession of raids and counter-raids over the following thirty years Saud–Wahhabi forces brought the whole region under their political and religious control. The small oasis village of Riyadh put up a stout resistance for many years, but in 1775 it too surrendered and became the capital of a new, unified Islamic state. Each settlement that was conquered had to swear allegiance to Ibn Abd al-Wahhab and Ibn Saud and undertake to wage jihad.[4] Those who refused to accept Islam and pay the *jizya* were to be executed. That included all Muslims who refused to accept Ibn Abd al-Wahhab's particular brand of Islam.

Ibn Abd al-Wahhab set out to create an Islamic state which resembled as nearly as possible the one established by Muhammad and the early caliphs. Everything that post-dated that time – including silk, tobacco, wine and hashish – was in principle banned. The Wahhabi regime was as religiously strict as Calvinist Geneva had been, and as suspicious and fearful. Volunteer groups, supported by the local ruler, enforced Wahhabi norms and made sure that everyone said their prayers five times a day. Such surveillance was made easier by the fact that Ibn Abd al-Wahhab insisted prayers could no longer be performed at home but had to be held communally. Just as the Génevois were encouraged to inform on their neighbours if they betrayed any hint of Catholic sympathies, so the inhabitants of the Wahhabi-controlled villages and towns were encouraged to tell the authorities of anyone they suspected to be lapsing from the true Muslim path.

Those ulema who disagreed with Ibn Abd al-Wahhab's form of Islam emigrated of their own accord or were forced to emigrate beyond the boundaries of Saudi–Wahhabi control. Some who did not leave were taken to Riyadh, where they were kept under house arrest. Amongst them was Ibn Abd al-Wahhab's brother Sulayman.[5]

Ibn Abd al-Wahhab died in 1792 at the age of eighty-nine, worn out by his zealotry, like Calvin. He was buried in an unmarked grave. His descendants, along with Ibn Saud's, still rule Saudi Arabia. And Islam is still divided on its attitude to Ibn Abd al-Wahhab and his practice of *takfir*, just as it was in the eighteenth century. In 2016, 200 Sunni clerics condemned Wahhabism as 'a dangerous deformation' of Sunni Islam, primarily because it sanctioned violence against non-believers and Muslims who rejected Ibn Abd al-Wahhab's interpretation. But al-Qaeda, Boko Haram in Nigeria, al-Shabaab in Somalia, the Taliban and the so-called Islamic State look to Ibn Taymiyya and to Ibn Abd al-Wahhab's practice of *takfir* to justify their murder of all those they have declared as infidels, including their fellow Muslims.

Six years after Ibn Abd al-Wahhab's death, Napoleon, 'the little crop-head', as he was called for his size and close-cut hair, invaded Egypt. The invasion was a deliberate attack on Britain's dominance of the Mediterranean, but it was also bringing the fruits of the Enlightenment to a benighted Islamic world. Or at least that is how the 29-year-old Napoleon, philosopher-general and disciple of Voltaire, saw it. And most of Europe agreed with him.

After the first terrifying months when French troops marched through Egypt, and panic-struck women fled unveiled from their homes, carrying only their children and with their baggage perched on their heads, Napoleon's second army invaded. This army consisted of 160 scientists, mathematicians, historians, astronomers, inventors, painters and archaeologists.

The European Enlightenment did not, of course, hurl its thunderbolt out of the blue onto an uncivilized Islamic world. Europe had been slowly extending its tentacles into the Islamic world through trade since the mid seventeenth century. Europeans, with their astonishing fashions and their dangerous ideas, were not strangers to Muslims. Powdered, bewigged merchants and diplomats from Britain, the Netherlands and France had been strutting the streets of the major port cities of both the Ottoman and Persian empires. The Ottomans had encouraged these merchants by granting enticing trade concessions, 'capitulations' they were called, in the form of lower tariffs and tax exemptions. But for the Ottoman Empire and indeed the wider Muslim world Napoleon's invasion was a shattering event. For the first time since the Crusades,

Europeans had conquered Islamic territory. The steady drip of Europe's increasing world dominance, which had begun with Spain's extraction of gold and silver from the Americas in the sixteenth century, had turned into a flood and could no longer be ignored.

One month after Napoleon's troops entered Cairo, his savants took over one of its palaces. There they created a showcase for the Enlightenment with a magnificent library, workshops, laboratories, observatory and botanical gardens. Muslim scholars were invited to the Institute of Egypt, as it was called, to marvel at the experiments in electricity, the microscopic lenses, the books ranging from natural history to a translation of the Quran into French. Among those invited were the 35-year-old cleric and historian Abd al-Rahman al-Jabarti and his pupil Hassan al-Attar.

Indicatively, the two men judged what they saw and heard by religious standards. How far were the technological innovations and Enlightenment ideas on display consistent with the principles of Islam? In the Islamic world, intellectual life was in the hands of the religious scholars. Outside their ranks few people could read and write. By the end of the eighteenth century only 3 per cent of the population in Ottoman Turkey and Egypt and the same percentage in the Iranian Empire were literate compared to 68 per cent of men and 43 per cent of women in England.[6]

Al-Jabarti (like his pupil) was educated at al-Azhar, probably the most renowned of Sunni Islam's mosque-universities, as it still is today, and the bastion of traditional Islam. But he saw that the key to Europe's success lay in its modern inventions and reforms. It was clear that the Islamic world must modernize or be swallowed up by Europe. Few but the ultra-traditionalists like Ibn Abd al-Wahhab in Arabia would have disagreed. The Ottoman Empire was in dire trouble. Russia had bitten large chunks out of it by taking control of the Crimea; internally it was facing an increasing number of rebellions from over-powerful local rulers and a population oppressed by heavy taxes. Economically, it was stagnating, caught in the claws of a world trade network controlled by Europe.

The older man acknowledged the efficiency of the French, notably displayed in their army – its drills, discipline and military strategies.

Napoleon's guns and highly disciplined troops had laid low the mamluks (the soldiers, formerly slaves, who effectively ruled Egypt) despite their dashing bravery, horsemanship and glittering scimitars. He admired the sheer drive of the French invaders: the way they renovated bridges, cut down trees to build wide boulevards, the windmills that they built 'turning in the wind in wondrous fashion'; he marvelled at the savants' willingness to share their knowledge:

> If they recognised in the visitor receptivity or knowledge, or a striving to study the disciplines of knowledge, they would be especially generous with their friendship and love for him. They would show him various printed books with all sorts of drawings and maps of countries, and regions, animals, birds and plants, histories of the ancients and the way of life of nations, stories of the prophets with pictures of them and their signs and miracles of the events of their nations – things astonishing to the mind.[7]

He admired their 'great inquisitiveness', their many marvellous and valuable instruments such as telescopes and watches.

But al-Jabarti also shared the view of the majority of the ulema and elite in his suspicion of, if not hostility to, Enlightenment ideas. The Enlightenment rested on the destruction of authority. It had pulled God down from his pedestal and replaced him with questioning, rational 'man'. The idea of unquestioning obedience, of faith in a supreme power, which is at the heart of monotheistic religions and especially of Islam, appeared totally at odds with Enlightenment thought. Islam's scholars were suspicious of *bid'a*, innovation and philosophy. Al-Jabarti rejected the enlightened, secular man who proclaimed his equality with his fellows and demanded his natural rights, including the right to religious freedom. 'Saying that [all people] are equal in the eyes of God the Almighty, this is a lie and stupidity. How can this be when God has made some superior to others…?' al-Jabarti asked, with considerable justification.[8]

His pupil al-Attar, on the other hand, was enthralled by the open-mindedness of the French. He was a regular visitor to the Institute, an ardent advocate of empirical thinking and became critical of the blinkered thinking of Islamic scholars. 'We have been dissuaded from the pursuit [of the empirical approach] because it has been considered an obstacle to God's law and to faith,' he declared.[9]

But al-Attar and his fellow modernists were not rejecting Islam, only trying to modernize it. They did not believe that a choice had to be made between Islam and the ideas coming from Europe. Enlightenment ideas of natural rights and equality squared with the principles of Islam, indeed were even derived from them. As the deists had done with Christianity so the modernists tried to strip Islam down to the general principles that could be extracted from the Quran, of charity, justice, obedience to God.

The French invasion did not last long, however. In 1801, only three years after their conquest, French troops surrendered to a combined British–Ottoman attack and pulled out of Egypt. The savants left too. They invited al-Attar to join them, but much though he loved their ideas and conversation, he was too attached to the Islamic world. His embrace of France, however, had made him unpopular among his fellow divines in Cairo. Though he would not follow the savants back to Paris, al-Attar left Egypt to pursue his studies in the Ottoman cities of Istanbul and Damascus.

The Ottomans, having been humiliated by the French, were now humiliated by the Arabs of Najd whom they had always regarded as uncouth semi-barbarians. In 1802, ten years after Ibn Abd al-Wahhab's death, 12,000 Saud–Wahhabi forces attacked the Ottoman-controlled city of Karbala in southern Iraq. It was the home of one of the Shiites' holiest places, the tomb of Husayn ibn Ali, martyr and third imam according to Shia Islam, who was the grandson of Muhammad and son of Ali.

The Ottoman garrison fled, leaving the Wahhabis free to butcher about 2,000 to 5,000 of Karbala's residents, many of them Shiite. For the Wahhabis, Karbala was a city of polytheists, whom it was therefore legitimate to kill. On top of which, troops had the opportunity to lay their hands on the enormous hoard of treasure housed in the shrine. Loot has always been one of the rewards of war and the Wahhabis – poor men scratching a living out of parched land – had taken a city which had more wealth than they had ever seen. For eight hours the troops abandoned themselves to an orgy of bloodletting and looting. 'Old people, women and children – everybody died at the barbarians' sword,' wrote the French consul, Jean-François Rousseau (not the author of *The Social Contract*). 'Their cruelty could not be satisfied, they did not cease their murders and blood flowed like water.'[10] According to Rousseau, it took 4,000 camels to carry away the gold, silver, emeralds, rubies, a pearl as big as a dove's egg, carpets and precious copies of the Quran which the Saud–Wahhabi army had looted from the shrine.

The following year, in 1803, forces led by the sons of Ibn Abd al-Wahhab and Ibn Saud took Mecca. It was hard to imagine a more humiliating blow to Ottoman prestige. The Ottoman sultan, 'the supreme caliph and the happy monarch of innumerable kingdoms, provinces and town, which evoke the envy of world sovereigns', as Selim III described himself, was the custodian of this holiest of cities and had been unable to save it.

The new Saud–Wahhabi regime promptly began to impose Wahhabi Islam on Mecca. It demolished mosques and mausoleums housing members of Muhammad's family and his close companions – they were venerating men other than Muhammad and were therefore polytheist. It forbade the sale of tobacco and banned the wearing of silk clothes. It abolished the weekly public prayer for the sultan and distributed copies of Ibn Abd al-Wahhab's writings to the ulema.

Unlike most of the Ottoman ulema, the Cairo religious scholar al-Jabarti was sympathetic to Ibn Abd al-Wahhab, and did not look down on him and his followers as barbaric and unscholarly. Al-Jabarti noted approvingly that Wahhabi authorities cracked down on 'illegal innovations' and the 'promiscuous meeting of men and women'.[11] He met two Wahhabi scholars in Cairo and was impressed by their learning.

In 1805, Muhammad's city of Medina, which was also under Ottoman guardianship, fell to the Wahhabis. The Ottomans felt compelled to act. The man they chose to crush the Wahhabis was Muhammad Ali, the luxuriantly moustachioed and bearded ruler of Egypt, which was theoretically a province of the Ottoman Empire but in practice was semi-independent. By 1818 the Wahhabis had been driven out of Mecca and Medina. Their ruler, Abdullah bin Saud, was taken in a cage to Istanbul and beheaded; Wahhabi religious leaders were executed. Muhammad Ali did not, however, have a large enough army to maintain control over the region. His troops were also engaged in trying to quell the Greeks' battle for independence from the Ottomans. Ali's forces withdrew from Arabia and the Saud–Wahhabis reinstalled themselves.

Muhammad Ali returned to the far more important task of making Egypt powerful enough to break away from the Ottoman Empire. Like his nominal sovereign the Ottoman sultan Mahmud II, Muhammad Ali was convinced that the Islamic world must shed its medieval skin or die. And he was ruthless in his breakneck race to modernize Egypt.

Thousands of peasants were press-ganged into building railways, telegraph lines and canals to water the vast cotton fields which Ali was planting all over the Nile Delta. About 20,000 men, women and children are thought to have died in the construction of just one canal. Peasants who fled their villages to escape the harsh land taxes were caught, chained by the neck, packed into boats and sent down the Nile to work on one of Ali's cotton farms. Veiled women were forced to work in the new cotton factories which employed the latest spinning, weaving and hydraulics technology imported from Britain.

Modernization is a disruptive and expensive business. To help fund it, Muhammad Ali nationalized Egypt's land, including 600,000 acres, about one fifth of all Egypt's land under cultivation, which had been given in religious endowments to the ulema. The land had been one of the ulema's major sources of wealth. To deprive them of this income was to inflict a massive assault on their power base. The State was taking over the Mosque. Al-Jabarti became one of Muhammad Ali's fiercest critics, while al-Attar became one of the ruler's closest friends.

In 1826 Muhammad Ali launched his invasion of Paris. A party of forty-three young men from Cairo's elite were sent to Paris to study Western ideas. What they learned in Paris, it was hoped, would qualify them to run a newly modernized Egypt. Al-Attar's pupil Rifa'a al-Tahtawi was selected to be their religious guardian. At that time not a single Muslim had settled in the city, according to Tahtawi, so this group of turbaned, robed figures must have made a strange spectacle in the Paris of Balzac and the restored Bourbon monarchy. Parisians and Londoners would become more used to such sights as an increasing number of Muslim students visited Europe.

In his memoir, *Takhlis al-Ibriz fi Talkhis Bariz* (sometimes translated as 'An Imam in Paris'), Tahtawi is struck by everything – the sheer number of institutions devoted to knowledge; that the French did not eat with their hands but with knives and forks; that the women revealed 'their face, head, the throat as well as what lies beneath it, the nape of the neck and what lies beneath it'.[12] Tahtawi was careful to ensure that the students were escorted in pairs to avoid the temptations of the all too seductive dark, foul-smelling, overcrowded medieval streets of Paris. As well as their studies in law, engineering and diplomacy, the Egyptians visited Paris's theatres. They also visited the Louvre where the newly built Egyptian galleries housed the treasures that Napoleon's archaeologists had brought back with them from their short sojourn in Egypt.*

During his five years in Paris, Rifa'a al-Tahtawi studied ethics, social and political philosophy and mathematics, and read the works of Voltaire and Rousseau. When he returned to Cairo in 1831 he was convinced that Islam had much to learn from Europe. He founded the School of Translators, where he supervised the translation of Voltaire and Montesquieu, histories and scientific treatises. In doing so he sparked off what has come to be known as the *Nahda*, a period of intellectual transformation in the Islamic world which lasted until the early twentieth century.

The *Nahda* was not a wholesale capitulation to European ideas, though it seemed that way to its critics. On the contrary, it was Islam's own Age of Enlightenment, according to those who contributed to it. Following Tahtawi's mentor al-Attar, its intellectuals believed that Islam

* It would be wrong to say these treasures were pillaged, since the Egyptians were amazed that anyone would be interested in studying these 'curious objects' and 'trivial details' as al-Jabarti called them.

and the Enlightenment were perfectly compatible, indeed that many of the Enlightenment's principles were Islamic ones.

Tahtawi had returned to Cairo a keen admirer of European ideas. Nonetheless, he remained a committed Sunni cleric. A witness of the July revolution of 1830 in which France had overthrown its Bourbon king, he was deeply, if not a little naively, impressed by France's 'complete justice on which the foundations of their political system rest. The reign of a tyrannical king or minister never lasts for very long with them, once it has become known that they have acted unjustly and oppressed the people.' Nevertheless, he noted disapprovingly that 'French justice is not based on divine works' and, more critically, that 'There are so few genuinely religious people in France that they are of no consequence.'[13]

Some of Tahtawi's ideas were astonishingly radical, but they were always put within an Islamic framework. He believed, for instance, in education for women, an idea that horrified most Muslims. But he justified it not on Western notions of equality and natural rights, but by citing the hadiths which showed that the Prophet's wives had been literate. And like the most traditional of clerics he was convinced that if it came to a conflict between what the dictates of reason suggested and what the Quran required, the Quran as the word of God must prevail and reason must be in error.

Islam was taking its own approach to the Enlightenment, but Europe was tightening its grip on the Islamic world nonetheless. In 1839, under European pressure, the Ottoman emperor, Sultan Abdulmejid I, made what was an extraordinary declaration of religious equality. The sultan was sixteen years old at the time. He looked, according to the English novelist Thackeray, one of the growing numbers of European tourists to visit Istanbul, 'like a young French roué worn out by debauch; his eyes bright, with black rings round them; his cheeks pale and hollow'.[14] Handsome, weak and easily led, Abdulmejid issued the Edict of Gülhane four months after he ascended to the throne.

The edict's purpose was, he said, 'to bring the benefits of a good administration to the provinces of the Ottoman Empire through new institutions'. He would abolish tax farming, reform military conscription, guarantee public trials to every accused person, outlaw executions without trial and establish security of property. But most radically of all he declared that 'these imperial concessions are extended to all our subjects, of whatever religion or sect they may be'. At a stroke, Abdulmejid had scythed through the millet system and the status of the *dhimmis* on which it was based.

Under the millet system which had been introduced in the early nineteenth century, the majority of the empire's non-Muslim subjects – the Greek Orthodox, Armenians and Jews – had been organized into three religious communities or millets; Catholics were soon recognized as forming their own separate millet. Each millet was administered by its own leader and was free to run its own schools, have its own courts where cases were tried according to its own religious law (except when a Muslim was involved, in which case sharia law prevailed) and raise and collect its own taxes. The millet system allowed a level of self-rule to religious minorities undreamt of in the West. But it was, in fact, simply a formalization and more tolerant version of the *dhimma* system under which Jews and Christians had been living in the Islamic world since the seventh century. Ultimately, the millet system was still based on the fact that non-Muslims were inferior to Muslims. They could live in their semi-autonomous communities but they were excluded from high office and still had to pay the *jizya*.

The Edict of Gülhane, however, decreed that henceforth Muslims, Jews and Christians were to be treated equally as subjects of the Ottoman sultan, not as members of separate religious communities. It was a body blow to the ulema and to ordinary Muslims who saw their position of superiority being stolen from them.

It was self-interest as much as noble Western principle that had prompted the 'Great Powers' – as Britain, France, Austria and Russia were called – to insist that Sultan Abdulmejid improve the *dhimmis*' lot. The constituent parts of the Ottoman Empire were fighting for their independence. Foreseeing rich pickings, Europe's empires were busy striking up alliances with minority religious communities around the

Ottoman Empire hoping to turn them into semi-client states. The French were courting the Maronites in Lebanon as well as Armenian and Syrian Catholics throughout the empire; Britain offered its protection to the Protestants and Jews and to the Druze in Lebanon; Russia was sidling up to the Greek Orthodox. It was in all of the Great Powers' interests to be seen to be furthering the lot of the *dhimmis*.

The sultan was in no position to refuse the Europeans. Financially overstretched, he needed Europe's support in his war against Muhammad Ali of Egypt. Abdulmejid also hoped that the emancipation of the *dhimmis* announced in the Edict of Gülhane would appease his Christian subjects enough that they would call a stop to the rebellions that were breaking out in the Balkans, where Christians were in the majority.

Christian/Muslim relations had broken down entirely when the Greek battle for independence broke out in 1821. Inspired by the French Revolution and Enlightenment ideas, and spurred on by the Greek Orthodox Church, Greek Christians had revolted against their humiliating status as *dhimmis*. But their revolt against the empire had enraged Muslims. Greeks were murdered in the streets of Istanbul, the patriarch of the Orthodox Church and three of his archbishops were dragged from their church and hanged; Orthodox clergy and Greek merchants were executed and imprisoned and their mansions looted; small boys played football with the heads of Greeks killed by Ottoman forces, that had been piled up outside the imperial gate of the Topkapi Palace.[15] Tens of thousands of Greek Christians – men, women and children, civilians as well as combatants – were massacred. In turn the Greek Christians massacred Muslims and Jews suspected of allying themselves with the Ottomans against the Greek rebels.

The era of Ottoman tolerance, the tolerance of the powerful, was drawing to an end, despite the Edict of Gülhane. In fact, the edict did the cause of religious equality no good. For Muslims, it was religiously wrong to consider *dhimmis* to be equal to Muslims. Furthermore, to accept religious equality was to accept being subjugated by a rival power, whose motives were certainly not disinterested when it pushed Enlightenment values down Muslim throats. The Enlightenment had arrived on horseback, with conquerors. Its principles of religious freedom and religious equality were forever after tarnished. They were associated with humiliation.

The Great Powers were using their devotion to the Enlightenment notion of 'equality' to assert their superiority over the Ottoman world. But the West did not even practise what it preached. In Britain, Austria and Hungary, Jews had still not gained civil parity, nor had Jews in the American state of New Hampshire. By the time of the Edict of Gülhane in 1839, British Catholics and black slaves in the British Empire had officially won their fight for emancipation – the former in 1829, the latter in 1833. But France under Napoleon had re-enslaved the black plantation workers it had freed in 1794 under Robespierre, though it was physically prevented from doing so in Saint-Domingue; France would not emancipate slaves again until 1848.

Nonetheless it was under European pressure that the Ottomans had officially freed white slaves in 1830. But though the reigning sultan, Abdulmejid's father Mahmud II, had closed down the slave markets where young and old, male and female, had stood naked to be examined by their prospective buyers, he continued to acquire slave women for his harem. The Ottomans saw no compelling moral reason to abolish slavery; sharia permitted slavery although it forbade the enslavement of Muslims. Slavery remained legal until the empire itself fell in 1918 after its defeat in the First World War.

For the ulema, who had seen their power being whittled away by the Ottoman emperor and the Egyptian governor Muhammad Ali, Enlightenment principles spelled the death of Islam. For many ordinary Muslims the Enlightenment brought oppression and hardship and a dizzying disruption of everything they knew. European principles went hand in hand with European modernization. Muslims were experiencing a speeded up Industrial Revolution, taking place within a generation rather than over a century as it had in Britain. Their soldiers, on the orders of the sultan, were now wearing European-style tunics and trousers, topped by a crimson fez. A fatwa declared the fez to be Islamic because it had no brim, and therefore did not prevent Muslim men from touching their foreheads to the ground when praying.[16] The alien sounds of Rossini and Donizetti drifted from the parade grounds. Government officials were ordered to abandon their sirwal (baggy trousers), caftans, turbans and slippers, and adopt frock coats, trousers, capes, black leather boots and fez. The wealthy were no longer sitting on cushions on the floor to eat but on chairs at tables, using knives and forks.

The Edict of Gülhane had launched a period of European-style reform and modernization of the Ottoman Empire which would become known as the Tanzimat (the reorganization or era of reforms).

On 5 February 1840, three months after the Edict of Gülhane had been announced, Jews in Damascus were accused of murdering a Catholic priest and his servant. Their blood, it was claimed, was to be used in a Passover ritual. Thirteen Jews were arrested and tortured. Outraged Muslims looted a local synagogue. Blood libel had been a commonplace in medieval Europe, but a rarity in the Islamic world. After the 'Damascus Affair', however, accusations of ritual murder were regularly levelled against Jews in the Ottoman provinces of Syria, Palestine and Egypt. It is hard not to connect this degradation of relations on the ground with the increased official status that the edict had offered Jews.

But the edict itself was not much more than a statement of intent: opposition to it meant that little was done to implement it. That changed, however, in 1856 when a new edict announced that measures would be taken to ensure that the promises made in the Edict of Gülhane would be put into effect.

It seemed to most Muslims that the sultan had yet again succumbed to European bullying. The Imperial Reform Edict emerged at the end of the incompetent mess that was the Crimean War with Russia. The Ottomans had come out the victors, but only thanks to their alliance with France, Britain and Austria, who were anxious to keep the Ottoman Empire from falling into the hands of the Tsar. Increasingly dependent on their European allies and heavily in debt to them, Sultan Abdulmejid reluctantly agreed to a package of reforms insisted on by Britain's prime minister, Lord Palmerston, and France and Austria. The sultan even agreed to the Europeans' more nakedly self-interested demand to allow foreigners to own property. The Ottomans did, however, refuse to abolish the death penalty for apostasy.

Sultan Abdulmejid was absent when religious and state dignitaries arrived in the pouring rain at the Topkapi Palace on 18 February 1856 to hear the Imperial Reform Edict read out: his baby daughter by his fifth wife had died the night before. European diplomats were also absent – it was considered wiser not to invite them, since their presence would only have underlined how much the edict was theirs, not the sultan's. But the ulema were present in their white and green turbans, along with the Ottoman ministers in their frock coats. They crowded into the palace's petition chamber to hear the sultan's edict read out. It applied, they were told, 'to all the subjects of my Empire, without distinction of classes or of religion, for the security of their persons and property and the preservation of their honour'. One clause spelled out the guarantee of religious tolerance demanded by the Western powers: 'all forms of religion are and shall be freely professed in my dominions, no subject of my Empire shall be hindered in the exercise of the religion that he professes, nor shall be in any way annoyed on this account.' The edict promised equality of access to education, government positions, and equality of treatment under the law. It would take another two years before Jews in Britain were fully emancipated.

The Imperial Reform Edict was greeted as a massive insult by most Muslims. They were to be put on an equal footing with those who were their inferiors. 'This is a day of weeping and mourning for the people of Islam,' was the reaction of most Muslims, according to Ahmed Cevdet, the Ottoman statesman and scholar, who was a major figure in the Tanzimat reforms.[17] Not even all the *dhimmis* or 'other than Muslims' as they were called, were happy with the edict. Equality was all very well but it depended who you were equal with. 'The government has made us equal with the Jews! We were satisfied with the superiority of Islam!' was how Ahmed Cevdet described the reaction of some of the Greek Orthodox clergy.

Religious tolerance had now become even more firmly attached, as far as many Muslims were concerned, to their humiliation by Western powers. The Europeans' arrogant sense of superiority towards Muslims who had once dominated much of the world, whose learning and culture had far outstripped the West's, was evident even amongst the tourists. They were told in the *Handbook to Egypt*, one of the most popular guide-books of the time, that 'The Egyptians … occupy a much lower grade in the scale of civilization than most of the western nations.'[18]

That the Imperial Reform Edict had been imposed by Europe was only too evident to the cognoscenti: the very wording of the edict deliberately echoed Jefferson's Virginia Bill of Rights of 1776 and France's Declaration of the Rights of Man and of the Citizen of 1789. In the preamble to the edict the sultan expressed his desire to effect 'the attainment of full happiness of all my subjects, who in my sight are all equal, and equally dear to me, and who [are] united to each other by the cordial ties of empire, under my protection'. It was a sort of Jeffersonian promise of life and the pursuit of happiness, of *egalité* and *fraternité*.

But missing from the edict is one word which is fundamental to both American and French declarations: the word 'rights'. Life, liberty and the pursuit of happiness are guaranteed by the State because they are the 'rights of man and of the citizen' according to the French Declaration, or 'inalienable' rights as the Virginia Declaration puts it. The Ottoman edict, however, speaks in terms of the sultan's wishes for his people; it is his wish that they should attain full happiness; it is because his subjects 'are equally dear to me' and united 'under my protection', that he bestows the gifts of equality. The sultan speaks in the language of a loving, omnipotent God – the people are equal amongst themselves but not with him; it is not their rights, but his beneficence which has secured them their liberties.

As for the *dhimmis*, they paid a dreadful price for their emancipation. True, they entered government service in far greater numbers; Sultan Abdulmejid in fact went out of his way to encourage *dhimmis* to join state educational institutions so that they would be well equipped to contribute to his modernization programme. At the School of Medicine which he founded, he even had a special kitchen set up to serve kosher food and insisted that the school employ a rabbi. But Muslim resentment against Christians and Jews grew steadily. It was *dhimmis*, not Muslims, who were the beneficiaries of the modernizing revolution that was ripping apart the world as they knew it; *dhimmis* were benefitting thanks to the support of the European powers, the colonizers and source of the Ottoman's humiliation. Britain and France relied on *dhimmis* to facilitate their all-important trade deals. These *dhimmis* were then able to enjoy the trade concessions that the European powers had wrung from the Ottomans. In customs duties alone, *dhimmi* merchants paid half what their Muslim counterparts were charged. As far as Muslim merchants were concerned, they were getting poorer, blocked from the most profitable trade with Europe, while *dhimmi* merchants got richer at their expense. When, on top of this economic superiority, the edicts eliminated – in law at any rate – the disadvantages which had always kept Christians and Jews inferior to Muslims, resentment against them intensified. After the Imperial Reform Edict sporadic violence against Jews occurred more frequently and more violently.

In Damascus, the growth in wealth and influence of the Christians, evidenced in their new houses and their new churches which would once have been forbidden under *dhimmi* regulations, had been particularly rapid. In the summer of 1860 young Muslim men began daubing crosses on the doors of houses in the Christian quarter.[19] When the Ottoman authorities arrested some of the perpetrators and ordered them to clean the streets, the mood rapidly grew nasty. A crowd gathered and demanded the boys' release. Years of resentment, fear of the cataclysmic changes that they were enduring while the Christians were the ones that were benefitting, burst out; Muslim mobs looted and set fire to the Christian quarter, killing at least several hundred Christians, though some put the numbers in the thousands. The violence lasted for eight days while the Muslim elite made no attempt to intervene.

The Tanzimat had done much damage to the *dhimmis* while only marginally improving their status. Nor had it saved the empire from collapse, as Abdulmejid had hoped. The sultan believed that by bettering the lot of Christians they would no longer feel the need to fight for their independence. But if anything the increased resentment they incurred as the result of their emancipation only furthered the Christians' desire to break away from the empire. Besides, it was clear that by reforming the millets, the sultan was bent on centralizing power, and the Christians wanted more, not less, control of their own affairs.

By the time Abdulmejid died from tuberculosis at the age of thirty-eight in 1861 rebellions, encouraged by the great powers, had broken out in Romania, Bulgaria and Macedonia. Greece had already been lost to the empire. The Ottoman government had become thoroughly Europeanized in an attempt to regain some of the power it had lost to Europe but as a result had lost more, not less, sovereignty to the European powers.

From the Ottoman Empire and its breakaway territory of Egypt to the Iranian Empire, Islamdom's rulers thought the only way to reclaim their position of world dominance was to beat the Europeans at their own game and modernize. Unfortunately, that only put them further in hock to Europe. Europe 'leveraged' its loans to gain control of the very modernizations that the Islamic world was trying to introduce – railways, shipping, the banking system and, in Egypt, the seventy-five-mile Suez Canal.

Tens of thousands died during the construction of the Suez Canal linking the Mediterranean with the Indian Ocean. The Egyptian governor, Ismail 'the Magnificent' – over-fed, over-confident and over-extravagant – spent millions on it and further millions rebuilding Cairo for the celebrations to mark the canal's opening. Ismail commissioned Verdi to write an opera for the occasion in 1869 but Verdi was too busy finishing *Aida*, and the select audience in Cairo's brand-new opera house had to listen to his existing opera, *Rigoletto*, instead. By 1875 Egypt was almost bankrupt and Ismail had to sell his shares in the Suez Canal Company. Britain's prime minister, Benjamin Disraeli, snapped them up immediately – the canal, he told Queen Victoria, must 'belong to Britain'. It was a pattern followed by all the European powers. The Ottoman Empire defaulted on its debts to Europe and as a result was forced to bow to British and French financial terms.

In the Iranian Empire the shah, like his Ottoman counterpart, was heavily in debt and was forced to grant countless concessions to the foreign powers. Britain and Russia were so powerful that their approval was necessary before the Tehran government could appoint a minister.

On 1 April 1873 a new play appeared in Istanbul. It was called *Vatan*, from the Arabic word *watan*, adapted to express the French idea of *Patrie*, of 'nation', an idea which was becoming increasingly potent in Europe (see Chapter 22). Until the nineteenth century *watan* had been used to mean place of birth or residence. The idea of nation, in the Romantic European sense of a community bound together by ethnicity and a common history and language within a specific territory, was alien to Muslims. Muslim rulers had defined their populations by their religion much more than by the territory in which they were born and lived. Muslim subjects in turn often thought of themselves as belonging to the *umma*, the worldwide community of Muslims, rather than belonging to a place, an almost feudal notion based as it is on land ownership. But this play, written by Namik Kemal, the 33-year-old son of the court astronomer, broke new ground in celebrating an Ottoman nationalist consciousness and patriotism.

The play is set during the Crimean War in the 1850s and tells the story of a group of Ottoman Muslim civilians who volunteer to defend the Bulgarian town of Silistra which is being besieged by the Russians. Young and old, they are prepared to die, not for religion but for their motherland. 'Should I sit comfortably in my home while the motherland is in danger? Should I stand still while the entire motherland is trembling?' asks the hero.[20] 'I was hungry when I came out from my mother's womb. It was the motherland that nourished me. I was stark naked, and it was the motherland that dressed me up… Why was I born if not to die for my motherland?' The play ends with the Russians fleeing and the victors shouting 'Long live the motherland! Long live the Ottomans!'

Staged at a time when the Balkan provinces were simmering with revolt, when the empire seemed totally in thrall to Europe, the play was an instant hit amongst Ottoman Muslims. They welcomed this injection of self-confidence, though ironically the play was based on a concept which came from Europe, the spirit of the nation. But *Vatan* was of course an indirect criticism of the sultan. Like his fellow 'Young Ottomans', Kemal attacked the sultan for being too weak against the European intruder and too strong and tyrannical against his own subjects. A few days after the play appeared, Kemal (no relation to the Mustafa Kemal who in 1934 would be given the title 'Atatürk', 'Father of the Turks') was put on a steamship and exiled to Cyprus. He left defiantly singing the Marseillaise (which he had translated into Turkish); its opening lines are 'Forward! Children of the nation'.[21]

A patriotic love of the empire, a sense of 'Ottomanness', was precisely what Sultan Abdulmejid had also intended with his emancipation of *dhimmis* and with his secular schools and university. But unlike the Young Ottomans he had hoped, admittedly under European pressure, to bind every one of his subjects to the empire and each other by a sense of being an Ottoman first rather than a Muslim, Christian or Jew. Abdulmejid had even presided over the creation of an Ottoman national anthem and an Ottoman national flag.

Abdulmejid's successor Abdulaziz had gone further. His 'Nationality Law' of 1869 applied the new legal concept of nationality to define who belonged to the Ottoman state. No reference was made to religion. The sultans were creating a nation and destroying a multicultural empire.

The millet system had not imposed assimilation, as had been the explicit requirement of the French delegates when France emancipated Jews in 1791. Instead it had recognized difference and managed it, as all empires have to do. But when the triumphant heroes of *Vatan* shouted 'Long live the Ottomans', they did not mean all the diverse ethnic and religious peoples who inhabited the empire. They meant Turkish Muslims like themselves who made up the majority. It is the glories of their ancestors, Turkish tribesmen who had spread out from Anatolia in the thirteenth century to create one of the largest and most powerful empires in the world, that Kemal celebrates. Indicatively, *Vatan*'s main character is called Islam Bey (Bey is a title given to senior officials in the Ottoman Empire) and his band of brave volunteers are all fellow Muslims. Islam Bey makes clear who the 'Ottomans' really were:

> The Ottomans talk as if they have no concern for the motherland. But when you show them the enemy, when they realize that the holy soil of the motherland is to be trampled under the filthy feet of the foreigners, then something happens to these people. At that time, the differences between me and the laziest peasant are dissolved. At that time, those wretched Turks wrapped in coarse wool and felt, those gentle, kind faced peasants, the desperate people whom we do not tend to tell apart from the harnessed oxen, disappear completely. In their place appears the spirit of Ottomanness, and the spirit of heroism.[22]

The 'spirit of Ottomanness' resides in the Turks.

As a foundational myth of a nation, *Vatan* is in its way the Turkish equivalent of the *Chanson de Roland*, the great propaganda myth of the Reconquista and of France, and just as exclusive. A sense of Turkishness and Turkish superiority found its earliest voice in Namik Kemal. It was echoed by his fellow Young Ottomans such as Ali Suavi who, though himself of Greek descent, boasted that 'in regard to their military, civilizing and political roles, the Turkish race was superior and more ancient than all the other races'.[23]

Neither Kemal nor the other Young Ottomans rejected the Enlightenment – in fact they considered some of its ideas vital to the revival of the Ottoman Empire. But following al-Attar and his pupil Rifa'a al-Tahtawi – the visitor to Paris who helped inspire the *Nahda* – their Enlightenment was never going to be a secular one, as had been the case in Europe. Kemal believed the State must be based on the sharia. He was passionately opposed to the secularization of the law which seemed to be occurring with the Tanzimat period of reform and modernization ushered in with the Edict of Gülhane in 1839.

Sharia law, he believed, could be quite in harmony with modernization if a distinction was made between those laws which were based on the essential principles of Islam as enunciated in the Quran and those which derived from the specific historical circumstances that Muhammad lived through. Kemal and the Young Ottomans believed in an Islamic Enlightenment. They hoped that it would persuade Muslims to look more favourably on modernization, which for many spelled European colonization and hardship. Islam would help the Ottomans to modernize, and modernization was essential if the empire was to stand up to the European powers. Islam thus became linked to the fight against Western colonialism.

The man who perhaps did more than any other Muslim to forge that link was the chain-smoking peripatetic political activist Jamal al-Din al-Afghani. He had been living in India at the time of the Indian Rebellion (Indian 'mutiny' according to the British) in 1857 and its savage suppression; he lived in Egypt during the 1870s when Egypt was in financial ruins and effectively controlled by Britain and France thanks to its governor Ismail the Magnificent's profligacy. A passionate opponent of European colonialism, al-Afghani believed that the Arabic world would have the strength to overcome the Western powers if it were united by Islam. But it would have to be a reformed Islam. Al-Afghani was as bitterly critical of the current state of Islam as he was of the profligate corrupt Muslim rulers who kowtowed to their European slave-masters. Like Ibn Taymiyya at the time of the Mongol invasions (see Chapter 10) Al-Afghani opposed *taqlid*, what he considered to be the blind unquestioning adherence by Muslim jurists and scholars to judgements and interpretations which had been made in medieval times and had then been set in stone. *Taqlid* had, he said, stifled Islamic debate and distorted true Islam. All Muslim states should be ruled according to sharia, but jurists must exercise *ijtihad* and not *taqlid*. They had to make a distinction between law based on the fundamental divine principles of the Quran and sunna and *fiqh*, the particular legal judgements made by jurists of the eighth and ninth centuries which Sunni jurists still insisted on following. In that way, sharia and the demands of a modern state were perfectly compatible. Al-Afghani may have been a fierce critic of European colonialism but he was also an admirer of European ideas and a believer in modernization. Like earlier

Muslim modernists such as al-Jabarti who visited Napoleon's Institute of Egypt in Cairo, al-Afghani was convinced that there need be no clash between the demands of a modern state and Islam, between reason and faith. Together with the Egyptian reformer Muhammad Abduh, another vital figure in the pan-Islamic and modernist movements, he propounded his views in the political newspaper, *al-Urwa al-Wuthqa* ('the firmest bond'), which the two men founded in 1884.

Al-Afghani was as unpopular amongst many of the ulema for his criticisms of Islam as he was amongst political rulers. With the encouragement of the ulema the authorities expelled him from Afghanistan, India, Egypt and Iran. In 1890 the Shah of Iran, Naser al-Din, granted a British company the monopoly on Iran's most important crop – tobacco. Although al-Afghani was by then an exile from Iran living in Iraq, he was nevertheless determined to stop 'this criminal' who was giving away Iran's precious assets to the 'foes of the faith'. Al-Afghani turned to the ulema and urged Mirza Shirazi, the Grand Ayatollah (the highest rank accorded to a Twelver Shiite cleric) to intervene. While the religious establishment was losing its authority in the Sunni Ottoman Empire, the opposite was occurring in Shia Iran. Since the religious scholar Majlisi had risen to become the most powerful religious figure in Iran at the end of the seventeenth century, the ulema had been making themselves into a body separate from – and as powerful as – the State (see Chapter 16). They still ran most of the Iranian Empire's schools, unlike the Sunni ulema in the Ottoman Empire; they were often the administrators of provincial cities; they were essential in the running of the bazaars, and their seals of approval had to be attached to the vital documents which governed everyday life, such as marriage contracts and deeds of possession.

In December 1891, Mirza Shirazi issued a fatwa forbidding the use of tobacco. Almost every man in Iran smoked but almost every man obeyed the fatwa; 'all the tobacco merchants closed their shops ... and no one smokes any more, neither in town, nor in the entourage of the Shah, even in his [harem]'.[24] The shah withdrew his concession to the British company. Mirza Shirazi then lifted his ban on tobacco. For al-Afghani it must have been the perfect proof of how the power of Islam could be enlisted to combat Christian Europe. Unfortunately, the success of the Tobacco Protest actually put Iran even more in debt to Britain: Iran needed to borrow yet more money in order to compensate the tobacco company's shareholders. Al-Afghani was later considered to have inspired the assassination of the shah in 1896.

Al-Afghani's pan-Islamism saw Islam as the way to unify the Islamic world against the Great Powers. So too did the Young Ottomans – but they combined religion with nationalism, the two most powerful and deadly social glues. Because, of course, to unify is to exclude. Kemal and the Young Ottomans were trying to fortify the Ottoman Empire by creating an 'Ottoman' who would fight fiercely for it. But this Ottoman was both a Muslim and a descendant of the Turkish tribesmen who founded the empire. 'Ottomans' shared a history, a language and a religion. That meant the non-Muslim, the non-Turk, was not part of the empire. The sultans, by abolishing the millet system, had in fact been trying to eliminate religious difference. The Young Ottomans were reintroducing it.

In 1882 Britain occupied Egypt and accelerated Europe's 'scramble for Africa'. By the end of the nineteenth century, the Ottoman Empire had lost Cyprus, Egypt, Algeria and Tunisia to Britain and France. The sick man of Europe, as Tsar Nicholas I called the Ottoman Empire, would never be well again. It was, said Thackeray, 'as rotten, as wrinkled and as feeble as the old eunuch I saw crawling about it [Topkapi Palace] in the sun', with his 'little fat white hands, and a great head sunk into his chest, and two sprawling little legs that seemed incapable to hold up his bloated old body'.[25]

Most of the Islamic world had become colonies of Europe. For many Muslims, European notions such as religious emancipation were fatally contaminated – yet another form of European imperialism imposed upon them. So indeed was liberalism in general. 'Your liberalness we see plainly is only for yourselves, and your sympathy with us is that of the wolf for the lamb which he designs to eat,' the Egyptian reformer Muhammad Abduh told a British official in 1895.[26]

The Young Ottomans were using Islam and nationalism to help the Islamic world regain its self-esteem. But nationalism was taking over from religion as the most effective way by which rulers could create an enemy and thereby unify their country. The consequences were catastrophic for the Armenians, the Assyrians and the Greeks of the Ottoman Empire, and for the Jews of the German Empire.

CHAPTER 21

EMANCIPATION AND THE FAILURE OF TOLERANCE

'Every people only remains a people so long as it possesses its own God and excludes all other gods without any reconciliation; so long as it believes that, with its God, it will vanquish and expel all the other gods from the world.'

– Dostoevsky, *The Possessed*, 1871

'The majority decide who the "alien" is; this, and all else in the relations between peoples, is a matter of power.'

– Theodor Herzl , *Der Judenstaat* (The Jewish State), 1896

IN 1743, MOSES BEN Mendel Dessau, the fourteen-year-old son of a poor Torah scribe, set off from his home town and walked to the Prussian city of Berlin. It was a journey of some ninety miles, but in the eyes of many Jews took on the epic dimensions of the journey that the biblical Moses took when he led the Jews out of captivity.

Like most Jewish boys Moses Dessau (named after the East German town of Dessau in which he was born) could barely speak German; he had had an exclusively religious education untouched by secular subjects such as mathematics, geography, European works of literature or philosophy, and had lived a life totally cut off from the gentile world.

As a Jew Moses had to enter Berlin at the Rosenthaler Gate, the only gate through which Jews and cattle could enter. He was stopped by a Jewish gatekeeper appointed to ensure that the number of Jews allowed to settle in the city was kept to the permitted level. The Prussian king Frederick II ('the Great' as he insisted newspapers call him, thanks to his military conquests) was turning Prussia into a major European power. And Jews were not Prussians. In some cities Jews were banned altogether or, as in Frankfurt, confined to a notoriously dark and horribly overcrowded disease-ridden ghetto; in Nuremberg 200 Jews were allowed to live in the city, but they had to live in the ghetto and even then could only trespass outside its walls if they were with a gentile. The enlightened Frederick II, however, one-time friend and patron of Voltaire, allowed 2,000 Jews to live in Berlin. Furthermore, they no longer had to wear an identifying yellow badge or be confined to a ghetto. Nonetheless the Jewish gatekeeper at the Rosenthaler Gate was under orders to forbid entry to 'non-useful Jews', such as beggars and hawkers. Moses was only permitted entry when he convinced the guard that he had come to Berlin to study the Torah.

Except for the 'court Jews', the financiers and traders to the local rulers of the 300 or so states that made up what was still known as the Holy Roman Empire, Jews lived segregated lives in communities defined by their Jewishness and their religious faith. The rabbi educated their sons, was their legal judge and their religious guide. They spoke Yiddish (literally 'Jewish'), a Hebrew-German dialect which dated from the ninth century. And they dressed differently, the men distinguished by their dark knee-length cloaks, long beards and flat black hats, the married women by their sombre clothes and headdress covering their hair.

But by the time of his death in 1786 Moses Mendelssohn (the Christian-German version of his name) had become famous throughout Europe as one of the leading figures of the German Enlightenment, renowned for his works on philosophy, theology and literary criticism. 'A small deformed Jew with a black goatee and a heavy hunchback', he was hailed as 'Germany's Socrates' or the 'Jewish Socrates' for his philosophical brilliance and erudition; he was the admired colleague and friend of the German Christian elite at a time when Christian–Jewish relations were virtually restricted to business transactions. Christians were drinking from porcelain teacups bearing his portrait; his high-cheekboned face stared out from vases and from countless engravings that graced the walls of Christian homes.

Moses, a contemporary of the Muslim Ibn Abd al-Wahhab, was, in the eyes of his admirers, leading the Jews out of the ghetto and into wider society. To his Jewish detractors, however, Moses was indeed leading the Jews out of their ghetto. But he was leading them down the slippery path of assimilation to where they would melt away into non-Jewish society, prepared to lose their identity for the sake of mere acceptance. Moses the Uncle Tom, the ingratiator,* or Moses the pioneer who opened the gates of the ghetto and showed how it was possible to be both Jew and an equal citizen in the non-Jewish world. Perhaps Mendelssohn had forgotten the history of Samuel Naghrela. Back in the eleventh century Samuel Naghrela, the most powerful political figure in Muslim al-Andalus, had thought, like Mendelssohn, that Jews could successfully integrate. He believed he had been accepted and was respected by the Muslim majority while not relinquishing his own Jewish identity. But it turned out he had only been tolerated after all. When his son Josef and fellow Jews broke the rules of the tolerance game by not accepting their inferiority, Josef and 4,000 Jews were massacred (see Chapter 6).

In many ways Mendelssohn bore witness to the blind naivety or perhaps essential lie at the heart of the Enlightenment dream of equality. He was, according to his critics, not becoming equal with gentiles but succumbing to the pressure of becoming like them. In theory the idea that all men were equal by virtue of being human and were therefore entitled to the same treatment was a glorious principle on which to build a society. And it was a significant advance on toleration. In reality, however, equality meant assimilation with the majority. But if your religion, the colour of your skin, your sex or sexual preferences, made

---

* Uncle Tom was the black slave hero of Harriet Beecher Stowe's anti-slavery novel, *Uncle Tom's Cabin*. Published in 1852, it was hated by pro-slavery white southerners in the United States. But it was also disliked by many black slaves for its depiction of Tom, who though he wanted freedom from his white masters, was still obligingly subservient and recognized his inferiority.

you unwilling or unable to assimilate, then, if you were lucky and were not killed or persecuted, you were still fated to be tolerated rather than treated as an equal. The same is often still true today.

As for Moses himself, he did not believe he was being forced to assimilate. On the contrary, he could be both a Jew *and* a German. He could be Moses ben Mendel Dessau (Moses son of Mendel from Dessau), the name he used when writing his theological works on Judaism. But he could also be Moses Mendelssohn, the Christianized version of 'son of Mendel'. The Jewish–Christian 'Mendelssohn' neglected, however, to recognize one important fact. He had adopted his new name because he thought his Jewish name might handicap his advancement in the Christian world.

Speaking the language of the Enlightenment, Mendelssohn was clear that Jews had the right to take their place amongst their fellow non-Jewish citizens in a shared world. In order to do so, Mendelssohn was convinced that Jews had to get out of the ghetto, metaphorically as well as physically. It was not just Christians who were keeping Jews in the ghetto, but Jews themselves. For thousands of years strict separation had been their stratagem to avoid disappearing into the wider community. But it was time to break down the barriers.

During his first seven years in Berlin, in the spare time he had from studying at the yeshiva, Mendelssohn unlocked the gates into the world of the Enlightenment. Unable to speak or read German when he arrived, educated only in the Torah, he now learned English, French and German, so that he could study the secular works of European non-Jewish scientists and philosophers.

In 1763 Mendelssohn won first prize in a competition set by the prestigious Academy of Sciences. His 'Treatise on certainty in metaphysical philosophy' beat into second place the essay by the emblematic philosopher of the *Aufklärung* (the German Enlightenment), Immanuel Kant. By the age of twenty-four Mendelssohn was friends with, and admired by, the greatest philosophers and literary figures of his time, not just Kant, but the philosopher and theologian Johann Gottfried Herder, the playwright Gotthold Ephraim Lessing (whom Mendelssohn allegedly met over a game of chess), the great poet Klopstock and the literary genius and polymath Goethe.

Frederick II's acknowledgement of Mendelssohn's genius was to elevate him from the status of 'tolerated Jew', a status which he shared with servants, to the status of 'extraordinary' protected Jew. This elevation put him on a footing with wealthy Jewish merchants, and indeed Mendelssohn was partner in a silk business. He was now entitled to live permanently in Berlin and to marry and have children. But he could not pass on to them his right to live in the city or to marry. And Frederick refused to allow Mendelssohn to become a member of the prestigious Academy of Sciences. Mendelssohn was still inescapably Moses ben Mendel Dessau, the Jew.

Frederick the Great was religiously indifferent, if not scornful of revealed religions, and declared that 'all religions must be tolerated'. He let the Huguenots, the French Calvinists, live in Berlin free from humiliating restrictions, but he would not do the same with Jews, limiting their numbers, restricting them to certain professions and insisting they pay the *Schutzgeld*, the tax for being a Jew (similar to the tax *dhimmis* had to pay). He declared that:

> We have too many Jews in the towns. They are needed on the Polish border because in these areas Hebrews alone perform trade. As soon as you get away from the frontier, the Jews become a disadvantage, they form cliques, they deal in contraband and get up to all manner of rascally tricks which are detrimental to Christian burghers and merchants. I have never persecuted anyone from this or any other sect. I think, however, it would be prudent to pay attention, so that their numbers do not increase.[1]

The king shared a deep inbuilt prejudice against Jews with his Christian subjects and most of Europe. Jews had been loathed, despised, resented and distrusted by Christian Europe for centuries. That almost innate visceral feeling did not disappear under the pure light of Enlightenment reasoning. Jews, said Kant, 'seek no civil honour, but rather wish to make up for their loss through the advantage of outwitting the people under whom they find protection'. Voltaire himself, the Enlightenment's intellectual superstar, shared the general antipathy towards Jews. 'You have surpassed all nations in impertinent fables, in bad conduct and in barbarism,' he told Jews in his 1772 essay 'One Must Take Sides'. 'You deserve to be punished, for this is your destiny.'

In 1779 Mendelssohn's admirer and friend Lessing staged his new play. *Nathan the Wise* was Lessing's plea for religious toleration and emancipation of Jews. Mendelssohn was the model for the eponymous hero. Benevolent and wise, Nathan is contrasted with the narrow-minded Christians who persecute him. The play was loathed by many who opposed Jewish emancipation and who condemned the play for attacking Christianity. Mendelssohn, touched and moved by the honour which he felt Lessing had paid him, was of course eager to defend the play, as were many Jews. But Lessing was deeply wounded by the attacks and never quite recovered his standing. The following year Mendelssohn and his wife and children, out walking on a summer's evening, were attacked by a gang of youths who hurled stones at them, shouting 'Juden! Juden!'

Even most of Mendelssohn's enlightened Christian friends, supporters of emancipation though they were, shared the general belief that Jews were morally inferior. The German historian and political writer, Christian Wilhelm von Dohm, and his fellow pro-emancipationists, differed from those more openly hostile to Jews only in believing that this inferiority could be remedied with emancipation. 'The moral turpitude in which that unfortunate nation [the Jews] is sunk', von Dohm wrote, was the result of Christian discriminatory regulations which had forced them into commerce and into social isolation. Enlightenment thinkers recognized the right of citizens to follow their own religious beliefs: it was universalism's concession to particularism.* But they asserted, with a superiority inherited over centuries of anti-Jewish prejudice, that in the process of assimilation, Jews would willingly abandon their religion.

* I am indebted to Tony Curzon Price for this aperçu.

'Driven by the innate human need for a loftier faith', Jews would inevitably turn to Christianity, according to Wilhelm von Humboldt, humanist, philosopher, diplomat and educational reformer.

The 'Jewish question' – how to treat Jews in the European state – was the burning issue of the late eighteenth through to the twentieth centuries. Answers ranged from deportation, to segregation and to the Nazis' 'final solution'. But for many enlightened Christians it was perfectly clear. To earn the right to become a citizen on a par with the gentile majority, Jews must abandon their difference, what made them Jews. The 'Jewish question' was, in fact, the assimilation question. For many Jews the real question was how much of their difference could be abandoned before Jews were no longer Jews but gentiles. Would commitment to the Enlightenment idea of equality actually mean embracing a universalism that ultimately would eradicate Jews and any minority?

Or was Mendelssohn correct, that actually there was no 'Jewish question' to be solved, that there need be no choice between being a Jew or a German? They could be German-Jews. It was this passionate conviction that inspired the *Haskalah* (from the Hebrew *sekhel*, meaning 'reason' or intellect), a Jewish version of the Enlightenment in which Mendelssohn played such a leading role. Mendelssohn and his fellow thinkers believed that Jews must embrace European culture and the wider world, but not at the expense of their own Jewish identity. Jews must have a secular education and learn European languages; they should stop speaking Yiddish and speak German instead, so that they did not cut themselves off from the wider community. But at the same time they must discover the riches of their own culture and study their own history. Mendelssohn actively promoted the revival of writing and reading Hebrew.

To that end he instituted the translation of the Torah, the first five books of the Hebrew Bible, into German. The Torah, known to Christians as the Pentateuch, was the Jewish child's introduction to their religion and to learning in general. Mendelssohn hoped his translation would enable young Jews to learn their religious tradition while at the same time learning it in the language of the society in which they lived. But just as Muslim modernizers like the reformer and political agitator al-Afghani (see Chapter 20) ran up against traditionalist Muslims and members of the ulema, so did Mendelssohn with the more traditionalist Jews and rabbis. It was a blasphemy to translate the Pentateuch into a secular tongue. Furthermore, Mendelssohn had undermined the rabbis' authority by failing to seek rabbinic approval as was customary.

While translating the Pentateuch, Mendelssohn also employed non-Jewish tutors to teach secular subjects, including science and geography, to his six children, his daughters as well as his sons. So did a growing number of the wealthy Jewish elite who shared his belief in the new potential role for Jews as part of, not separated from, the rest of society. They began to found schools with a secular as well as religious educational programme, and even schools which were exclusively secular. It was a trend which gained momentum throughout the nineteenth century. Jews were becoming secularized. Was this the price of their acceptance within the gentile world?

When Mendelssohn died in 1786 the 'Jewish question' had become more, not less, of an issue for gentiles and Jews alike. Jews were fighting for their emancipation. There was increasing mixing between Christians and Jews, of the wealthier sort anyway. Jews and gentiles sat together at the theatre, went to the same coffee houses, spoke the same language, dressed in the same fashions. Jews strolled alongside gentile Germans in Berlin's parks from which they had been previously banned. The men were dressed in powdered wigs and knee-length breeches, the women in hoop skirts, silk gowns and elegant hats that no longer covered all their hair as tradition had demanded. And the cream of Europe's Christian intellectuals were attending salons hosted by the most brilliant Jewish women in Berlin, amongst them Mendelssohn's daughter Brendel. It seemed that Mendelssohn's project was working: Jews were breaking out of the ghetto and finally beginning to be treated as equals.

But were they Jews any longer? They had abandoned Yiddish for German, religious education for a secular one; the men had even given up their beards for a clean-shaven Christian look. Mendelssohn's critics needed only to point to his children to show how dangerously misguided

Mendelssohn had been. Out of the six, four of them converted to Christianity, most notoriously Brendel, his eldest and most beloved child.

Like all of his children, Brendel was given a secular education. She was taught to speak and read in German, was steeped in the ideas and literature of the times. The more of this wider European culture she absorbed, the more she distanced herself from traditional Jewish practices. In 1794 she discarded her Yiddish name in favour of the Christian one, Dorothea. Soon after, she discarded her Jewish husband in favour of a gentile, the poet, literary critic and philosopher, Friedrich Schlegel. Schlegel was twenty-five, eight years younger than Dorothea, and handsome. Dorothea, intelligent, unconventional, straining at what she perceived as her Jewish leash, fell in love with him and his ideas, as he did with her. To the outrage of her family and friends, they became lovers; her marriage, she told her friends, had felt like 'slavery'. Two years later she was granted a divorce. From then on the couple lived a peripatetic life moving in Europe's intellectual circles. In Paris, Madame de Staël became their friend and patron. In 1804, the couple moved to Cologne where Jews had only just been readmitted after being expelled back in 1424. Following Napoleon's invasion in 1797, the city had been forced to comply with French law. Since France had emancipated Jews, Cologne could no longer forbid Jews to settle there. Dorothea, however, converted to Protestantism and married Friedrich in the cathedral. When her husband later converted to Catholicism, she did too, in 1808.

Brendel Mendelssohn, now Dorothea Schlegel, the daughter of the man who believed he could make a new type of citizen, a German-Jew, had done precisely what Mendelssohn's Jewish opponents had feared and predicted. She had disappeared into the Christian world and, worse still, was not the only one to do so. Almost all of her close friends, part of the Jewish elite who, like Dorothea, had been given a secular education and hosted prestigious salons, were doing precisely the same thing: first Christianizing their name, then converting to Christianity, then marrying a gentile who was usually wealthy, prominent and often aristocratic. Henriette Herz, hostess of the literary salon where Dorothea had met Schlegel, converted; Sara Meyer became Sophie Meyer and later Sophie von Pobeheim; her sister Marianne also converted and married Prince von Reuss; Rahel Levin, a writer who presided over one of the most famous salons in Europe, changed her name to Antonie Robert, converted and married Karl August Varnhagen von Ense.[2] Dorothea's own sister converted to Catholicism, one of her brothers, Nathan, converted to Lutheranism, the other, Abraham, to Calvinism; Abraham's son Felix, the future violinist and composer, would be baptized and marry a Huguenot.

Up to one quarter of Berlin's Jewish families and about the same proportion in other cities was affected by the *Taufepidemie*, the epidemic of baptisms.[3] It only ended in the 1830s with the influx of more traditional Jews escaping persecution in Russia. Moses Mendelssohn notwithstanding, it was still a handicap to be a Jew in Berlin. Christianity was the passport to success – to aristocratic husbands for Jewish women, to university and careers for Jewish men. Wealthy Jews had indeed broken out of the ghetto, but only to exit the Jewish world altogether and become Christian, swept up in the desire and pressure to assimilate.

Even many of those Jews who had retained their Jewish faith had Christianized their religion, in the horrified eyes of more traditional Jews. Mendelssohn had firmly believed that Jews must adhere to Jewish law – he himself was a punctilious observer. But a fundamental tenet of the *Haskalah* was that it was possible, and important, both to retain a Jewish identity and yet integrate into the wider gentile world. Like many contributors to the movement, Mendelssohn recognized that strict observance of the law was a major obstacle to Jews taking their place in Christian society – furthermore it contributed to the tide of conversions to Christianity. An anonymous writer in 1792 described the difficulties that observing Jewish law posed for a young Jewish apprentice working for a non-Jewish craftsman. He 'could not partake of the meals of the non-Jewish household, his day of rest was different, and his daily prayer interfered with his work'.[4]

Mendelssohn and his fellow reformers took the route followed by the deists and Muslim modernists. They whittled Judaism down to its fundamentals. Under this distinction, Reform Jews adapted or even abandoned some of the law. Muslims had tried to reconcile Islam with modernization; Reform Judaism tried to do the same.

On 17 July 1810, Israel Jacobson, wealthy philanthropist, Hebrew scholar and admirer of Mendelssohn, opened a synagogue in the town of Seesen in today's north-west Germany. It is considered to be the day when Reform Judaism was born. A boys' choir sang hymns in German accompanied by an organ; prayers were said in German as well as Hebrew and Aramaic. The liturgy was abbreviated and the rabbi gave his sermon in German. Jacobson believed it would make religious services more understandable and Judaism a less alien presence in the Christian world. Over the next ten years synagogues in Berlin and Hamburg followed Jacobson's example and introduced choirs and mixed seating (men and women had always sat separately in the synagogue).

Traditional Jews were appalled. They condemned any deviation from Jewish tradition as blasphemous. In the desire to adapt to changing times, to make practising Jews' lives compatible with the requirements of living in a gentile world, Reform Jews had created a non-Jewish Protestant-style religion. The traditionalists, called Orthodox by their opponents, formed themselves into separate communities. A rift was opening up between Reform and Orthodox Jews. In 1875 a formal schism was effected in Prussia when Orthodox Jews declared Orthodoxy to be a separate religion from the Reform.

In the Russian Empire, most Jews retained their traditional Judaism. But although Orthodox rabbis in Germany managed to persuade the authorities to shut down a few Reform synagogues, most Jewish communities adopted Reform. Nowhere did the Reform movement flourish more than in America where thousands of Jews from central and eastern Europe had been settling since the mid-1800s. By 1880, 90 per cent of American synagogues were Reform and had taken on such Protestant colouring that its men and women sat together in pews, clutching their hymnals as the organ blared. By the end of the century many Reform synagogues had rejected circumcision as barbaric, switched the Sabbath to Sunday and abandoned the strict regulations surrounding the Sabbath and the laws on family purity. The bar mitzvah, celebrating the young Jewish boy's coming of age, was replaced with a Christian-style confirmation ceremony. In German synagogues the Hebrew language was removed from the liturgy.

It seemed to many Jews that the Enlightenment would not let them be Jews. They could not be equal but different; they could only be equal by being the same. As Enlightenment citizens, Jews were to be humans, but 'human' meant European and Christian, or if not a practising Christian, then certainly the product of a Christian education and culture. Ottomanists of the Islamic Enlightenment similarly assumed that 'Ottoman man' was actually 'Turkish man' (see previous chapter). If Jews were to take their place alongside their fellow citizens, they must assimilate – there was to be no emancipation without assimilation. But of course assimilation only went one way – from Jew to Christian, and not the other way round.

Even Napoleon, the conqueror of Europe, hailed by Jews in the Holy Roman Empire and northern Italy as their emancipator, expected Jews to lose their identity. In the states he conquered between 1800 and 1815, Jews became equal citizens with Christians overnight. Jews were granted almost complete emancipation in Prussia in 1812. States were reluctantly forced to free Jews from the ghetto, or as in the case of Cologne, where Dorothea Mendelssohn-Schlegel converted to Protestantism, lift their ban on Jewish residency. But Jews must stop being Jews and become 'good citizens' just as revolutionary France had demanded Jews should do when it granted them full citizenship in 1791. They were, Napoleon said, 'the most despicable of mankind'. As he put it in a letter to his Minister of the Interior Jean-Baptiste de Nompère de Champagny in 1806, they must 'cease to have Jewish interests and sentiments; their interests and sentiments will be French'.[5] The nation is clearly positioned as the substitute to Judaism. In other words, the nation is also a jealous God, a monotheism.

It was partly to address complaints from French gentiles that emancipated Jews were not after all melting away but were still using rabbinical courts, refusing to intermarry, and maintaining their old occupation of moneylending at interest, that Napoleon passed his *Décret infâme*, as it was called by Jews, in 1808. The decree restricted Jews' rights of residency unless they became peasants or craftsmen, cancelled all debts owed to Jews by non-Jewish married women, soldiers and minors, and annulled any debts owed to Jews who charged more than 10 per cent interest. When Napoleon fell in 1815, the old order scrambled to reassert itself. As in the Islamic world, emancipation of Jews was associated with foreign occupation and Jews themselves were seen as the beneficiaries and allies of the conquerors, indeed as having made money from the Napoleonic Wars. In Rome, the pope ordered the rebuilding of the ghetto. But the Jews' fight for their emancipation continued.

The shock of Napoleon's invasion also prompted Prussia and the territories that made up the Holy Roman Empire to rethink their status. Instead of being semi-independent states under the loose suzerainty of the Holy Roman emperor, would they not be far more powerful and capable of resisting an enemy such as Napoleon if they united as a nation? But what defines a nation? It was while Berlin was under Napoleonic occupation that Johann Fichte, friend of Friedrich and Dorothea Schlegel, provided an answer.

Like many who had enthusiastically greeted the French Revolution, Fichte had watched with dismay as it spiralled down into the Terror. He was sadly disillusioned with the Enlightenment ideals in the name of which the revolution had been fought. His vision of the nation, outlined in a series of lectures published in 1808, expressed a new anti-Enlightenment Romantic spirit. The 'nation' is a set of people, he said,

> … who speak the same language, are joined to each other by a multitude of invisible bonds by nature herself, long before any human art begins; they understand each other and have the power of continuing to make themselves understood more and more clearly; they belong together and are by nature one and an inseparable whole.[6]

So Fichte summed up all the inchoate, amorphous, mystical, magical and nostalgic elements which imparted a sense of 'we-ness', which made nationalism so attractive and so lethal. As a means of uniting people together in a group and thereby creating the enemy outside, nationalism was as powerful as religion, if not more so. Back in the eleventh century the Church and Europe's secular rulers were already appealing to a sense of national pride in their call to arms against the Muslims, witness the *Chanson de Roland* (see Chapter 7). But that national pride was firmly based on a devotion to Christianity and the Church, on the conviction held by each nation that it was particularly favoured by God. Religion and nationalism were linked together as binding agents. In the nineteenth century, however, Romantic nationalism displaced religion and the Church and became the sole binding social force (though without being tempered by religion's moral strictures). Temporal and spiritual needs were supplied – for the insiders – by just one entity, the father- or motherland (the choice of parent varying according to each country's custom).

The legacy of war, the requirements of modernization, the principles of the Enlightenment and its religious scepticism had combined to ensure that rulers recognized the necessity of downplaying religious difference and tolerating minorities. Pragmatics and principle had combined to shift religion to a less prominent position. Rulers found in nationalism the tool that replaced religion when they needed to whip up the support of their people.

It was this belief in a national spirit, which was unique to those people who shared it and was what differentiated them from other nations, each with their own national spirit, that inspired the Grimm brothers. Their collected German folk tales were stories which expressed the spirit and culture of the German *Volk*. Nationalism led to a revival of enthusiasm for the *Chanson de Roland*, France's eleventh-century national epic; it led to the transcription of *Beowulf*, the Anglo-Saxon epic, which encapsulated England's own national spirit, albeit a Germanic freedom-loving, democratic one. It led Wagner to believe that those who were ethnically different could not comprehend the artistic and cultural meaning inherent in national culture. A Jew, he thought, could not become a great composer because rootlessness precluded real musicianship.

At the same time that Fichte was propounding a national romanticism, his friend Schlegel was laying the foundations of literary romanticism with his cult of the genius artist pursuing their own unique creative path. Romanticism's glorification of feeling stood against the cool rationalism of the Enlightenment. The exclusiveness of the Romantic nationalist against the inclusiveness of the enlightened universalist. Both Fichte and Schlegel seemed to be explicitly rejecting the Enlightenment, which was ironic in Schlegel's case, since his father-in-law Moses Mendelssohn had been a key figure in the Jewish Enlightenment.

But in fact romanticism was a rebellious child of the Enlightenment, not unrelated to it. Romanticism's homage to the creative genius of the individual, and the genius of the nation, grew out of the primacy which the Enlightenment gave to the individual and their right to be free to flourish. Nationalist breakaway movements claimed a universal right – the right to be free and independent – on the grounds of particularism, that they represented a set of people who shared the same spirit born of a particular history, culture and language.

Jews in the nineteenth century were caught in a double bind – as European minorities still are today. They had to be both the universal Enlightenment citizen and the particularist Romantic citizen. If the qualification for emancipation, for claiming the rights to which the universal citizen was entitled, was to share a common 'spirit' then that, as far as many nationalists were concerned, certainly disqualified Jews. Fichte called the Jews a 'state within a state'; to emancipate Jews would undermine the German state, he wrote, unless it were possible 'to cut off all their heads in one night, and to set new ones on their shoulders, which should contain not a single Jewish idea'. That was the poison at the heart of nationalism.

The problem for Jews was that in some ways Fichte was right. Jews were indeed a 'nation' in the Romantic nationalist sense. Indeed, it could be said that the biblical Moses's gift to world history was the formula for creating a nation: gathering a people in the face of a common oppressor (Pharaoh), galvanizing them with the prospect of a promised land and giving them a jealous God, supplier of law, to hold the group together. Jews did not just have their own religion but also shared a common descent, history, attachment to a cultural heritage: they did in effect share that ineffable spirit of a nation. Theodor Herzl, founder of political Zionism, would adopt this nationalist idea and fight to create a physical territory where the Jews, a spiritual nation, could become a physical nation.

But Romantic nationalism was a useful tool for those who hated the social and political advances that Jews were making across Europe. In 1867 the emperor Franz Josef I had emancipated all Jews in the Austro-Hungarian Empire; Jews in Italy had been emancipated by 1870. Across the continent, Jews were increasingly mingling with Christians. Condemned for centuries for their self-imposed differentiation from Christians, Jews were now being resented for their assimilation, for becoming equal if not superior to Christians.

German opponents of emancipation turned to the new doctrines of Romantic nationalism. Jews might gain legal parity with Christians, but they would never be able to integrate. Jews were indelibly other, even if they took on all the colouring of Christians, even their religion. Wealthy, beautiful, witty, intellectual Jewish women might open their doors to all the Christian luminaries of Europe, but they were still Jewesses. 'Their dress, however splendid it may be, has nevertheless retained certain Jewish traits as has their physiognomy,' wrote a prominent Berlin lawyer, Karl Grattenauer, in one of the first attacks on Jewish assimilation and emancipation, published in 1781.[7] 'Their language is still the wretched stammering jargon which, though they try to modernise it in conversation with Christians, they still use among themselves; filth and uncleanliness prevails among them and they cannot cover it with their great pomp.' The European world was still a virulently Christian one. Being a Jew, said Rahel Varnhagen von Ense, née Levin, hostess of one of the most glittering salons in the early nineteenth century, and close friend of Dorothea Schlegel, was 'a curse which the children of its adherents vainly try to flee in all quarters of the globe'.

Attacks on assimilated Jews, because of their 'alien essence', became more widespread and more virulent after 1871, when Germany's thirty-nine states (there had been about 300 at the end of the eighteenth century) united to form a single nation. Under the new constitution citizenship was independent of religious confession. The Jews of Germany had been emancipated. They had become too useful to the industrialization that was under way in many German cities and too sizeable a minority to risk alienating them by denying them equal rights. Besides, the Enlightenment climate of opinion was still a powerful enough force in Germany that keeping the Jews to a politically limited and socially inferior status was considered incompatible with the principle of 'natural rights' and equality.

The new Germany – it called itself the Second Reich or empire – was rising from the ashes of the First Reich, the Holy Roman Empire. But it was a nation, not a multicultural empire. Otto von Bismarck, its brilliant, despotic creator and ruler, chief minister of Prussia and now Chancellor of Germany, set out to mould the different states into a united single entity. To do so he used the increasingly popular idea of nationalism. The people were one united body because they had been bound together over centuries by invisible threads of culture, language, history and religion – in a word, by their 'Germanness'. For Bismarck, however, that Germanness was Prussian and he determinedly set out to create a Germany in the image of Prussia: authoritarian, militaristic, conservative and Protestant, like Bismarck himself.

Eight years after German unification, Heinrich von Treitschke, one of Germany's leading liberals, professor of history and editor of a prestigious Berlin journal, wrote an editorial condemning the 'Jewification' of German society. 'What we have to demand from our Jewish fellow-citizens is simple,' he wrote, 'that they become Germans, feel themselves simply and justly as Germans… for we do not want thousands of years of Germanic civilization to be followed by an era of German-Jewish mixed culture.'[8] Treitschke had, like so many liberals, fallen under the spell of Romantic nationalism, and had shown how easily it could slip into anti-Jewishness. The Jews were too different; they were seen as being contrary to the spirit of the German nation, as getting in the way of the new Germany's cohesion. 'The Jews are our misfortune,' Treitschke declared.

The dreadful irony was that probably more than any other Jews in Europe, German Jews wholeheartedly loved the culture of their nation. By 1860 only 25 per cent of German Jewish children were being educated in Jewish schools. The other 75 per cent were receiving a secular education. Wealthy Jews spoke fluent German. The astonishing speed and visibility of Jewish assimilation at the end of the nineteenth century, their success in fields previously barred to them – law, medicine, journalism, commerce – only increased hostility towards them amongst the non-Jewish majority. Like many Muslims in the Ottoman Empire, German Christians watched indignantly as Jews, hitherto their despised inferiors, were permitted to become their formal equals before the law and, more galling still, sometimes their superiors professionally, financially and socially.

Anti-Jewish feeling had always been fiercest at times of economic crisis. The 1870s and 1880s, when a financial depression hit Europe, were no exception. Political parties expressing opposition to Jews grew in popularity in Germany, Austria and France.

In 1879, Wilhelm Marr, a journalist and erstwhile left-wing radical, founded the League of Anti-Semites and introduced the word Antisemitismus, anti-Semitism, into politics. Marr coined this new word to define what had hitherto been called Judenhass because he wanted to emphasize that this was hatred of a race – not just of a religion.

In the eighteenth century linguists had begun to make a distinction between languages with Aryan and with Semitic roots. It was then assumed, wrongly, that there were two separate 'racial' groups corresponding to that distinction. Jews were Semites, racially distinct from Aryans. That belief gave yet more strength to the nationalist arguments of those opposed to the Jews' emancipation. Romantic nationalism had excluded Jews from the German nation on the grounds that they did not share the Germans' national spirit. But since this idea was so ineffable, it left open the possibility that if Jews converted to Christianity and shed their Jewish customs, they too could share the German spirit and become part of the nation. But if Jews were also racially distinct, then however

Christian they became they would never be able to integrate. Jews were inescapably different physically from gentiles.

Marr was living in a time of intense social and economic upheaval when political divisions were becoming sharper and nastier. Even the physical landscape was becoming unrecognizable. Berlin itself was changing from the demure, small capital of Prussia, 'with rough streets, muddy and lantern-lighted', into what Mark Twain, who lived in Berlin in 1891, called 'the Chicago of Europe' (Chicago having the reputation of being the most modern city in the world). A foul-smelling city stinking of excrement seemed to be modernizing overnight. Ever more people were drawn to this booming city, and packed ever more tightly into tenement houses which lined the new ruler-straight streets. From a population of 412,000 in 1849, Berlin had grown to over 1 million by 1880 and had become the most densely populated city in Europe. Joining the competition for housing and work were, of course, Jews. Their presence in Berlin had increased from about 19,000 in 1860 to 54,000 in 1880.

Marr accused Jews of deliberately setting out to create the social and political tensions bedevilling Germany in order to dominate it. Before long, he warned in his pamphlet 'The Way to Victory of Germanism over Judaism', 'there will be absolutely no public office, even the highest one, which the Jews will not have usurped'. The pamphlet was so popular that it went into its twelfth edition the year it was published in 1879. For Marr and his League of Anti-Semites, the Jews had to be defeated and the only way to do so was to eliminate them.

It was not a big leap from Marr to Hitler. Nor for that matter, from Dostoevsky to Hitler. Dostoevsky, that superb writer who could understand the mind of a murderer and probably wrote better than any other novelist about the torments and ecstasies of religion, was also a rabidly anti-Semitic pan-Slavist. He believed that all the Slav peoples of eastern and central Europe shared a common national spirit and should be united. 'What if there were not three million Jews but three million Russians in Russia, and there were eighty million Jews?' he asked in *A Writer's Diary*. 'Well, how would they treat Russians ... wouldn't they skin them altogether? Wouldn't they slaughter them to the last man, to the point of complete extermination…?' Dostoevsky, like so many anti-Semites, was convinced that Jews were involved in a worldwide conspiracy to dominate the world. 'Their reign, their complete reign is approaching!' he warned. 'What is coming is the complete triumph of ideas before which sentiments of humanity, the thirst for truth, Christian feelings, the national and popular pride of European peoples, must bow.'

In 1881 Alexander II, Tsar of Russia, was assassinated. One of his assassins was a Jewish woman, Gesya Gelfman. Under the guise of patriotic fury, anti-Semitism found its voice. Newspapers published inflammatory anti-Semitic articles; posters appeared calling on the Russian people to attack Jews. A great wave of pogroms followed.

Pogroms were not new in the Russian Empire. They had been occurring for over a hundred years, ever since Russia began encroaching west into Poland and Lithuania, where the highest concentration of Jews had previously lived (the result of the uniquely tolerant policy of Poland to Jews). Hundreds of thousands of Jews suddenly became part of an empire which had previously had almost no Jews at all. By the late nineteenth century about 45 per cent of the world's Jews were living in the Russian Empire, the largest Jewish population in the world. The majority of them were corralled into the 'Pale of Settlement' set up by the empress Catherine 'the Great' in western Russia, today's Ukraine, Belarus and Poland. Most Jews were forbidden to live outside the Pale. It would become the site of Russia's worst pogroms at the end of the nineteenth and early twentieth centuries.

Pogroms – from the Russian, meaning storm or devastation – were disorganized mass acts of killing Jews. Police and soldiers sometimes joined in the attacks. But even when the authorities did not actively connive in the pogroms, they did little to prevent the orgies of murder. In the early twentieth century thousands of Jews were killed in the pogroms, thousands of homes and businesses were wrecked. 'Beat up the yids and save Russia' was the battle cry.

Patriotic fury initially provided an excuse, even a justification, for the pogroms. But they were also the product of the helpless rage felt by many

Russians at their economic circumstances. They were struggling with the consequences of rapid industrialization, with a desperate competition for jobs made fiercer when the serfs flooded the labour market after their emancipation in 1861. Poor Jews were resented by poor Russians for taking their jobs and their homes. Wealthy Jews were resented for being too economically successful and exploiting the poor.

The growing number of populist revolutionary groups only contributed to the rising tide of anti-Semitism. As socialists/communists, they damned Jews for being the quintessential capitalists, squeezing money out of the poor. And this despite the fact that large numbers of Jews were joining revolutionary socialist movements in protest against the social and economic hardships they were enduring. Jews were no less critical of the authorities than other left-wing radicals were, and perhaps more so as they became disillusioned with the pace and results of their emancipation.

The Jews could not win: they were condemned as capitalists by the left, as revolutionaries by the right, or in an oxymoronic amalgam as 'Bolshevik bankers'. That phrase was used as recently as the 1980s by the French populist right-winger and founder of the Front National, Jean-Marie Le Pen.

The noose around Jews was tightened still further by Tsar Alexander III, whose father had been assassinated in 1881. He renewed the ban on Jewish settlement and ownership of property outside towns. As a result hundreds of thousands of Jews were forced to move from the countryside and crowd into the cities, only exacerbating the hostility towards them of non-Jews. Quotas were imposed on the number of Jews admitted to high schools and universities and into certain professions. Konstantin Petrovich Pobedonostsev, close adviser to Alexander III, made the government's intentions towards Jews quite clear: 'One third will die out, one third will leave the country and one third will be completely dissolved in the surrounding population,' he declared.

Between 1881 and the outbreak of the First World War in 1914, over 2.5 million Jews are thought to have left Russia and central and eastern Europe for the United States and cities in Germany and Austria. It only exacerbated the rising tide of anti-Semitism in western Europe. The *Ostjuden*

(Jewish immigrants from eastern Europe, usually Yiddish-speaking) were despised, even by western European Jews, for their backwardness and traditionalism. In Western eyes, they epitomized all the grotesqueries of the Jew that had been depicted in cathedral statues, medieval manuscripts and would soon populate the cartoons of Nazi newspapers.

But it was the Dreyfus Affair that finally convinced many Jews that Mendelssohn's dream of being accepted by Christians as equals was never going to be realized.

In 1894 the French army began to suspect that one of their military officers was passing secrets to the German Embassy in Paris. Suspicion fell on a minor French officer, Captain Alfred Dreyfus. Dreyfus had the misfortune to be a Jew and a wealthy Jew at that. He was generally disliked, considered to be cold, over-ambitious, and standoffish. There was little evidence to convict him of treason but in the anti-Semitic climate of the times, and despite his fierce patriotism and protestations of innocence, Dreyfus was found guilty. His medals and insignia were stripped from him before massed ranks of silent soldiers, while a jeering crowd spat at him and shouted 'Jew' and 'Judas!'[9] Torn from his wife and two children, Dreyfus was imprisoned on Devil's Island, a penal colony off the coast of South America. Shackled to his bed at night, the works of Tolstoy, Nietzsche and Shakespeare were his only consolation.

The case split France apart. On the one side were those who hailed the conviction of the Jew Dreyfus as striking a blow for Christian France, as being part of the rearguard action to preserve or restore the *Ancien Régime*, the true France. On the other were those who fought to save Dreyfus from what they saw as an appalling miscarriage of justice fuelled by an anti-Semitism which had no place in a France refashioned on the principles of equality, liberty and fraternity. The affair divided even the Impressionists – pro-Dreyfus (Dreyfusard) Pissarro and Monet passionately at odds with anti-Dreyfusard Degas and Renoir. Foremost amongst the anti-Dreyfusards was, however, the Catholic Church, which was still deeply anti-Semitic (almost a third of the anti-Semitic books published in France between 1870 and 1894 were written by Catholic priests) and bent on re-establishing its pre-eminent position as embodying the spirit of the French nation.

Two years after Dreyfus had been condemned to exile for life, the chief of army intelligence, Lieutenant Colonel Georges Picquart, uncovered the real culprit, Major Ferdinand Walsin Esterhazy, a drunk and a gambler who was constantly in debt. Picquart, though an avowed anti-Semite, was brave and honest enough to recognize the injustice that had been done and to bring it to the attention of his superiors. But it cost him his career. The army establishment refused to accept the evidence. Reinforced by the anti-Semitic tirades of the Catholic newspaper *La Croix*, and with vociferous public support, a military court acquitted Esterhazy, while Picquart was transferred to Tunisia and sentenced to sixty days' imprisonment. In an open letter to France's president, Félix Faure, entitled '*J'Accuse*', Émile Zola, famed for his naturalist novels, accused the highest levels of the army of anti-Semitism and of colluding in a cover-up.

Zola was convicted of libel and fled to England where he spent nine miserable months in the London suburb of Upper Norwood. But Zola had not risked his career in vain. Dreyfus was brought back from exile and put on trial again. Though the army could not bring itself to declare him innocent, it set him free because of what it called 'extenuating circumstances'. After five years, the awkward, unpopular Dreyfus was released from his hell and found himself to be the hero of the left. He had to wait, however, until 1906 before the army officially declared him innocent and promoted him along with his courageous defender Lieutenant Colonel Picquart. Picquart went on to become Minister of War in 1906. Dreyfus fought in the First World War and died in 1935, an officer of the Legion of Honour, France's highest order of merit. The Catholic Church, on the other hand, fared less well in its fight with the Enlightenment Republic. In 1905 France declared itself to be a secular state – so far it is still the only country in Europe to have done so. France, said Aristide Briand, the future prime minister, who guided the Separation of the Churches and the State bill through the French Assembly, 'is not anti-religious… It is un-religious'. Church schools were closed down, religious orders were expelled from the country, and if they were not purged from the army, Catholics found their promotion was blocked.

Though the majority of France was still Catholic, though Pope Pius X warned that the bill was 'as disastrous to society as it is to religion', French secularism had broad popular support, including from that segment of society which, standardly, can be expected to be the most conservative, the peasantry. French peasants on the whole supported the secularists because they feared the Church would connive in the restoration of the *Ancien Régime* and with it the feudal dues (including payment of tithes and forced labour) that had bedevilled their existence.

During the Revolution and since then, when France had switched back and forth between being a republic and being a monarchy, the Church had been in league with the monarchy waiting for any opportunity to bring back the old order. '*Le cléricalisme, voilà l'ennemi*', Léon Gambetta, one of the greatest advocates for separation and for a democratic republic, told the Chamber of Deputies in 1877. During the tragedy of Captain Dreyfus which had split France politically between left and right, the Church had aligned itself squarely with the anti-Dreyfusard, monarchical right.

The Dreyfus Affair had also revealed the anti-Semitism at the heart of the French establishment. It made a deep impression on the 34-year-old Theodor Herzl, Paris correspondent for the *Neue Freie Presse*, a newspaper which was as prestigious in the Austro-Hungarian Empire as *The Times* was in England. The child of Jewish parents who had moved to Vienna from Hungary, Herzl had initially been convinced that assimilation was the only path to emancipation. Though radical German nationalists were questioning whether Jews could ever share the German national spirit, Herzl still believed Jews could. He was steeped in German-Jewish Enlightenment culture.

But in trying to assimilate, Herzl fell into the dreadful trap that lies in wait for the assimilationist. He had taken on the anti-Semitism of the gentile world that had been hidden at the heart of the Enlightenment and was becoming only too apparent in the Romantic nationalism that was co-existing awkwardly with it. Like Mendelssohn's friend Christian Wilhelm von Dohm and many other Christian sympathizers, Herzl believed that Jews were indeed morally inferior, but not because of any innate flaw in their character. Centuries of oppression by Christians had turned them into a shiftless, alien people, unmanly, cowardly and servile. But, he said, such 'shameful Jewish characteristics' could be shed and Jews would then become civilized Europeans. Herzl, though he himself was an atheist, even considered a mass conversion of Jews to Christianity, but gave up the idea as impracticable. He became that creature so despised by the anti-assimilationists, the 'self-hating Jew'. 'Anti-Semitism did not succeed until the Jews began to sponsor it,' was a popular Viennese joke at the end of the nineteenth century, according to the Austrian author and playwright Arthur Schnitzler.

While studying law at the University of Vienna, Herzl joined one of the belligerent, hard-drinking, hard-fencing German nationalist student fraternities that were becoming so popular in Austria. Its motto was *Ehre, Freiheit, Vaterland* (Honour, Freedom, Fatherland). Like his near-contemporaries Mahler and Freud, Herzl was committed to pan-Germanism and the transformation of the Austro-Hungarian Empire, where Germans and German culture predominated, into part of a greater Germany.

Sporting a sash of black, red and gold across his chest, brandishing an ivory-tipped walking stick, an obligatory duelling scar on his left cheek though his poor performance in his trial dual nearly cost him his membership, Herzl was the assimilated Jew personified. But it was, according to Herzl, when he saw the epaulettes torn from Dreyfus's shoulders, heard the mob shouting 'death to the Jews', and read the anti-Semitic venom spewed out from newspapers like the Catholic *La Croix* that he realized the futility of assimilation. Dreyfus, who was an ardent patriot, who shouted 'Long Live France! Long live the Army!' as he was being publicly humiliated and stripped of his office, would always be suspect in a gentile world. Jews would never be accepted. The only solution, Herzl concluded, was the nationalist one: Jews must have a nation of their own.

In 1896 he published *Der Judenstaat* (The Jewish State), his manifesto for political Zionism.*

> We have sincerely tried everywhere to merge with the national communities in which we live, seeking only to preserve the faith of our fathers. It is not permitted us. In vain we are loyal patriots, sometimes super-loyal; in vain do we make the same sacrifices of life and property as our fellow citizens; in vain do we strive to enhance the fame of our native lands in the arts and sciences or their wealth by trade and commerce. In our native lands where we have lived for centuries we are still decried as aliens, often by men whose ancestors had not yet come at a time when Jewish sighs had long been heard in the country. The majority decide who the 'alien' is; this, and all else in the relations between peoples, is a matter of power.

Jews were attacked for being rootless cosmopolitans, citizens of the world who had no loyalty to any nation They were also attacked for being citizens of a separate nation within a nation. They were too universalist and too nationalist. They were filthy capitalists or dangerous revolutionaries. They were suspected of conspiring to take over the Christian world, or told that however much they tried they could not assimilate. They were accused of not assimilating enough, while their fellow Jews accused them of assimilating too much. And the leitmotif to it all, they were Christ-killers in a Christian world.

Herzl the German nationalist became Herzl the Jewish nationalist and began to drum up support from senior Jewish and non-Jewish figures. Amongst those Jews who still passionately believed in assimilation, Herzl's views caused outrage. The editor of Herzl's own paper, the *Neue Freie Presse*, forbade his journalists to use the word Zionism; Herzl was sarcastically hailed as 'His Majesty', the King of Zion. And indeed

---

* 'Zion', literally a fortress on the hill of Mount Zion in Jerusalem, soon came to be used synecdochically for Jerusalem or the biblical land of Israel.

he did have a majestic bearing with his 'high forehead, his clear-cut features, his long and almost blue-black beard and his deep-blue, melancholy eyes', according to the Austrian Jewish novelist Stefan Zweig, who met Herzl at the *Neue Freie Presse* where Herzl was the leading arts columnist.

In 1896 Herzl made a proposal through the Grand Vizier of the Ottoman Empire to the sultan Abdulhamid II. Jews would pay off the empire's foreign debt in exchange for an outpost of the empire, Palestine. After all, in 1561 the sultan Suleiman I had given his Jewish counsellor Joseph Nasi authority to set up a Jewish homeland in Tiberias (see Chapter 15). Abdulhamid II, however, refused to meet Herzl, but sent his reply which Herzl noted down in his diary: 'While I am alive I would rather push a sword into my body than see the land of Palestine is [sic] taken away from the Islamic State.'[10]

Rejected by the sultan, Herzl tried to enlist the support of Kaiser Wilhelm II, Emperor of the Second Reich and King of Prussia; Herzl also approached Joseph Chamberlain, one of the most prominent British politicians of his day; he even tried the pope, Pius X. Kaiser Wilhelm dismissed the idea; the British offered him a Jewish homeland in Uganda; Pope Pius X refused to give his support until the Jews accepted the divinity of Christ.

It was not until 1934 that Jews got a homeland – in the Soviet Union. Stalin wanted to set up a Jewish autonomous region in the almost uninhabited area of Siberia on the borders with China so as to prevent China from taking over the area. To further this 'Soviet Zion', Soviet officials toured not just the Soviet Union but the Jewish communities of Germany, America and Argentina to recruit immigrants, in open competition with the Zionists who were encouraging Jews to settle in Palestine. And thousands of Jews did indeed emigrate from elsewhere in Russia and from beyond its borders, escaping the Depression of the 1930s for the chance of farming the bleak Siberian steppes. By 1934, when the Soviet authorities declared the territory – the size of Switzerland – the Jewish autonomous region or oblast of Birobidjan (or Birobidzhan) about 20,000 Jews were living there. But two years later they were caught up in Stalin's purges, classed as counter-revolutionaries and saboteurs and sent to the gulags or liquidated. The Jewish Autonomous Republic of Birobidjan still exists today and, apart from Israel, is the only Jewish territory with an official status, but it is home to fewer than 2,000 Jews.

Herzl had swapped the Enlightenment's supposedly inclusive universalism for nationalism's avowedly exclusive particularism. The Enlightenment had failed to resolve the tension between universal man in whom difference had been magically rubbed out, and the real man in all his glorious differences of culture and religion. The Enlightenment smoothed over this problem with a dangerous sleight of hand which in fact covertly maintained its own form of intolerance. Its 'universal man' had to be male, white, heterosexual and from a European Christian culture. The West is still struggling with the fact that tolerant, inclusive, universal enlightenment still walks hand in hand with intolerant, exclusive nationalism, though both are tugging in opposite directions. Jews in nineteenth-century Europe bore the costs of this. So today do Muslims. They are distrusted in the West because they are not considered to share the particularist national spirit. Essential to that spirit, ironically enough, is considered to be the inheritance of Enlightenment universalism to which Islam – modernists not withstanding – is said to be inimical.

That said, it was under the banner of the Enlightenment that former slaves, Jews and Catholics lived in Protestant countries at the end of the nineteenth century with more freedoms and rights than they had ever done before. Within less than a hundred years, however, murderous extremism would be back – both in Europe and the Ottoman world.

CHAPTER 22

THE GENOCIDAL CENTURY

'As long as your ideology identifies the main source of the world's ills as a definable group, it opens the world up to genocide.'

– Stephen Pinker, interview with J.P. O'Malley, 9 November 2011

'What is to be done, O Moslems? For I do not recognize myself.
I am neither Christian, nor Jew, nor Gabr [Zoroastrian], nor
Moslem.
I am not of the East, nor of the West, nor of the land, nor of the
sea; …
My place is the Placeless, my trace is the Traceless…'

– Rumi, 1207–1273

THE FIRST GENOCIDE OF the twentieth century began with the arrest and deportation of 250 Armenians on the night of 24–25 April 1915. It was followed a month later by a law which allowed the Ottoman authorities to deport anyone they considered a threat to national security. Soon after, diplomats were sending reports of death marches, massacres and concentration camps. Railroad workers described seeing families crammed into cattle trucks. 'There is a consensus that all deportees are doomed to die,' wrote one German diplomat in October 1915. 'Nothing less than the destruction of an entire people is at issue.'[1]

Tens of thousands of corpses were reported to be piling up outside concentration camps. One witness described seeing starving camp inmates searching horse manure for grains. By 1923 about 1.5 million

Assyrian,* Armenian and Greek Christians had been slaughtered. That it bore such resemblances to the Nazi Holocaust was not coincidental. The Nazis explicitly looked to the Ottomans' treatment of the Armenians, 'the Jews of the Orient', as they called them, as a model for how to 'solve' the 'Jewish question'.

It was the fact that neither the Ottoman nor the Nazi authorities could be prosecuted for their responsibility in organizing a programme to eliminate millions that prompted a Polish lawyer, Raphael Lemkin, to campaign for a new crime to be recognised by international law. He coined a word for this crime, 'genocide', from the ancient Greek word *genos* (race, tribe) and the Latin *cide* (killing). In 1948 the United Nations agreed to recognize genocide, which it defined as 'acts committed with intent to destroy, in whole or in part, a national, ethnical, racial or religious group' as a crime under international law. Turkey has, however, always denied that it was guilty of genocide.

How did the Ottoman Empire, an empire which like all empires was designed to put up with its minorities, become so murderously intolerant? Because it was fearful, in decline, and no longer had the security of superiority which is a necessary ingredient for imperial tolerance.

At the end of the nineteenth century, the Ottoman Empire had been defeated by the Russian Empire and was haemorrhaging territory. Serbia, Romania, Montenegro, Bulgaria and Albania had been swept up in the tide of nationalist fervour engulfing western Europe. They had all followed Greece and won their independence. The empire had lost virtually all of its European territory. It was increasingly dominated by the European powers who were trying to manipulate the wars of independence to their own advantage, grabbing territory (Cyprus, Egypt, Algeria and Tunisia) or at least economic control, for themselves.

In the 1890s, the Armenian Christian communities in the eastern regions of the empire had also taken up arms. They were tired of being overtaxed by the authorities, of being the constant victims of kidnappings

---

* The Assyrians are an ethnic group who claim descent from the ancient Assyrians of what is now Iraq, Turkey and Egypt.

and raids by local Kurdish Muslim tribesmen. The savagery with which the Armenian struggle for independence was put down shocked even the Russian and European powers, used though they were to their own pogroms against Jews. About 80,000 to 300,000 Armenians are estimated to have been murdered between 1895 and 1896.

The sultan, Abdulhamid II, was rapidly losing support not only amongst the Great Powers, but amongst his own military officers, civil servants and intellectuals, who became known as the Young Turks. In July 1908, a group of officers, members of a secret revolutionary group, the Committee of Union and Progress (CUP), revolted against the sultan and demanded that he reinstall rule by parliament. Mutinies and strikes in support of their revolution spread across the empire. In the face of such opposition, the sultan capitulated and announced that parliamentary elections would be held.

In the early hours of 29 April 1909 the 76-year-old sultan, hunched and cadaverous, was put on a train bound for Salonica in Greece along with his immediate family. Abdulhamid II had turned down Herzl's offer to pay off the Ottoman Empire's debt in exchange for Palestine (see Chapter 22); his palace had been a monument both to European art and to the glorious colours, arabesque curves and textiles beloved of Islamic artists; he had had the Quran read to him every night along with the (translated) Sherlock Holmes stories. The Young Turks replaced him with his brother Mehmed V who was both plumper and more amenable to their insistence that he abandon authoritarian rule and accept the new constitutional spirit of the times.

But the deposition of a sultan had not solved the empire's desperate problems. Young Turks were divided as to how the empire could be saved. Should it become an improved version of what empires are anyway, a multicultural, multi-religious confederation of semi-autonomous provinces; or should it transform itself into a nation, uniting under one culture and one religion?

The solution was clear enough to the Committee of Union and Progress (the CUP), the party which had engineered the coup and which was becoming the dominant voice of the Young Turks. The empire had tried tolerance when it announced the Edict of Gülhane in 1839 and its follow-up the Imperial Reform Edict of 1856. It had hoped that by emancipating the *dhimmis*, it would put a stop to the Christian-dominated provinces' bids for independence. Religion would no longer be the marker of a community, effectively separating each community off from the others and fostering a desire for independence. Instead, the empire's subjects would unite as Ottomans, not divide as Christians, Jews and Muslims, nor split along ethnic divisions which mirrored the religious divisions. As far as the CUP was concerned, that attempt had failed disastrously. 'The sheriat [sharia], our whole past history, and the sentiments of hundreds and thousands of Musselmans and even the sentiments of the *Giaurs* [a derogatory term for non-Muslims] themselves, who stubbornly resist every attempt to Ottomanize them, present an impenetrable barrier to the establishment of real equality,' said Mehmed Talaat, the leader of the CUP.[2]

In 1910, speaking through its official organ, *Tanin*, the CUP 'confessed that its measures to bring about the union of the different communities had failed'.[3] The CUP would continue 'to pursue the cause of unity', *Tanin* declared, but 'in a different way'. That different way was to be 'Turkification'.

The CUP had wholeheartedly embraced the ideas of sociologist and political activist Mehmed Ziya Gökalp (Gökalp, meaning 'sky hero', was his pen name). He believed that the empire would not survive unless it became a nation, in the German Romantic sense of nation. Gökalp, the father of Turkish nationalism, was the Ottoman version of Germany's Fichte. Indeed Gökalp specifically acknowledged his debt to the German Romantic's idea of nationhood. For Gökalp the Turkish 'nation' was not just a piece of territory in which people lived under one political system; it was 'a shared consciousness' of a people whose nomadic ancestors had ridden out of Central Asia and founded the great and glorious Ottoman Empire at the beginning of the fourteenth century.

Namik Kemal had begun the transformation of the empire into a Turkish nation with his play *Vatan* in 1873 (see Chapter 21). Until the onslaught of nationalism, the idea that the Ottoman Empire was

'Turkish' was scarcely entertained. It was usually called 'the lands of Islam', 'the Imperial realm', 'the divinely guarded realm', and was understood to mean the whole of the empire and not simply the area inhabited by the Turkish nation. Anecdote has it that when a group of Turks in Paris were asked what nation they belonged to, they replied that they were Muslims; when told that Islam was a religion, not a nation, they then replied that they were Ottomans (the name comes from Osman, the founder of the dynasty); but it never crossed their minds to say that they were Turks.[4] In secular schools, pupils were never taught about 'Turkish' history; the history they learned was usually the history of the European powers. If the word 'Turk' was used it was as a term of abuse, meaning barbaric and uncouth. But under the spell of nationalism, the hitherto uncivilized Turkic tribesmen were being transformed into a united noble heroic race; according to Gökalp, they were, in fact, the 'supermen' that Nietzsche had written about, a concept that would be taken up and distorted by Nazi ideology.

If the Turkish-Muslim people could be imbued with a pride in themselves, a sense that they were bonded together as a people by centuries of history which had made them courageous and selfless, many hoped they would have the strength and unity necessary to save a dying empire. But on the basis of Romantic nationalism Young Turks constructed a hideous syllogism and pursued it to its logical conclusion: a nation needs the strength of unity; unity comes from a people that is homogeneous; therefore, a strong nation must subjugate, expel or, if necessary, exterminate those who are different. 'Just as there could be no shared lover, there could be no shared homeland,' said Gökalp.[5] The homeland 'gathers in all the Turks and excludes foreigners'. Or, as Hitler put it in his party's manifesto of 1920: 'Only a member of the race can be a citizen. A member of the race can only be one who is of German blood, without consideration of creed. Consequently, no Jew can be a member of the race.' At a CUP meeting to discuss what should be done with the non-Muslims, the *ghiaurs*, who refused to be Turkified and wanted to maintain their own religious communities, the options discussed were compulsion, exile or extermination.

Any opposition to Turkification was effectively crushed when the

CUP engineered a coup in July 1913. Three men, Mehmed Talaat, Ismail Enver and Ahmed Djemal (usually known as Cemal), effectively ruled the empire. Of the 'Three Pashas' (pasha being the honorific for a high-ranking official) Talaat Pasha, the CUP leader, was the ablest and the man considered to be most responsible for the Armenian genocide. His enemies called him the 'gypsy' because of his swarthy complexion; the American ambassador Henry Morgenthau described him as a man of 'bulldog rigidity'.

The Three Pashas were ardent nationalists. They believed they could save the Ottoman Empire by redrawing it as a national Turkish one. It was with that vision that they allied themselves with the German Empire and entered the First World War in 1914.

Inevitably Christians in the Ottoman Empire were caught up in the conflict. The Allies urged Armenians and Assyrians to join with them in fighting the Ottomans. The Russians promised them their autonomy and about 150,000 Armenians signed up. It was not, then, surprising that Enver Pasha, the Ottoman minister of war, branded Armenians as collaborationists and a threat to the security of the empire. He also included Assyrians and, for good measure, Greeks.

On 24 April 1915, when Allied troops were landing at Gallipoli, Talaat Pasha ordered the arrest of several hundred Armenian community leaders and intellectuals in Istanbul – the arrest which opened this chapter. All Armenian conscripts in the Ottoman army, about 250,000 men, were consigned to forced-labour battalions. They were killed soon after on the orders of Enver Pasha, as were the Armenians who had been rounded up in Istanbul. 'Revenge, revenge, revenge… There is no other word,' he said.[6] Revenge for the Armenians' struggle to secede from the empire, for their collaboration with the Russian army, for their economic success.

Muslim animosity towards Christians had only been exacerbated by the numbers of Muslims who had been forcibly expelled or had been forced to flee the savagery of the newly independent Christian Balkan states in the early twentieth century. Around 850,000 Muslim refugees were resettled in the Ottoman Empire in Christian, often Armenian, villages where the Muslims were usually noticeably poorer than their Armenian neighbours. The Three Pashas responded by pursuing an economic policy of elevating Turkish Muslims and eliminating – metaphorically at first – their Christian competitors. Turkish Muslim guilds were set up with specific instructions to exclude Christians and Christian property was seized. 'My province has been cleansed of Christian elements. The merchants and business owners, who two years ago were 80 per cent Christian, are now 95 per cent Muslim and 5 per cent Christian,' reported the governor general of the Syrian province of Aleppo, Mustaf Abdulhak, in 1916. Abdulhak played a prominent role in the genocide, as did the muhacirs (the refugees from the Balkans).

But economic restrictions on Christians did not go far enough. And so the Three Pashas authorized mass deportations, in actuality death marches, to concentration camps in the Syrian desert. Whole villages were ordered to pack up their possessions and join the vast processions heading for the desert under police guard. Thousands of men, women and children were massacred or died along the way from heat, exhaustion and starvation; the women were often raped.

German consuls based near the concentration camps in Aleppo and Mosul sent horrified reports back to Germany of the atrocities being committed by their Ottoman allies. They were told not to interfere as it would endanger German–Ottoman relations. But as with the Nazi Holocaust, this genocide had its soul-stirring heroes; men like the Ottoman governor Mehmet Celal Bey, dubbed the Ottoman Schindler, who saved thousands of Armenian lives by defying deportation orders. Such bravery, however, could not outweigh the massacres, the rapes and the drownings of thousands of women and children who, according to an American consul, 'were loaded into boats and taken out to sea and thrown overboard'.

In overall charge was Talaat Pasha. A former telegraph operator, he had a telegraph machine installed in his home from where he could transmit 'sensitive' instructions. 'The work must be done now,' said Talaat. 'After the war it will be too late.'[7]

The Ottoman Empire surrendered to the Allies on 30 October 1918. On the night of 2 November 1918, the Three Pashas stepped onto a

German submarine which was docked at Istanbul's harbour and slipped away to Berlin. A court martial convened under British insistence in Allied-occupied Istanbul found the three men guilty of 'the massacre and destruction of the Armenians'; they were condemned to death *in absentia.*

Three years later Talaat Pasha, who was living under an assumed name in Berlin, was gunned down as he stepped out of his house to take a walk in the Tiergarten. His assassin was an Armenian engineering student, Soghomon Tehlirian. Tehlirian was an agent of a special operation set up by the newly independent Armenian Republic to assassinate the men held responsible for the genocide. His orders were: 'blow up the skull of the Number One nation-murderer and… don't try to flee. You stand there, your foot on the corpse and surrender to the police, who will come and handcuff you.' The trial of Tehlirian was intended to tell the world of the scale of the crimes committed against the Armenians. Exactly as intended, the resultant trial became in fact a trial of Talaat Pasha and not of the Armenian gunman. 'I have killed a man. But I am not a murderer,' Tehlirian told the judge at his trial.[8] After hearing that his mother and two brothers had been murdered on one of the death marches, while two of his sisters had been raped, it took the jury just one hour to acquit him on grounds of temporary insanity. The other two members of the triumvirate, Enver Pasha and Cemal Pasha, were assassinated a year later in 1922.

At the time, some of Germany's right wing, including Hitler's party, the National Socialist German Workers' Party, claimed that the Pashas had been justified in massacring Armenians. Armenians had collaborated with the Allies and had no loyalty to the Ottoman Empire; they were a greedy, clannish people without a homeland. Today the Turkish government still refuses to acknowledge that what happened to the Armenians was 'genocide'; nor will the United Kingdom, Israel or the United States (unlike Canada, Russia and most European states), on the grounds that it would not be helpful to the cause of Turkish–Armenian relations.* The Turkish government refers to 'Armenian allegations' or 'the so-called

* The legislatures of forty-eight out of the fifty US states have individually recognized the events of 1915 to 1923 as genocide. But US presidents have consistently refused to do so, including Presidents Obama and Trump.

Armenian Genocide'. In Ankara, Turkey's capital since 1923, one of its principal avenues is still named after Talaat. The historian Taner Akçam, on whose work *From Empire to Republic* I have relied heavily, has the brave distinction of being the first Turkish scholar openly to acknowledge that the Turks committed the crime of genocide.

The Ottoman Empire itself, the sick man of Europe, died at the end of the First World War. So too did the Austro-Hungarian Empire. The old order collapsed in the mass slaughter of the First World War. From Istanbul to Vienna, the rulers of the old world were stepping onto trains, steamships – even submarines – and heading into exile. In his memoirs the writer Stefan Zweig recalls a March afternoon in 1919 when his train stopped at a small Austrian station on the borders with Switzerland, and he noticed an unusual amount of people lining the platform. The reason became clear, Zweig explained, when in the train opposite,

> I recognised Emperor Karl [the Austro-Hungarian emperor] standing very erect beside his black-clad wife Empress Zita... he stood at the window of the train, a tall grave man, looking for the last time at the mountains, the buildings and the people of his land... All of us there felt that we were witnessing a tragic moment in history. The police and the soldiers ... looked away in embarrassment, unsure whether or not to give him the old salute of honour ... no one said a word, and so we suddenly heard the quiet sobbing of the old lady in mourning, who had come heaven knows how far to see 'her' emperor for the last time.

The signal was given, the train started. 'At this moment the Monarchy, almost one thousand years old, was truly at an end.'*

On 15 May 1919, under the protection of British, French and American warships, a Greek army crossed the Aegean Sea and invaded part of

* It is quite possible that this 'recollection' was actually an irresistible piece of poetic licence on Zweig's part. Zweig, ch xiii, *The World of Yesterday: Memoirs of a European*, trans. Anthea Bell, Pushkin Press, 2009.

Anatolia, the heartland of the old Ottoman Empire. General Mustafa Kemal masterminded the resulting war to defend the territory against the Greeks. A brilliant soldier who had secured the Ottoman Empire's only major victory during the First World War, the Gallipoli campaign, Mustafa Kemal defeated the Greeks and retained control of Anatolia. Alone of all the defeated powers after the First World War, Mustafa Kemal was in a strong enough position to reject the humiliating terms imposed by the Allies and impose his own. The Allies recognized the independence of the new Republic of Turkey. Admittedly, the Ottoman Empire had been much reduced in size; nonetheless, what was left of it had retained its independence. In 1923, Turkey and Greece agreed to settle their differences with a ruthless exchange of religious populations.*

Mustafa Kemal was elected as the first president of the Republic of Turkey on 29 October 1923. In 1934 he was given the surname Atatürk, 'Father of the Turks', by the Grand National Assembly (the Turkish parliament), in recognition of the role he played in the creation of Turkey.

On 3 March 1924 the Assembly announced that 'all members of the deposed Ottoman dynasty are forever forbidden to reside within the frontiers of the territory of the Turkish Republic'. Abdulmecid II and his family (two wives and two children) were informed of the decision that very day. At dawn the next morning, they were driven to an out-of-the way station outside Istanbul, where their presence would attract no alarming demonstrations. It is said that the Jewish stationmaster made tea for his distinguished passengers. When Abdulmecid thanked him, the stationmaster replied, with tears in his eyes, that it was the Jews who should be thanking him and his family for having welcomed Jews into the empire after their expulsion from Spain in 1492. Abdulmecid and his family left on the Orient Express bound for Paris.

In the same year, 1924, the Assembly drew up a constitution for the new Republic. It followed along the Enlightenment lines of the American

* According to the agreement, those Greek Orthodox that had survived the Armenian genocide, and had not already fled, were expelled from Turkey and allowed to settle in Greece. In exchange 355,000 Muslims were expelled from Greece and allowed to resettle in Turkey.

and French Declarations in its assertion of the equality of all citizens and their freedom of conscience. 'The people of Turkey, regardless of religion or race, are Turks as regards citizenship,' it declared. 'No one shall be compelled to worship, or to participate in religious rites and ceremonies, or to reveal religious beliefs and convictions, or be blamed or accused because of his religious beliefs and convictions.' 'It is not our intention to curtail freedom of worship', Atatürk wrote, 'but rather to ensure that matters of religion and those of the state do not become intertwined.'[9]

The Young Ottomans and the Young Turks had been convinced that while the empire had to modernize, that modernization had to be done within the context of Islam. Atatürk, on the other hand, was equally convinced that the only way Turkey could modernize itself was by breaking free from Islam. Traditional Islam was antithetical to all that Atatürk wanted Turkey to be. It was, he thought, mere superstition, and acted as a brake on a Turkey that must embrace science and reason so that it could take its place in the modern world.

For Atatürk and the Kemalists traditional Islam was fatally linked with backwardness and resistance to the republic. In much the same way French republicans viewed Catholicism as an enemy of the new order. But there was this fundamental difference. In France, secularization, which was officially announced in 1905, was broadly supported. In Turkey, on the other hand, secularism was imposed from on top by a small elite. Between 1924 and 1934 Turkey underwent a tsunami of secularization. A month after Abdulmecid and the imperial family had vanished from Turkey for ever, Atatürk lifted the ban on alcohol. A heavy drinker himself (and heavy womanizer) Atatürk would die of cirrhosis of the liver in 1936. His legalization of alcohol was followed by a systematic attack on the educational and judicial roles of the ulema. Madrasas and religious schools were closed down and replaced by a single system of public education which followed a secular curriculum. Thousands of new schools were opened all over the country and primary education was made free and compulsory. Instruction in religious culture and morals would be one of the compulsory lessons in the curricula of primary and secondary schools but it would be conducted under State control.

Most cataclysmic of all, in 1926 the Assembly announced that Turkey would no longer be ruled according to the sharia. The Ottoman Empire had always operated a dual legal system: an empire-wide secular system concerned with all criminal, administrative and commercial affairs and a particularistic religious one under the millet system, where each recognized religious community ruled themselves according to their own religious laws. For Muslims it would have been unthinkable for their family and religious lives not to be regulated according to sharia law. Most Muslims indeed would have seen themselves as living in a society where God was sovereign ruler. Now Atatürk was declaring that God's word as reflected in the sharia was to be replaced with a set of civil laws modelled along the lines of Switzerland's Swiss Civil Code, which had its basis in Roman law. Sharia courts were abolished. At a stroke, God's word, and that of his judicial interpreters, had been set aside.

Women were now recognized as equal to men before the law, an emancipation which put Turkey in advance of many Western countries. Women could get a divorce and marry a non-Muslim man; polygamy was banned. In 1934 Turkish women won the right to vote in parliamentary elections and to be elected as deputies. Seventeen women were elected the following year. Amongst those who had lobbied for the vote was Atatürk's own wife (he married only once but divorced after two years), a wealthy, multilingual woman who studied law in Paris and London and wore a scarf rather than the hijab. Women in France, by contrast, had to wait another ten years before they were entitled to vote.

In 1928 the word 'Islam' was removed from the Turkish Constitution, as were all references to an Islamic state. Atatürk's secularism was part of a radical programme which was wrenching people from their old identity and forcing them into a new and totally alien one. Suddenly they found themselves to be members of a secular, Westernized state. Their Islamic calendar, where time had started ticking from the birth of Muhammad, was abandoned in favour of the Gregorian calendar which dated events from the birth of Christ. The muezzin still called them to prayers, but in Turkish, not in Arabic. Their day of rest was switched from Friday, the day of public prayers, to Sunday. In 1927 Atatürk banned the turban and the fez (which had itself been forced on Muslims by Sultan Mahmud II in 1829 as part of his modernization drive) and made it compulsory to wear a Western hat. The fez, he said, 'sat on the heads of our nation as an emblem of ignorance, negligence, fanaticism, and hatred of progress and civilization'.[10] Thirty-four men were executed for refusing to comply with the law, presumably because their refusal was seen as a protest against Kemalist secularization.*

In 1928, the same year that Turkey dropped all reference to Islam from its constitution, a young Egyptian school teacher and religious leader, Hassan al-Banna, founded the Muslim Brotherhood and spearheaded the transformation of Islam into a means of waging ideological war against the West. Banna is considered to be one of the founding fathers of 'Islamism'. He takes his place alongside his contemporary the Shiite cleric Ruhollah Khomeini, future leader of the 1979 Iranian Revolution; Sayyid Qutb, who joined the Muslim Brotherhood in 1950 after Banna's assassination; and Abul A'la Maududi, the Indian reformer whose ideas were incorporated into the constitution of the Islamic Republic of Pakistan, 1973, according to which Pakistan was to be an Islamic state. Banna advocated the Islamization of the state, which would be ruled according to the sharia. If state and society became truly Islamic, he believed, the Muslim world would be strong enough to defeat colonialism.

Banna experienced the evils and humiliations of colonialism at first hand when in 1927 he was appointed Arabic teacher at a primary school in the town of Ismailia on the Suez Canal. After a series of uprisings, strikes and demonstrations, Egypt had just won its independence from Britain. Nominally, anyway. Britain still maintained its grasp on the most valuable asset it possessed in Egypt, the Suez Canal. In Banna's new

* Atatürk also frowned on headscarves as being similarly backward-looking. Today, the issue is still a deeply divisive one in an ostensibly secular country where 95 per cent of the population are Muslims. Until 2013 women were banned from wearing veils in all public institutions despite widespread public protest, including from women themselves who demanded their right to wear the hijab. Under President Recep Tayyip Erdoğan this ban has been gradually lifted.

home of Ismailia, signs of British domination were visible everywhere. It was home to the largest British military base in Egypt and centre for the administration of the canal; every business and public utility was in British, or certainly foreign, hands; English and other Europeans crowded the streets where even the street signs were written in English. Banna was deeply affected, not just by Egypt's visible subjugation to the West but by the decadence with which he felt Muslims had been infected. They had been seduced into losing their commitment to Islam.

Young, wildly fervent and an excellent speaker, Banna began preaching in coffee houses and private homes, and soon gathered a following. He wrote in his memoirs, *Mudhakkirat*, that in 1928 he had been approached by six Muslims who worked for the Suez Canal Company. 'We are weary of this life of humiliation and captivity,' they told him. 'Arabs and Muslims in this country have no status or dignity. They are but hirelings depending on these foreigners.' Their plea prompted Banna to set up the Muslim Brotherhood. Its founding manifesto was: 'Allah is our goal, the Prophet our model, the Quran our constitution, the Jihad our path and death for the sake of Allah the loftiest of our wishes.'

Banna had been deeply influenced by the late nineteenth and early twentieth-century pan-Islamists al-Afghani, Muhammad Abduh and Rashid Rida. Like them he wanted to liberate the Islamic world from the indignity of colonialism, and like them he believed that the way to do so was through Islam. But, more conservative than al-Afghani and Abduh, he did not agree with their 'modernist' belief that the sharia was perfectly consistent with Western Enlightenment ideas as long as a distinction was made between law based on divine principles of the Quran and sunna, and *fiqh*. The first of the Islamists, he wanted to reconstruct society politically, economically and culturally so that it would be truly Islamic, rooted in the Quran and sunna, emulating the practices of Muhammad and the first Islamic rulers and stripped of its Western influences. Islam, he believed, was the answer to all the Muslim world's ills. But that meant soldering politics and religion back together again as they had been at the birth of Islam.

As well as the traumas of colonialism, Egypt had been undergoing the social upheavals of rapid modernization which had forced thousands to leave their villages, ripped up families and created a growing divide between rich and poor. The world economic crisis only exacerbated social tensions and increased the levels of dire poverty. Though secularization in Egypt had not been nearly as radical as Kemal was making it in Turkey, the authority of the ulema had been severely undermined, leaving ordinary Muslims rudderless. In Egypt, as in Turkey, secularism was a top-down affair, associated with colonial subjection.

Like Khomeini, Banna was a populist and he offered Muslims an extraordinarily attractive mix of religious conservatism and social radicalism rooted in Islamic principles of equality. He promised to 'improve the situation of the peasants and industrial workers', to create more jobs and employ the jobless, and to spend the proceeds of the zakat (a proportion of their wealth that every Muslim is required to give to charity) on welfare projects dedicated to helping the poor. Banna also promised 'To reform the law in such a way that it will be entirely in accordance with Islamic legal practice; To bring to trial those who break the laws of Islam, who do not fast, who do not pray, and who insult religion'; and to make religious teaching 'the essential subject matter to be taught in all educational establishments and faculties'.[11]

The Muslim Brotherhood rapidly gained a mass membership; by 1938 it had about 20,000 members in Egypt and had branches in Syria, Iraq, Yemen and of course Palestine. It was thanks to Banna's passionate adoption of the Palestinian cause that the society grew so spectacularly from a small socio-religious group to a mass political movement.

The rise of the Nazis in Germany had led to an increasing number of Jews emigrating to Palestine where they were buying up land with the explicit goal of setting up a Jewish state. In 1936 Palestinian Arabs revolted against British rule and its acceptance of the concept of a Jewish 'national home'. Banna, who was equally opposed to British rule in Egypt, passionately supported the Palestinians. In May 1936 he demanded that the British government put an immediate end to Jewish immigration to Palestine and extolled 'the heroic struggle' of 'our brave Palestinian brothers', who were playing their part in the struggle of the entire Islamic Arab *umma* against 'the Jewish injustice', 'British oppression', and 'the violent, murderous hand of imperialism'.[12] He called on Egyptian merchants to boycott Jewish traders, whom he called 'the aggressors and usurpers'. As Muslim protests against Zionism intensified so did attacks on Egyptian Jews, who were all lumped together as Zionists. Student nationalist demonstrators were heard shouting 'Jews get out of Egypt and Palestine'.

Crucially, Banna saw the Palestinian cause in terms of a jihad, in the sense of armed warfare against the infidels. It was the duty of every Muslim to help his co-religionists in preventing the occupation of Muslim territory by infidel conquerors. Banna's belief that the true Muslim was a jihadi soldier whose duty was to fight to defend Islam has been a major influence on today's jihadis.

In his determination to vanquish Western intellectual, political and economic colonialism, Banna is considered to have found common cause in the 1930s with the German Nazi party. Certainly both shared a hatred of Jews. Banna saw Jews not just as invaders of Palestine with the implicit support of the British, but as colluders with the British colonialists in Egypt and as deeply associated with all that he objected to in the Enlightenment and the West – its scepticism and decadence.

It was of course in Hitler's interests to encourage this anti-British, anti-Jewish Islamic movement which commanded such a huge following. In 1933 the German government established a special Arab press service and in 1935 opened a branch of the German News Agency which subsidized anti-British organizations, including the Muslim Brotherhood. The Nazis are said to have loaned German officers as advisers to the militia organization which Banna founded in 1940 to wage jihad against the British and Jews in Palestine.[13]

But though the Brotherhood was in close co-operation with the Grand Mufti of Jerusalem, Hajj Amin al-Husayni, because of his fierce opposition to Zionism, and British colonialism, Banna never praised Germany, as the mufti did in 1943 for having 'very clearly recognized the Jews for what they are and resolved to find a definitive solution for the Jewish danger that will eliminate the scourge that Jews represent in the world'.[14] Nor did Banna actively collaborate with the Nazis as the mufti did. Banna was always critical of the Nazis' supremacist nationalism, which was, he said, 'racial self-aggrandizement to a degree which leads to the disparagement of other races, aggression against them and their victimization for the sake of the nation's glory'.[15] Banna advocated equal rights for all citizens regardless of their race. Nonetheless he believed in a discrimination based on religion. Inevitably. Since he insisted on the application of sharia law and of the establishment of a state which approximated as closely as possible to that established by Muhammad and his Companions, the inequality of the *dhimmi* would perforce have to be reintroduced.

Banna was assassinated in 1949, in retaliation for the assassination of the Egyptian prime minister Mahmud Fahmi al-Nuqrashi by a Muslim Brother. Banna's ideological baton was taken up by Sayyid Qutb, who joined the Muslim Brotherhood in 1950. Qutb took the Brotherhood along a far more radical and anti-Semitic line. He would be responsible for a distinctly Islamist anti-Semitism.

•

When Hitler came to power in 1933, Germany was collapsing politically and economically. Between 1919 and 1933, ten governments had come and gone. Strikes and armed uprisings had led many Germans to fear that they too would suffer a communist revolution as the Russians had in February and October 1917. That prospect looked all the more likely since capitalism seemed to be failing so catastrophically. The hyperinflation of the 1920s was only succeeded, after a brief recovery, with hyper-unemployment. By 1932, 6 million Germans, about 30 per cent of the population, were unemployed, and families were going hungry.

Under such circumstances, what easier way for a politician, especially one in a new era of mass democracy, than to offer a desperate and distressed people an enemy, a sacrificial victim? This book has been littered with the dead bodies of scapegoats. They have always been the crudest but often most effective way of gaining support in times of trouble.

By the end of the 1930s the Nazis had created a mass party. Working, merchant and ruling classes joined together in targeting the Jews as their common enemy. Many on the German left saw Jews as the arch-capitalists and consequently blamed them for the economic sufferings they were enduring. Many on the right were convinced that Jews were bent on turning the world communist. The fact that some leading Bolsheviks were Jews was proof enough. But White Russian émigrés (opponents of the Bolsheviks) fanned the flames. They brought with them from Russia the *Protocols of the Elders of Zion*, purportedly the minutes of a meeting where Jewish leaders discussed their strategies for taking over the world. It was, of course, a forgery. But it became a massive seller in the United States, in Britain, continental Europe and across the Arab world, confirming suspicions that Jews were indeed bent on destroying the Christian world. 'The rats are underneath the piles. The Jew is underneath the lot,' as T.S. Eliot put it in his 1920 poem, 'Burbank with a Baedeker: Bleistein with a Cigar'.

Hitler's party was united not only by hatred of Jews, but also by worship of Hitler. Anyone who watches Leni Riefenstahl's two documentaries, *Triumph des Willens* (Triumph of the Will), made in 1935, and *Olympia*, a celebration of the Olympic games, made in 1938, will get a glimpse of the religious passion with which German fascism was imbued. Tellingly, this religion swept away all sense of the individual. Vast black and white close-ups of noble Aryan faces, indistinguishable one from the other, gaze with undiluted happiness into the distance. Young and old exercise in perfectly co-ordinated groups and go joyfully out on their healthy walking holidays. Nazi banners flutter triumphantly in the breeze (never mind that a member of the inferior races, a black man from America, became the most successful athlete of the 1936 Olympic games). And benignly watching over them all is Hitler, their God who is creating for them a Germany made up exclusively of the racially pure Aryan master race.

If the Christian clerical hierarchy did not actively back the Nazis' anti-Semitism, they certainly were not vociferous in opposing it. 'Where is merciful God, where is He? … For God's sake, where is God?' cried one concentration camp inmate forced to watch a child not heavy enough to be suffocated by the gallows struggling for breath for thirty excruciating minutes. He should have cried 'Where are the Churches?' Though individual Catholic and Protestant priests committed great acts of bravery and spoke out from the pulpit, the leaders of the Catholic and Protestant Churches never did, or they couched their condemnation in such general terms that it had little impact. The record of the Catholic and Protestant Churches in Germany is a dismal story of compromise, evasion and silence.

Protestant churches were divided on their response to the Nazis. The Deutsche Christen, German Christians, embraced Nazism. They forbade any acknowledgement of the Judaic origins of Christianity. They called themselves the SA of Jesus Christ (the SA were the *Sturmabteilung*, the Brownshirts, the paramilitary wing of the Nazi party, later superseded by the SS), and believed that Hitler was 'greater than Christ himself'.[16] The Confessing Church, on the other hand, condemned the Deutsche Christen as heretics and opposed Hitler's attempt to unify all Protestant churches into a single pro-Nazi Church. The Confessing Church has the honour of including amongst its members Dietrich Bonhoeffer, executed for his role in the conspiracy to overthrow the regime, and Martin Niemöller, who spent seven years in Dachau and Buchenwald concentration camps for his criticisms of Hitler. Yet these two men were not typical: evangelical Church leaders preferred to avoid incurring the wrath of the Nazi state.

Within the Catholic Church, there were priests who were outspokenly haters of Jews. The Austrian bishop Alois Hudal wrote in praise of Hitler and the Nazi party. Ivan Šarić, Bishop of Sarajevo in Croatia, was an outspoken supporter of the fascist ultra-Catholic Ustaše government which murdered about 32,000 Jews along with over 300,000 Serbs, Roma and opponents of the regime. In his diocesan newspaper a Catholic priest wrote: 'The Jews have led Europe and the world towards disaster… There is a limit to love. The movement to free the world of Jews, represents the movement for the restoration of human dignity.'[17] After the war, Šarić was one of the many who escaped along the ratlines, the underground escape routes for Nazis to Latin America with which some senior members of the Vatican were deeply involved.

As for Pope Pius XII, opinion is still bitterly divided. At a time when a moral voice was so desperately needed, Pope Pius XII signally failed to provide one.[18] While he excommunicated communists after the war, the pope never excommunicated Nazis and never overtly condemned them. Was this the most appalling moral failure? Was the pope determined to preserve his institution from attack by the Nazis at all cost? Or was he, as his defenders argue, painfully maintaining silence from fear of making the plight of the Jews even worse? Thousands of Jews were, in fact, sheltered in convents, monasteries and parish churches, often on the pope's urging. Critics paint him as cold and aloof, authoritarian and disdainful; defenders as mild, shy and saintly. According to Albrecht von Kessel, aide to the German ambassador to the Vatican, the pope was haunted by the question of whether he should act on his knowledge of the Holocaust. Indeed, he 'almost broke down under the conflicts of conscience. I know that he prayed, day by day, week by week, month by month for the answer.'[19]

Any suggestion that the pope was not aware of the Nazis' murderous policies was firmly rejected by the International Catholic–Jewish Historical Commission (ICJHC), a group of three Jewish and three Catholic scholars appointed in 1999 by the Vatican. Indeed, it noted that in January 1941 Konrad von Preysing, Bishop of Berlin, wrote in a letter to the pope: 'Your Holiness is certainly informed about the situation of the Jews in Germany and the neighbouring countries.' Preysing was one of the few senior figures in the church to speak out against the Nazis and their genocidal policies. His cathedral administrator, Bernhard Lichtenberg, ran the bishop's aid organization which secretly gave help to those being persecuted. Lichtenberg was arrested in 1941 for preaching against the Nazis and for his open support for Jews. He died on the way to Dachau concentration camp.

In June 1941 Vichy France (the part of France which was unoccupied by the Germans but which in fact bought its 'independence' by capitulation to Nazism) introduced anti-Jewish laws modelled on the Nuremberg Laws. The Nuremberg Laws, instituted by the Nazis in Germany in 1935, deprived Jews of citizenship, prohibited any non-Jewish German from marrying a Jew and outlawed sexual relations between Jews and

Germans. Asked for the Catholic Church's response to Vichy's new laws, the pope replied that the Vatican condemned racism but did not consider the legislation in conflict with Catholic teaching – as long as it was carried out with 'charity' and 'justice'.

In October 1941, the assistant chief of the US delegation to the Vatican, Harold Tittman, asked the pope to condemn the atrocities; the Vatican's response was that it had to remain neutral and that the pope would endanger Jews and Catholics by speaking out. But bowing to pressure from London, Washington and Moscow, the pope did refer in his Christmas Eve broadcast of 1942 to 'the hundreds of thousands who through no fault of their own, and solely because of their nation or race, have been condemned to death or progressive extinction'. He never specifically referred to Jews, however. Nor did he in 1940 when, with reference to Germany's extermination of Jews in Poland, he condemned 'the horror and inexcusable excesses committed on a helpless and a homeless people'. The Vatican defended its conduct on the grounds that it was quite clear that the Pope was referring to Jews. Besides, said the pope, 'I have already done so much.'

But if the Vatican claimed that this was speaking out, then, said Albert Camus, the French novelist, journalist and philosopher,

> I assure you that millions of men like me did not hear it and that at that time believers and unbelievers alike shared a solitude that continued to spread as the days went by and the executioners multiplied... What the world expects of Christians is that Christians should speak out, loud and clear, and that they should voice their condemnation in such a way that never a doubt, never the slightest doubt, should rise in the heart of the simplest man.[20]

Diplomats from Britain, the United States, Poland and Brazil, Jewish communities from Costa Rica to Canada, begged the pope to condemn the Nazi extermination of Jews. Some of the pope's own bishops and cardinals also urged him to speak out, as did Andrey Sheptytsky, Archbishop of the Greek Orthodox Church of Ukraine. He was one of the few church leaders in Nazi-occupied Europe openly to defend Jews. He threatened his flock with excommunication if they participated in any way with the destruction of Jews, ordered his monasteries to hide Jewish children, sent an official letter to Hitler and Himmler protesting against German treatment of Jews, and wrote to the pope describing the Jews' plight. The pope told the archbishop that he should 'bear adversity with serene patience'.

According to his critics Pius XII's main priority was to preserve a strong Germany as a bulwark against Communism. Although from 1935 onwards the highest Vatican officials considered Nazism and Communism equally diabolical, the pope feared Communism more. If Communism won, the Church would simply not survive; Nazism, on the other hand, would die with Hitler.

And so the pope kept silent, even though many amongst the Nazi leadership were virulently anti-Christian and antagonistic toward any institution that threatened their own supremacy. Christianity for the Nazis was also fatally contaminated by its Jewish origins. Furthermore its values of humility, love and peace were deeply antithetical to the imagined proud warrior spirit of the German *Volk*. There was, said the propaganda minister Joseph Goebbels, an 'insoluble opposition between the Christian and a heroic-German world view'.[21]

The Nazis had embarked on a policy of repression of religions in Germany: Jehovah's Witnesses (many of whom died in concentration camps), the Bahá'í faith, the Seventh-Day Adventist Church and the Salvation Army were all banned. But since the majority of Germany's 67 million people were Christians, Hitler, who had been brought up a Catholic, decided it was politically wiser to restrain his more aggressively anti-Christian radicals such as Goebbels, Himmler and Martin Bormann. Jews, it is worth noting, made up less than 0.75 per cent of the population (around 500,000 people).[22] The majority of Europe's 8 million Jews lived in central and eastern Europe.

Nonetheless the hostility of the Nazis to the Church was clear. It was to keep them at bay that the Vatican had signed a concordat in 1933 agreeing that its priests in Germany would stay out of politics. In return the Nazi government would respect the Church's autonomy. The concordat effectively silenced all vocal opposition to Nazism from the Catholic hierarchy. Bishops in Germany who had hitherto supported the Catholic centre party's opposition to a bill giving Hitler near dictatorial powers, were told to withdraw their opposition and to look more favourably on national socialism. As a result, the enabling act was passed which declared that the National Socialist German Workers' Party, the Nazi party, was the only legally permitted party in the German state. Hitler, of course, did not stick by his side of the agreement. He closed down Catholic schools, Catholic associations and publications; Catholic priests and nuns were arrested, often on charges of homosexuality, and joined the 5,000 to 15,000 gay men and lesbians who were taken to concentration camps: it is not known how many died.

No one can condemn Church leaders for wanting to protect their flocks. The Catholic and Protestant Churches feared that if they openly attacked the Nazis, the Nazis would take their revenge on Christians. But it was also the sheer desire to preserve their own institutions that led the leaders of Germany's Churches to keep their mouths shut. Even Britain's minister at the Vatican, the Protestant Sir D'Arcy Godolphin Osborne, who described Pius XII as 'the most warmly humane, kind, generous, sympathetic (and, incidentally, saintly) character that it has been my privilege to meet', was shocked.[23]

After the Nazis had invaded Rome in 1943, Osborne wrote in his diary that he was 'revolted' by the Vatican's 'apparently exclusive preoccupation with the effects of the war on Italy and the possibilities of the bombardment of Rome'. The pope was more concerned to prevent the physical destruction of Vatican City than to save the Jews who were being carted away to the gas chambers of Auschwitz from the Roman ghetto in Trastevere. The protection of Rome was 'a matter of conscience for Us', Pius XII wrote in a letter to Bishop Konrad von Preysing in 1944. Rome, he said, had been 'the centre of Christendom since the beginning of the church of Jesus Christ'.[24] More than a thousand Jews in the ghetto were captured by the SS.

It should be noted that about 4,000 Roman Jews were sheltered in Catholic churches and monasteries owned by the Vatican. Praiseworthy, of course, but indicative of the Vatican's wartime policy.[25] The Vatican only offered succour to Jews in secret.

In 1949, the pope declared that any Catholic who professed Communist doctrine, or who propagated 'the materialistic and anti-Christian teachings of communism', would be excommunicated. By contrast, the most powerful religious institution in the world never came out in forthright condemnation of the Nazis and their genocidal policies; it offered no moral guidance. Indeed in 1933, the pope had encouraged Germany's bishops to rescind their prohibition against Catholics joining the Nazi party, although the bishops had in fact pre-empted him and already withdrawn their ban.[26] Pius XII did not threaten Catholics with excommunication for joining the Nazi party, or for participating in mass murder, nor were any Catholics excommunicated after the war for their part in the Holocaust.

After the war, Pius XII even intervened on behalf of convicted Nazi war criminals, asking Washington and London to reduce their sentences. On the basis of documents released by the British Public Records Office and the Argentinian government it is also likely that the pope knew of the involvement of some members of the Vatican in the ratlines, the underground escape routes for Nazis which enabled many hundreds of Nazi war criminals to escape to Catholic Latin America. The ratlines were in the main organized by Franciscan friars from Croatia. During the war the friars had been heavily involved with the ultra-Roman Catholic and ultra-nationalist Ustaše government which had killed hundreds of thousands in concentration camps and massacres. British and American intelligence and diplomatic services were convinced that the Vatican was sheltering war criminals and even saw them being driven in Vatican cars. But when Sir D'Arcy Osborne requested permission for British military police to raid Vatican buildings where it was thought war criminals were sheltering, he was refused. Josef Mengele, Klaus Barbie and Adolf Eichmann were among those who escaped along the ratlines.

Pope Pius XII died in 1958. Moves for his canonization began in 1965. One of the four stages towards declaring him a saint was taken in 2009 when he was pronounced 'venerable'. But in 2014 Pope Francis blocked the next stage, 'beatification', on the grounds that this required a proven miracle, which had not yet been forthcoming.

By the time of the death of Pius, the Church had moved significantly in its stance towards Jews. In 1965 the Second Vatican Council had declared that even though the Jewish authorities and those who followed them 'pressed for the death of Christ; still, what happened in His passion cannot be charged against all the Jews, without distinction, then alive, nor against the Jews of today'.

In absolving 'all Jews' from responsibility for Christ's crucifixion, the Declaration on the Relation of the Church with Non-Christian Religions upturned a belief which had been held by the Church since the Gospel of John. Furthermore, the Declaration discarded the belief that all non-Catholics were heretics bound for hell by announcing that, 'She [the Vatican] regards with sincere reverence those ways of conduct and of life, those precepts and teachings which, though differing in many aspects from the ones she holds and sets forth, nonetheless often reflect a ray of that Truth which enlightens all men.'

Heretics would not burn in hell, but nor was the Vatican renouncing its conviction that it is the only church of God. How could any monotheism do that? The Vatican, said the Declaration, 'proclaims, and ever must proclaim Christ "the way, the truth, and the life" (John 14:6), in whom men may find the fullness of religious life, in whom God has reconciled all things to Himself'. All Jews were not Christ-killers; Judaism had some elements of truth – after all, Christianity sprang from it – but for their salvation Jews still needed to become Christians. If Christianity was the truth, then those who lacked Christianity were not necessarily bad, but were certainly deprived, and to that extent inferior.

This belief was evident in the Prayer for the Jews. The prayer, which dates back to at least the eighth century, is part of the annual Good Friday service, read out in every Catholic church in the world. Originally it said:

> Let us pray also for the faithless Jews (*perfidis Judæis*) that Almighty God may remove the veil from their hearts so that they too may acknowledge Jesus Christ our Lord... Almighty and eternal God, who dost not exclude from thy mercy even Jewish faithlessness: hear our prayers, which we offer for the blindness of that people.*

In 1959 the phrase 'faithless Jews' was removed from the prayer and in 1965 reference to the Jews' blindness was also deleted. By 1970 the prayer made no mention of conversion although in 2008 it was briefly reinserted into the Latin version of the Mass by the traditionalist Pope Benedict XVI. Today Catholics pray 'for the Jewish people, the first to hear the word of God, that they may continue to grow in the love of his name and in faithfulness to his covenant'.

It was not until 1998 that the Vatican was prepared to acknowledge that there was a question that needed to be answered about 'whether the Nazi persecution of the Jews was not made easier by the anti-Jewish prejudices imbedded in some Christian minds and hearts. Did anti-Jewish sentiment among Christians make them less sensitive, or even indifferent, to the persecution launched against the Jews by National Socialism when it reached power?'

Sadly the answers it provided in 'We Remember: A Reflection on the Shoah' (the Holocaust), the document published by the Vatican in 1998, let the Church off the hook. But it is as far as the Church has ever gone in acknowledging its own particular, and Christianity's in general, responsibility for the anti-Semitism that has cursed European Jews for nearly two thousand years, and that contributed to the deaths of 6 million in the Second World War. According to 'We Remember', which was issued under the aegis of Pope John Paul II, the history of relations between Jews and Christians 'has been quite negative' – an understatement to say the least.

> In the Christian world – I do not say on the part of the Church as such – erroneous and unjust interpretations of the New Testament

---

* For more on this prayer, see Chapter 5.

> regarding the Jewish people and their alleged culpability have circulated for too long, engendering feelings of hostility towards this people... In times of crisis such as famine, war, pestilence, or social tensions, the Jewish minority was sometimes taken as a scapegoat and became the victim of violence, looting, even massacres.

Note that 'We Remember' blames the 'Christian world', not the Church, for anti-Judaism. Furthermore it claims that hostility to Jews was 'essentially more sociological and political than religious', though as this book has consistently shown, the political and the religious are impossible to disconnect.

'We Remember' then gets to the heart of the matter: 'The fact that the Shoah took place in Europe, that is, in countries of long-standing Christian civilization, raises the question of the relation between the Nazi persecution and the attitudes down the centuries of Christians towards the Jews.' But having had the courage to ask the question, it then absolves the Church of all responsibility. 'The Shoah', it says, 'was the work of a thoroughly modern neo-pagan regime. Its anti-Semitism had its roots outside of Christianity and, in pursuing its aims, it did not hesitate to oppose the Church and persecute her members also.' The Holocaust's roots were in a 'false and exacerbated nationalism' rather than in a religious anti-Judaism.

The Nazis' hatred of the Jews, it is true, was not religious. Nonetheless it fed into a centuries-old hatred which had always found its justification, if not its inspiration, in Christianity and in the institution of the Church. 'We Remember' ignores the fact that the Church had played a vital part in the long history of the use of anti-Semitism in European power politics.

As for the Church's conduct during the war, here the Vatican does apologize. But it makes its *mea culpa* for the failure in courage of ordinary Catholics, rather than for any failures it might itself have committed. While 'We Remember' notes that after the war Jewish leaders had thanked many of the Catholic laity, churchmen and even Pope Pius XII himself, for saving 'hundreds of thousands of Jewish lives', it acknowledges that 'alongside such courageous men and women, the spiritual resistance and concrete action of other Christians was not that which might have been expected from Christ's followers'. These Catholics were too frightened to protest though they were no doubt horrified by what was happening to their Jewish neighbours. 'We deeply regret the errors and failures of those sons and daughters of the Church.' But on the Pope's failure to deliver an outright condemnation of the Nazis, 'We Remember' is notably silent.

CONCLUSION

'It is not the dogmatic believer who insists that the sacred texts are divinely inspired and true, who tries to model his life on the ethical requirements of those texts, and who seeks to impose these requirements on the entire society who is unusual. The liberal who supposes that his sacred texts are actually human constructions of differing moral worth, whose religion makes little difference to his life, and who is quite happy to accept that what his God requires of him is not binding on other members of his society: this is the strange and remarkable creature.'

– Steve Bruce, *Fundamentalism*, 1955

WHAT A PITY THAT the world is round. 'If its surface were an unbounded plane,' as Immanuel Kant, the great philosopher of the Enlightenment, observed, 'people could be so dispersed on it that they would not come into any community with one another, and community would not then be a necessary result of their existence on the earth.' However, Kant himself lived in a round world: he was shockingly anti-Semitic but at the same time a friend of Moses Mendelssohn, the proponent par excellence of Jewish assimilation whom we met in Chapter 21.

Groups will form, and groups will run up against other groups. And groups must share an earth. So no one can avoid the question of how we – all of the 'we's, be they exclusive, overlapping, territorial, religious or whatever – can rub along together.

Following the horrors of the Second World War, when humankind – or at least the Western world – was forced to confront the depths to which it could sink, the victors thought that human rights could solve the problem.

> All human beings are born free and equal in dignity and rights. They are endowed with reason and conscience and should act towards one another in a spirit of brotherhood ... Everyone is entitled to all the rights and freedoms set forth in this Declaration, without distinction of any kind, such as race, colour, sex, language, religion, political or other opinion, national or social origin, property, birth or other status.

These words could have flowed straight from the quill pens of the eighteenth-century French and American Enlightenment thinkers. In fact, they are from the Universal Declaration of Human Rights (UDHR) signed in 1948 by members of the newly formed United Nations, the international governmental organization, founded to maintain international peace. The UDHR would stand up to the horrors of the early twentieth century rather as the Peace of Westphalia's moves towards toleration did to the hundred years of the Wars of Religion and their carnage.

That same year, 1948, the state of Israel was founded. For those few European Jews who had survived the Shoah, the establishment of Israel marked the victory of Herzl's arguments against the sham equality of assimilationism (see Chapter 21).

Both Israel and the UDHR enshrined a spirit of 'never again'. But the founding of Israel has, in fact, been one of the proximate causes of a hitherto unknown level of violence against Jews in the Muslim Arab world, sometimes becoming a specifically Islamist anti-Semitism which has tragically borrowed from Europe's age-old characterization of Jews as a malign, controlling and treacherous group. Sadly 'never again' has happened all too frequently since 1948. The genocides have not ceased. Violence against groups on the basis of their religion is on the rise. And that is the inevitable result of an upsurge in fundamentalism, or, as it is often called, religious traditionalism.

Traditionalists believe that their religion contains the essential truths and is the answer to all the world's evils. Their role is to restore it to its purest form by faithfully following a literalist reading of scripture, and in the case of Muslims by imposing sharia and returning the world to the way it was under Muhammad in the seventh century. Believing that they possess the sole truth, fundamentalists/traditionalists tend to be intolerant of those with different opinions and interpretations. At the extreme end of the fundamentalist spectrum are the terrorists, like members of ISIS, who believe that they have a religious duty to kill those who stray from the 'true' path of Islam.

Apostasy, blasphemy and atheism are in principle punishable by death in twelve Muslim countries.[1] Saudi Arabia and Iran officially impose the death penalty for apostasy, though it is rarely put into effect; in Pakistan blasphemy but not apostasy is a capital offence

Serious discrimination against minority religions is still legally enforced in nearly all Islamic countries. Saudi Arabia, for example, forbids non-Muslims from worshipping in public, and bans the building of Christian churches. According to a report commissioned in 2018 by the British foreign secretary, Jeremy Hunt, Christians, the most oppressed religious group in the world, suffer the worst persecution in the Middle East and North Africa.[2]

Persecution in the region ranges from routine discrimination in education, employment and social life, incitement to hatred through media and from the pulpit, detention, imprisonment, kidnapping, extrajudicial killings to genocidal attacks against Christian communities. Over the past two decades, millions of Christians have been uprooted from their homes. As a result, the report claims, the number of Christians in the region has fallen to four per cent of the population compared to twenty per cent at the beginning of the twentieth century.

The upsurge in fundamentalism has not, however, occurred solely in the Islamic world. Israel has also witnessed a rise in fundamentalism and so too has the United States, a surprisingly traditional country, especially in comparison with the countries of western Europe. Christian fundamentalists have reacted forcefully to what they see as the decline of America, as a result of, in their eyes, an erosion of its Christian values. Though the bombing of abortion clinics and the hate demonstrations against homosexuals are rare, American Christian fundamentalists, like Islamists, tend to believe that the reassertion of religion in its purified form will 'make America great again'. They are increasingly capturing the political right in the US and exporting their policies to other countries. With the active encouragement of American evangelists, who see homosexuality as a major factor in the breakdown of society, Kenya, Uganda and Nigeria have introduced or maintained anti-gay legislation.*

Nonetheless, the most intolerant countries in the world today are Muslim, according to the Pew Research Center, an American non-partisan social research organization.

So to return to the questions posed at the beginning of this book. Does Islam pose a threat to the liberal values of the West today? Are Muslim habits of thought and behaviour inimical to modern Western ones?

Let us go back to that optimistic proclamation of faith in the power of human rights, the UN Declaration of Human Rights of 1948. For many signatories the UDHR was the Enlightenment's gift to the world. Belief in the equality of all humans, in their equal claim to freedom and dignity, would overcome the catastrophes caused by divisions based on race, religion and sex. The world would be united in solidarity and fellow feeling. Together the world would achieve *liberté*, *egalité* and *fraternité*.

---

* Homosexuality is a criminal offence in the majority of Muslim countries in the Middle East and in Africa. It is still punishable by death under sharia law in Iran, Sudan, Saudi Arabia, Yemen, parts of Somalia and northern Nigeria (annual report, 2017, by the International Lesbian, Gay, Bisexual, Trans and Intersex Association). Nor are Christian countries immune from anti-homosexual legislation. Gay sex is a criminal offence throughout the Commonwealth Caribbean, where Christians form the majority of the population, including Jamaica, Barbados and Grenada; only Bahamas, Belize and Trinidad and Tobago have decriminalized homosexuality. In 2013 Russia enacted a law prohibiting any positive mention of homosexuality in the presence of minors. The Vatican has declined to condemn the criminalization of homosexuality.

For large swathes of the Muslim world, however, the Declaration was part of the continuing march of the 'Enlightenment on horseback', where the horse is more visible – and more threatening – than the light. In the eyes of its Muslim critics, the UDHR simply exposed what they always saw as the fatal hypocrisy at the heart of the Enlightenment – the West talks about universal rights, but what it really means is the imposition of Western values on the rest of the world. The Universal Declaration of Human Rights is not talking about 'human' rights but rights which specifically apply to a Western post-religious world. It thereby excludes about 1.8 billion Muslims for whom religion is the air they breathe, and shows no consideration for a traditional set of values by which a large part of the world has lived for centuries. Saudi Arabia abstained from voting in favour of the UDHR on the grounds that it violated sharia law.*

In 1969 forty-five Muslim countries and those countries that had a substantial Muslim community founded the Organization of Islamic Co-operation. The organization states that it is 'the collective voice of the Muslim world' and works to 'safeguard and protect the interests of the Muslim world in the spirit of promoting international peace and harmony'. Fifty-six of its fifty-seven members are also members of the UN, but indicatively they are all signatories to the Universal Islamic Declaration of Human Rights (UIDHR) which they signed in Cairo in 1981.

It is worth comparing the UIDHR with the UN's UDHR which was drawn up in 1948. In many ways the two documents are very similar. The Cairo declaration begins by stating: 'All men are equal in terms of basic human dignity' and goes on to forbid 'discrimination on the basis of race, colour, language, belief, sex, religion, political affiliation, social status or other considerations'. Not so different from the UDHR which states 'All human beings are born free and equal in dignity and rights' (although the use of 'human beings' rather than 'men' is significant), and that 'Everyone is entitled to all the rights and freedoms set forth in this

* Seven other countries also abstained, including the Soviet Union, Poland, Czechoslovakia and South Africa; but none of the fifty-eight members of the United Nations at the time, including Iran and China, voted against the declaration.

Declaration, without distinction of any kind, such as race, colour, sex, language, religion, political or other opinion, national or social origin, property, birth or other status.'

Both declarations agree on equality before the law, the presumption of innocence until proven guilty, freedom of movement, the right to education, and the banning of slavery. The Cairo declaration also specifically cites colonialism as 'being one of the most evil forms of enslavement', and prohibits it. But where they markedly diverge is that Allah takes centre place in the Cairo declaration; equality is an equality before God, not before one's fellow human: 'All the rights and freedoms stipulated in this Declaration are subject to the Islamic Shari'ah', states article 24 of the UIDHR, and it concludes by stating that 'The Islamic Shari'ah is the only source of reference for the explanation or clarification of any of the articles of this Declaration.' By contrast, Christianity does not get a mention in the United Nations document. It is not God but our common humanity that gives us equal rights.

This fundamental distinction between the two declarations determines their differing stances on religious freedoms, and on the status of women: the one based on divine revelation, transmitted by the Prophet Muhammad in the seventh century (admittedly mediated by human interpreters), the other based on an accumulated body of thinking by flawed humans which has gradually become accepted over the centuries.* 'Woman is equal to man in human dignity, and has her own rights to enjoy as well as duties to perform', the Islamic declaration states, and continues 'The husband is responsible for the maintenance and welfare of the family.' Woman's rights are clearly different from man's and the man is the domestic boss. The United Nations declaration, on the other hand, refers to the 'equal rights of men and women'. Neither document addresses the question of homosexuality.

---

* The Quran refers to the man's duty to slap his wife if he fears her 'high-handedness' (4:34) and that a son should receive two shares of inheritance for every one share given to a daughter (Quran 4:11). See for example Quran 9:29 for reference to the differential treatment of non-Muslim People of the Book who must pay the *jizya* in return for protection.

Religious freedom, according to the UN, is a human right. 'Everyone has the right to freedom of thought, conscience, and religion. This right includes freedom to change his religion or belief, and ... to manifest his religion or belief in teaching, practice, worship, and observance.' According to the Universal Islamic Declaration of Human Rights freedom of expression is permissible only in so far as it 'would not be contrary to the principles of the Shari'ah' or 'violate sanctities and the dignity of Prophets, undermine moral and ethical Values or disintegrate, corrupt or harm society or weaken its faith'.

So there is indeed a clash of values. It is only in the light of the continuing centrality of a particular conception of the divine in the Muslim world that one can remotely understand the motivation for Ayatollah Khomeini's fatwa in 1989 declaring that Muslims had a duty to kill the author Salman Rushdie on the grounds that his novel, *The Satanic Verses*, was blasphemous; or the jihadists who gunned down the French cartoonists at *Charlie Hebdo* in 2015 for their blasphemous cartoons of Muhammad.

But it would be wrong to classify this clash as one between Islam and the West or between a religious and a secular world. It is, in fact, one between the traditional and the post-traditional.

From at least the eighteenth century, Islamic modernizers/reformers believed that the idea of human rights trumpeted by the West was perfectly compatible with Islam, indeed that Western Enlightenment thinkers even got their inspiration from Islam (see Chapter 20). Modernizers believed, and still believe, that the essential principles underlying sharia law, which include the ideas of human dignity and equality, must be divorced from *fiqh*, the detailed rules and regulations that were elaborated by Muslim jurists in the specific historic circumstances of the seventh to tenth centuries.

To distinguish between principles and circumstance, however, might be relatively easy for the modernizers, but is not possible for the traditionalists, for many of whom every ruling of sharia law is sacred and immutable. That belief essentially erases the potential for compromise since any deviation from the sacred law is to contradict the word of Allah and his mouthpiece Muhammad.

Traditionalist Muslims therefore could not possibly agree with the UN's special rapporteur appointed to examine religious persecution and discrimination around the world. In 1981 the rapporteur announced that 'freedom of religion or belief can never be used to justify violations of the rights of women and girls, and that it can no longer be taboo to demand that women's rights take priority over intolerant beliefs used to justify gender discrimination'. The blithe assumption that women's rights naturally trumped religious diktat was indicative of what Said Rajaie-Khorassani, the post-revolution Iranian representative to the UN, characterized as the relativistic 'secular understanding of the Judeo-Christian tradition', which could not be implemented by Muslims without flouting Islamic law.[3]

Just as a distinction can be made between the principles on which sharia law must be based and specific laws and regulations made in relation to the particular circumstances of the times, so a distinction must be made between Muslim states (ones where many or most citizens are Muslim) and Islamist states (those which favour a strict implementation of sharia and a government firmly based on a traditionalist Islam). It is equally important to distinguish between ordinary professing Muslims and Islamists who are political traditionalist radicals. Militant Islamists believe that sharia law is the answer to all the world's ills and that it should therefore be imposed throughout the world, in its specifics as they were elaborated in medieval times as well as in its broad principles. They naturally see the West as the enemy of Islam, and cannot even take the step of tolerating the West as the 'other'. Islamists do indeed pose a threat to post-traditionalist ways of life in the West, just as they do to non-Islamist Muslims in Muslim countries. But when those threats are clear, no special law or principle is needed to counter them – just the standard laws by which a country protects its people. Murder is murder; a threat is a threat... The state and the law does not need to know what the motivations or reasons were.

Far more difficult to resolve is the question of traditionalist Muslims who harbour no aggression towards the West, live in the West, yet insist on traditional practices that many liberals abhor (or at least are troubled by), such as the wearing of the burqa or the ritual slaughter of animals.

In 2002 the German newspaper *Allgemeine Zeitung* listed the sort of questions that Western liberals agonize over. The list was cited by the German philosopher and sociologist Jürgen Habermas in his essay on tolerance.[4] It included the following questions: Does a Muslim employee have the right to briefly interrupt his work time in order to pray? Does a Muslim pupil have the right to be exempted from PE classes because she is not allowed to show herself to other pupils wearing sports clothes? May Muslim pupils wear headscarves in class? And what if the woman concerned is a teacher at a government-owned school? Should the law be different for nuns than it is for a Muslim teacher? Should muezzins be allowed to broadcast their call to prayer by loudspeaker in German cities just as churches are allowed to ring their bells? Should foreigners (a direct translation here) be allowed to ritually slaughter animals although it contravenes the local animal protection regulations?

In other words: to tolerate or not to tolerate? How tolerant are Western countries prepared to be in the face of the intolerant, or conversely, how intolerant should the West be in order to preserve its tolerance? And, on their side, how tolerant should traditionalists be of the modern context in which they live? Who will compromise, say, on the slaughter of animals? The imam or rabbi and their congregations who want to follow their religious laws and therefore do not stun the animal before killing it, or the majority who believe that slaughter without pre-stunning causes additional suffering? Questions of tolerance rapidly become knotted and foggy.

But what I hope this book has shown is that the question – to tolerate or not to tolerate? – is the wrong one to be asking. What we really need to do is get out of the tolerance game.

Over the course of the seventeen hundred years covered by this book, there has been a slow and incomplete transformation of tolerance into something better. The Muslim states of the Mediterranean and near-beyond were more tolerant than Western Christendom ever was. Unlike the Islamic world, all factions within Western Christendom made systematic political use of the demonization of the other. The centuries of violence unleashed as a result led, internally, to the effective victory of sovereign, often national, powers and their adoption of doctrines of toleration, most notably under the 1648 Peace of Westphalia. The spirit of the combative group that had been whipped up to such effect by the medieval Church was, however, transferred to these new units in the form of nationalism – which over time has become as much a source of intolerance as religion.

The words tolerance and intolerance still pervade the discussion, but as this gallop through Muslim and Christian attitudes to religious minorities has shown, tolerance is not a virtue, and the tolerated do not want to be tolerated.

Despite the fear, misunderstanding and consequent hatred of the other which still bedevils us, the world has come a long way since the signing of the UN Declaration of Human Rights in 1948. In the West there has been a significant shift not towards tolerance but towards equality, even affirmation, of groups who have historically been despised or persecuted for their difference. However, there are always lines drawn in the sand, saying this far and no further. Political correctness, ironically, has developed its own limits of tolerance, always increasing the domains from which it is acceptable to exclude. No platform, or deplatforming, denies an individual or organization the right to speak because of their quite literally intolerable views – racist or homophobic opinions, for example. The self-styled home of tolerance has grown its own exclusive fundamentalism.

The West has been wrong to pride itself on its tolerance – not because it has *not* been tolerant, but because that is not what we should be proud of. What the West should celebrate is not tolerance but the three cardinal political virtues – liberty, equality and solidarity, or fellow feeling – which we have come to value as the post-traditional ideals, even if in practice we frequently fall far short of these ideals.*

So when I walk down the street and see a woman wearing a burqa, I do not need to feel that I am in the impossible position of having to choose between my feminism and my liberalism. The question is not whether to tolerate or not tolerate the wearing of the burqa, but whether

* These three core values enjoy remarkable support on both the left and right, although Conservatives will often prefer to call 'solidarity' something like 'social cohesion', and left and right will disagree on how best to realize them and their relative order of importance.

the wearing of the burqa contravenes the fundamental values by which we want to live: liberty, equality and fellow feeling. Western countries should acknowledge their commitment to the task of furthering the realization of these virtues.

There can be no general rule by which to decide all the thorny issues that arise in a multi-religious society. But if we remember that the purpose of public policy in our countries is to move towards a truer realization of the ideals of liberty, equality and solidarity then when it comes to particular cases, such as a ban on the burqa, the way forward becomes clearer. The issue has been debated across Europe. Six European countries – France, Belgium, Austria, Denmark, Latvia and Bulgaria – have banned the burqa in public places. The UK has not done so – yet.

Looked at in the light of the three cardinal virtues – avowedly Enlightenment virtues – the burqa can be seen as injurious to the equality of men and women and to fellow feeling between the sexes. Of course, there is also an argument that to ban the burqa is a straightforward violation of liberty and might only increase the sense of inequality experienced by Muslims in relation to dominant Western society. And if a ban means that women in traditionalist homes are confined indoors because they were not allowed to wear the burqa outside, the longer-term progress of equality and solidarity would be slowed down. A political judgement still has to be made because there is no neutral course of action – even to do nothing is a choice in that it means the acceptance of the status quo. Of course, whatever judgement is made will infringe to some degree on at least one of the three core values. Trade-offs are central to the politics of post-traditional, Enlightenment societies, but at least they can be made within a framework we understand.

But are we not back to the clash of civilizations between the Western world which prizes Enlightenment values, and the Islamic world which does not? The Islamic modernists al-Afghani, Muhammad Abduh and their successors did not believe there was a clash. Nor did the former US president Barack Obama. In 2009 he addressed Al-Azhar University in Cairo, the centre of Sunni Muslim learning, and said this:

> I reject the view of some in the West that a woman who chooses to cover her hair is somehow less equal, but I do believe that a woman who is denied an education is denied equality … Our daughters can contribute just as much to society as our sons, and our common prosperity will be advanced by allowing all humanity – men and women – to reach their full potential. I do not believe that women must make the same choices as men in order to be equal, and I respect those women who choose to live their lives in traditional roles. But it should be their choice.[5]

Obama believes in our core Enlightenment values. But he does not want to be the American imperialist intent on imposing those values on traditionalists in the Islamic world. He is looking for the common ground on which Enlightenment and Islamic values coincide.

In the light of the UN and Cairo Declarations of Human Rights, his presentation of equality between men and women is a subtle and useful one. A personal choice made by a woman to wear the burqa or hijab is not necessarily a sign of inequality, he says, and so there need not necessarily be a conflict between sharia law and the values of religious liberty and equality. But, furthermore, since the Cairo declaration asserts the equal dignity of men and women, the proposition that the denial of education is a denial of equality is a position on which traditionalists and post-traditionalists can hope for agreement. The appeal to 'our common prosperity' through the ability of each to attain 'their full potential' is an appeal to solidarity – it is a common prosperity – and it is also an appeal to the universalist conception of the good and united society that Muhammad so clearly endorsed against the tribalism that surrounded him.

There is much that seeks common ground in Obama's speech. And yet it also has bite. In traditional societies, women are usually the largest group that is dominated by the status quo, or, as many post-traditionalists would see it, by men. So to demand of the highest seat of Sunni learning that the benefits of learning be extended to women is no small demand. It gives support to probably the most progressive force in the traditionalist world today – the education of women. Having established common ground, Obama pushes where, pragmatically, he is likely to have the greatest impact. This is not because of a special preference for education, or for equality over liberty, or for solidarity between the sexes over other forms of fellow feeling, but because this is what is likely to make the most difference in that place, to that audience. Obama is able to combine an attitude of respect with one of high expectation: he points to the direction of travel that Al-Azhar should support – a direction consistent with its own values while also absolutely aligned with Obama's.

Obama is setting a fine example of the way forward on the global political scale. He is not pontificating about the equality of women – that would be the Enlightenment on horseback yet again. But nor is he saying he tolerates or respects the unequal treatment of women, the condescending or multi-culturalist relativist approach, which pretends to make no moral judgement on others while often being implicitly condescending in its own way – allowing the 'primitive other' to adhere to their traditional customs while doing nothing to help those, usually women, who bear the brunt of them. Obama is not insisting on assimilation; he is expecting traditionalist Muslims will educate women not because it is an Enlightenment value but because it furthers the cause of women's equality – which is a Muslim value as much as it is an Enlightenment one.

But how do we – each of us, as we go about our daily business – share this spherical planet? I have a friend, a passionate white secular feminist, who is enraged by the veil. One day in London she was on the Tube and found herself sitting beside a woman in a hijab. Unable to contain herself (she rarely can), she asked the Muslim woman – who, it transpired, was from the Gulf and worked in the medical profession – how she could wear the veil. The two got talking. They have been close friends ever since, though one still wears her headscarf and the other is still a secular feminist.

My friend was not in a mind to tolerate or not tolerate: her anger did not translate into an abstract pseudo-paradox about tolerating the intolerant. She has a visceral sense of the need for solidarity and wanted to advance the cause of equality between the sexes – in this situation by making her case against the wearing of the veil. Over the years, their relationship has become one of love and respect. And I imagine that each has moved the other – not to some military-sounding 'middle ground', as if every belief is a gun-encampment to be taken or negotiated over during the truce, but rather to a deeper understanding of the common humanity they share. Indeed, they share much more than an abstract humanity – both my irritable secularist and her friend who wears the hijab are jointly engaged in the battle for gender equality that so many women are fighting. Perhaps they have different ideas of what that equality might look like, but they both agree that it is important.

What is the moral of this tale? That if we are to have any chance of living together we need not just genuine mutual respect, but also an avowed and confident acknowledgement of what we expect from those with whom we deeply disagree. Respect is great but it does not move things forward, it is an attitude towards the other and their opinions as they are. Expectation, on the other hand, goes beyond the status quo and looks to the future, to how things will develop. My friend's expectation is that her Muslim sister will gradually lift her eyes towards greater equality and greater liberty and remove her veil. No doubt conversely, the woman in a hijab may expect to bring her new friend closer to God. The point about the way out of the trap of tolerance is precisely that it requires not just respect, but also a confidence in where you stand. In stating your expectations, you both affirm what you believe and by doing so avoid being condescending – the fault that is common to both the attitude of tolerance and of multi-cultural relativism.

When the veil between people is lifted and we live in mutual respect and expectation, then Enlightenment flourishes, not galloping on horseback, but picking its careful way through this treacherous terrain.

ENDNOTES

Chapter 1: The Birth of Persecution: The Roman Empire turns Christian

1 Mary E. Smallwood, *The Jews Under Roman Rule*, Brill, 2014, pp. 83,147–8, 348.
2 *Apologeticus XL*; available at http://www.sacred-texts.com/chr/ecf/003/0030046.htm (accessed 1 April 2019).
3 Eusebius, *History of the Church*, VIII, vii.
4 'Edict of Milan'; available at https://sourcebooks.fordham.edu/source/edict-milan.asp (accessed 1 April 2019).
5 Eusebius, *Life of Constantine*.
6 *Codex Theodosius,* XVI.i.2; available at http://penelope.uchicago.edu/~grout/encyclopaedia_Romana/greece/paganism/paganism.html (accessed 1 April 2019).
7 Libanius, *Orations*, 30.8.
8 Smallwood, p. 508.
9 Ambrose funeral oration, *On the Death of Theodosius* (34), 395.

Chapter 2: Muhammad's Edict of Toleration

1 Weber, *Religion of China*, 1915, cited in Robert I. Moore, *The Formation of a Persecuting Society*, Blackwell, 1987, p. 105.
2 Ibn Ishaq, *The Life of Muhammad*, A. Guillaume, Oxford University Press, 1955, p. 145.
3 As described by the late nineteenth-century travel writer, Charles Montagu Doughty, in his *Travels in Arabia Deserta*, vol. 1, Cosimo Classics, 1888, p. 3.
4 Ibn Ishaq, pp. 232–3.
5 Gerhard Bowering (ed.), *The Princeton Encyclopedia of Islamic Political Thought*, Princeton University Press, 2013, p. 454.
6 Ibn Ishaq, pp. 304, 354.
7 *Sahih al-Bukhari*, 2301.

Chapter 3: The Price of Toleration: The *Dhimmi* in the Islamic Empire

1 Cited by Bernard Lewis, *The Jews of Islam*, Princeton University Press, 1984, p. 63.

2 From the Pact of Umar, cited by Tritton, pp.13–14.
3 *Sahih al-Bukhari*, 5902.

Chapter 4: Islam's Inquisition

1 Guy Le Strange, *Baghdad During the Abbasid Caliphate: From Contemporary Arabic and Persian Sources*, Clarendon Press, 2017, pp. 37 ff.
2 Al-Tabari, *The History of al-Tabari*, vol. XXX, *The Abbasid Caliphate in Equilibrium*, trans. C.E. Bosworth, University of New York Press, p. 321. 1989.
3 Cited by John Nawas, 'A Reexamination of Three Current Explanations for Al-Ma'mun's Introduction of the Mihna', *International Journal of Middle Eastern Studies*, vol. 26, 1994, p. 621.
4 Ibn al-Jawzi, *The Life of Ibn Hanbal*, trans. Michael Cooperson, New York University Press, 2016, p. 104.
5 Cited by Michael Cooperson, *Classical Arabic Biography*, Cambridge University Press, 2004, p. 114.

Chapter 5: The Problems of Assimilation: Willing Martyrs

1 Al-Jahiz, cited by Amira K. Bennison, *The Great Caliphs*, I.B. Tauris, 2009, p. 125.
2 Leonard B. Glick, *Abraham's Heirs*, Syracuse University Press, 1999, p. 51.
3 From *The Deeds of Emperor Louis*, written by Thegan, bishop of Trier in 836–7, in Thomas F.X. Noble (trans.), *Charlemagne and Louis the Pious*, The Pennsylvania State Press, 2009, p. 203.
4 Ibid., p. 188.
5 Cited by the tenth-century Muslim historian al-Masudi in his *Meadows Of Gold*, written *c.*947.
6 Cited by Bennison, p. 127.

Chapter 6: Austerity in England and the Papal Battle for Supremacy

1 *Dictatus papae*, 1075.
2 First Deposition and Banning of Henry IV by Gregory VII, 22 February 1076; available at http://avalon.law.yale.edu/medieval/inv04.asp (accessed 1 April 2019).
3 Oliver J. Thatcher and Edgar Holmes McNeal (eds), The Oath of King Henry, in *A Source Book for Mediaeval History: Selected Documents illustrating the history of Europe in the Middle Ages*, Charles Scribner's Sons, 1905, p. 160; available at https://archive.org/details/asourcebookform03mcnegoog/page/n9 (accessed 1 April 2019).

4 Cited by Barlow, p. 51.

5 Cited by Bernard Lewis, *Islam in History*, Open Court Publishing, 1993, pp. 168–71.

6 Cited by Norman A. Stillman, *The Jews of Arab Lands*, Jewish Publication Society of America, 1979, p. 225.

7 See the historian R.I. Moore's hugely influential *The Formation of a Persecuting Society*, first published in 1987.

Chapter 7: The Crusades: The Church Finds its Enemy

1 Ermenfrid Penitential, 1067; see H.E.J. Cowdrey, 'Bishop Ermenfrid of Sion and the Penitential Ordinance following the Battle of Hastings', *Journal of Ecclesiastic History*, vol. 20, no. 2, October 1969 , pp. 225–42.

2 *Song of Roland*, trans. John O'Hagan, verse xcii, available at https://sourcebooks.fordham.edu/basis/roland-ohag.asp (accessed 1 April 2019).

3 Ibn Khaldun, *Prolegomena: An Introduction to History*, cited by Elbaki Hermassi, 'Leadership and National Development in North Africa: A Comparative Study', University of California Press, 1972, p. 18.

4 *Song of Roland*, O'Hagan, verse cxiii; available at http://www.sacred-texts.com/neu/roland/rol01.htm (accessed 1 April 2019).

5 Early twelfth-century Regulations for the Market at Seville, cited by Lewis, 1984, p. 38.

6 Cited by Edward Peters, *The First Crusade*, University of Pennsylvania Press, 1998, p. 31.

7 Steven Runciman, *A History of the Crusades*, vol. I, Appendix II, Cambridge University Press, 1951, pp. 336–7.

8 *Historia Hierosolymitanae expeditionis* (History of the Expedition to Jerusalem), cited by Robert Chazan (ed.), *Church, State and Jew in the Middle Ages*, Behrman House, 1980, p. 71.

9 Albert of Aix, Medieval Sourcebook; available at https://sourcebooks.fordham.edu/source/1096jews.asp (accessed 1 April 2019).

10 Fulcher of Chartres, *A History of the Expedition to Jerusalem, 1095–1127*, cited by August C. Krey, *The First Crusade: The Accounts of Eyewitnesses and Participants*, Princeton University Press, 1921, p. 134.

11 Cited by Peters, 1998, p. 144.

12 Richard A. Fletcher, *Moorish Spain*, Weidenfeld & Nicolson, 1992, p. 118.

13 Rosamond McKitterick and R. Collins, *The New Cambridge Medieval History*, vol. II, Cambridge University Press, 1990, p. 551.

14 Glick, pp. 123 ff.

15 Mark R. Cohen, *Under Crescent and Cross*, Princeton University Press, 1994, p. 182.

16 Cited by Stillman, p. 247.

17 Cited by Stanley Lane-Poole, *Saladin and the Fall of the Kingdom of Jerusalem*, G. P. Putnam's Sons, 1906, p. 298.
18 *Kamil*, XI, 362, cited by Carole Hillenbrand, *The Crusades*, Routledge, 2000, p. 316.

Chapter 8: The Moneylender

1 See Jonathan Riley-Smith, *The First Crusade and the Idea of Crusading*, University of Pennsylvania Press, 1986, p. 89.

Chapter 9: Enemies Within: The Heretic, the Leper, the Sodomite and the Jew

1 From the thirteenth-century *Chronica Majora* by Matthew Paris, cited by E. Denison Ross. 'An Embassy from King John to the Emperor of Morocco', *Bulletin of the School of Oriental Studies*, vol. 3, no. 3, 1924, pp. 555–9.
2 Cited by Ross, p. 556.
3 The papal bull annulling Magna Carta issued by Pope Innocent III on 24 August 1215; available at https://www.bl.uk/collection-items/the-papal-bull-annulling-magna-carta (accessed 1 April 2019).
4 Chazan, p. 173.
5 Cecil Roth, *A History of the Jews in England*, Clarendon Press, 1941, pp. 44–5. Though written in 1941 this text is still invaluable.
6 See Sara Lipton, *Dark Mirror*, Metropolitan Books, 2014.
7 Jacques de Vitry, *Oriental History*, cited by John Boswell, *Christianity, Social Tolerance and Homosexuality*, University of Chicago Press, 1980, p. 281.
8 Edward Peters, *Inquisition*, University of California Press, 1989, p. 59.

Chapter 10: The Mongols and the 'Closing of the Door'

1 Cited by the assassins of Egyptian President Anwar Sadat in their jihad manifesto *Al-Farīḍa al-ghā'iba* (The Neglected Duty), 1981.
2 Cited by W.B. Bartlett, *The Mongols*, Amberley Publishing, 2009, p. 151.
3 Giovanni da Pian del Carpine, *The History of the Mongols*, in *The journey of William of Rubruck to the eastern parts of the world, 1253–55*, trans. William Woodville Rockhill, Hakluyt Society, 1942, p. 63.
4 Rockhill, pp.221, 208, available at https://archive.org/stream/journeyofwillia00ruys/journeyofwillia00ruys_djvu.txt (accessed 1 April).
5 Hugh Kennedy, *The Court of the Caliphs*, Routledge, 2004, p. 239.
6 Cited by M. Perlmann, 'Notes on Anti-Christian Propaganda in the Mamluk Empire', *Bulletin of the School of Oriental and African Studies*, vol. 10, no. 4, 1942, p. 850.
7 See, for example, Jonathan Riley-Smith, *The Crusades, Christianity and Islam*, Columbia University Press, 2008, p. 97.

8 *Summa Theologica*, 1–2.19, 5.
9 See F.E. Peters, *The Monotheists*, vol. 2, Princeton University Press, 2003, p. 117.
10 See Cecil Roth, 1941, pp. 76–85.
11 From Raphael Holinshed's *Chronicles of England, Scotland and Wales*, 1587, cited by James Shapiro, *Shakespeare and the Jews*, Columbia University Press, 1996.
12 Simon Dubnow, *History of the Jews in Russia and Poland*, The Jewish Publication Society of America, 1916, vol. 1, pp. 16–18.
13 Jakob von Königshofen, 'The Cremation of Strasbourg Jewry, St. Valentine's Day, February 14, 1349—About the Great Plague and the Burning of the Jews', cited by Jacob R. Marcus, *The Jew in the Medieval World*, The Union of American Hebrew Congregations, 1938, p. 45.

Chapter 11: The Black Death: An Experiment in Tolerance

1 *The Decameron*, trans. with an introduction and notes by G.H. McWilliam, Penguin Books, 1995, pp. 209–10.
2 *Decameron*, p. 212.
3 *Decameron*, pp. 206–7.
4 'The Cremation of Strasbourg Jewry, St. Valentine's Day, February 14, 1349—About the Great Plague and the Burning of the Jews', cited by Marcus, 1938, p. 47.
5 Ibid, p. 47.
6 Ibn Khaldun, *The Muqaddimah*, i, 64, cited by Ann K.S. Lambton, *State and Government in Medieval Islam*, Oxford University Press, 2004, p. 153.
7 For what follows I have relied on Michael Dols, 'Comparative communal responses to the Black Death in Muslim and Christian societies', *Viator*, vol. 5, 1974, pp. 269–88.
8 *The Travels of Ibn Battuta*, trans. H.A.R. Gibb, GoodWord, 2000, p. 23.

Chapter 12: Inquisitions and Expulsions

1 See Henry Kamen, *The Spanish Inquisition*, Weidenfeld & Nicolson, 1997, chapters 9–10.
2 Peters, 1989, p. 87.
3 Norman Roth, *Conversos, Inquisition and the Expulsion of the Jews from Spain*, University of Wisconsin Press, 1995, p. 376.
4 Cited by Kamen, p. 241.
5 Cited by Helen Rawlings, *The Spanish Inquisition*, Blackwell, 2006, p. 38.
6 Erika Rummel, *Jiménez de Cisneros*, Arizona Center for Medieval and Renaissance Studies, 1999, p. 16.
7 Chazan, p. 321.

8 Cited in *The Jewish Encyclopedia*, ed. Isidore Singer, Funk & Wagnalls, 1912, vol. 2, p. 460.
9 Cited by Lewis, 1984, pp. 135–6.

Chapter 13: The Reformation's War Against the Catholic Church

1 For this and the following cases see B. Ann Tlusty (ed.), *Augsburg During the Reformation Era*, Hackett Publishing, 2012, pp. 215 ff.
2 Cited by Tlusty, p. 249.
3 Cited by Tlusty, p. 29.
4 Cited by Tlusty, pp. 29–31.
5 Benjamin J. Kaplan, *Divided by Faith*, Harvard University Press, 2007, p. 55.
6 Bernard Cottret, *Calvin: A Biography*, trans. M. Wallace McDonald, William B. Eerdmans Publishing, 2000, pp. 174–5.
7 Cited by Cottret, p. 190.
8 Cited by Cottret, pp. 224–5.
9 Cited by Kaplan, p. 19.
10 *Concerning Heretics: Whether they are to be persecuted and how they are to be treated*, published 1554, the year after Servetus was burned at the stake.
11 *Concerning Secular Authority*, 1523.
12 Cited by Roland H. Bainton, *Here I Stand*, The Beacon Press, 1953, p. 390.

Chapter 14: The Ghetto

1 Cited by Cecil Roth, *The House of Nasi*, The Jewish Publication Society of America, 1948, p. 127.
2 Martin Brecht, *Martin Luther*, vol. III, *The Preservation of the Church, 1532–1546*, trans. James Schaaf, Fortress Press, 1999, p. 351.
3 See Tlusty, pp. 186–90.
4 Cited by Brian Pullan, *The Jews of Europe and the Inquisition of Venice, 1550–1670*, I.B. Taurus, 1983, p. 158.
5 Israel Abrahams, *Jewish Life in the Middle Ages*, Dover Publications, 2004, p. 81.
6 See Abrahams, pp. 77, 147.
7 Cecil Roth, 1948, p. 115.
8 Cited by Cecil Roth, 1948, p. 118.
9 Lewis, 1984, p. 131.

Chapter 15: The Religious Wars of Europe

1 Geoff Mortimer, *Eyewitness Accounts of the Thirty Years War 1618–48*, Palgrave Macmillan, 2002, p. 33.

2 Peter H. Wilson, *Europe's Tragedy*, Penguin, 2010, p. 783.
3 Peter H. Wilson, *The Thirty Years War*, Palgrave Macmillan, 2010, p. 262.
4 For extracts from Dobel's diary, see Wilson, *The Thirty Years' War*, ch. 16, p. 146.
5 Wilson, *Europe's Tragedy*, p. 784.
6 See Zwierlein in Olaf Asbach and Peter Schröder, *The Ashgate Research Companion to the Thirty Years' War*, Routledge, 2014, pp. 231–44.

Chapter 16: Sunnis vs Shiites

1 See for example, Samuel Huntington, *The Clash of Civilizations and the Remaking of World Order*, Simon & Schuster, 1996; Roger Scruton, *The West and the Rest: Globalization and the Terrorist Threat*, ISI Books, 2002; Bernard Lewis, *What Went Wrong? The Clash between Islam and Modernity in the Middle East*, Weidenfeld & Nicolson, 2002; Ayaan Hirsi Ali, *The Caged Virgin: An Emancipation Proclamation for Women and Islam*, Free Press, 2006; and Niall Ferguson, *Civilization: The West and the Rest*, Penguin, 2011.
2 Cited by Stefan Winter, *The Shiites of Lebanon Under Ottoman Rule*, Cambridge University Press, 2010, p. 15.
3 Roger Savory, *Iran Under the Safavids*, Cambridge University Press, 1980, p. 28.
4 Colin Turner, p. 86. *Islam Without Allah? The Rise of Religious Externalism in Safavid Iran*, Routledge, 2001, p. 86.
5 Turner, p.83; Rosemary Stanfield-Johnson, 'The Tabarraiyan and the early Safavids', *Iranian Studies*, vol. 37, no. 1, March 2004, p. 48.
6 Rula Jurdi Abisaab, *Converting Persia*, I.B. Tauris, 2004, p. 19.
7 Cited by José Cutillas Ferrer, 'War and Diplomacy: A Letter describing Shah Tahmasp I and His Ministers', in Enrique García Hernán, José Cutillas Ferrer and Rudi Matthee (eds), *The Spanish Monarchy and Safavid Persia in the Early Modern Period: Politics, War and Religion*, Albatros, 2016, p. 36.
8 Anthony Black, *The History of Islamic Political Thought*, Edinburgh University Press, 2011, p. 231.
9 Ferrer, p. 37.
10 Abisaab, p. 128.
11 Evliya Çelebi, *An Ottoman Traveller: Selections from the Book of Travels of Evliya Çelebi*, ed. and trans. Robert Dankoff and Sooyong Kim, Eland Publishing, 2011, p. 60.

Chapter 17: The Puritan who Fought the Puritans

1 For much of what follows on Williams I have relied on John M. Barry, 'God, Government and Roger Williams' Big Idea', *Smithsonian Magazine*, 2012.

2 Andrew R. Murphy, *Conscience and Community*, Penn State University Press, 2001, p. 44.
3 Lewis Hanke, 'The Dawn of Conscience in America: Spanish Experiments and Experiences with Indians in the New World', *Proceedings of the American Philosophical Society*, vol. 107, no. 2, April 1963, p. 89.
4 Edwin S. Gaustad, *Roger Williams*, Oxford University Press, 2001, pp. 28, 26.
5 Roger Williams, *The Bloudy Tenent of Persecution, for Cause of Conscience*, ed. Richard Groves, Mercer University Press, 2001, pp. 154–5.
6 Records of the colony of Rhode Island and Providence Plantations in New England, ed. John Russell Bartlett, cited in Murphy, p. 67.
7 Murphy, p. 68.
8 Anthony Gill, 'Religious Pluralism, Political Incentives, and the Origins of Religious Liberty', in Allen D. Hertzke (ed.), *The Future of Religious Freedom*, Oxford University Press, 2013, p. 114.
9 See John Lilburne, *The Free-Mans Freedome Vindicated*, June 1646.
10 See Jerome Friedman, *Miracles and the Pulp Press During the English Revolution: The Battle of the Frogs and Fairford's Flies*, University College London Press, 1993, pp. 171–5.
11 Cited by John Coffey, *Persecution and Toleration in Protestant England, 1558–1689*, Routledge, 2000, p. 148.
12 Cited by Isaac Levitats, *The Jewish Community in Russia, 1772–1844*, Columbia University Press, 1943, pp. 20–21.

Chapter 18: America Writes God out of the Constitution

1 Letter to the physician and social reformer Benjamin Rush, 1803.
2 Hasia R. Diner, *The Jews of the United States, 1654 to 2000*, University of California Press, 2004, p. 22.
3 For a good description of New Amsterdam at the time, see Edwin G. Burrows and Mike Wallace, *Gotham: A History of New York City to 1898*, Oxford University Press, 1999, pp. 50–60.
4 Burrows, p. 60.
5 Diner, p. 14.
6 Thomas Jefferson, *Notes on the State of Virginia*, 1785.
7 From the records of the First Federal Congress debates on the Constitutional Amendments, 1789; available at http://candst.tripod.com/1stdebat.htm (accessed 1 April 2019).
8 Benjamin Franklin, *The Autobiography of Benjamin Franklin*, available at http://www.ushistory.org/franklin/autobiography/page38.htm (accessed 1 April 2019), p. 37.
9 Thomas Paine, 'Of the Religion of Deism compared with the Christian Religion, and the superiority of the former over the latter'.

10 Thomas Paine, *The Age of Reason, Part One*, 1794.
11 Cited by Brooke Allen, 'Sensibility and Sense', *The Hudson Review*, vol. 59, no. 3, 2006, p. 493.
12 Cited by Dennis C. Rasmussen, *The Pragmatic Enlightenment*, Cambridge University Press, 2014, p. 170.
13 Franklin, p. 37.

Chapter 19: Robespierre's New Religion

1 The following is taken from a contemporary description of the civic festival at Châlons-sur-Marne held to inaugurate a temple to the Supreme Being, in Isaac Kramnick (ed.), *The Portable Enlightenment Reader*, Penguin Books, 1995, pp. 168–73.
2 For much of what follows on emancipation, I have relied on I. Hersch, 'The French Revolution and the Emancipation of the Jews', *Jewish Quarterly Review*, vol. 19, no. 3, April 1907, pp. 540–65.
3 Frank Tallett, 'Dechristianizing France: The Year II and the Revolutionary Experience', in Frank Tallett and Nicholas Atkin (eds), *Religion, Society and Politics in France Since 1789*, Hambledon Press, 1991, p. 6.
4 Tallett, p. 5.
5 7 May 1794, address to the Committee of Public Safety.
6 Carlyle, *The French Revolution: A History*, vol. III, Chapman & Hall, 1842, p. 330.
7 Cited in Ruth Scurr, *Fatal Purity*, Chatto & Windus, 2006, p. 296.
8 Cited by Simon Schama, *Citizens*, Knopf, 1989, p. 855.

Chapter 20: Ibn Abd al-Wahhab vs the Islamic Enlightenment

1 Michael Crawford, *Ibn 'Abd Al-Wahhab*, Oneworld Publications, 2014, p. 51.
2 Cited by Crawford, p. 93.
3 Crawford, p. 104.
4 Ibid., pp. 156–7.
5 Ibid., p. 115.
6 Christopher de Bellaigue, *The Islamic Enlightenment*, Bodley Head, 2017, p. xi.
7 All quotations in this paragraph are taken from al-Jabarti, *Al-Jabarti's History of Egypt*, ed. Jane Hathaway, Markus Wiener, 2009, pp. 191–4.
8 Al-Jabarti, *Napoleon in Egypt: Al-Jabarti's Chronicle of the French Occupation*, ed. and trans. Shmuel Moreh, Markus Wiener, 1993, p. 31.
9 Cited by de Bellaigue, p. 28.
10 Cited by Alexei Vassiliev, *The History of Saudi Arabia*, Saqi Books, 2000, p. 167.
11 Al-Jabarti, 2009, p. 241.

12 Rifa'a al-Tahtawi, *An Imam in Paris*, trans. Daniel L. Newman, Saqi Books, 2011, p. 261.
13 Ibid., p. 249.
14 William Makepeace Thackeray, *Notes of a journey from Cornhill to Grand Cairo*, Chapman & Hall, 1846, p. 113.
15 Philip Mansel, *Constantinople: City of the World's Desire, 1453–1924*, John Murray, 1995, p. 242.
16 Ibid., p. 236.
17 Cited by Lewis, 2002, p. 93.
18 Cited by Andrew Beattie, *Cairo: A Cultural and Literary History*, Signal Books, 2005, p. 147.
19 For my account of this massacre I have followed B. Masters, *Christians and Jews in the Ottoman Arab World*, Cambridge University Press, 2001, pp. 163–4.
20 Namik Kemal, [*Vatan*] 'Motherland, or Silistra', trans. Ahmet Ersoy, in Balázs Trencsényi and Michal Kopecek (eds), *National Romanticism: The Formation of National Movements*, Central European University Press, 2007, pp. 489–92.
21 De Bellaigue, p. 97.
22 Kemal, p. 492.
23 Cited by Taner Akçam, *From Empire to Republic*, Zed Books, 2004, pp. 249–50.
24 See de Bellaigue, p. 260.
25 Thackeray, pp. 130, 134.
26 Cited by Yvonne Haddad, 'Muhammad Abduh: Pioneer of Islamic Reform', in Ali Rahmena (ed.), *Pioneers of Islamic Revival*, Zed Books, 2005, pp. 35–6.

Chapter 21: Emancipation and the Failure of Tolerance

1 From Frederick the Great's 'Testament Politique', 1778, cited in Giles MacDonogh, *Frederick the Great: A Life in Deed and Letters*, Phoenix Publishing, 2000, p. 347.
2 See Deborah Sadie Hertz, *Jewish High Society in Old Regime Berlin*, Syracuse University Press, 2005, ch. 6, for more on Jewish salon women.
3 See J. Katz, *Out of the Ghetto*, Syracuse University Press, 1973, pp. 120–1.
4 Cited by Katz, p.131.
5 Cited in *Mind of Napoleon: A Selection of His Written and Spoken Words*, ed. and trans. J. Christopher Herold, Columbia University Press, 1955, p. 115.
6 Johann Gottlieb Fichte, *Addresses to the German Nation*, trans. R.F. Jones and G.H. Turnbull, Chicago, Open Court Publishing, 1922, Thirteenth Address, para. 198, pp. 223–4.
7 Katz, p. 86.
8 November 1879 edition of *Preussische Jahrbücher* (Prussian Annals), cited in Marcel Stoetzler, *The State, The Nation, The Jew*, University of Nebraska Press, 2008, p. 1.

9 For a good summary of the Dreyfus Affair, see Adam Gopnik, 'Trial of the Century: Revisiting the Dreyfus affair', *New Yorker*, 28 September 2009.
10 Theodor Herzl, *The Complete Diaries of Theodor Herzl*, vol. I, ed. Raphael Patai, trans. Harry Zohn, Herzl Press and Thomas Yoseloff, 1960, pp. 378–9.

Chapter 22: The Genocidal Century

1 M. Kuckhoff, German consul, cited by Israel W. Charny (ed.), *Genocide Studies*, vol. III, *The Widening Circle of Genocide*, Transaction, 1994, p. 105.
2 Cited by Akçam, p. 130.
3 Ibid, p. 130.
4 See Akçam, p. 119.
5 Cited by Akçam, p. 138.
6 Akçam, p. 95.
7 Cited by Vahakn N. Dadrian, *The History of the Armenian Genocide*, Berghahn Books, 1995, p. 207.
8 From the transcript of the defence district attorney's summing-up of Tehlirian's trial; available at http://www.cilicia.com/armo_tehlirian.html (accessed 1 April 2019).
9 Cited by Andrew Mango, *Atatürk: The Biography of the Founder of Modern Turkey*, Overlook Press, 1999, p. xx.
10 Bernard Lewis, *The Emergence of Modern Turkey*, Oxford University Press, 1961, p. 263.
11 The Muslim Brotherhood, 'Toward the Light', 1936.
12 Cited in Israel Gershoni and James P. Jankowski, *Confronting Fascism in Egypt: Dictatorship versus Democracy in the 1930s*, Stanford University Press, 2009, p. 371.
13 See Gudrun Krämer, *The Jews in Modern Egypt, 1914–1952*, I.B. Tauris, 1989, p.151 and Matthias Küntzel, 'National Socialism and Anti-Semitism in the Arab World', *Jewish Political Studies Review*, vol. 17, nos. 1-2, Spring 2005. Küntzel, a German political scientist, has, however, been criticized by some scholars, such as Krämer and Wild, for insisting that the Brotherhood's anti-Semitism originated in fascism more than in anti-colonialism.
14 Cited by Gilbert Achcar, *The Arabs and the Holocaust*, Chastleton Travel, 2010, p. 157.
15 Cited by Stefan Wild, 'National Socialism in the Arab near East between 1933 and 1939', *Die Welt des Islams*, vol. 25, nos. 1–4, 1985, p. 138.
16 Stefan Zweig, *The World of Yesterday*, trans. Anthea Bell, Pushkin Press, 2009, p. 377.
17 Cited by Ronnie S. Landau, *The Nazi Holocaust*, I.B. Tauris, 1992, p. 237.
18 See Michael Phayer, *The Catholic Church and the Holocaust, 1930–1965*, Indiana University Press, 2000, pp. 67–7.

19 Cited by Susan Zuccotti, *Under His Very Windows*, Yale University Press, 2000, p. 60.

20 Albert Camus, in a statement made at the Dominican Monastery of Latour-Maubourg in 1948.

21 Radio interview, 1939, cited by Ian Kershaw, *Hitler: A Biography*, W.W. Norton & Co., 2008, pp. 381–2.

22 According to the 1933 census, see *The Holocaust Encyclopedia*, available at https://encyclopedia.ushmm.org/content/en/article/germany-jewish-population-in-1933 (accessed 1 April 2019).

23 Cited by Zuccotti, p. 60.

24 Cited by Phayer, Pius XII, 88.

25 William Patch, 'The Catholic Church, the Third Reich, and the Origins of the Cold War: On the Utility and Limitations of Historical Evidence', *The Journal of Modern History*, vol. 82, no. 2, June 2010, p. 413.

26 Patch, p. 403.

Conclusion

1 *Freedom of Thought*, annual report 2018, International Humanist and Ethical Union.

2 Bishop of Truro's Independent Review for the Foreign Secretary of FCO Support for Persecuted Christians, Interim Report, May 2019, https://christianpersecutionreview.org.uk/interim-report/#articleAnchor99 (accessed 9 May 2019).

3 'Universal Human Rights and "Human Rights in Islam"', David Littman, *Islam Watch*, 13 January 2008.

4 D. Grimm's list is in the *Frankfurter Allgemeine Zeitung*, 21 June 2002, cited by Jürgen Habermas, 'Religious Tolerance: The Pacemaker for Cultural Rights', *Philosophy*, vol. 79, no. 307, January 2004, p. 13.

5 *New York Times,* 4 June 2009, available at https://www.nytimes.com/2009/06/04/us/politics/04obama.text.html (accessed 1 April 2019).

SELECTED BIBLIOGRAPHY

Abd Allah ibn Buluggin, *The Tibyān: Memoirs of 'Abd Allāh B. Buluggīn, Last Zīrid Amīr of Granada*, trans. Amin T. Tibi, Leiden, Brill, 1986.

Abisaab, Rula Jurdi, *Converting Persia: Religion and Power in the Safavid Empire*, London, I.B. Tauris, 2004.

Abrahams, Israel, *Jewish Life in the Middle Ages*, London, Macmillan, 1896; New York, Dover Publications, 2004.

Ahmad, Barakat, *Muhammad and the Jews: A Re-Examination*, New Delhi, Vikas Publishing House, 1979.

Akçam, Taner, *From Empire to Republic: Turkish Nationalism and the Armenian Genocide*, London, Zed Books, 2004.

Allen, Brooke, 'Sensibility and Sense', *The Hudson Review*, vol. 59, no. 3, 2006, pp. 491–9.

Andersen, Magnus Scheel, 'Ummah and the Jews in the constitution of Medina', 2010. Available at: https://www.academia.edu/9385682/Ummah_and_the_Jews_in_the_Constitution_of_Medina (accessed 1 April 2019).

Anderson, Perry, 'The Feudal Synthesis', extract from *Passages from Antiquity to Feudalism*, New York, Verso Books, 1996. Available: www.versobooks.com/blogs/3247-the-feudal-synthesis (accessed 1 April 2019).

Arjomand, Said Amir, 'The Constitution of Medina: A Sociolegal Interpretation of Muhammad's Acts of Foundation of the "Umma"', *International Journal of Middle East Studies*, vol. 41, no. 4, November 2009, pp. 555–75.

Arjomand, Said Amir, 'Two Decrees of Shah Tahmasp Concerning Statecraft and the Authority of Shaykh 'Ali al-Karaki', in *Authority and Political Culture in Shi'ism*, trans. and ed. S. A. Arjomand, State University of New York Press, 1988, pp. 250–62.

Asbach, Olaf, and Peter Schröder, *The Ashgate Research Companion to the Thirty Years' War*, Abingdon, Routledge, 2014.

Badar, Mohamed, Masaki Nagata and Tiphanie Tueni, 'The Radical Application of the Islamist Concept of *Takfir*', *Arab Law Quarterly*, vol. 31 (2017), pp. 132–60.

Ashtiani, Julia (ed.), *Abbasid Belles Lettres, The Cambridge History of Arabic Literature*, Cambridge, Cambridge University Press, 2011.

Bainton, Roland H., *Here I Stand: A Life of Martin Luther*, Gibraltar, The Beacon Press, 1953.

Bainton, Roland H., *Hunted Heretic: The Life and Death of Michael Servetus, 1511–1553*, Gibraltar, The Beacon Press, 1960.

al-Balādhurī, *The Origins of the Islamic State: Translation with Annotations, Geographic and Historic Notes of the Kitāb Futūḥ al-Buldān of al-Imâm abu-l'Abbâs Aḥmad ibn-Jâbir al-Balâdhuri*, trans. Philip Khuri Hitti, New York, Columbia University Press, 1916.

Barkey, Karen, 'Islam and Toleration: Studying the Ottoman Imperial Model', *International Journal of Politics, Culture, and Society, The New Sociological Imagination II*, vol. 19, no. 1/2, December 2005, pp. 5–19.

Barlow, Frank, *Thomas Becket*, London, Weidenfeld & Nicolson, 1986.

Bartlett, W.B., *The Mongols: From Genghis Khan to Tamerlane*, Stroud, Amberley Publishing, 2009, p. 151.

Barry, John M., 'God, Government and Roger Williams' Big Idea', *Smithsonian Magazine*, 2012. Available at: http://www.smithsonianmag.com/history/god-government-and-roger-williams-big-idea-6291280/ (accessed 1 April 2019).

Bennison, Amira K., *The Great Caliphs: The Golden Age of the 'Abbasid Empire*, London, I.B. Tauris, 2009.

Berkey, Jonathan P., *The Formation of Islam: Religion and Society in the Near East, 600–1800*, Cambridge, Cambridge University Press, 2003. Available at: https://ia802708.us.archive.org/29/items/originsofislamic00balarich/originsofislamic00balarich.pdf (accessed 1 April 2019).

Berkey, Jonathan P., 'Islam', in Robert Irwin (ed.), *New Cambridge History of Islam*, vol. IV, Cambridge, Cambridge University Press, 2010, pp. 17–59.

Bernstein, R.B., *The Founding Fathers: A Very Short Introduction*, Oxford, Oxford University Press, 2015.

Bird, H.W., 'Diocletian and the Deaths of Carus, Carinus and Numerian', *Latomus*, vol. 35, 1976, pp. 123–32.

Black, Anthony, *The History of Islamic Political Thought: From the Prophet to the Present*, Edinburgh, Edinburgh University Press, 2011.

Blaydes, Lisa, and Eric Chaney, 'The Feudal Revolution and Europe's Rise: Political Divergence of the Christian West and the Muslim World before 1500 CE', *The American Political Science Review*, vol. 107, no. 1, February 2013, pp. 16–34.

Blumenthal, Uta-Renata, *The Investiture Conflict: Church and Monarchy from the Ninth to the Twelfth Century*, Philadelphia, University of Pennsylvania Press, 1988.

Bonner, Michael, *Jihad in Islamic History: Doctrines and Practice*, Princeton University Press, 2006.

Bori, Caterina, 'A New Source for the Biography of Ibn Taymiyya', *Bulletin of the School of Oriental and African Studies*, vol. 67, no. 3, 2004, pp. 321–48.

Boswell, John, *Christianity, Social Tolerance and Homosexuality: Gay People in*

Western Europe from the Beginning of the Christian Era to the Fourteenth Century, Chicago, University of Chicago Press, 1980, 2015.

Bowering, Gerhard (ed.), *The Princeton Encyclopedia of Islamic Political Thought*, Princeton University Press, 2013, p. 454.

Brecht, Martin, *Martin Luther*, vol. III, *The Preservation of the Church, 1532–1546*, trans. James Schaaf, Minneapolis, Fortress Press, 1999.

Brown, Peter, 'St Augustine's Attitude to Religious Coercion', *Journal of Roman Studies*, vol. 54, 1964; reprinted in Peter Brown, *Religion and Society in the Age of Saint Augustine*, New York, HarperCollins, 1972.

Bukay, David, 'Peace or Jihad? Abrogation in Islam', *Middle East Quarterly*, vol. 14, no. 4, 2007, pp. 3–11. Available at: http://www.meforum.org/1754/peace-or-jihad-abrogation-in-islam#_ftnref59 (accessed 1 April 2019).

Burrows, Edwin G. and Mike Wallace, *Gotham: A History of New York City to 1889*, Oxford University Press, 1999.

Cabaniss, Allen, 'Paulus Albarus of Muslim Cordova', *Church History*, vol. 22, no. 2, June 1953, pp. 99–112.

Carlyle, Thomas, *The French Revolution: A History*, vol. III, London, Chapman & Hall, 1842.

Castellio, 'Concerning Heretics: Whether they are to be persecuted and how they are to be treated', 1554, available at https://www.colorado.edu/neh2015/sites/default/files/attached-files/castellioonheretics-i.pdf (accessed 1 April 2019).

Çelebi, Evliya, *An Ottoman Traveller: Selections from the Book of Travels of Evliya Çelebi*, ed. and trans. Robert Dankoff and Sooyong Kim, London, Eland Publishing, 2011.

Charny, Israel W. (ed.), *Genocide Studies*, vol. III, *The Widening Circle of Genocide*, New Brunswick, Transaction, 1994.

Chazan, Robert (ed.), *Church, State, and Jew in the Middle Ages*, New Jersey, Behrman House, 1980, p. 173.

Cheney, C.R.,, *King John and the Papal Interdict*, Manchester, Manchester University Press, 1948.

Coffey, John, *Persecution and Toleration in Protestant England, 1558–1689*, Abingdon, Routledge, 2000.

Cohen, Mark R., 'The Neo-Lachrymose Conception of Jewish-Arab History', *Tikkun*, 6.3, 1991, pp. 55–60.

Cohen, Mark R., *Under Crescent and Cross: The Jews in the Middle Ages*, Princeton, Princeton University Press, 1994.

Cohen, Mark R., 'The "Golden Age" of Jewish-Muslim Relations: Myth and Reality', in *A History of Jewish-Muslim Relations: From the Origins to the Present Day*, Abdelwahab Meddeb and Benjamin Stora (eds), Princeton, Princeton University Press, 2013, pp. 28–38.

Cohn, S., 'The Black Death and the Burning of the Jews', *Past & Present*, vol. 196, no. 1, 2007, pp. 3–36.

Collins, Roger, 'Spain: The northern kingdoms and the Basques, 711–910', in R. McKitterick (ed.), *New Cambridge Medieval History*, vol. II, Cambridge, Cambridge University Press, 1995, pp. 272–89.

Commins, David, *The Wahhabi Mission and Saudi Arabia*, London, I.B. Tauris, 2006.

Cook, M.A., *The Koran: A Very Short Introduction*, Oxford, Oxford University Press, 2000.

Cook, Michael, *Understanding Jihad*, Berkeley, University of California Press, 2005.

Coope, Jessica A., *The Martyrs of Cordoba: Community and Family Conflict in an Age of Mass Conversion*, Lincoln, University of Nebraska Press, 1995.

Cooperson, Michael, *Classical Arabic Biography: The Heirs of the Prophets in the Age of al-Ma mūn*, Cambridge, Cambridge University Press, 2004.

Cooperson, Michael, *Al-Ma'mun (Makers of the Muslim World)*, London, Oneworld Publications, 2005.

Costen, Michael, *The Cathars and the Albigensian Crusade*, Manchester, Manchester University Press, 1977.

Cottret, Bernard, *Calvin: A Biography*, trans. M. Wallace McDonald, Grand Rapids, William B. Eerdmans Publishing, 2000.

Crawford, Michael, *Ibn Abd Al-Wahhab*, London, Oneworld Publications, 2014.

Crone, Patricia, *Slaves on Horses: The Evolution of the Islamic Polity*, Cambridge, Cambridge University Press, 1980.

Crone, Patricia, *Medieval Islamic Political Thought*, Edinburgh, Edinburgh University Press, 2004.

Dadrian, Vahakn N., *The History of the Armenian Genocide: Ethnic Conflict from the Balkans to Anatolia to the Caucasus*, New York, Berghahn Books, 1995.

de Bellaigue, Christopher, *The Islamic Enlightenment: The Modern Struggle between Faith and Reason*, London, Bodley Head, 2017.

de Ste. Croix, Geoffrey E.M., 'Why Were the Early Christians Persecuted?', *Past & Present*, vol. 26, 1963, pp. 6–38; reprinted in Michael Whitby (ed.), *Christian Persecution, Martyrdom, And Orthodoxy*, Oxford, Oxford University Press, 2006.

de Ste. Croix, Geoffrey E.M., 'Aspects of the "Great" Persecution', *Harvard Theological Review*, vol. 47, no. 2, April 1954, pp. 75–113.

Diner, Hasia R., *The Jews of the United States, 1654 to 2000*, Berkeley, University of California Press, 2004.

Dobson, R.B., *Jews of Medieval York and the massacre of March 1190*, York, St Anthony's Press, 1974.

Dols, Michael W., 'The Comparative Communal Responses to the Black Death in Muslim and Christian Societies', *Viator*, vol. 5, 1974, pp. 269–88.

Donner, Fred McGraw, *The Early Islamic Conquests*, Princeton, Princeton University Press, 1981.

Donner, Fred McGraw, *Muhammad and the Believers: At the Origin of Islam*, Cambridge MA, The Belknap Press of Harvard University Press, 2010.

Doyle, W., *Oxford History of the French Revolution*, Oxford, Oxford University Press, 1989.

Drake, H.A., 'Lambs into Lions: Explaining Early Christian Intolerance', *Past & Present*, vol. 153, no. 1, November 1996, pp. 3–36.

Drake, H. A., 'The Church, Society and Political Power', in Augustine Casiday and Frederick W. Norris (eds), *Cambridge History of Christianity*, vol. 2, Cambridge, Cambridge University Press, 2007, pp. 403–28.

Duffy, Eamon, *Saints and Sinners: A History of the Popes*, New Haven, Yale University Press, 1977, 2014.

Efron, John M., *The Jews: A History*, Abingdon, Routledge, 2016.

Einhard, *Vita Karoli Magni, Life of Charlemagne (814–830)*, in Thomas F.X. Noble (trans. and ed.), *Charlemagne and Louis the Pious: Lives by Einhard, Notker, Ermoldus, Thegan, and the Astronomer*, Pennsylvania, Penn State University Press, 2009.

Elukin, Jonathan, *Living Together, Living Apart: Rethinking Jewish-Christian Relations in the Middle Ages*, Princeton, Princeton University Press, 2007.

Esposito, John, *Oxford History of Islam*, Oxford, Oxford University Press, 2000.

Eusebius, *Martyrs of Palestine*, composed some time after 311. Available at: https://people.ucalgary.ca/~vandersp/Courses/texts/eusebius/eusempaf.html (accessed 1 April 2019).

El Fadl, Khaled Abou, *The Place of Tolerance in Islam*, Boston, Beacon Press, 2002.

Fairey, Jack, *The Great Powers and Orthodox Christendom: The Crisis over the Eastern Church in the Era of the Crimean War*, Basingstoke, Palgrave Macmillan, 2014.

Farrin, Raymond (ed.), *Abundance from the Desert: Classical Arabic Poetry*, New York, Syracuse University Press, 2011.

Ferrer, José Cutillas, 'War and Diplomacy: A Letter describing Shah Tahmasp I and His Ministers', in Enrique García Hernán, José Cutillas Ferrer and Rudi Matthee (eds), *The Spanish Monarchy and Safavid Persia in the Early Modern Period: Politics, War and Religion*, Berkhamsted, Albatros, 2016, pp. 29–40.

Fichte, Johann Gottlieb, *Addresses to the German Nation*, trans. R.F. Jones and G.H. Turnbull, Chicago, Open Court Publishing, 1922, Thirteenth Address, para. 198, pp. 223–4.

Firestone, Reuven, *Jihad: The Origin of Holy War in Islam*, Oxford, Oxford University Press, 1999.

Fletcher, Richard A., *Moorish Spain*, London, Weidenfeld & Nicolson, 1992.

Franklin, Benjamin, *The Autobiography of Benjamin Franklin*. Available at: http://www.ushistory.org/franklin/autobiography/page38.htm (accessed 1 April 2019).

Frend, W.H.C., 'The Failure of the Persecutions in the Roman Empire', *Past & Present*, vol. 16, November 1959, pp. 10–30.

Friedmann, Yohanan, *Tolerance and Coercion in Islam: Interfaith Relations in the Muslim Tradition*, Cambridge, Cambridge University Press, 2003.

Garnsey, Peter, 'Religious Toleration in Classical Antiquity' in W.J. Sheils (ed.), *Persecution and Toleration*, Ecclesiastical History Society (Summer Meeting 1983), 1984.

Gaustad, Edwin S., *Roger Williams: Prophet of Liberty*, Oxford, Oxford University Press, 2001.

Gill, Anthony, 'Religious Pluralism, Political Incentives, and the Origins of Religious Liberty', in Allen D. Hertzke (ed.), *The Future of Religious Freedom: Global Challenges*, New York, Oxford University Press, 2013, pp. 107–27.

Giovanni da Pian del Carpine, *The History of the Mongols*, *c.*1248, in *The journey of William of Rubruck to the eastern parts of the world, 1253–55*, trans. William Woodville Rockhill, Hakluyt Society, 1942, p. 63. Available at: https://archive.org/stream/journeyofwilliam00ruys/journeyofwilliam00ruys_djvu.txt (accessed 1 April 2019).

Glick, Leonard B., *Abraham's Heirs: Jews and Christians in Medieval Europe*, New York, Syracuse University Press, 1999.

Goddard, Hugh, *A History of Christian-Muslim Relations*, Edinburgh, Edinburgh University Press, 2000.

Goitein, S.D., *A Mediterranean Society: An Abridgement in One Volume*, Berkeley, University of California Press, 1999.

Goldschmidt, Arthur, and Lawrence Davidson, *A Concise History of the Middle East*, New York, Avalon Books, 2006.

Gran, Peter, 'Tahtawi in Paris', *Al-Ahram Weekly Online*, no. 568, 10–16 January 2002. Available at: http://weekly.ahram.org.eg/Archive/2002/568/cu1.htm (accessed 1 April 2019).

Guibert of Nogent, *A Monk's Confession: The Memoirs of Guibert of Nogent*, *c.*1115, trans. and with an introduction by Paul J. Archambault, Pennsylvania, Penn State University Press, 1995, p. 30.

Habermas, Jürgen, 'Religious Tolerance: The Pacemaker for Cultural Rights', *Philosophy*, vol. 79, no. 307, January 2004, pp. 5–18.

Haddad, Yvonne, 'Muhammad Abduh: Pioneer of Islamic Reform', in Ali Rahmena (ed.), *Pioneers of Islamic Revival*, London, Zed Books, 2005, pp. 30–63.

Hamilton, Bernard, 'The Albigensian Crusade and Heresy', in David Abulafia (ed.), *New Cambridge Medieval History*, vol. V, Cambridge, Cambridge University Press, 1999, pp. 164–81.

Hanke, Lewis, 'The Dawn of Conscience in America: Spanish Experiments and Experiences with Indians in the New World', *Proceedings of the American Philosophical Society*, vol. 107, no. 2, April 1963, pp. 83–92.

Hashmi, Sohail H. (ed.), *Just Wars, Holy Wars and Jihads: Christian, Jewish, and Muslim Encounters and Exchanges*, Oxford, Oxford University Press, 2012.

Heck, Paul L., '"Jihad" Revisited', *The Journal of Religious Ethics*, vol. 32, no. 1, 2004, pp. 95–128.

Heck, Paul, *Common Ground: Islam, Christianity and Religious Pluralism*, Washington, DC, Georgetown University Press, 2009.

Hersch, I., 'The French Revolution and the Emancipation of the Jews', *Jewish Quarterly Review*, vol. 19, no. 3, April 1907, pp. 540–65.

Hertz, Deborah Sadie, *Jewish High Society in Old Regime Berlin*, New York, Syracuse University Press, 2005.

Hertzke, Allen (ed.), *The Future of Religious Freedom: Global Challenges*, Oxford, Oxford University Press, 2013.

Herzl, Theodor, *The Complete Diaries of Theodor Herzl*, vol. I, ed. Raphael Patai, trans. Harry Zohn, Herzl Press and Thomas Yoseloff, 1960, pp. 378–9.

Hillenbrand, Carole, *The Crusades: Islamic Perspectives*, Abingdon, Routledge, 2000.

Hillgarth, J.N. (ed.), *Christianity and Paganism, 350–750: The Conversion of Western Europe*, Philadelphia, University of Pennsylvania Press, 1986.

Hodgson, Marshall G.S., *The Venture of Islam: Conscience and History in a World Civilization*, vol. I, Chicago, University of Chicago Press, 1977. Available at: https://ia601003.us.archive.org/6/items/TheVentureOfIslamClasicalAgeVol1MarshallHodgson/The_Venture_of_Islam_Clasical_Age_Vol-1_Marshall-Hodgson.pdf (accessed 1 April 2019).

Holland, Tom, *In The Shadow Of The Sword: The Battle for Global Empire and the End of the Ancient World*, London, Abacus, 2012.

Hoyland, Robert, G. (ed.), *Seeing Islam as Others Saw it: A Survey and Evaluation of Christian, Jewish, and Zoroastrian Writings on Early Islam*, Princeton, The Darwin Press, 1997.

Hsia, R. Po-Chia (ed.), *A Companion to the Reformation World*, Hoboken, Blackwell, 2004.

Ibn Battuta, *The Travels of Ibn Battuta*, trans. H.A.R. Gibb, New Delhi, GoodWord, 2000, p. 23. The full title of Ibn Battuta's work is *A Gift to Those Who Contemplate the Wonders of Cities and the Marvels of Travelling*; it is usually referred to as 'The Travels'.

Ibn Ishaq, *The Life of Muhammad: A Translation of Isḥāq's Sīrat Rasūl Allāh*, with Introduction and Notes by A. Guillaume, Oxford, Oxford University Press, 1955. Available at: http://www.justislam.co.uk/images/Ibn%20Ishaq%20-%20Sirat%20Rasul%20Allah.pdf (accessed 1 April 2019).

Ibn Khaldun, *The Muqaddimah: An Introduction to History*, trans. Franz Rosenthal, Princeton, Princeton University Press, 1967.

Ibn Shaddad, *The Rare and Excellent History of Saladin*, trans. Palestine Pilgrims' Text Society, Committee of the Palestine Exploration Fund, 1897, p. 24. Available at: https://ia802205.us.archive.org/18/items/lifesaladin00condgoog/lifesaladin00condgoog.pdf (accessed 1 April 2019).

Ibn al-Jawzi, *The Life of Ibn Hanbal*, trans. Michael Cooperson, New York, New York University Press, 2016.

ICJHC, International Catholic–Jewish Historical Commission, 'The Vatican and the Holocaust: A Preliminary Report. Submitted to The Holy See's Commission for Religious Relations with Jews', October 2000. Available at: http://www.jewishvirtuallibrary.org/preliminary-report-on-the-vatican-during-the-holocaust-october-2000-2#3 (accessed 1 April 2019).

al-Jabarti, *Napoleon in Egypt: Al-Jabarti's Chronicle of the French Occupation*, ed. and trans. Shmuel Moreh, Princeton, Markus Wiener, 1993.

al-Jabarti, *Al-Jabarti's History of Egypt*, ed. Jane Hathaway, Princeton, Markus Wiener, 2009.

Jansen, Johannes J.G, 'Ibn Taymiyyah and the Thirteenth Century: A Formative Period of Modern Muslim Radicalism', *Quaderni di Studi Arabi*, vol. 5/6, 1987.

Johnson, James Turner, and John Kelsay (eds), *Cross, Crescent, and Sword: The Justification and Limitation of War in Western and Islamic Tradition*, Westport, Greenwood Press, 1990.

Johnson, James Turner, and John Kelsay (eds), *Just War and Jihad: Historical and Theoretical Perspectives on War and Peace in Western and Islamic Traditions*, Westport, Greenwood Press, 1991.

Kamen, Henry, *The Spanish Inquisition: A Historical Revision*, London, Weidenfeld & Nicolson, 1997.

Kaplan, Benjamin J., *Divided by Faith: Religious Conflict and the Practice of Toleration in Early Modern Europe*, Cambridge MA, Harvard University Press, 2007.

Karabell, Zachary, *People of the Book: The Forgotten History of Islam and the West*, London, John Murray, 2007.

Katz, J., *Out of the Ghetto: The Social Background of Jewish Emancipation, 1770–1870*, New York, Syracuse University Press, 1973.

Kemal, Namik, [*Vatan*] 'Motherland, or Silistra', trans. Ahmet Ersoy, in Balázs Trencsényi and Michal Kopecek (eds), *National Romanticism: The Formation of National Movements*, Budapest, Central European University Press, 2007, pp. 488–92.

Kennedy, Hugh, 'Muslim Spain and Portugal: Al-Andalus and its Neighbours', in David Luscombe and Jonathan Riley-Smith (eds), *New Cambridge Medieval History*, vol. IV, part 1, 2004, pp. 599–622.

Kennedy, Hugh, *The Court of the Caliphs: The Rise and Fall of Islam's Greatest Dynasty*, London, Weidenfeld & Nicolson, 2004.

Kennedy, Hugh, *The Prophet and the Age of the Caliphates: The Islamic Near East from the 6th to the 11th Century*, Abingdon, Routledge, 2004.

Kramnick, Isaac (ed.), *The Portable Enlightenment Reader*, London, Penguin Books, 1995.

Küntzel, Matthias, 'National Socialism and Anti-Semitism in the Arab World', *Jewish Political Studies Review*, vol. 17, nos. 1–2, Spring 2005, pp. 99–118.

Kuru, Ahmet T., *Secularism and State Policies toward Religion: The United States, France and Turkey*, Cambridge, Cambridge University Press, 2009.

Lambert, Frank, *The Founding Fathers and the Place of Religion in America*, Princeton, Princeton University Press, 2006.

Landau, Ronnie S., *The Nazi Holocaust: Its History and Meaning*, London, I.B. Tauris, 1992.

Lane Fox, Robin, *Pagans and Christians in the Mediterranean World: From the Second Century AD to the Conversion of Constantine*, London, Penguin Books, 1988.

Lane-Poole, Stanley, *The Story of Cairo*, London, J.M. Dent, 1902.

Lane-Poole, Stanley, *Saladin and the Fall of the Kingdom of Jerusalem*, *Heroes of the Nations*, vol. 24, London, New York, G.P. Putnam's, 1906.

Lapidus, Ira M., 'The Separation of State and Religion in the Development of Early Islamic Society', *International Journal of Middle East Studies*, vol. 6, no. 4, October 1975, pp. 363–85.

Lapidus, Ira M., *A History of Islamic Societies*, Cambridge, Cambridge University Press, 1988

Lapidus, Ira M., 'Muslim Cities and Islamic Societies', in Ira M. Lapidus (ed.), *Middle Eastern Cities: A Symposium on Ancient, Islamic and Contemporary Middle Eastern Urbanism*, Berkeley, University of California Press, 1969, pp. 47–79.

Le Strange, Guy, *Baghdad during the Abassid Caliphate from Contemporary Arabic and Persian Sources*, Oxford, Clarendon Press, 1900.

Levy-Rubin, Milka, *Non-Muslims in the Early Islamic Empire: From Surrender to Coexistence*, Cambridge, Cambridge University Press, 2011.

Lewis, Bernard, *Islam in History: Ideas, people and events in the Middle East*, Chicago, Open Court Publishing, 1993.

Lewis, Bernard, *The Jews of Islam*, Princeton, Princeton University Press, 1984.

Lewis, Bernard, 1961, *The Emergence of Modern Turkey*, Oxford, Oxford University Press, 1961.

Lipton, Sara, *Dark Mirror: The Medieval Origins of Anti-Jewish Iconography*, New York, Metropolitan Books, 2014.

Little, Donald P., 'Did Ibn Taymiyya Have a Screw Loose?', *Studia Islamica* 1975, 41:93-111.

Little, Donald P., 'Coptic conversion to Islam under the Bahri Mamluks, 692–755/1293–1354', *Bulletin of the School of Oriental and African Studies*, vol. 39, no. 3, 1976, pp. 552–69.

Lowenstein, Steven M., *The Berlin Jewish Community: Enlightenment, Family, and Crisis, 1770–1830*, Oxford, Oxford University Press, 1994.

Loyn, H.R., *The English Church, 940–1154*, London, Pearson Education, 2000.

Maalouf, Amin, *The Crusades through Arab Eyes*, London, Saqi Books, 1984.

MacDonogh, Giles, *Frederick the Great: A Life in Deed and Letters*, London, Phoenix Publishing, 2000.

MacMullen, Ramsay, *Christianizing the Roman Empire: A.D. 100–400*, New Haven, Yale University Press, 1977.

Al-Makrisi, *Essulouk li Mariset il Muluk* (The Road to Knowledge of the Return of Kings), in Henry G. Bohn (ed.), *Chronicles of the Crusades*, 1848; reissued New York, AMS Press, 1969, pp. 535–56.

Mango, Andrew, *Atatürk: The Biography of the Founder of Modern Turkey*, New York, Overlook Press, 1999.

Mansel, Philip, *Constantinople: City of the World's Desire, 1453–1924*, London, John Murray, 1995.

Marcus, Jacob R., *The Jew in the Medieval World: A Source Book 315–1791*, New York, The Union Of American Hebrew Congregations, 1938.

Marrus, Michael R., *The Holocaust in History*, London, Weidenfeld & Nicolson, 1988.

Marsham, Andrew, *Rituals of Islamic Monarchy: Accession and Succession in the First Muslim Empire*, Edinburgh, Edinburgh University Press, 2009.

Masters, B., *Christians and Jews in the Ottoman Arab World: The Roots of Sectarianism*, Cambridge, Cambridge University Press, 2001.

al-Masudi, *The Meadows of Gold: The Abbasids*, trans. P. Lunde and C. Stone, London, Kegan Paul, 1989.

McKitterick, Rosamond, *The Frankish Kingdoms under the Carolingians 751–987*, Abingdon, Routledge, 1983.

McKitterick, Rosamond and Collins, R., *New Cambridge Medieval History*, vol. II, Cambridge, Cambridge University Press, 1990.

Melchert, Christopher, 'Religious Policies of the Caliphs from Al-Mutawakkil to Al-Muqtadir, AH 232–295/AD 847–908', *Islamic Law and Society*, vol. 3, no. 3, 1996, pp. 316–42.

Menoca, Maria Rosa, *The Ornament of the World: How Muslims, Jews, and Christians Created a Culture of Tolerance in Medieval Spain*, New York, Back Bay Books, 2003.

Mitchell, Richard Paul, *The Society of the Muslim Brothers*, Oxford, Oxford University Press, 1993.

Moore, John C., *Pope Innocent 3rd 1160/61–1216: To Root Up and to Plant*, Leiden, Brill, 2003.

Moore, Robert, I., *The Formation of a Persecuting Society: Authority and Deviance in Western Europe 950–1250*, Hoboken, Blackwell, 1987.

Moreno, Eduardo Manzano, 'The Iberian Peninsula and North Africa', in Chase Robinson (ed.), *New Cambridge History of Islam*, vol. I, Cambridge, Cambridge University Press, 2011, pp. 581–621. Available at: https://archive.org/stream/TheNewCambridgeHistoryOfIslamVolume1/The_New_Cambridge_History_of_Islam_Volume_1#page/n611/mode/1up (accessed 1 April 2019).

Mortimer, Geoff, *Eyewitness Accounts of the Thirty Years War 1618–48*, Basingstoke, Palgrave Macmillan, 2002.

Murphy, Andrew R., *Conscience and Community: Revisiting Toleration and Religious Dissent in Early Modern England and America*, Pennsylvania, Penn State University Press, 2001.

An-Na'im, Abdullahi Ahmed, 'Islamic Foundations of Religious Human Rights', in John Witte and Johan D. van der Vyver (eds), *Religious Human Rights in Global Perspective: Religious Perspectives*, vol. 1, Kluwer Law International, 1996, pp. 337–60.

Nawas, John, 'A Reexamination of Three Current Explanations for Al-Ma'mun's Introduction of the Mihna', *International Journal of Middle Eastern Studies*, vol. 26, 1994, pp. 615–29.

Nawas, John, 'The Mihna of 218 A.H./833 A.D. Revisited: An Empirical Study', *Journal of the American Oriental Society*, vol. 116, no. 4, 1996, pp. 698–708.

Nelson, Janet L. (ed., trans. and annotated), *The Annals of St-Bertin: Ninth-Century Histories*, vol. 1, Manchester, Manchester University Press, 1991.

Neusner, Jacob, *God's Rule: The Politics of World Religions*, Washington, DC, Georgetown University Press, 2003.

Nirenberg, David, *Communities of Violence: Persecution of Minorities in the Middle Ages*, Princeton, Princeton University Press, 1996.

Nirenberg, David, 'The Birth of the Pariah: Jews, Christian Dualism, and Social Science', *Social Research*, vol. 70, no. 1, Spring 2003, pp. 201–36.

O'Connell, D.J.K., 'Pius XII: Recollections and Impressions', *Irish Quarterly Review*, vol. 47, no. 188, Winter 1958, pp. 361–8.

Paris, Matthew, *Matthew Paris's English history from the year 1235–1273*, trans. the Rev J.A. Giles, London, Henry G. Bohn, 1854. Available at: https://archive.org/stream/matthewparisseng03pari/matthewparisseng03pari_djvu.txt (accessed 1 April 2019).

Paris, Matthew, *Chronicles of Matthew Paris: Monastic Life in the Thirteenth Century*, ed., trans. and with an introduction by Richard Vaughan, Basingstoke, Palgrave Macmillan, 1984.

Patch, William, 'The Catholic Church, the Third Reich, and the Origins of the Cold War: On the Utility and Limitations of Historical Evidence', *The Journal of Modern History*, vol. 82, no. 2, June 2010, pp. 396–433.

Peters, F.E., *Islam: A Guide for Jews and Christians*, Princeton, Princeton University Press, 2003.

Peters, F.E., *The Monotheists: Jews, Christians, and Muslims in Conflict and Competition*, vols 1 and 2, Princeton, Princeton University Press, 2003.

Peters, Edward, *The First Crusade: 'The Chronicle of Fulcher of Chartres' and Other Source Materials*, Philadelphia, University of Pennsylvania Press, 1998.

Peters, Edward, *Inquisition*, Berkeley, University of California Press, 1989.

Peters, Edward (ed.), *Heresy and Authority in Medieval Europe: Documents in Translation*, Philadelphia, University of Pennsylvania Press, 1980.

Phayer, Michael, *The Catholic Church and the Holocaust, 1930–1965*, Bloomington, Indiana University Press, 2000.

Poliakov, Léon, *The History of Anti-Semitism: From Mohammed to the Marranos*, New York, Vanguard Press, 1974.

Pullan, Brian, *The Jews of Europe and the Inquisition of Venice, 1550–1670*, London, I.B. Tauris, 1983.

Rapoport, Yossef, and Shahab Ahmed (eds), *Ibn Taymiyya and His Times*, Oxford, Oxford University Press, 2015.

Rasmussen, Dennis C., *The Pragmatic Enlightenment: Recovering the Liberalism of Hume, Smith, Montesquieu, and Voltaire*, Cambridge, Cambridge University Press, 2014.

Rawlings, Helen, *The Spanish Inquisition*, Hoboken, Blackwell, 2006.

Riley-Smith, Jonathan, *The First Crusade and the Idea of Crusading*, Philadelphia, University of Pennsylvania Press, 1986.

Riley-Smith, Jonathan, *The Crusades, Christianity and Islam*, New York, Columbia University Press, 2008.

Ross, E. Denison, 'An Embassy from King John to the Emperor of Morocco', *Bulletin of the School of Oriental Studies*, vol. 3, no. 3, 1924, pp. 555–9.

Roth, Cecil, *A History of the Jews in England*, Oxford, Clarendon Press, 1941.

Roth, Cecil, *The House of Nasi: The Duke of Naxos*, Philadelphia, The Jewish Publication Society of America, 1948.

Roth, Norman, *Conversos, Inquisition and the Expulsion of the Jews from Spain*, Madison, University of Wisconsin Press, 1995.

Roth, Norman, *Jews, Visigoths, and Muslims in Medieval Spain: Cooperation and Conflict*, Leiden, Brill, 1994.

Rummel, Erika, *Jiménez de Cisneros: On the Threshold of Spain's Golden Age*, Arizona Center for Medieval and Renaissance Studies, 1999.

Runciman, Steven, *A History of the Crusades*, vol. I, *The First Crusade and the Foundation of the Kingdom of Jerusalem*, Cambridge, Cambridge University Press, 1951.

Ruthven, Malise, 'Islam and the State', *CM* (*Critical Muslim*), vol. 14, April–June 2015, pp. 37–51.

Savory, Roger, *Iran under the Safavids*, Cambridge, Cambridge University Press, 1980.

Schama, Simon, *Citizens*, New York, Knopf, 1989.

Scruton, Roger, *The West and the Rest*, London, Continuum, 2002.

Scurr, Ruth, *Fatal Purity: Robespierre and the French Revolution*, London, Chatto & Windus, 2006.

Sebeos, *The Armenian History*, attributed to Sebeos, trans. and with notes by R.W. Thomson, Liverpool, Liverpool University Press, 1998. Available at: https://erevangala500.com/upload//pdf/1323119797.pdf (accessed 1 April 2019).

Serjeant, R.B., 'The "Sunnah Jāmi'ah" Pacts with the Yat͟hrib Jews, and the "Taḥrīm" of Yat͟hrib: Analysis and Translation of the Documents Comprised in the So-Called "Constitution of Medina"', *Bulletin of the School of Oriental and African Studies*, vol. 41, no. 1, 1978, pp. 1–42.

Smallwood, E. Mary, *The Jews under Roman rule: from Pompey to Diocletian: A study in Political Relations*, 1981, Leiden, Brill; reprinted 2014.

Song of Roland, trans. John O'Hagan, Digireads.com, 2004.

Southern, R.W., *Western Society and the Church in the Middle Ages*, London, Penguin, 1970.

Stanfield-Johnson, Rosemary, 'The Tabarraiyan and the early Safavids', *Iranian Studies*, vol. 37, no. 1, March 2004, pp. 47–71.

Stillman, Norman A., *The Jews of Arab Lands: A History and Source Book*, Philadelphia, The Jewish Publication Society of America, 1979.

Stillman, Norman A., 'The Jew in the Medieval Islamic City', in Daniel Frank (ed.), *The Jews of Medieval Islam: Community, Society, and Identity*, Leiden, Brill, 1995, pp. 3–13.

Stoetzler, Marcel, *The State, the Nation, the Jew: Liberalism and the Antisemitism Dispute in Bismarck's Germany*, Lincoln, University of Nebraska Press, 2008.

Straumann, Benjamin, 'The Peace of Westphalia (1648) as a Secular Constitution', History and Theory of International Law Series, IILJ Working Paper 2007/7.

al-Tabari, *The History of al-Tabari*: see vol. VII for Battle of Badr, *The Foundation of The Community*, trans. W. Montgomery Watt and M.V. McDonald, New York, University of New York Press, 1987; vol. XXXII, *The Reunification of the Abbasid Caliphate*, trans. C.E. Bosworth, New York, University of New York Press, 1987; vol. XXXIV, *Incipient Decline*, trans. Joel Kraemer, New York, University of New York Press, 1989.

Taitz, Emily, *The Jews of Medieval France: The Community of Champagne*, Westport, Greenwood Press, 1994.

al-Tahtawi, Rifa'a, *An Imam in Paris: Account of a Stay in France by an Egyptian Cleric (1826–1831)*, trans. Daniel L. Newman, London, Saqi Books, 2011.

Tallett, Frank, 'Dechristianizing France: The Year II and the Revolutionary Experience', in Frank Tallett and Nicholas Atkin (eds), *Religion, Society and Politics in France Since 1789*, London, Hambledon Press, 1991, pp. 1–29.

Thackeray, William Makepeace, *Notes of a journey from Cornhill to Grand Cairo*, published under the name Mr M.A. Titmarsh, London, Chapman & Hall, 1846.

Tierney, Brian, *The Crisis of Church and State, 1050–1300*, Toronto, University of Toronto Press, 1988.

Tlusty, B. Ann (ed. and trans.), *Augsburg During the Reformation Era: An Anthology of Sources*, Indianapolis, Hackett Publishing Company, 2012.

Toch, M., 'The Jews in Europe 500–1050', in P. Fouracre (ed.), *New Cambridge Medieval History*, vol. I, Cambridge, Cambridge University Press, 2005, pp. 545–70.

Tritton, A.S., *The Caliphs and their Non-Muslim Subjects: A Critical Study of the Covenant of Umar*, Oxford, Oxford University Press, 1930. Available at: https://archive.org/stream/caliphsandtheirn029590mbp/caliphsandtheirn029590mbp_djvu.txt (accessed 1 April 2019).

Turner, Colin, *Islam Without Allah? The Rise of Religious Externalism in Safavid Iran*, Routledge, 2001.

Vassiliev, Alexei, *The History of Saudi Arabia*, London, Saqi Books, 2000.

Walzer, Michael, *On Toleration*, New Haven, Yale University Press, 1997.

al-Waqidi, *The Life of Muhammad: Al-Wāqidī's Kitāb al-Maghāzī*, ed. Rizwi Faizer, trans. Rizwi Faizer, Amal Ismail and AbdulKader Tayob, with an introduction by Rizwi Faizer and Andrew Rippin, Abingdon, Routledge, 2011.

al-Waqidi, *Islamic Conquest of Syria* ('Futuhusham'), trans. Mawlana Sulayman al-Kindi, London, Ta-Ha Publishers, 2000.

Wasserstein, David, *The Rise and Fall of the Party-Kings: Politics and Society in Islamic Spain, 1002–1086*, Princeton, Princeton University Press, 1985.

Watt, Montgomery, *Muhammad in Mecca*, Oxford, Clarendon Press, 1953.

Watt, Montgomery, *Muhammad at Medina*, Oxford, Oxford University Press, 1956.

Wild, Stefan, 'National Socialism in the Arab near East between 1933 and 1939', *Die Welt des Islams*, New Series, vol. 25, nos. 1–4, 1985, pp. 126–73.

William of Newburgh, *The Church Historians of England*, vol. IV, part II, trans. Joseph Stevenson, London, Seeley's, 1861, chs 1, 7–11. Available at: https://sourcebooks.fordham.edu/basis/williamofnewburgh-four.asp (accessed 1 April 2019).

Williams, Roger, *The Bloudy Tenent of Persecution, for Cause of Conscience: discussed in a Conference Between Truth and Peace*, ed. Richard Groves, Macon, Mercer University Press, 2001.

Williams, Stephen, and Gerard Friel, *Theodosius: The Empire at Bay*, New Haven, Yale University Press, 1995.

Wilson, Peter H., *Europe's Tragedy: A New History of the Thirty Years War*, London, Penguin, 2010.

Wilson, Peter H., *The Thirty Years War: A Sourcebook*, Basingstoke, Palgrave Macmillan, 2010.

Winter, Stefan, *The Shiites of Lebanon under Ottoman Rule, 1516–1788*, Cambridge, Cambridge University Press, 2010.

Wolf, Kenneth Baxter, *Christian Martyrs in Muslim Spain*, Cambridge, Cambridge University Press, 1988. Available at: http://libro.uca.edu/martyrs/martyrs.htm (accessed 1 April 2019).

Zuccotti, Susan, *Under His Very Windows: The Vatican and the Holocaust in Italy*, New Haven, Yale University Press, 2000.

Zweig, Stefan, *The World of Yesterday: Memoirs of a European*, trans. Anthea Bell, London, Pushkin Press, 2009.

ACKNOWLEDGEMENTS

To my wonderful agent Ivan Mulcahy; James Nightingale, sensitive and patient editor; Lisbet Rausing, the learned and discerning reader that every writer should have; Terence Mitchison whose erudition always amazes me; Tariq al-Timimi for his invaluable corrections; Yossef Rapoport, Dov Samet, Malise Ruthven and Anthony Grayling for their generous advice; Jeremy O'Grady, another brilliant editor; Jane O'Grady for her love and support; my copy-editor Katherine Ailes for not letting me get away with anything; to Rachel Wright for the proofreading and Chris Bell for the index; and of course Tony Curzon Price – I couldn't have written the book without him

INDEX

A NOTE ABOUT THE AUTHOR

Selina O'Grady was a producer of BBC1's moral documentary series *Heart of the Matter*, presented by Joan Bakewell, Channel 4's live chat show *After Dark* and Radio 4's history series *Leviathan*. She is the author of *And Man Created God* and has written for the *Guardian*, *Mail on Sunday*, *Independent*, *Literary Review* and *The Oldie*.